The Politics of Social Knowledge

The Politics of Social Knowledge

Larry D. Spence

The Pennsylvania State University Press
University Park and London

To Burt Alpert

Whose work, courage, genius, and friendship
made it possible for me to see the world
in a more productive way.

Library of Congress Cataloging in Publication Data

Spence, Larry D
  The politics of social knowledge.

  Includes bibliography and index.
  1. Political science. 2. Political socialization.
3. Knowledge, Theory of. I. Title.
JA74.S654   300'.1   77-10543
ISBN 0-271-00521-1

Preface

Rouze up, O young Men of the New Age! Set your
foreheads against the ignorant Hirelings! For we
have Hirelings in the Camp, the Court and the University, who would, if they could, for ever depress
Mental and prolong Corporeal War.
                    William Blake, Preface to *Milton*

This volume focuses on the problems of epistemology involved in demonstrating the theoretical possibility and practical necessity of creating a
classless society. It is meant to be read as a critical examination of some
problematic assumptions of Western political thought. It attempts to
account for the persuasiveness of these assumptions, to argue for their
rejection, and to outline an alternative approach to political theory.
While research and experiments in the social sciences over the last sixty
years are cited in the text, there is no attempt to prove or demonstrate
the argument. Rather, I have tried to show a plausible alternative that
should be researched, criticized, and tested. I have written as persua-
sively and forcefully as I can, aiming to engage others in dialogue and
to make it easier for them to see my mistakes. Politeness and
overqualification do not a scientific discourse make. An open mind is
demonstrated by the capacity to alter ideas in the face of counterargu-
ment and evidence, not by false humility or lack of commitment. If I
didn't think I am right I would not write the book. If I didn't know that
my ideas are limited and to some unknown degree in error, I would
not strive to write as clearly as I can. Therefore, the tone of the book is
combative and critical.

The book is not strictly philosophical, being an essay about epistemology rather than a technical treatise in epistemology. I do not deal
with the philosophical literature on whether or not social science is
possible or what degree of rigor it might attain, but instead with the
political and social problems of epistemology. I leave to my philosophical colleagues the important and nagging issues of the foundations of

human knowledge. My aim is for a strictly working or journeyman philosophy.

All wisdom begins with what we have inherited from the past. The aim of this book is not the rejection of that heritage but its improvement. The quest for the knowledge of values that can enrich and enhance our social and political lives is an old one. The many false starts and failures should goad us to increase our efforts and never to accommodate our imaginations or seek fanciful escapes. The struggle with the past is only a struggle against its content of acquiescence and against that arrogance which ignorance so often wears. While I am not kind to traditional Western political thought, I believe it to be fundamental and crucial to the improvement of the human lot. But it demands more than the study of the so-called masters; it requires our willingness to philosophize and to create theories just as they did.

The documentation is designed to press the reader to examine sources and to reinterpret them if necessary. I have not tried to deal with all possible counterarguments and evidence but only with what seemed important. Likewise, I have tried to limit supporting evidence to that which fleshes out the argument and its implications. The notes are not intended as badges of scholarship or signs of erudition but as a sample of the information available to social thinkers who wish to proceed beyond the accepted wisdom of the past. While this information is often scattered, obscure, strange, and currently neglected, that deficiency is due to the task division of modern academia rather than to the information's lack of importance. Sticking my nose into other peoples' fields of inquiry will, no doubt, get it snapped at. Such discomfort is worthwhile if it results in increased interdisciplinary dialogue and better understanding.

I have written the book more out of driven need than design. Since I first publicly questioned the inevitability of hierarchy in human organizations in a graduate seminar at Berkeley, I have found it difficult to obtain reasoned discussion of the issues involved. These issues, while politically and emotionally volatile, had to be brought to the level of public discourse or I would have been left to a life of carping. It is my goal to put the issue of hierarchical organizations on the agenda both of the social sciences and of American society. The time, I hope, is opportune.

It is difficult for me to acknowledge all who have contributed to this work. Friends, teachers, colleagues, and students too numerous to mention will find scattered throughout the book bits and pieces I have eagerly seized from them. Even if my memory does not allow an accounting of all these borrowings, I am grateful and would like nothing better than to be able to list the hundreds of individuals who have helped me. Several people have contributed so significantly to the work by reading and criticizing it that they deserve special recognition. Robert Biller, Andŕe Orriane, Michael Weinstein, and Sheldon Wolin have made helpful suggestions concerning the manuscript. My thanks are due the Lifwynn Foundation, its director, Hans Syz, and especially its secretary, Alfreda S. Galt, for valuable bibliographic help in researching the chapter on Trigant Burrow. I have also benefited from fierce arguments with John Schaar and Muzafer Sherif over the central themes of the book. John M. Pickering of The Pennsylvania State University Press has been an exemplary editor and friend and has much improved both substance and style. Kathy McNitt did the original typing—which meant correcting my wretched spelling—cheerfully, for the most part. My good friends and colleagues Peter Kardas, Lin Nelson, Norm Bowen, and Pat Bowen have served loyally as cheerleaders and spiritual advisers in addition to offering their intellectual stimulation. Special thanks are due to the woman I love and to the workers of the Heaven Hill Distillery of Bardstown, Kentucky—over the years, they have given me more solace than inspiration.

L.D.S.

April 1976
Milesburg, Pennsylvania

Contents

Introduction

The Myth
of
Natural Hierarchy

The evolution of a science of humanity has been blocked by persistent assumptions about the nature of the human species and human societies. The species has been judged as wanting in motivation, character, and intelligence. As Freud put it succinctly, "men are not naturally fond of work, and arguments are of no avail against their passions."[1] A second entrenched and destructive assumption is the conviction that human societies are inevitably hierarchical. Both assumptions have assumed the structure and power of myths in that there are no facts known or imaginable that can falsify them, no events or actions that could result in their modification. Offer a counterexample of a work-loving, responsible, intelligent person and you will have found an "exception" produced in spite of human nature by the determination and wisdom of the socializing agents of hierarchical institutions. Find a group of cooperating producers without structured positions of domination and you will have only failed to see the hidden hierarchy and the totally conformist nature of their behavior. The combined myths of unreliable men and women enlightened and ennobled by an omniscient hierarchy of administrators is so much an implicit part of the perspective of the social investigator as to be immune to minimal criticism. To challenge these myths is to undergo the risks involved in taking stands against the political and academic institutions of our age.

My thesis is that social investigators must and can divest themselves of their traditional epistemological premises if they are to achieve the ability to contribute to social knowledge. These blocking premises are based on a presumption that some individual member of our species can make meaningful moral evaluations of the species—more explicitly, that some one of us can validly impose his or her judgment upon the rest of us. This defective judgmental stance is necessary to the myth of the inevitability of hierarchy. It expresses a claim to a kind of divine right of knowing which presumes that definitive and accurate judgments can be made without evidence or criticism. It involves the faith that a minority of men and women can become unhuman or superhuman knowers and actors. Compared with these superhumans of fantasy, immediate mankind appears stupid, lazy, stubborn, and greedy. Thus, if the social investigator begins from such a supernatural and dogmatic stance it is inevitable that he will perceive a need for hierarchy (literally, the rule of the sacred) in all human organization and will lend himself to the production of self-serving justifications for elite domination. It matters not whether the investigator declares mankind to be inherently good or inherently evil—in either case such judgments are justifications and motivations for the design or defense of social structures that are meant to restrain, remake, or restore human beings according to some timeless principles. These justifications reduce the premise to absurdity. And when we come to understand that the species with its needs and capacities can be the only source of valid criteria for the evaluation of social institutions, only then, we can begin the work of discovering human nature and eschew the tendentious task of reforming it.

My own perspective on these issues is derived from the attempt to demonstrate, theoretically, the feasibility of classless societies. The goal or dream of a communal society of producers, free of all structures of domination and exploitation, is an old one. But for nearly 5,000 years this dream has been derided and attacked with little regard for standards of logic, evidence, or common fairness. In their writings, great political thinkers in the Western world have been motivated to oppose the popular expression of these ideas in times of social degeneration and upheaval. Most of these writers have attempted to show not only that such dreams are hopelessly naive but also that those who believe them or say they believe them are either wicked usurpers or the foolish pawns of more disguised ambitions. Many critics of the dream have been Utopians—creating immaculate, abstract designs of societies that inflame the intellect as they chill the heart. But while the Utopian goals of justice, harmony, or peace have never been considered pernicious, the goal of an egalitarian social order has been rejected by many of the most idealistic political thinkers.

The very fierceness of the rejections has always intrigued me and suggests something about the perennial attraction of the communal dream. To repudiate the hope of organized freedom and community, it appears, the rejectors must learn to curb some of their strongest needs and to deny some of their most prevalent desires. But those who learn to curb also learn to regard the curbed part of themselves as against reason, morality, and order, wherefore those who continue to dream and hope can be seen only as threatening enemies rather than as innovators. The more eloquent and persuasive such enemies become, the more the hierarchists must resist them. The very fury of the attacks on egalitarian ideals is evidence of the pain and rage involved in the destructive accommodation to the myths of hierarchy.

Faced with opponents who use without scruple every skill of learning, manipulation, and warfare, revolutionaries and anarchists have found it difficult enough merely to proclaim their beliefs. Out of the difficulties, words like *freedom, fraternity, community, brotherhood,* or *equality,* and descriptive formulas of the dream like "all power to the people," "down with the state," "expropriate the expropriators" come to be charged as if with magical qualities. These qualities have been used to bolster the spirits and stiffen the wills of men and women engaged in struggles so desperate that the destruction of their class opponents has seemed to be the immediate and only requisite for the realization of their dreams. While the intent and spirit of these words and slogans are clear, their sacred character has both prevented serious consideration of the means of implementation and made it easy for them to be subverted in practice while ritualized in theory. On them, the victims of hierarchy set up counter hierarchies. From the Sun City of the workmen and slaves of ancient Pergamon through Robespierre to Lenin and Mao Tse-tung, the egalitarian dream has foundered on a complex reality that is always intractable to magic slogans and wishful thinking. The resulting betrayal of the social dream of a producers' commune is, I hope, to be avoided in the future. Our century has seen the fearful human price in lives, in hopes, in imagination, and in increased brutalization of existence that such betrayals exact. But this avoidance will not be accomplished by denying the dream or by condemning each new generation of dreamers. The dream will not die so long as the race lives. Its endurance and its strength are witness to the strong biological capacities and needs that it expresses. It is pernicious to mankind only as long as it remains a mere dream with all the escapism, denial, and liturgy—in short, all the enervating qualities—that mere dreams involve.

Challenging the age-old identification of order and organization with hierarchy, as well as the judgmental stance on which it rests, is like attempting to pull up a weed in a garden only to find its root system so intertwined that removal entails the destruction of the very garden. The conceptual uprooting I am attempting involves the destruction of important beliefs and socially accepted wisdom as well as the debunking of the pretensions of great men and powerful thinkers. But keep the crude analogy in mind—for I hope to replant many of the productive ideas and practices of the old garden in a new and healthier setting where they can grow straight and strong. This work is an effort to realize that hope. It exhibits much negativity and, I fear, much ill-tempered impatience toward our common culture. These result from the effort involved in plowing the ground for the new crop, for the replanting, rather than from any fury of laying waste with whatever instrument is at hand. My efforts are radical in that they go to roots; and they are destructive, in that they uproot assumptions of the past in order that these may be criticized in the daylight of the present. But my efforts do not comprise terrorism in any form. What I hope to do is deny, or to call into serious doubt, the litanies and dogmas of class society—so that we may as citizens and scientists look with fresh eyes, think with fresh brains, and speak with fresh words upon the political world around us. Of course, were it not for the efforts of ancestors this would not be possible. If we do not equal them there will be less possibility for critical reevaluation in the future world of our descendants.

Having described the mythical structure of our assumptions about mankind and organization in the first chapter of this book, I take up the problem of social ignorance in chapters 2 and 3. Pervasive evidence of social ignorance in the form of false accounts and false descriptions of the social and physical environment is the most often cited and perhaps strongest case for the assumption of human depravity. But social ignorance is a complex phenomenon. Indeed the traditional ways of describing it and accounting for it—from Plato's myth of the cave to the latest research in political socialization—are involved in unavoidable paradoxes. For if he contends or demonstrates that human beings cannot be trusted to learn the truth about themselves and the world, the social investigator must invoke some special dispensations or ecstatic maneuvers to free himself from the defect common to the species. These maneuvers of purification, transcendence, or polygonal vision always involve authority claims that cannot be evaluated, even in theory. Thus accounts of social ignorance make social knowledge impossible and we are left only with the medicinal lies of those who know what is best for us.

The persistent assumption of social investigators that humans are an unreliable or defective species seems related to the fact that most social investigators are reformers. So long as human institutions function well, interest in investigating them wanes. It is in time of crisis that the need for analysis becomes pressing. The social investigator must then try to understand why things are going badly—discovering missing information about the social world, or correcting misinformation. His first problem is to deal with his own and others' social ignorance. The archetypal reformer, Socrates, began by simply trying to demonstrate the fact of social ignorance. His own superiority rested on his insight that while all Athenians were ignorant, he knew his ignorance. This seems like a reasonable start—but look where it leads. The reformer begins with an experience of fallibility; suddenly his eyes are opened, he awakes from dogmatic slumbers, or he is goaded to novel action. He discovers that there have been severe defects in the way he has understood the world. He looks for such defects in the way others understand it. As a reformer, he hopes to remedy the defects, to change the way people think and act upon the world. Hence he must present to the community his findings on ignorance and his suggestions for change.

At the point of his presentation the investigator/reformer meets apathy (at best) and myriad defenses of traditional social wisdom. He discovers not only that such wisdom is in error but also that it is dogmatically held and defended even to death. Confronted with subtle and ingenious arguments justifying the older view of social wisdom, he can only argue that if others would doubt their premises and accept his, they might see the world in a better and more useful way. If only others would tentatively see the social world from his new perspective, they would grasp the importance and the value of what he has to offer. Unfortunately, his opponents are stubborn on this point, arguing that the adoption of the social investigator's perspective must be avoided at all costs because it represents a distorted vision based on the perverse biases of a reformer. Thus the churchmen refused to look into Galileo's telescope, not because they were afraid that they would find evidence to refute their theories but because they did not wish to be deceived by the known visual distortion of that crude instrument.

The social investigator can counterattack at this point by analyzing the all-too-human sources of his opponent's perspective. He can point out that the accepted perspective also is limited and distorting. Having made these charges and accepted what they entrain, the social investigator seems to face a world in which truth is only a label for a party line. At this point he has several options and must choose one of them: he may rethink the assumptions he has made about the species, society, and knowledge; or he may be reduced to cynicism; or he may proclaim some extrahuman foundations for his knowledge—scripture, revelation, demons, facts, or other. If he claims extrahuman support, he has taken the first step toward proclaiming a new dogmatism with all its attendant implications of propagandizing and heresy hunting. Thus the medicinal lie is the opiate of the social investigator. The content of the lie is always the declaration of the generalized and nonspecific superiority of some members of the species over the rest. The result is a renewed call for a class-structured society.

The major difference between the social investigators of the ancient world and those of today is that the ancients wished to change or improve the content of the social myths on which they assumed social action and social institutions had to be based, whereas modern social investigators in the field of socialization research are interested only in the techniques of producing consensual lies. Socialization, or more exactly, social indoctrination, is taken as an end in itself identical with the social propensities of the species. According to this view, stable institutions are possible only so long as indoctrination is complete and the same lies are believed by nearly everyone. Social knowledge exists only in terms of knowing the techniques of socialization. More importantly, social knowledge has nothing to do with the criticism or improvement of social values. The entire realm of the content of social myths is thus rendered immune from scientific investigation. However, the propositions about human nature, human learning, and human knowledge on which socialization theories are based are generally in error or vacuous. Investigations of these propositions have resulted in evidence contradictory to what socialization theories suggest. For example, adult character structure is assumed to have some crucial relationship to the child-rearing practices of weaning, potty training, and sexual initiation—but the relationship has as yet failed to be empirically demonstrated.

Socialization theories answer any and all questions we might ask about the social and political behavior of men and women—but so would a theory of fairy godmothers. These theories are useful only as sets of names for the variance left unaccounted for by our current inadequate descriptions of social structures and processes. The theories' failures to provide us with anything approaching reasonable guides toward developing social knowledge or improving social practice is due to their invidious presumption that the human brain is a passive recording instrument. This "bucket theory" of mind not only fails to account for the way human beings actually learn but also leads to activities, policies, and institutions that produce learning behavior analogous to that of decorticate robots. Socialization theories result in desocialization because they imply that all consensual behavior is relative and therefore to be managed and manipulated. According to this view "freedom means social indoctrination." But for the citizen to know that he or she is indoctrinated is to undermine the effectiveness of the indoctrination. Thus either socialization theories are false or else are destructive and subversive to the necessary consensus that social and political stability require.

In chapters 4 and 5, we analyze the role of cognitive structures in human learning. The relationship between organizational and cognitive structures is examined in an attempt to understand the experiential basis for invidious theories of human nature. Hierarchical organizations mean cognitive damage to the human organism that must live and work within them. The members of such organizations are consequently made less responsive to themselves and their environment, more restricted in the scope of their actions, more cautious in their aspirations, and rigidly narrow in their cognitive structures. The distribution of the cognitive damage differs according to the individual's position in the hierarchy. With respect to concrete action, the degree of insensitivity, repetitiousness, and rigidity is greater in the incumbents of the upper levels of the hierarchy and less in those of the lower levels. With respect to abstract thought, the degree of insensitivity, repetitiousness, and rigidity is greater in the incumbents of the lower levels and less in those of the higher levels. The differences reflect the elite's isolation from the demands of environmental adaptation and the different survival requirements at the various levels. The general result is nonadaptable and nonproductive individuals. While the cost of sustaining such individuals is high and requires some degree of exploitation in a hierarchy, dependent upon what resources are available, exploitation is not the primary goal of hierarchical structures. Although we can find greedy and even rapacious men and women predominating at upper levels—and also thriving throughout the middle and lower levels—I believe such greed to be largely compensatory. The understanding of compensatory behavior—the attempt to satisfy one human need by substituting gratification of another need—and its accompanying fantasies is perhaps a key to understanding the culture of class societies. While it appears that a greedy, superstitious, and pitiless human being is ideally suited to hold elite office, we often find unselfish, skeptical, and tolerant individuals doing just as well. The differences are only in styles of compensation. The form of the adaptation involved—consisting of the repetitious and unwavering application of a given formula or principle to all situations—remains the same whether the content of that formula is greed or altruism.

Because of the cognitive damage required for adaptation to the conditions of hierarchies, knowledge appears to be harmful to individuals within such organizations. They behave much as do persons suffering from temporary or permanent disabilities of the brain or other organs who defend themselves from the catastrophic confrontation with their disability. Defenses such as retreat, apathy, and denial are biologically functional in hierarchical situations but they have dangerous political implications. Harmful or damaging social contexts are likely to lead to censored aspirations and obstacles against awareness rather than to critical assessments and needed reforms. The apathy, dogmatism, resistance to change, and ignorance attributed to human nature are more the result of the formation of narrow cognitive structures under the survival demands of specific social contexts than the result of any inherent propensities of the species. Organizational contexts characterized by dissembling or disguise of crucial features, overrepetition of behavior patterns, and overmotivation or frustration result in functional brain damage. If we are to attempt the production of social knowledge, we must challenge the usefulness and meaning of such contexts. We must ask ourselves, in the words of Montague Ullman:

> How do we as students of behavior, unwittingly, by virtue of the theories we develop and the explanations we offer, allow for the continued generation of further social blindness? In short, how do we add to the problem? Are we engaged in a theory building that perpetuates the social scotoma . . . ?[2]

Experimental evidence from animal psychology indicates that learning consists in changing from one general, purposive pattern of behavior to another and another until a given problem of an organism's survival is solved. The findings of David Krech, E. C. Tolman, and others emphasize the important dynamic role of cognitive postulates in this process. Perception in this view is an event in which the organism frames a satisfactory internal matching response to environmental stimuli. Learning then is a self-activated, seeking process rather than a passive reception and recording of data. Because of human verbal capacities, we can articulate cognitive postulates in the form of theories that greatly expand our learning potential over that of other animals. Such articulation allows us to examine our cognitive structures for relevance, consistency, and adequacy before testing them in practice. Testing enables us to experiment without the threat of potentially fatal failures. We can use articulated theories to systematically investigate the world in a cooperative manner rather than simply respond individually to the contingencies of our experiences and ignorance. Theories perform three functions in this learning process. They provide us with an intelligible vocabulary for public discourse; they provide models of stable environmental patterns that allow us to predict the outcomes of our actions; and they provide us with schemata of investigation that enable us to look for missing information in a systematic way. While often treated as a mystery and often seen as a threatening or debilitating activity, theorizing is both a reasonable and necessary human enterprise involving skills and procedure that can be improved in practice. Specifically, the theorist should be in proximate contact with the objects and process he wishes to describe and understand, and the theorist should always begin with metaphors and models abstracted from human activities and techniques. Just as industrial techniques have provided us with the basic theoretical models of the physical sciences, so may social techniques provide us with the models needed for the development of the social sciences. While the quality of human life is dependent upon the quality of our theories of the environment and society, theorizing should be understood to be a necessary but not a governing or ruling social activity.

Traditionally, political theorists have responded to periods of massive political and social breakdown by analyzing institutional failures and articulating new visions of political possibilities. In the last three chapters of the book we undertake an analysis of this heroic style which attempts to reconstruct a shattered world. Insofar as the heroic or epic theorist creates a new order by prescribing perceptions, responses, and values, he fosters pathological social learning rather than development. Political order based on such prescriptions is only chaos in disguise because it maximizes social entropy in the form of cognitive hegemony, behavioral conformity and the accompanying suppression of novelty, variety, and information. Political theorists obsessed with order have failed to provide us with a means of producing social knowledge. In view of this failure, some political scientists recently have looked to the physical sciences for a more fruitful if less heroic model of the theoretical enterprise. Unfortunately few have gotten further than reading philosophers of science. Specifically, the ambiguous works of Thomas Kuhn have influenced the discussions of epistemology and theory construction in political science in the last decades.

Kuhn's description of the scientific enterprise confirms the need for heroism and dogmatism in the production of knowledge. While his work contains insights and is quite plausible on the surface, it fails to substantiate a need for cognitive hegemony and the hierarchical social organization required to maintain it. The apparent success of *The Structure of Scientific Revolutions* is due to its pervasive ambiguity of purpose, definition, and execution. Kuhn's theory of scientific development boils down to little more than a blind faith that sufficient environmental and social variation will occur to save scientists from perishing in the lockstep of dogmatic ignorance. From this failure we conclude that cognitive hegemony in science is more a fantasized need than an actual requirement, and that it is entirely vicious as a regulatory principle. While Kuhn may well be describing the deplorable bureaucratization of scientific research that exists today, his prescriptions for the most part are mystifying and even destructive of the knowing activity.

The traditional treatment of social ignorance has dealt with symptoms but not with the underlying biological disturbances of the human species. This was the view of the American social psychologist Trigant Burrow, whose life work was an attempt to describe the social pathologies of the human species. Beginning as an orthodox psychoanalyst, Burrow broke with Freud as he concluded that so-called normal behavior constituted not health but a social neurosis. He argued that the existence of this social neurosis demanded the development of laboratory techniques of group observation and analysis. In short, Burrow wanted society to be analyzed with the same thoroughness and uncompromising methodical care that Freud advocated for the analysis of the individual. He wished to establish a biological, as opposed to a social or conformist, standard of health.

Understanding neurosis as a result of the repression of people's fundamental social instincts, Burrow rejected individualism as a delusion and the taking of individuals as the unit of analysis in social research as fallacious. He argued that this delusion arose from the interdiction of organic responses by means of moralistic evaluations. Such interdictions cause a split between the human organism's responses to the environment and the verbal symbols utilized to describe that environment. Thus aspects of the environment are labeled "good" or "bad" not because of any relationship they bear to the biological life of the species but because of the personal advantage to be gained (in the form of various social and economic rewards) from agreeing with judgments. The social world resulting from this symbolic conditioning or autistic image of dependence is one in which ideas apparently determine behavior and the primary motivating force is the advantage of the individual ego. Social knowledge, of course, is impossible in such a world.

Burrow believed that this situation was the result of an evolutionary *faux pas*— namely the development of symbolic capacities in human beings resulting inevitably in the substitution of the partial, abstract processes of the symbolic system for the organism's total physiological pattern of response. However, the substitution of affective symbols for organic response occurs only within certain social contexts that Burrow failed to investigate. He mistook a necessary condition of the social neurosis—man's symbolic capacities—for the cause. But it is one thing to understand that a given species is susceptible to certain diseases and/or is debilitated by specific environments, yet quite another matter, as we have argued, for a species member to judge that species to be defective. Human beings cannot fly, nor do they act always as my limited imagination would want them to. Nevertheless they are not defective birds nor stubborn fools. As a seminal thinker, Burrow pushed into uncharted grounds with vigor and yet significant restraint. He left no cult behind. In recognizing the pervasiveness of the disturbance of the species and our inability to deal with this disturbance on a purely symbolic level, Burrow pointed the way to developing a new perspective from which to deal with social ignorance. As he indicated, we must develop laboratory techniques of direct group observation and experimentation, learn to avoid "semiomorphism," or the erroneous investment of the symbol with substance, and create inclusive schemata of social investigation that deny to the social investigator any fixed point of view or absolutist sanctuary. For we are dealing with an epidemic, not with a fallen creature, and the thrust of our efforts should be in terms of research rather than in terms of redesigning human beings.

In an effort to achieve a superior perspective, the heroic social investigator tries to separate himself from the social context he wishes to describe and explain. But such a perspective precludes any critical examination of the investigator's assumptions. In short, it requires the end of social investigation in any form other than cooking experience to fit the categories of the framework of research. The paradoxes of the heroic perspective—that ignorance is the basis of knowledge, that science is achieved at the cost of dogmatism, that the investigator avoids or escapes from that which he wishes to study, among many—all suggest that this view is symptomatic of pathogenic conditions. It has features similar to that perspective or outlook often labeled schizophrenic. R. D. Laing argues that what we have come to label madness is not a disease but an attempt to get well under pathogenic conditions. I suggest that this is a fruitful way of understanding the heroic perspective—as an attempt to produce social knowledge under conditions interdicting such knowledge. Exploring the phenomenon called schizophrenia can help us understand the limits of the heroic perspective and likewise something of the conditions that require the development of social ignorance.

For example, Gregory Bateson and his associates found that certain patterns of communication called "double binds" are associated with the occurence of schizophrenia. The preconditions of double binds—namely, prohibitions against altering the social context, leaving the context, or commenting on the paradoxical injunctions encountered in the context—are found wherever the control of human behavior is attempted in the name of order or some other social value. Any social structure or political institution that involves rules against altering the rules promotes disturbed communication. Communication disturbances, like double binding, require that people learn to suppress, distort, or discount their perceptions. The result is a severe loss in the individual's ability to distinguish what is real from what is fantasy. Social control—the direction of human behavior by a person or persons designated as superior—is a goal both false and impossible to achieve.

It is a false goal because over time it would entail restricting the range of future adaptation to that circumscribed by a few minds—a restriction that in all likelihood would entail the extinction of the species. Social control can be achieved only in ritual forms in which the overcompetent image of the ruler or administrator is maintained by means of paradoxical injunctions, overrestrictive contexts, and the resulting loss of ability to accurately perceive and evaluate. The price of social control is the continual and mundane demonstration of the citizen's inadequacy and error. Thus stability is purchased at the cost of the continual degradation of the members of the organization. Life is possible in such contexts of control, but living in them means learning not to see, not to feel, not to judge, not to discriminate. The resulting schizophrenic responses to such contexts represent a derangement of human theoretical capacities. As a substitute for incoherent losses and needs, the building of symbolic representations of the world proceeds, but the theoretical structures produced are not tools to guide learning and action but only ideologies of despair and consolation.

We must move from the goal of social control to that of controlling our political institutions and social contexts. For the attempt to control human behavior is only a symptom of social ignorance. Insofar as we do not understand and cannot control our organizational structures we attempt to remake human nature to fit the dictates of our ignorance. Social scientists can better serve the communities of mankind—they can resist and describe the institutional concealment and prohibitions, demanded by hierarchical organizations, against critical discourse concerning the communication disturbances. In this way they can help shatter the mind-forged manacles that debilitate our theoretical capacities. Further, social scientists must continually conceive of and try out alternative institutional structures and social contexts that are more conducive to the essential developmental processes of life. Organizations are to be designed not to shape men and women but to enable them to live out the problems of life with acumen and honor. The goal of the social investigator has always been to free mankind from its delusions. Once it is understood that delusions and deception cannot be employed in this ambitious and necessary undertaking, we will perhaps be on the way to a history made and fashioned with all the skill, love, and sense of beauty of which the species is capable. What remains then is the adventure of details. As Brecht wrote in conclusion to his poem "A Worker Reads History":

"So many particulars,
So many questions."

1   Escaping Myth: An Introduction to Epistemological Problems of the Social Sciences

> . . . if we have any chance at all to rediscover some value in collective life, we must reject past and present myths and attain full consciousness of the political reality as it actually exists.
> —Jacques Ellul, *The Political Illusion*

Orthodox political thought is based on the assumption that all viable forms of human organization are hierarchical—structured by scales of positional authority, specialized tasks, positional rewards, and restricted communication roles. Less technically, it is assumed that a social structure implies: a chain of command; an unequal if not skewed distribution of work, leisure, skills, and rewards; and functional ignorance expressed in a consensus of values, motivations, and cognitive maps. Since the birth of civilization this assumption has been supported by myths as well as by religious doctrines. Despite the announcement in the seventeenth century that all foundations of human thought must be subjected to the canons of rationality and despite the subsequent efforts to introduce and use more rigorous methods in the study of politics and society, the assumption has rarely been questioned and the myths remain intact in substance although rearticulated in the more modern and formal mode of reasoned arguments. This persistence suggests that the methodological and epistemological problems of theory and research in the social sciences involve more than logic, language, quantification, and enthusiastic empiricism.

Arguments for the Necessity of Hierarchy

The arguments supporting the necessity of hierarchical political and social structures are basically four, although they are seldom found pure or even alone. The first two arguments are based on interpretations of human nature, the third on ontological assumptions, and the fourth on empirical evidence. We will label these arguments: (1) psychological, (2) contractual, (3) metaphysical, and (4) empirical.

The Psychological Argument Schematically the first or *psychological argument* goes like this:

1. There is a single, common and unchanging human nature.
2. A basic feature of that nature is to always seek power (or domination) over others.
3. Power by definition requires submission.
4. Only a few can possess power at any given time because an increase in power means an increase in submission such that the powerful must seek always to thin their own ranks.
5. *Therefore:* Hierarchy is inevitable because the few will rule and the many will submit if men act according to their nature.

The difficulty with this argument is that it ends with a social structure requiring two kinds of human nature—a power-seeking nature and a submissive nature. Thus, Aristotle proclaims such a duality in his distinction between the rationality of the natural citizen and the natural slave. Plato suggests that there are three kinds of human nature, although he admits this proposition to be a lie. And, the conclusion contradicts the first premise of a single and fixed human nature. There remains another way out, however. We can alter the argument this way:

5. *(alternative:)* If all men seek power at all times, then social power, in the sense of stable dominance and order, is impossible to achieve.
6. Some men must forgo seeking power and submit (at least temporarily), allowing others to achieve it.
7. *Therefore:* Hierarchy is inevitable if men are to act according to their nature and live in society.[1]

The problem here is that most men must act most of the time counter to their own natures, suggesting extreme social instability. Hierarchical stability requires, then, a dual morality. That is, a ruler will act according to human nature, but a citizen will act to suppress human nature. The ruler's morality demands hypocrisy.[2] The citizen's morality demands lifelong unrelieved submission or, if temporary submission, then also hypocrisy, since it is likely that someone who has learned to deny his nature will be incapable of asserting the power needed to preserve the political equilibrium. In this world the danger to hierarchical society, as Mosca and Pareto pointed out, is the development of humanitarian sensibilities among the powerful few and the recurrence of power lust and resentment among the powerless many.[3] No coherent set of ethical rules or guides to successful political action can follow, since the argument implies that all men at some time must necessarily act both according to and counter to their own nature. This hidden contradiction in the argument allows us to derive any rules of conduct and to justify any course of action.

The Contractual Argument The second or *contractual argument* is usually seen in opposition to the first argument. It runs:

1. All men are created free and equal.
2. Freedom means the absence of restraints.
3. A society is a contractual system of rules or restraints limiting the freedom of each member in order to ensure the survival of all.
4. Society is necessary to human life—for various reasons according to different theorists, but all based upon conjectures about what "absolute freedom" would mean. Thomas Hobbes envisioned such freedom as "a war of all against all" while other writers emphasized other possibilities (such as madness) which Hobbes mentions in passing.[4]
5. Since (1, 2, 3, 4,) some men must be chosen (elected, appointed, self-appointed, etc.) to legislate and administer the rules of the social contract. Again Hobbes' formulation is the most concise: (A) Society is a contractual system; (B) contracts can be guaranteed only when there is an enforcing power or sovereign; (C) therefore, a sovereign power is necessary if men are to have a social existence.
6. *Therefore:* A political hierarchy is inevitable given the nature of men and their need for society.

Another part usually accompanying this argument points out that other prerequisites of society, like money and systematic incentives, also result in nongovernmental hierarchies. But the end point is always the same—that hierarchies, while social conventions, are nevertheless necessary to social existence given human nature.[5]

The contract argument has difficulties similar to the psychological argument. Being human results in self-contradicting behavior. Men are naturally "free and equal" and yet require social structures based on coercion and inequality. It follows that only rulers come near to acting rationally, in that they can at once maximize their freedom, avoid the degradation of subordination, and still get the benefits of social membership. Just as the tyrant is the only patriot in a despotic state, so the sovereign (whether president, king, or party secretary) is the only citizen in a republic. Popular sovereignty is a logical development of the argument, but it must be noted that democracy based on the contract argument is a means of universalizing the ruling function either symbolically through periodic voting or actually through rotation of office. In any case, all men are to rule not because they are competent or deserving, but because becoming rulers is the only way they can be human. Political thinkers in this tradition, from Locke on, have recognized this need and offered various opinions on whether only a few, many, or all could become rational and human.

Again, it is impossible to base a consistent set of ethics or guidelines for political efficacy on this argument, since to act freely as an equal is likely to result in ostracism or jail whereas to act socially is to go against one's basic nature. The political world based on this argument would be a zero-sum game for each individual—a world as much fraught with power struggles as the one based on the psychological argument. Indeed, the two arguments are usually found fused and men are at once proclaimed free and equal and condemned as knaves. In this contractual world the danger is the combination of the drive for freedom and equality and the need for social hierarchy since hierarchy makes each man a potential tyrant (or, via the drive for equality, a participator in tyranny) constantly tempted by the means to tyrannize embodied in political institutions. This tendency is the significant (if mostly missed) point of James Madison's *Federalist 10*.[6] Paradoxically, the contractual world that begins by positing human freedom and equality looks very much like the elitist world that begins by positing a lust for power and necessary inequality.

The Metaphysical Argument   The third argument is *metaphysical*. It proceeds in this manner:

1. The natural state of things in the universe (including men) is chaotic.[7]

2. Men (or organisms) cannot survive under conditions of chaos, but require a minimal order.[8]

3. Order is an artificial and improbable structure imposed by an agency possessing and expending great amounts of force or energy; that is, order is hierarchical.

4. An established order always contains an often hidden, but continuous fermentation of chaos.

5. As energy is expended, order collapses and all reverts eventually to primordial chaos.

6. Human societies require massive and powerful control units to attempt the ultimately impossible tasks of maintaining order.[9]

This argument is close to what Kant called the "physico-theological proof" of God's existence. For if the natural state of the world is disorder and if we observe order, then there must be an agency of order available, that is, something that is naturally orderly. Previously such a naturally orderly agent was considered supernatural. Modern versions assert instead that organic substances for finite periods of time are orderly, while ultimately succumbing to the basic trend toward chaos. But if men (as organisms) are natural agents of order, then control units are hardly necessary and the argument's conclusion is contradicted. Or to put it another way, if order is hierarchical and men are naturally orderly, the hierarchies will persist in human society without special efforts. Again, this statement results in a contradiction of the conclusion that massive and powerful control units are required for ordered societies. To go further: if men (like everything else) are natural agents of chaos, then it is not possible for them to order anything. Thus, putting some chaotic agents in charge of other chaotic agents is fruitless.

In recognition of this rebuttal a cynical version of the argument exists in the form of *the principle of the fewest sons of bitches;* thus: Since it is the nature of men to steal, kill, cheat (that is, increase chaos) at every opportunity, the chances for survival are enhanced if a few men are designated a government with certain rules as to where, when, and how the cheating, killing, and stealing are to be done. The supposition is that getting robbed and beaten by a few men at designated times and places is better than getting it from all sides at all times and at any place.[10]

The metaphysical argument, like the physico-theological proof of God's existence, rests basically on the analogy with human tool making—more specifically, machine building. A working machine implies a designer, a builder, and a tender. Thus, an ordered society implies an agency or agencies of design, creation, and maintenance. However, the environment always appears chaotic relative to the artifical order of a machine. When we assume that society is like a machine we imply that nonsociety in the forms of individual members and materials is chaotic. The mechanical analogy thus carries the contradictory implication that men are agents of order when they rule and agents of chaos when they do not rule, whatever the empirical case may be.

The Empirical Argument The *empirical* argument remains. This argument is not logical in form, but instead rests on a series of "facts" that need only to be recognized and interpreted. This argument begins by asserting that all known human societies are and have been hierarchical in form, consisting at least of two classes, the rulers and the ruled.[11] Or this assertion may be modified to say only that efficient, successful, or persistent human organizations, whether large or small, are hierarchical. Still another variant says that all modern and hence surviving human institutions are hierarchies. From these facts is derived the generalization or law that human organizations are necessarily hierarchical in form. This generalization is taken as an empirical proposition presumably to be discarded as soon as we find a counterinstance of a nonhierarchical organization. A more general version of the argument insists that all organized systems are hierarchical in form, whether cells, shell fish, or the Shell Oil Corporation.[12] Presented with these facts and the empirical generalizations based on them, we are left only with the task of understanding why hierarchy is the universal form of organization and describing how it works.

The difficulties with this argument arise when we try to conceive of a counterinstance, that is, a nonhierarchical society, organization, or system.[13] For example, when cases of nonhierarchical societies such as those of the Congo Pygmies or the Alaskan Eskimo are cited, they are rather summarily dismissed as based on inadequate observations.[14] The implication is that if we persist long enough in our observations of any functioning human organization and if we are honest, intelligent, good, and scientific we will discover its hidden hierarchical form despite any contrary appearances. Often the possibility of nonhierarchical forms is ruled out by defining such a form by impossible conditions. Svalastoga constructs an egalitarian model of society based on perfect permeability, that is, zero correlation between the status of parents and children.[15] Such a condition is, of course, impossible or at any rate nonsensical, requiring a complete lack of interaction between parents and children. A carpenter's son is more likely to become a carpenter if only because of access to the information and tools of that profession. Some correlation is always to be expected and it might even be quite high in an egalitarian social order. Given the tautological relationship between organization and hierarchy (based, of course, on the actual experience of living in class-structured societies), nonhierarchy is an imaginary nonentity. The perception of a nonhierarchical social order would be analogous to running across a white raven. We can either reformulate our definition of a raven or organization to include the new instance or we can invent new categories such as albino bird or spontaneous group. Our original definitions of ravens as black birds or organizations as hierarchies can thus easily remain unchanged.[16]

The Unfalsifiable Nature of the Arguments

Each of the arguments outlined admits of no falsification. Power is defined so amorphously in the case of the psychological argument as to include all forms of human interaction. This amorphous nature of power seems to hold even when rigorous and formal definitions are attempted. For example, Robert Dahl defines power this way: "A has power over B to the extent that he can get B to do something that B would not otherwise do." This seems at first to be intuitively correct. However, consider this example: B is dressing to go out. He is preparing to wear a new suede coat. A comes into the room and announces, "It is raining." B thereupon puts on a raincoat, digs an umbrella out of the closet, and decides not to wear his new coat. According to Dahl's formulation, A has exerted power over B. But if that is the case, then any human interaction must be a power relationship since as far as we know all such interactions (except perhaps the most trivial like passing on the street) involve some change in the plans and actions of the individuals involved. Not only does Dahl imply that all interactions are power relationships, but he also has rendered nonpower relationships impossible to conceive. But in their absence, the concept of power cannot discriminate. It has no boundaries and is, therefore, scientifically useless. Nor can the concept be saved by substituting a softer word like "influence" or a less emotional word like "control." The difficulty is due not to semantics but to the underlying assumption that all human relationships are power relationships.

Most writers would agree with Dahl that 'the main problem . . . is not to determine the existence of power but to make comparisons."[17] I maintain that the ubiquitous existence of power cannot be demonstrated unless the concept is defined in a bounded way, nor can power relationships be adequately described. Obviously, there is no society without interaction and, therefore, without power so defined. Further, if all interactions are power transactions, then all social forms are necessarily scalar.

The contract argument depends on a nonsensical and nonempirical definition of freedom. For, if freedom is the absence of restraint, only a billiard ball in a gravityless vacuum is free. Men seeking to become billiard balls (hard, smooth, insensitive to the environment) not only need restraining lest they destroy themselves and others, but moreover can approximate their goal only by achieving a hierarchical position freeing them from the demands of learning. There is no empirical access to the "natural" state of the universe and the postulation of natural chaos required by the metaphysical argument can in no way be tested, since the occurence of chaos precludes the possibility of perceiving. By assuming organization to mean hierarchy, as in the empirical argument, we rule out the possibility of finding any nonhierarchical social forms on *a priori* grounds, since all societies are organized unless in the throes of civil war or natural disaster. Each argument turns on a sleight of mind—loose definition, untestable assumption, tautological proposition, or nonsensical concept—that makes their conclusions unfalsifiable. Although any or all of these arguments are used by those calling themselves scientists, they do not admit of empirical tests. They cannot be wrong, but neither can they usefully guide novel operations. To grasp them adds nothing to the efficacy of our social practice, although it may be reassuring. These arguments are certainties or, in other words, myths.

The inevitability and necessity of hierarchy as a human organizational form remains a basic metaphysical postulate of modern social science. As metaphysical doctrine supported by myths, it has not been subjected to any rigorous analysis or careful formulation that could lead to the possibility of an observational test by those calling themselves scientists or behaviorists. While current opinion has it that the social sciences are largely free of metaphysics, myths, animistic notions, superstitions, or the like, and that social scientists think of such things as typical of ancient and primitive societies, we see that social myths, which if not new are dressed in new garments, remain basic to the conceptual framework of current thought and investigation. Further, these myths are so pervasive as to be treated often as elaborations of fact, while the hierarchical assumption they support is taken as a general law of social and political phenomena.

Notice what happens if we attempt to object to any of these arguments by citing counterevidence. Confronted with the psychological argument we might cite, say, paternal, altruistic, masochistic, ascetic, or loving behavior as instances of actions not seeking power. Doing this threatens to refute the proposition that all men seek power. But our adversary can point out that all our instances are only devious forms of power seeking. Parents care for children so as to mold them. Men give in order to obligate, deny themselves in order to consume. And so on. Further, sick individuals even devise perverse forms of power in which they appear to be victims, for in this view the masochist controls his torturer as surely as the sadist dominates his victim. All of these reinterpretations of our counterinstances now support the power proposition, implying that humans are so prone to seek power that they do it continuously and in fantastic forms. This kind of rebuttal is the clue that we are dealing with myth and not with empirical propositions. P. K. Feyerabend writes, "A myth . . . is not merely a dream or a piece of poetry whose distinctiveness from a true account of the universe is clearly realized. It is itself supposed to be such a true account; it is supposed to be in agreement with the facts."[18]

The arguments we are examining are myths because there are *no* facts—known, unknown, or imagined—with which they are not in agreement. Their propositions and conclusions are certainties because of their logical forms. What begin as theories of human behavior or propositions based on observation become myths through logical manipulation. Feyerabend describes the operation of turning theories into myths this way: "A is proposed. O turns up and threatens to refute A. Now B is proposed. B gives a new account of O according to which O now supports rather than eliminates A."[19] The resulting myth has the logical form of the proposition "tomorrow it will either rain or not rain." No matter what happens—draught, tornado, or any other event—the proposition will be true. It is a certainty. Feyerabend's point is that all certainties result from the logical manipulations of men and not from the isomorphism of theory and reality. He writes that "certainty is not something that exists independently of the human will but rather is a reflection of the way in which we (consciously or unconsciously) proceed."[20] The myths of hierarchy fit the facts of our social lives and human history, but they fail, just as our meteorological certainty fails, to provide any rational guides to action. These myths can be used (and have been used) to justify any and all actions, just as they can give *a posteriori* explanations of any social occurrence. They are psychologically and sociologically reassuring. Indeed, they give the impression of brute fact. So long as there is no need to alter our social practice—to evolve, to learn from experience, to develop—such myths function as universes of discourse rendering experience verbally intelligible. As soon as the need for social change arises their practical value and empirical content are exposed as inadequate. They not only become obstacles to the development of scientific knowledge, but also are indeed the verbal means of denying the possibilities of change. So long as the myths of hierarchy function as the most basic premises of the social sciences they must remain apologetics, teaching every man, in Montesquieu's words, "new reasons . . . to love his prince, his country, his laws."[21] Thus they restrict the range of human adaptation and rationalize the mad schemes of rulers.

The Failures of the Social Sciences

These functions of reconciling men and women to the status quo while limiting their aspirations to the results of available practice are contrary to the social functions of a productive science. The physical sciences are not always productive, but what we appreciate about them is the new possibilities of human adaptation that they open. When most success-ful, the physical sciences lead to changes in both the material and social environment of human life. They are productive in the sense of intro-ducing novel objects and operations into the world. We do not build monuments to the men who denounced Galileo, derided Newton, laughed at Pasteur, or thought Einstein crazy. But in the social sciences such men are so honored. Most political thinkers from Plato to Weber have proclaimed limits to practice and looked backward to perfection. Change has been equated with chaos and novelty with sin. Or when recognized by enlightened and Utopian thinkers, change has been wor-shiped as an end in itself, ruling out any possibility of making rational judgments about concrete innovations. Thus, change—in the form of the violent imposition of abstract bureaucratic designs ruling out fur-ther change—has been advocated by nearly all theorists, while change in the form of novelty and increased repertoires of responses has been condemned. The result is the conditions leading to the recurring com-plaint that while our knowledge of the environment has increased our knowledge of the human species and the social techniques based on that knowledge remains (despite the exaggerated claims of contempo-rary grant-seekers) at about the same level as the corresponding knowl-edge of the ancient Greeks or even of the ancient Mesopotamians.

Jacques Ellul remarks: "Politically man lives on certain connotative stereotypes without doctrinal content (democracy, republic, fascism, social justice and so on) which cannot help him understand or inter-pret events."[22] Harold Innis attempts to focus on the responsibility for this situation by asserting that "absorption of the social scientist in bureaucracy in the present crisis has left the community exposed to a flood of arrant nonsense."[23] Both authors attest the failure of social sciences in our time. And yet never has there been such an emphasis on method, rigor, empirical observation, data collection, replication, mathematization, and the development of social technology. Since these trends are now nearly half a century old, it is important to note their failure to free the social sciences from stereotypes, myths, or arrant nonsense. While the ancient despots of the Tigris and Eu-phrates river valleys could always hire an astrologer or soothsayer to advise them to do as they wished and add the approval of the heavens to their whims, modern officials can always find a political scientist, sociologist, or psychologist to confirm their impulses and lend to their fancies the authority of computers and abstruse formulas. No amount of preaching or practicing the so-called scientific method has aided in escaping mythology.

Indeed, it may be that political scientists, for example, found it at-tractive to adopt the logical positivist interpretation of scientific method because it added authoritativeness to their pronouncements, just as scripture was attractive for the same reason to twelfth-century political theorists. John Gunnell considers this adoption of philosophical doctrine on *a priori* grounds paradoxical in those calling themselves empiricists.[24] It is easier to understand this paradox if we suppose that political scientists were more interested in finding a mantle of respectable authority than a rigorous method of investigation that would lead to the challenge of many cherished political and social myths.

Many methods in the social sciences seem to be litanies. Philosophical doctrines are repeated at the beginnings and ends of articles and books, and mathematical techniques are discussed and displayed in such a way as to urge the acceptance of otherwise questionable assumptions and conclusions. The doctrines are often *non sequiturs* or platitudes unrelated to the problems at hand. Likewise, the mathematical techniques are often inappropriate. A new generation of more seriously trained mathematicians is now appearing in the discipline of political science, and their devastating critiques of a generation of supposedly sound scientific research is becoming an open scandal.

The obstacles to social knowledge must have something to do with things other than precise operational definitions, testable propositions, and formalization. For the very authors who prescribe such practice boldly assert the infallible myths of hierarchy. Feyerabend's description of intellectual practices under the hegemony of a theory turned myth gives a good picture of the state of contemporary social science:

> The conceptual apparatus of the theory having penetrated nearly all means of communication, such methods as transcendental deduction and analysis of usage, which are further means of solidifying the theory, will be very successful. Altogether it will seem that at last an absolute and irrevocable truth has been arrived at. Disagreement with facts may of course occur, but, being now convinced of the truth of the existing point of view, its proponents will try to save them with the help of *ad hoc* hypotheses. Experimental results that cannot be accommodated, even with the greatest ingenuity, will be put aside for later consideration. The result will be absolute truth, but at the same time, it will decrease in empirical content to such an extent that all that remains will be no more than a verbal machinery which enables us to accompany any kind of event with noises (or written symbols) which are considered true statements by the theory.[25]

This noisy ignorance is both reassuring and despairing. It both denies social dissolution and laments human failings. The failure it represents cannot be too strongly emphasized, for that failure is the beginning of wisdom, and not, as many seem to think, the end of reason.

The Critical Attitude

Feyerabend holds that a way out of this situation is the adoption of what he calls (after Karl Popper) a "critical attitude."

> All that is required is the realization that however basic and obvious a certain belief may seem and however great its appeal to those who have adopted it, *one* of the possible ways of getting out of trouble is the elimination of this belief and its replacement by something different.[26]

In the social sciences, what is needed (and quite generally so) are new and different theories of human action and social processes. But given this need we are at a loss how to proceed, for simply to change beliefs, conceptual frameworks, or vocabularies can merely be another way of avoiding problems. Feyerabend responds to this difficulty by requiring such alternative theories to be (1) counterintuitive or significantly different from established belief and (2) falsifiable or having a large number of statements which could count as refuting evidence. According to him, theories and facts are so interdependent that the facts required to falsify one theory may be discovered only within the conceptual structure of a countertheory.[27] For example, the myths of hierarchy we have examined point to a systematic selection, observation, and analysis of certain facts (such as the persistence of domination, competition, and manipulation in human affairs) that verify their truth as absolute and irrevocable. It is necessary to adopt a different theory of political and social organization in order to observe and analyze a body of facts (such as the seemingly remarkable persistence of fraternity, productive cooperation, and reliable communication in human relationships) sufficient to constitute refuting evidence. Further, such a countertheory should be factually adequate, that is, account for most of the known facts of the old mythology but lead ultimately to findings inconsistent with formerly accepted empirical propositions and predictions. In terms of social theory this would mean that a successful countertheory would increase the range of social possibilities and not simply substitute one conceptual and institutional hegemony for another.

A "critical attitude" may be a necessary condition of the development of knowledge but it is not sufficient. Merely adopting new vocabularies, models, or analogies that are themselves "certainties" incapable of falsification is another form of dogmatism. "All they do," writes Feyerabend, "is describe ordinary and well-known things in an extraordinary and not so well-known fashion."[28] The literature of the social sciences is rank with new theories today. Most of these are novel only in the sense of restating old clichés in new forms with new symbols. This old-stuff/new-expression formula is apparently what is meant by "middle-range" or "empirical" theory. This may be a more or less conscious strategy of preserving an area of creativity in a time when invention often invites bureaucratic intervention, or it may be taken as evidence of the social determination of ideas. In Weber's words, "Concept-construction" (or theory building) "depends upon the setting of the problem and the latter varies with the content of culture itself."[29]

The contemporary setting of the problem for social scientists is the university. Whether from necessity or expendiency, they tend to investigate their subject matter in the library and the study rather than in the field or in the laboratory. They either choose to learn or must learn about society by means of books and various reports and almost never by direct observation or participation. Thus the resultant version of the "critical attitude" found in the social sciences today prescribes a retreat from empirical observation, experience, and skill consistent with this setting. As he detects the interrelationship of theory and fact and seeks to devise a different theoretical perspective, the "critical" social scientist tries to ignore, deny, or flee from the facts of the social situation in which he lives. This removal can take the form of a Baconian purification of the mind's idols, the disciplined detachment of Mannheim's intellectual, or the abstraction of Marcuse's "negation." In each case, the social investigator must be removed from participation in the situation in order to approximate what Merleau-Ponty caricatured as an "absolute spectator."[30]

This prescription apparently requires some form of death as a prerequisite for social knowledge—since a human organism that ceases to participate and respond to the world thereby ceases to live. Emile Durkheim pronounced this suicidal need to free the social scientist from the constraints of his culture and society in this manner:

> The impulses of common sense are so deeply ingrained in us that it is difficult to eradicate them from sociological discussion. When we consciously free our thoughts of them, they still mold our unconscious judgments; and against such error we have no defense. Only long and special training can teach us to avoid it. The reader must bear in mind that the ways of thinking to which he is most inclined are adverse, rather than favorable, to the scientific study of social phenomena; and he must consequently be on his guard against his first impressions.[31]

Such advice has led to the strange situation in which social scientists literally know less and less about the detailed operations of the organisms and organizations they profess to describe. The adoption of the philosophical doctrines of logical empiricism as a means of attaining objectivity in research has either drastically circumscribed research or directed it away from empirical concerns and cases.[32] In the social sciences, self-styled empiricists are constantly telling everyone what they must or must not see. Such empiricism in political science, for example, has meant an increase in abstract, ambiguous, and formal pronouncements and a decrease in actual content. Textbooks, journals, and lectures read or sound grand (if faintly Hegelian) and yet are distinctly lacking in empirical statements. Psychologists study rats and pigeons, economists construct vast Platonic theories, political scientists concentrate on slavishly correlating the occurence of various phenomena while maintaining studied indifference to relevance or social desirability. Sociologists appear to remain the least scientistic and still go out in the field as do the anthropologists, but both appear to be ashamed and are turning increasingly to computer simulation and other techniques of investigation that avoid empirical contamination.

The Promise of the Social Sciences

In this century man has learned that his knowledge is much more a creation of his own imagination and technology than a reflection of the ultimate structure of reality. Physicists were the first to formulate this insight and it is gradually being absorbed by the social sciences. This recognition has shattered beliefs held to be certain as well as the belief in the possibility of certainty itself. Despite the dilemmas created by man's discovery that he (not some supernatural force) is the source of the patterns of his perceptions, his operations, and his institutions, a recurring theme of optimism is found in many writers today. For example, Feyerabend writes:

> So far man was only responsible for acting or not acting in accordance with a certain code. The code itself was "given" by the basic myth and is unalterable. Now it is admitted that man is the creator even of the most basic rules of behavior and therefore responsible of them too. This is the step from childhood into maturity.[33]

This idea is repeated, for example, by men as diverse as Marshall McLuhan and B. F. Skinner. McLuhan declares: "Hitherto most people have accepted their cultures as a fate like climate or vernacular; but an empathic awareness of the exact modes of many cultures is itself a liberation from them as prisons."[34] Skinner expresses the theme differently in this form: "We are all controlled by the world in which we live, and part of that world has been and will be constructed by men. The question is this: are we to be controlled by accident, by tyrants, or by ourselves in effective cultural design."[35]

All this is an echo of Marx's prophecy of the end of the prehistory of determinism and the beginning of history as a species-directed process. Much is promised by such millenarian statements, but so far the discovery of man's responsibility for his own fate has resulted in a widespread retreat from using that discovery. We need to find out more about the particular limits that social and physical context place on thought as well as to explore the possiblity of actively designing and living the codes and institutions of culture. We must recognize that the creation of a body of social knowledge—a set of models, explanations, and other pattern statements which would enable men and women to act collectively in new ways that would meet the requisites of human life—is a direct threat to all existing political structures, however idealistic their ideology or benign their goals. Myths about the profane nature of man and the sacred forms of organization, on the contrary, promise stability, if not stagnation.

In this discussion I have used the modern myths of hierarchy as an example of political certainties that cannot be challenged empirically because of their logical form. This fact of logic is only a reflection of the fact that they cannot be critically challenged by any group of social scientists in any country in the world today without fear of some form of retribution. As Laing notes, it is easy for us to see that social science is impossible in contemporary Russia or China unless those countries undergo extensive political change, but it is rare for us to understand that the same is true of our own and other nations of the so-called free world. The paradigm situation for contemporary social scientists is that they can remain investigators of political and social processes and structures so long as they forgo attempts to create a body of useful knowledge. Instead of trying to deny or escape this situation through compulsive ritual in the form of methods, or through fantasies in the form of negations, we should acknowledge the insight of the archeologist V. Gordon Childe that "a precondition for the perfection of knowledge . . . is the realization of the ideal society."[36]

The goal of perfect, certain knowledge is as false as the chilling idea of a perfect society. It leads to the ossification of intellectual life. Better knowledge than we have and better societies than we have are real possibilities and they are interconnected. Better social knowledge, I argue, is knowledge that expands the present repertoire of human social possibilities and further increases the range of future adaptation. It is novel, relevant, and reliable. Better societies are those that are flexible, complex, and responsive enough to be adaptable to the needs of human beings and the changing demands of the physical environment. Finally, we should recognize that the knowledge—its precision of detail, its levels of complexity, its relevance, and its reliability—required for beginning the conscious design, evaluation, and eventual redesign of social and political institutions is far beyond the competence of any elite and demands cooperative efforts on an unimagined scale.

2 Social Ignorance and the Social Investigator

> When precedents fail to assist us, we must return to
> the first principles of things for information, and
> *think,* as if we were the *first men* that thought.
> —Thomas Paine

In the matrilineal societies of the Trobriand Islands, physiological paternity is not recognized. It is inconceivable to the Trobrianders that males cause pregnancy. When the anthropologist Bronislaw Malinowski discovered this piece of social ignorance, he tried to correct it. However, the Trobrianders labeled any discussion of the matter "missionary talk." Such talk to them added up to an absurd theory of paternity which they easily refuted with contradicting facts. One Trobriander asserted, "the missionaries are mistaken; unmarried girls continually have intercourse, in fact, they overflow with seminal fluid, and yet have no children."[1] Malinowski had to admit that such were the facts. Other evidence brought to his attention included a blind, deformed near-idiot woman named Tilapo'i. This woman was considered too repulsive for any male to come into contact with and yet she had a child. Albino women were considered unfit for intercourse, but they too were cited as evidence, since many of them bore children. One of Malinowski's native friends, Layseta, recounted that he had been absent from his wife for more than a year and found two children when he returned. When the anthropologist questioned others about this, hinting that the children were not Layseta's, he found that no one understood what he was talking about. He also learned that if pregnancy occurred during a premarital alliance, the male would leave the woman and refuse to marry her because she had broken the taboo against pregnancy outside of marriage.

This is an example of social or ritual ignorance, and such ignorance involves a set of problems in what I call social epistemology. For a

Trobriander to challenge the prevailing theory of exclusive maternity would be to challenge many of the central institutions and practices of that society, such as polyandry, matrilineal inheritance, clandestine adultery, and premarital promiscuity. Further, it would also challenge even more fundamental postulates about the nature of reality and the basic techniques of survival. Thus those most likely to guess the truth—the adulterous wife, the albino's lovers, or the swain of Tilapo'i—are those who would suffer punishment or degradation for stating it. Under these conditions rational, logical, or empirical arguments for paternity are refuted with equally rational, logical, and empirical arguments. The Trobrianders had learned well to defend their beliefs because they were frequently challenged by missionaries. Malinowski noted the Christian dogma of the trinity and Christian patriarchal sexual morality simply do not make any sense in a matrilineal society. Thus physiological paternity must be one of the basic principles proselytized. However, the natives considered the correct view of the missionaries as part of the set of antagonistic myths they were preaching. Thus the theory seemed to them to be only a self-serving ideology.

Ritual Ignorance

The Trobriand theory of exclusive maternity is unfalsifiable, but not because of any faulty logic or poor articulation. Nor is the theory a belief which they often disregard in practice, as some evidence might suggest. For example, Malinowski notes that Trobrianders also assert that virgins cannot give birth, condemn unmarried mothers, and insist on the need for a male in every family, much as we do. All of these conclusions are reached by a kind of reasoning much different from ours. That is, virgins cannot give birth because their vaginas have not been dilated; families must have fathers for sociological reasons. Practice is explained in conformity with belief, even those practices that we maintain on the basis of different beliefs. What is difficult to understand is that physiological paternity is taken into account in Trobriand practice and theory while it is simultaneously denied. As Malinowski states it:

> Thus, though the natives are ignorant of any physiological need for a male in the constitution of the family, they regard him as indispensable socially. This is very important. Paternity, unknown in the full biological meaning so familiar to us, is yet maintained by a social dogma which declares: "Every family must have a father; a woman must marry before she may have children; there must be a male to every household."[2]

Although the world of the Trobriander and our world seem to be conceptualized in radically different ways, our practices in regard to unmarried mothers and the necessity for fathers are identical. Thus we assume that either they understand paternity as we do or that they suppress their knowledge of it.

The Trobrianders pay for their belief in exclusive maternity with faulty breeding practices. Pigs are among their most valued possessions. Malinowski says that the ideal is to possess strong, healthy pigs of a good breed. While the flesh of the village or domestic pigs is a delicacy, the flesh of wild or bush pigs is taboo. But the Trobrianders castrate all the male village pigs. Thus the bush pigs sire all the offspring. When Malinowski pointed this out he was not understood. Indeed, one informant used the pigs as falsifying evidence against the missionary theory. Witness: "From all male pigs we cut off the testes. They copulate not. Yet the females bring forth."[3] Although European pigs are highly valued and worth many times more than a village pig, the Trobrianders did not breed them since they castrated the males. Malinowski cites these examples from pig-raising practices as crucial evidence that Trobrianders do not just give lip service to the idea of exclusive maternity, but that there is a depth and tenacity to the belief.

In one of the first articles written by Malinowski, he himself was misled about the Trobriand beliefs in the area of pig raising by a statement of one of his informants which went: "They copulate, copulate, presently the female will give birth."[4] He interpreted this to mean that copulation caused pregnancy. He later came to understand that it means that vaginal dilation is necessary to pregnancy. Dorothy Lee argues that both interpretations are wrong and that the sentence represents only simple temporal sequence without any sense of causation.[5] She remarks that "this cultural stress on simple sequence rather than causal relationship may acccount for the Trobrianders' ritual ignorance of physiological paternity."[6] Lee perceives an "absence of a cause-and-effect pattern of thought" and notes that "Trobriand culture has no convention for motivating action in terms of ends."[7] This logic without causality is mirrored in Trobriand ethics. For example, nearly all exchange in this society is in the form of giving. But such giving is never done with the expectation of a gift in return, even though there is always sooner or later such a gift. Lee concludes that "the activity, then, which is mostly highly sanctioned among the Trobrianders is futile giving."[8] Bateson labels Trobriand culture, as revealed in magical practices, as "semi-Pavlovian." He remarks that "it appears from Trobriand magic that these people continually exhibit a habit of thinking that to act as if a thing were so will make it so," or that " 'salivation' is instrumental to obtaining 'meat powder.' "[9]

Rules of Social Ignorance

Notice that having begun with an erroneous notion of exclusive maternity we have become involved in questions of animal husbandry, logic, ethics, and effective action. Any correction of the Trobrianders' theory of procreation would involve changes in their practices of pig raising, in their magical procedures, in the structure of their language, and in their valuation of actions. I am not familiar enough with descriptions of the society to speculate on the relationship of all these to their social structure, but I assume that they are connected and consistent with it. Thus what appear to be simple, empirical statements about procreation are based on an entire system of ethics, logic, and metaphysics. These statements are then in no sense value-neutral though their connections with the dominant values of the society are not apparent. That is, they appear neutral just as many of our descriptive statements of the world and our society appear neutral within the framework of social postulates and practices in which they are asserted. To challenge such statements often seems perverse, if not ideologically motivated. Thus to demand of social science that it stick to crude empirical description is then to demand that it become deliberately ignorant of the problems of social epistemology and to tie it blindly to the beliefs and structures of the status quo.

These problems are complex. Erroneous beliefs like those of the Trobrianders are often explained as the results of the process of socialization—meaning that the members of a society have been conditioned by the reward-and-punishment structures of their culture to see the world and to talk about it in designated ways. It is this simplistic account of cultural beliefs that I wish to criticize. For in this case, Trobriand culture both denies physiological paternity and takes account of it at the same time. There is not simply a rote formula or an opinion about procreation, there is a structure of explanation that accounts for all available evidence—even the evidence that we would count as falsifying. Stanislaw Ossowski writes that "an intellectual scheme that is rooted in the social consciousness may within certain limits successfully withstand the test of reality. In time of need, arguments or interpretations can always be found to invalidate inconvenient facts."[10] But Ossowski is again too simplistic. It is not, in this case, just that facts are ignored; rather, most are interpreted in the light of the theory as confirming evidence. Empirical events like copulation, pregnancy, and childbirth are not denied—they just are not connected in the same way we would connect them. The important point is to note that in this example we find again the structure of a myth as Feyerabend described it, that is, a theory that accounts for all facts and all possible facts. For, while it might be possible to educate a Trobriander in biological science and genetics, such education would entail teaching an entirely different way of life. This teaching is possible only if there *is* an entirely different way of life, possibly via immigration or social change. Thus it is extremely difficult for a Trobriander to come up with a theory of physiological paternity and even more difficult to vindicate within Trobriand culture his or her reasons for doing so.

The situation of social ignorance is convoluted and difficult. Laing conceives of the context of such ignorance as governed by a set of rules:

> Rule A: Don't.
> Rule A1: Rule A does not exist.
> Rule A2: Rule A1 does not exist.[11]

In the Trobriand case, Rule A says, "don't recognize physiological paternity." Rule A1 says that there is no rule against recognizing such a fact (that is, there is no such fact, as the evidence clearly shows). Rule A2 then says that there is neither a rule against recognizing such a rule as A1 nor a rule A. In other words, at this level, the Trobriander would just not understand what was meant, as was the case when Malinowski questioned his informant about who fathered his children or asked a chieftain why he ate the offspring of bush pigs. Laing continues:

> In order to comply with the rules, the rules have to be broken. Even if one could wash one's brain three times a day, part of oneself must be aware of what one is not supposed to know in order to assure the continuance of those paradoxical states of multiplex ignorance, spun in the paradoxical spiral that the more we comply with the law the more we break the law. . . . [12]

Sartre's analysis is similar. He calls the situation one of bad faith. At first glance, bad faith appears to have the structure of a falsehood; or, in terms of socialization theory, it appears to be the adherence to cultural values in the face of facts. But Sartre points out that an individual in such a situation must know the "truth" in order to effectively hide or deny it. Sartre notes, "I must know in my capacity as deceiver the truth which is hidden from me in my capacity as the one deceived."[13] That is, what is involved is an "unwillingness-to-see," not an "inability-to-so-see."[14]

The rules of what Lee called ritual ignorance are not transmitted by an oral or written tradition. They are not imposed or adopted from some source outside of the individual. Such rules are self-initiated and self-imposed. They are viable techniques of survival under certain conditions. The human being cannot learn not to learn, as the neurophysiologist Grey Walter points out.[15] If the human species were that simple it would have long ceased to exist. For, caught up in delusions of gods, demons, and heroic figures, it would have forgotten to provide itself with the daily sustenance of food, love, shelter, and work that it requires for survival. Social ignorance then is the result of a process that involves the individual actively, not just passively. The delusions of humanity may be opiates, but they are opiates produced by that same humanity and never simply purchased or absorbed.

Social Epistemology

Social epistemology as a study deals with the social context in which ignorance pays off and the means by which men and women learn to lie to themselves and yet retain enough grasp of reality to perform the actions necessary to survival. I introduce the term advisedly because I wish to indicate the relationship between methodological and metaphysical issues in the sciences and the social context in which they arise. Also I wish to distinguish a viewpoint different from that of the more conventional sociology of knowledge and socialization theories. The basic premise of these viewpoints is that ideas are existentially determined. This premise implies that thinking is not something that one does, but something that happens because of outside or environmental causes. Although the terms *sociology of knowledge* and *socialization* are quite recent, the outlines of this approach to understanding the relationship between social structure and cognitive structure are as old as Western traditional political thought itself.

Plato's famous allegory of the cave is a depiction of the problems faced by a social investigator in attempting to demystify the beliefs and unravel the rules of ritual ignorance of hierarchical social structures. According to Plato, the philosopher (or social investigator) finds himself in the following situation: The routines and rules of social life chain people in such a way that they can see only the shadowy representations of unseen manipulators. Their surroundings are in darkness and offer few clues for understanding. The social investigator somehow (by some terrific exertion of will, some divine or accidental intervention, or perhaps some startling discovery of hitherto overlooked data) finds his chains broken and turns to discover first the mechanisms of delusion—the manipulators, their tools of manipulation, and the source of the persuasiveness of the images they project. Second, he discovers a way out of the cave of his society and thereupon escapes the images of culture to emerge with great pain into the real world of sunlight. But with this miraculous escape the investigator's work has only begun. For now he must return to the darkness to teach his fellow citizens or inmates what he has learned.

What he has learned is not clear. Some might say that the investigator must return to teach his fellows about the higher reality of the sunlit world and the limited cave structure in which they are entangled, in order to help them build a new social structure congruent with the truth. Others understand the allegory to mean that the investigator must return to the cave, strengthened by his vision, to resolutely maintain the necessary delusions on which the order of the social cave is based. That is, he returns as a wise guardian of delusion, understanding both the appeal of skepticism and criticism and the necessity for suppressing them.[16] The radical or revolutionary investigator returns to change society drastically, making it conform with the new vision of truth. The conservative investigator returns to bolster conventional values as a means of maintaining the fundamental necessity of social order. Neither task is easy, as Plato notes. He foresees the social investigator will be laughed at, derided, and perhaps even killed.

Paradoxes of the Social Investigator

Plato's allegory raises four important epistemological issues that any social investigator must confront. The investigator must account for: (1) the general state of social delusion; (2) his own method of escape; (3) his resulting social ineptitude; and (4) the reluctance of others to follow his example and perhaps more significantly their hostilities to his attempts to enlighten them and/or lead them to freedom. To account for these is a formidable task of explanation. This task haunts all social investigation. It involves unavoidable paradoxes. First we must demonstrate the social function of delusions and the pervasiveness of a human capacity for delusion and deception. Human beings must be understood as needing and capable of an extraordinarily high level of lying and ignorance. We must show not only that lies and delusions can occur among people but that they occur with ease and little cost. Men and women must be understood as both dissemblers and fools; and these characteristics must be recognized as functional for the survival of the species.

Then we must demonstrate some means or method by which such delusions can be discovered to be false and/or can be escaped. Such methods presuppose a human capacity for knowledge and the motivation to develop accurate descriptions of the social world. Indeed this capacity and motivation must be large and strong in order for a social investigator to be successful in the face of the difficulties created by the pervasive and functional nature of social delusions. Therefore we must show not only that dissembling and foolish human beings are sometimes capable of truth and wisdom but also that they are capable of actively seeking such things for long periods of time despite the strictures (both social and biological) against such activities. In short, our method of escaping social delusions must be powerful enough to radically transform human nature even as the occurrence of the escape indicates that human nature must be different from what we supposed in the first place. But having demonstrated that delusions can be escaped, we must again explain why so few escape them and, more importantly, why our new found methods of escape are resisted by others. If there is a capacity and motivation for knowledge requisite to devising the means of escaping social ignorance, it must be rare or weak since so few respond.

But now we must again account not only for human error but also for the apparently conscious choice of an inferior existence based on ignorance instead of an existence based on knowledge. We must show either that ignorance is bliss and that social investigation is a perverse activity or that we cannot, except in special instances, discriminate between ignorance and knowledge—in which case the social investigator's claims to knowledge are dubious. Finally we must try to believe that the escape from delusion is something worth doing and that the price we pay for such an escape in terms of personal failure and even mental suffering is worth paying. That is, if the quest for social knowledge is a nonhuman or even an antihuman endeavor, how can we take it up or recommend it? For those who achieve such knowledge seem to be beings outside or beyond the politics of a human community. Like Aristotle's apolitical man, they are either revolutionary beasts or founding gods. The deeds they accomplish or recommend are bloody and awful. The social orders they map out or leave behind are based on a new social ignorance that specifically forbids the kinds of active quest of knowledge the investigators pursued. As these heroes stride off the stage they leave behind a structure of paradoxes promising new and endless tragedies of insight, insurrection, and enforced ignorance.

These paradoxes are the first clue that Plato's hallowed and influential way of explaining social ignorance is not satisfactory. We could stop with that profundity. However, it is my view that the task is impossible or at least mired in paradox because the situation has been improperly described. The descriptions and explanations of the problems of social knowledge derived from Plato throughout the history of Western political thought all fail because they do not take into account the limitations of the hierarchical context of knowing. That is, they assume the given context as the only reality rather than as a particular kind of social structuring with a situational logic that entails systematic ignorance. Thus the form of explanation is to indicate a special methodology of escape, while describing a pervasive and determining system of delusion. These special methodologies all share the false assumption that the central problem in knowing is the avoidance of error. We will look at three attempts at such explanations—Francis Bacon's, Karl Marx's, and Karl Mannheim's.

The Relationship of the Social Investigator to Society

"The only theory of knowledge which can be valid today is one which is founded on that truth of microphysics: the experimenter is part of the experimental system," declares Sartre.[17] The relationship between the social investigator and the system he is observing is quite close, as Plato pointed out. One sees quite easily that the very closeness of this relationship is what seems to make the quest for social knowledge hazardous. One does not, however, so easily see why this is so or whether it is necessarily so. The truth that Sartre alludes to is difficult to interpret even on the level of microphysics. Bohr's conception of complementarity (that it is necessary to picture microphysical events in seemingly contradictory ways if we are to account for them) and Heisenberg's uncertainty principle (that it is impossible to attribute to a particle a precise motion and an exact location at the same time) have been interpreted to be statements about the structure of subatomic events, or as statements about the limitations of human perception. Quantum theory may tell us only how we must talk about certain kinds of micro events, or it may tell us something about the events themselves. Generally, quantum theory has been interpreted in a purely epistemological way. It has seemed to buttress the crude positivistic notion that only those things exist which we can measure, and that only those statements are meaningful which we can verify. That is, one of the results of recognizing that the investigator is part of the experimental system may be to derealize knowledge to the point that it becomes something like an image projected onto the physical or social universe. Certainly this theory of knowledge is not one of the sort for which Sartre is looking. Another way of interpreting quantum theory, however, implies that the world is structurally indeterminate and that our notions of Newtonian physics are naive and fixated, if not simply erroneous. This interpretation has important implications for social epistemology, as we shall see. Usually it is ignored or taken to imply the terror of ultimate chaos.

The nature of the relationship between the social investigator and society is crucial. There are several ways of formulating this relationship and the resulting problems for social knowledge. Does this relationship entail the probability of distortion because of the inherent limitations and cognitive vulnerability of human beings or the massive effects of institutional conditioning or the threats and sanctions anticipated because of the effect of social knowledge upon the power distribution in the social structure?

Theological Epistemology

The problem of the perceptual limitations and susceptibilities of the investigator has been most forcefully described by Francis Bacon, although his formulation owes much to the Judeo-Christian notion of man's fallen nature. According to the Baconian view, the human organism is a bundle of passions and appetites, vain myths, and paradoxical laziness. Men and women tend to perceive the world in the most self-satisfying, self- and group-aggrandizing and yet effortless manner they can achieve. This natural way of viewing reality is thus determined by a set of preconceived notions consisting of clichés, superstitions, traditions, so-called common sense, and other social dogmas that are easily learned and simple to apply. These notions, or "idols" as Bacon called them, are apparently created by fancy—that is, by simply guessing or speculating about the nature of things in some way divorced from any experience except that of the joy and security of social conformity. The human organism is thus a self-serving, inertia-loving entity. Each individual from birth onward is seeking a cave of delusion in order to escape the demands of learning. For Bacon the problem is not only how to escape this collective cave but how to motivate people, against their nature, to want to escape.

Bacon's method for escaping the limitations of being human has been called "epistemological protestantism."[18] It involves a process of first systematically cleansing and polishing the mind and then passively exposing it to the true light of facts. According to Bacon, knowledge cannot be achieved through the impure works of the mind driven by the passions. The source of knowledge comes from without—from without society and without our efforts, if only we learn to attend to the world of fact with patience and purity. Bacon's method is a spiritual exercise that he described as "the true and legitimate humiliation of the human spirit," the "true end and termination of infinite error," and as the "legitimate, chaste, and severe course of inquiry."[19] According to him, the "uniqueness of what he called the "inductive method" was "that it seeks for the sciences not arrogantly in the little cells of human wit, but with reverence in the greater world."[20] All this implies, and Bacon believed, that the mind is basically an adequate instrument of knowledge if purified and "restored to its perfect and original condition." Even so, the active mind was the major source of error and delusion (or as Bacon put it, "the human intellect makes its own difficulties,")[21] while the source of knowledge was the world of material things and processes. The humiliation and cleansing of the mind led to a direct and unmediated communion with nature. Symbols of the success of Bacon's method as ideology, if not a canon of modern investigation, are today found in the immaculate white vestments and thick eyeglasses of the scientist, as popularly imagined.

But why should anyone subject himself to such humiliation? If human beings are so easily deluded because of their inordinate appetite for power and demand for recognition, qualities that move them to seek closed conceptual caves, why should they submit themselves to the severity of Bacon's method? The answer is that the humiliation required is only temporary. Submission to the method eventually results in the acquisition of theoretically unlimited power. Thus human nature—lazy, greedy, and vainglorious as it is—could realize its goals of unlimited power and sloth only by submitting itself to the severe and chaste discipline of the inductive method. But problems remain. Bacon maintains that what corrupts intellect in the first instance is the desire for power, ease, and abundance. It is difficult to see why these desires would not be still corrupting after a period of chastity. Bacon's formula appears to simplify rather than cure mankind's supposed defects. In a sense, therefore, it is prophetic. The adoption of Bacon's method may well lead to extensive and arrogant corruption.

The problems for social knowledge and scientific knowledge in general, which Bacon saw—the pervasiveness of dogma, superstition, the inventive but vain speculations of the academic world, and the heavy burden of tradition—are real enough.[22] His sense that these problems are due in part to a neglect of and in part to a bias against the painstaking manipulation and observation of material environment is quite promising.[23] However, his paradoxical combination of humility and arrogance, self-effacement and power lust, make the enterprise of the social and physical sciences appear almost impossible, except as limited instruments at the service of domination. Perhaps this appearance results from Bacon's solution to the problem of the social distortion of knowledge having more to do with the informational problems of hierarchical administrators than with the actual difficulties of social investigation. As the physician William Harvey put it, "He writes philosophy like a Lord Chancellor."[24] In a hierarchical structure, subordinates tend to tell superiors what they want to hear. Thus, an administrator's wishes, fancies, and whims—insofar as they are known to subordinates—become obstacles to his gaining needed information. The logic of the administrator's position promotes delusions of grandeur and paranoia. Periodic humiliation is a much needed therapy in such a situation. Bacon's lasting impact on the formulation of the epistemological problems of the social sciences is due to this need. His inductive canon with its built-in informational overload, its prescriptive humiliation, and its grandiose promise of unlimited power provides a framework for understanding the epistemology of the administrative context.

Using Bacon's method means learning to see social processes from the perspective of this context. It enables the intellectual symbol worker to grasp the logic of the administrator.

The administrative perspective seems objective, since it is impersonal. At the same time, the premises and logic of this perspective limit knowledge to what is useful to the ruling function. Rather than increasing the range of adaptive responses of men and women in society, Baconian social science merely increases the range of administrative responses to human demands. It is hard for the social scientist who has undergone "true and legitimate humiliation" to understand that those who are administered may judge him to be biased and even corrupted. Given his assumptions, he is pure, without biases, and the rewards he reaps are only the just fruits of a true method. Further refinements of Bacon's epistemology at the hands of Hobbes, Freud, and contemporary behavioralists have not changed this self-certainty. We begin with man, a fallen creature hardly capable of knowing at all, so beset is he by passions and appetites that run counter to his own survival. This fallen nature can be saved only by chastising it by means of a severe method while pandering to its perverse demands. But these expedients hardly seem a solution. The description of the fallen creature's derangement from Bacon to Pareto easily persuades one that the case is hopeless. Of course, that conclusion is heresy. Bacon's method of objectivity in research demands a paradoxical faith in both man's degradation and his capacity for purification. This faith, which underpins Bacon's optimistic declaration that knowledge is power, is more likely to lead to the converse notion that power is knowledge. Thus chaste and severe humiliation may pass easily into an epistemological terror, resulting in mind-forged manacles.

Mechanical Epistemology

Marx's position in the historical development of these issues is complex, contradictory, and difficult. Many of his statements form the major premises of the sociology of knowledge. When he declared that "life is not determined by consciousness, but consciousness by life," Marx seems to be well within the environmentalism of the liberal tradition. For this statement implies that human improvement is to be achieved by institutional improvement, and that human derangement is caused by perverted institutions. However, Marx is also one of the few major political thinkers to stress the idea that men produce their own delusions and to view ideology, sometimes, as a mass product rather than as the imposed outlook of the ruling few. Marx approaches the issue this way—we find mankind believing in gods, devils, private property, and other apparitions because the condition in which people live demands such delusions for survival. In his early writings he stated:

> . . . *Man makes religion;* (religion does not make man). Religion is indeed man's self-consciousness and self-awareness so long as he has not found himself or lost himself again. But *man* is not an abstract being squatting outside the world. Man is *the human world,* the state, society. This state, this society, produce religion which is an *inverted world consciousness,* because they are an *inverted world.* Religion is the general theory of this world, its encyclopedic compendium, its logic in popular form, its spiritual *point d'honneur,* its enthusiasm, its moral sanction, its solemn complement, its general basis of consolation and justification. It is the *fantastic realization* of the human being inasmuch as the *human being* possesses no true reality.[25]

I understand this dense passage to mean that what Marx later called ideology is not just a social lie and a source of error, but a social image and a source of information about the logic of the social situation. Ideology (such as religion) is a product of human effort and intelligence. It contributes to the survival of the species. But as a symbolic representation of the world such ideology is inverted in that it appears to be the conscious driving force of human life, much as the commands of the administrative class appear to be the directing force of that life. The relationship between the actual world of the producer and the fantastic world of religion is upside down because the producer's world is upside down.

Burt Alpert has labeled the intellectual products of this situation "inversions," which implies, according to him, that they must be dealt with, even rehabilitated, rather than simply discarded.[26] Alpert cites the same passage from Marx as the most comprehensive notice of the concept to be found. The Marx-Alpert conception of inversion by no means denies the influence of conceptual structures on the situation— that is, inversions are not simply passive reflections but are the way in which the community officially perceives and communicates about the situation. Marx initially treats private property as an inversion:

> *Private property* is, therefore, the product, the necessary result, of *alienated labour;* of the external relation of the worker to nature and to himself. . . .
>
> We have, of course, derived the concept of *alienated labour (alienated life)* from political economy, from an analysis of the movement of *private property.* But the analysis of the concept shows that although private property appears to be the basis and cause of alienated labour it is rather a consequence of the latter, just as the gods are *fundamentally* not the cause but the product of the confusion of human reason. At a later stage, however, there is a reciprocal influence.

Only in the final stage of the development of private property
is its secret revealed, namely, that it is on one hand the *product* of
alienated labour, and on the other hand the means *by* which
labour is alienated, the *realization of this alienation.*[27]

Marx points out that while it appears that gods, superstitions, and
the like confuse human reason, the actual situation is that they are the
products of confused reason. While the concept and institution of private property appear to be the cause of alienated labor—of a human
expression distorted to the status of a means—alienated labor is the
product of an alienated condition. Over time, however, the situation
grows more complex—gods, superstitions, religions become the confused means by which men understand their situation, just as private
property becomes the means by which the human being becomes alienated from his labor, his product, his fellow producers, and his species.
To attack an inversion is to attack the world in which inversions are the
intellectual product. Or as Marx put it following the cited passage: "To
struggle against religion is, therefore, indirectly a struggle against *that
world* whose spiritual *aroma* is religion."[28] To demystify and criticize
ideology is accordingly a means of struggle. Thus many of Marx's own
works are titled or subtitled "critique," and in September 1843 he wrote
to Arnold Ruge that the task of radical philosophy was the "relentless
criticism of all existing conditions."[29] In this vein Marx continued:

Reason has always existed, but not always in rational form. The
critic, therefore, can start with any form of theoretical and practical consciousness and develop the true actuality out of the
forms *inherent* in existing actuality as its ought-to-be and goal. . . .

Social truth, therefore, can be developed everywhere out of
this conflict of the political state with itself. Just as *religion* is the
table of contents of the theoretical struggle of mankind the *political state* is that of the practical ones.

Marx in the same letter further argues that a necessary part of the
struggle to change society is to take part in theoretical and practical
controversies, that is, to "enter into these political problems, which
crass socialists regard as below their dignity. . . . Nothing prevents us,
therefore, from starting our criticism with criticism of politics, with
taking sides in politics, hence with actual struggles. . . ."

Again the confused way in which men and women think and talk
about their world as well as the contorted way in which they struggle
with it are taken as the basic starting point of thought and action. The
investigator does not try to get out of the cave of social delusion but
tries to understand it by entering into its controversies, conversations,
and petty squabbles. In Plato's allegory the inhabitants of the cave pass
the time by identifying passing shadows and trying to remember long
sequences of their occurrence. We can imagine that many controversies

over identification and sequence might occur just because shadows—
ill-defined and limited in detail—are involved. While Plato notes that
the enlightened investigator becomes inept at this, Marx suggests that it
is through participating and therefore exacerbating the contradictions
of the situation that social truth is developed. The cave's prisoners
might discover by such means that they are watching shadows or apparitions that do not have the same characteristics as their own material
bodies. The investigator does not turn away from social delusions to
seek truth; he plunges into them, exposing their contradictions, fool-
ishness, falsehoods, and tendentious character. Marx calls this action
"criticism in a hand-to-hand fight."[30]

What has been quoted emphasizes once again Marx's position at this
time concerning the reality of ideology or consciousness and its intimate connection with the logic and structure of the social situation.
While ideology represents a misstatement of social reality, it also must
contain or imply a statement of the situation. Thus when the master
tells the slave how well he is being treated the statement calls attention
to the fact of some real concession that the slave has forced, plus the
fact of deprivation. In other words, people do not proclaim or drama-
tize their generosity except as a defense of cupidity. Generosity speaks
for itself. Likewise, if a major part of the political education of citizens
consists in learning about their freedom, we may conclude that a situation of unfreedom is the common lot punctuated by instances of freedom; and these instances can be interpreted as freedom for all. But
again freedom speaks for itself. However, to speak of freedom requires
that it be present in some instance. Thus the critic who proclaims such
a situation one of unfreedom will be easily refuted by concrete examples based on the instances of freedom that occur. If he is to cling to
his partially correct analysis, he will have to deny the status of these
examples and will be forced in the direction of idealism.

But this dialectical view of ideology is only one side of Marx's position. It is the most positive side and the side most influenced by Feuerbach. Its most complete and enthusiastic statement comes at the end of
the letter to Ruge.

> We do not tell the world, "Cease your struggles, they are stupid;
> we want to give you the true watchword of the struggle." We
> merely show the world why it actually struggles; and the aware-
> ness of this is something the world *must* acquire even if it does
> not want to.
>
> The reform of consciousness exists *merely* in the fact that one
> makes the world aware of its consciousness, that one awakens
> the world out of its own dream, that one *explains* to the world
> its own acts. Our entire purpose consists in nothing else (as is
> also the case in Feuerbach's criticism of religion) but bringing

the religious and political problems into the selfconscious human form.[31]

Marx concludes that "... mankind does not begin any *new* work but performs its old work consciously." And he goes on to declare: "To have its sins forgiven, mankind has only to declare them for what they are." This task of self-understanding parallels the Freudian idea of therapy. In psychoanalysis, the patient is aided in understanding the nature of his symptoms and their causes. The symptoms themselves, however, are not treated. Thus water phobia is not treated by demonstrating again and again that water is not threatening, but by aiding the patient to see what fear is represented by the phobia—that is, what fear is simultaneously not recognized and dealt with by means of the phobia. Marx writes that "religious suffering is at the same time an *expression* of real suffering and a *protest* against real suffering." He continues:

> Religion is the sign of the oppressed creature, the heart of a heartless world, and the soul of a soulless condition. It is the *opium* of the people.[32]

The last phrase is the one most often quoted and interpreted to mean that religion (or other ideology) is fed to the people to make them feel good and keep them quiet. It seems clear in the context, however, that Marx means something different by the metaphor. Religion is an opiate in the sense of a medicine which gives symptomatic relief, but Marx does not at this point challenge the reality of such relief. He does not say that religion is not an aid to survival, only that it is a limited aid to a limited survival. Criticism of religion is an "embryonic criticism of this vale of tears." But criticism must be directed against the conditions that require illusion. Marx argues that it is not enough to relieve men of their consolations. "Criticism has plucked the imaginary flowers from the chain, not in order that man shall bear the chain without caprice or consolation but so that he shall cast off the chain and pluck the living flower," Marx announces. He moves on in the essay to unmask the secular form of human self-alienation by means of criticizing German politics and law. This analysis leads to "tasks which can only be solved by means of practical activity." At this point comes Marx's famous dictum that "the arm of criticism cannot replace the criticism of arms."[33] Thus while criticism is the beginning of the struggle it must become, according to him, a "material force," and this progression is possible only when critical theory has been adopted by the masses. No passage better demonstrates Marx's basic dilemma. For while he proclaims that radical theory ends "with the categorical imperative to overthrow all those conditions in which man is an abased, enslaved, abandoned, contemptible being," he proceeds to treat the proletariat in a contemptuous manner, proclaiming that "revolutions need a *passive* element, a *material* basis." This element is the proletariat, not because of its special human qualities, but because of its "radical chains." The quality of the proletarian class that is most attractive to Marx is its "total loss of humanity."

Abolition of the Proletariat

That is a terrifying indictment of any class. We might assume that a radical, such as Marx, would use it to describe a class which deals exclusively with delusions, deceits, and idealizing phrases—the ruling class. Removed from the fundamental activity of human life (productive labor), divorced from creative contact with the social and physical environment, existing parasitically off the mental and material products of others, the ruling class is a class of aliens. Marx comes close to saying this at times.[34] As a class that has totally lost humanity, the ruling class is null in revolutionary potential. It has no competence, no experience, no responsiveness to bring to the task of rebuilding society. But Marx's description of the proletariat is paradoxically meant as a statement of its special revolutionary feature. The proletariat is passive, is a blank, is a total loss, but is of the stuff that philosophers require to realize their ideas. While proclaiming that "man is the highest ideal being for man" and that "no type of enslavement can be abolished unless *all* enslavement is destroyed," Marx concludes: "Philosophy can only be realized by the abolition of the proletariat, and the proletariat can only be abolished by the realization of philosophy."[35]

This eventuality does not seem to be a bargain for the proletariat. While the philosopher does the thinking or is the "head of the emancipation," the proletariat, as always, does the dirty work. For its pains it gets abolished, that is, "raised" to the level of the investigator-theorist-critic-philosopher. In the letter to Ruge, Marx saw the critic as a part of the struggle of emancipation, but now the critic becomes a Platonic director of the struggle. But with this exalted role come limitations in the range of creative activity.

Enter the Historicist

How can the investigator be sure that he has gone to the root and is not simply contributing new inversions to the collective delusions of society? Marx says that theory becomes a material force, that is, is true if it is capable of seizing the masses. The investigator criticizes ideology, offering a new interpretation of the situation based on internal evidence and on the external evidence that ideology may lead him to seek and hopefully find. The validity of his interpretation is based on its acceptability to the masses. To make the case stronger, we might add that not only must the theory be acceptable to the proletariat, it must be useful in the struggle to achieve the emancipation of the species. Therefore, history is the final judge of the critical theorist's work.

There are many problems with this explanation. For one, since the masses or proletariat are passive and totally devoid of humanity—in fact, defined as radical not by what they do and think but by the form of their domination—they are not likely to discriminate well between valid and invalid theories. Given Marx's description of this class, we could make a good case that fascism would be as likely to seize them as would socialism or liberalism. Thus the proletariat is not a reliable judge of the validity of theory. Later, when the historical proletariat did in fact reject Marx's theory, he began to write about "false consciousness." This concept makes Marx's doctrines unfalsifiable at this level. He can proclaim that he is speaking for the proletariat whatever the consciousness of the proletariat may actually be. Like Plato, he has to make some parts of reality into appearances in order to negate evidence against his own claims. His theory, again like Plato's, becomes more abstract, idealistic, esoteric, and removed from empirical contamination. If the proletariat cannot judge, we are left only with history, and if history is the judge, the investigator is left with the midwife's role.

Thus the investigator becomes the historicist, who cannot create or add to our social knowledge by teaching us new techniques or suggesting institutional redesign, but who predicts the gross outlines of the future.[36] Once this predicting or prophesying is completed, the actual task of politics becomes that of easing the birthpangs of that future. The investigator's consciousness is determined by the historical situation in which he lives. If he is sensitive to this situation—sees through its appearances to the reality of the historical forces at work—he will be able to make statements about what is coming like a tour guide. The social investigator is only a mouthpiece of history—a priestess of Delphi, or a Hegelian owl flying into the future.

Marx never completely abandoned the activist or materialist side of his thinking—the notion that men themselves make history. But he does often seem to have abandoned the notion that ideology is something produced by mankind as a means for its own survival. In *The German Ideology* (1845-1846), Marx and Engels proclaim:

> The ideas of the ruling class are, in every age, the ruling ideas: i.e., the class which is the dominant *material* force in society is at the same time its dominant *intellectual* force. The class which has the means of material production at its disposal, has control at the same time over the means of mental production, so that in

consequence the ideas of those who lack the means of mental production are, in general, subject to it.[37]
Ideology is therefore a means for control and rule and not a means for survival. While ideas may be radical to the extent that they are useful in class struggle, they remain as cognitive commodities to be created and imposed by the ruling class or the revolutionary vanguard. But since there is no way of testing ideas, except in the forge of history, they must be held on faith alone. It is for this reason that Marxism appears to have the structure of a chiliastic religion rather than that of a political philosophy.[38] This religious aspect is anti-intellectual and antiscientific. Social science becomes an impossibility; there is left only the clash of ideas representing the political and social aspirations of various classes and groups. Radical thought and belief occur, not as a rational process, but as a reflex to conditions of repression and exploitation.

The Marxian formula thus becomes: (1) ideas are conditioned by the social situation; (2) in order to change ideas the social situation must be changed; (3) in order to change the social situation, men must perceive that it needs to be changed and, perhaps, that it can be changed; (4) the perception of the need for change is determined by the human suffering caused by the situation. While men play a part in this scheme, their part is that of a transmission belt transforming the contradictions of the social condition into grievances that motivate mass movements. Worse still, the formula involves a paradox. Ideology or distorted consciousness of the world results because the social situation inflicts damage on people, according to Marx's concept of inversion. This indicates that worsening social conditions will likely lead to more distorted conceptualizations of the situation, not to a revolutionary consciousness. The only way we can make sense of Marx at this point is to assume he thought that damage to the human organism up to a point inhibited social knowledge, but that after reaching a point of some intensity damage makes social knowledge likely and possible. Another solution would be to understand that the class of maximum suffering, the proletariat, is subject to delusions, while the revolutionary social investigator escapes these delusions because he does not suffer and yet identifies with the proletariat. This solution is the foundation of the notion of a revolutionary vanguard developed by Lenin. Thus the richness of Marx's earlier thought on the issues of social epistemology is transformed into a sterile Hegelianism.

The Possibility of a Natural Science of Man

In fact, Marx never gives up his earlier insights. His fecundity as a thinker is due to his reluctance to accept the offered resoluton of these difficulties to be found in the mechanistic schemes of Engels and other Marxists. Marx indeed was no Marxist. His 1845 "Theses on Feuerbach" contains the means to criticize Engels, Lenin, and other determinists. Marx wrote:

> The materialist doctrine concerning the changing of circumstances and education forgets that circumstances are changed by men and that the educator must himself be educated. This doctrine has therefore to divide society into two parts, one of which is superior to society.[39]

Marx ended the thesis with the famous remark that "the philosophers have only *interpreted* the world in different ways; the point is to change it."[40] In this context his slogan does not mean that philosophers have no intellectual role in the project of change, that philosophy should cease and street fighting begin. Rather it indicates that social knowledge is part of the practice of social change. Only if we interpret the remark in this way can we understand why Marx spent his energies in attempting to demystify political economy and to explain the structure and process of capitalist society.

Marx was not a Utopian devising a perfect society of the future, but neither was he a mere political agitator or soothsayer. He attempted to be a social scientist and his attempt implies that subjectively, at least, he considered thought to be a form of practice and therefore to be judged on the basis of its results rather than on its consistency or esthetic appeal. Indeed, his vision of the possibility of a natural science of man in the manuscripts of 1844 is vital. In a few paragraphs, Marx outlined a critique of the "abstract materialist or idealist" orientation of the natural sciences. Asserting that "one basis for life and another for science is *a priori* a falsehood," he went on to declare that "science is only genuine science when it proceeds from sense experience, in the two forms of *sense perception* and *sensuous* need; i.e., only when it proceeds from nature."[41] This statement is in serious disagreement with the traditional explanations of social knowledge. The joining of perception and need, observation and emotional reaction, in the process of knowing is the beginning point of a different and more productive approach to the problems of social epistemology.

The problems of social epistemology dance through the writings of Marx. He does not solve them, but from time to time he does bring them into focus. In consequence, he is difficult to understand at times and one cannot utilize him as a model of social investigation. Having once left his native Germany and the active participation in political struggles that informed his earlier thought, Marx grew more and more detached from the social conditions he attempted to describe. Seated day after day in the British Museum, he became more removed from sensuous existence and practical activity. Despite his insights, he found himself in the same situation as Plato's philosopher-king. Blinded by the possibilities he has seen beyond the cave, he perceives the resistance of the proletariat to his ideas as institutional corruption rather than as due to the errors of his own idealistic fancy. Marx ceased to learn. His theory therefore became an unfalsifiable statement of timeless categories to be imposed upon those proletarians presenting a total loss of humanity.

Employee Epistemology

The sociology of knowledge is most often associated with the name of Karl Mannheim. To date, Mannheim's formulation of this approach to the problems of social epistemology is the most complete, and at the same time confusing. He is often taken to task by current writers, and indeed the sociology of knowledge as an intellectual enterprise has progressed little since his efforts and now finds itself in some disrepute. However, many of Mannheim's conclusions, descriptions, and models have become dogmatic assumptions in current discussions of epistemological issues in the social sciences. For Mannheim, social ignorance is the result of what he called "social conditioning" rather than of any deliberate manipulation on the part of directing elites, governing bodies, or institutions. Within the structures of institutions, the daily routines and operations of life combine to determine the form and scope of knowledge. Conditioning is required for survival of a routine or of a structure. Given a social situation without conflicts or instability, social knowledge would result from the appropriate indoctrination. That is, social ignorance is not a problem for the social investigator unless there is conflict or some impetus to change. Mannheim writes: "As long as the same meanings of words, the same ways of deducing ideas are inculcated from childhood on into every menber of the group, divergent thought processes cannot exist in that society"[42]

Mannheim believes that the situation is one of competing systems of thought rather than one of uniform delusion in a closed cave. The social investigator in the twentieth century does not face a single massive delusional system that he must escape; he faces a situation in which there are as many delusional systems as there are competing social groups. In fact, to talk of delusional systems no longer makes sense because there is no basis on which to proclaim social knowledge. The social investigator's claim becomes only another shout in the din. Mannheim redefines the problem by avoiding the question of delusions and focusing on the mechanical links between the social situation and social knowledge. The sociology of knowledge has "the task of solving the problem of the social conditioning of knowledge."[43]

Instrumental Knowledge

Mannheim assumes first that all knowledge is instrumental; that is, he assumes a hierarchical social structure in which men compete for scarce resources. In this context, all action is distrustful or agonistic, and all politics is distributive. Thinking is always subordinate to the primary quest for goods and power. The resulting function for the intellectual is "The verbalization of motives rather than production of ideas which may create motives."[44] Under these conditions there is no such thing as a true idea or theory, but only successful or unsuccessful ones. The social investigator's own claims to truth can be validated only if it can be shown that they lead to some successful change in the distribution of power.

Mannheim does not propose to leave the cave of social ignorance. For unlike Plato, Bacon, and the Hegelian Marx, he understands that the cave represents the limits of both knowledge and life. Any other kind of knowledge that is possible in the situation would be other than human knowledge. Absolute knowledge would require an absolute being. Staying within the cave, the social investigator's more modest job is to attempt to provide some illumination in the darkness. Mannheim writes "The false ideal of a detached, impersonal view must be replaced by the ideal of an essentially human point of view which is within the limits of a human perspective, constantly striving to enlarge itself."[45] In other words, we must "accept the phenomenon of knowing as the act of a living being."[46]

Human beings view the world through a perspective based upon their own experience, desires, and needs. Mannheim uses the metaphor of human vision to illuminate this point. When we look at any three-dimensional opaque object, we can see only the near side of it. And assuming the object to be hollow, we cannot see the inside of it when seeing the outside of it, nor vice versa. But given this limitation, we still possess a knowledge of such objects that might be called objective. That is to say, we can mentally add the "pictures" or mental representations of the object that we might obtain from various perspectives into a single image of it. For example, having examined a tomato from all sides, cut it open, and so on, we can be said to know tomatoes. We know that tomatoes are not hollow, that they are spherical, not hemispherical, without having to investigate each particular tomato we encounter. Mannheim suggests that social knowledge would be of the same form, that is, we can collect descriptions or representations of a phenomenon reported from different perspectives. We can then synthesize these descriptions to gain an idea of the actual or "objective" nature of the phenomenon.[47]

The perspective of a social observer, which Mannheim describes as

" . . . the manner in which one views an object, what one perceives in it, and how one construes it in his thinking,"[48] is not something that is easily changed. For in Mannheim's view, perspective is determined by one's situation in the social structure, that is, by one's competitive position and interests. Social conditioning cannot be escaped. We cannot will a perspective that would lead to a valid synthesis. However, some perspectives may be more strategic than others in terms of such a synthesis. What Mannheim calls "a detached perspective" can be gained. In this case, Mannheim writes: "a valid synthesis must be based on a political position which will constitute a progressive development in the sense that it will retain and utilize much of the accumulated cultural acquisitions and social energies of the previous epoch."[49] This stipulation implies that a collective set of positions, such as a class, can lead to a perspective from which a valid synthesis is possible if such a class is rising, that is, being politically successful. But such a success is useful in this way only if it involves the preservation of culture. Thus Mannheim is not arguing that might equals correct knowledge, but that political success requires a minimal amount of valid political knowledge. In times of crisis, when political development is demanded for the survival of a society, those elements of a society who possess an anticipatory map of that development are the elements likely to become ascendant. Mannheim suggests that power in the long run goes to those who have the knowledge, that is, a theory that promises a new form of society or a theory that will *conserve* society. This is a modified restatement of the Marxist position.

Mannheim is impressed by the possibilities for synthesis involved in attaining a more detached perspective. He says such a perspective can be gained by individual mobility within the class structure, by the shifting of class position, or through conflict of classes leading to vigorous criticism of each perspective. The possibility of conflict leading to criticism is, for Mannheim, most likely to lead to a full development of social knowledge. This likelihood is particularly strong if there exists what he calls, after Alfred Weber, "a socially unattached intelligentsia." Within this "relatively classless stratum," the conflict of classes is turned into a conflict of ideas.

The modern inteligentsia is not manned primarily by any one class, as was the ancient priesthood, but is recruited from all social strata. Thus, while intellectuals may attach themselves to the political fortunes of, say, the social class of their origins within their own stratum, they will find other intellectuals attached to other classes. But each intellectual, no matter what his conditioning interests, must develop and articulate reasons and justifications for his affiliation as well as develop what we might call a winning strategy. Thus, the various classes and interest groups in a society are forced to become more aware of the assumptions about the social world which their interests demand, of the kinds of actions required to satisfy their interests, and finally, of how their interest and its accompanying perspective differs from that of others. The existence of an intelligentsia means to Mannheim that intellectuals might achieve "the discovery of the position from which a total perspective would be possible. Thus they might play the part of watchmen in what otherwise would be a pitch-black night."[50]

Watchmen in the Night

The watchman position is one achieved when the social investigator recognizes that he is not involved in setting the norms or goals of a society or its members, but rather in discovering what Mannheim called structural relationships. Like Weber, Mannheim says that the social investigator cannot prescribe interest, but can only point out that the adoption of "this or that set of interests implies also that you must do this or that to achieve them, and that you must know the specific position you occupy in the whole social process."[51] We see then that a total perspective is an abstract perspective, and that the position from which such a perspective is possible is one above or beyond the arena of political conflict. What Mannheim has told the social investigator is how to get out of the system intellectually without removing himself politically. By narrowly focusing on devising technical means instead of ends (a relatively simple task compared to, say, what was required of the philosopher-king, or of Bacon's scientist, or of Marx's theoretical activist), the social investigator finds himself removed intellectually from the conditioning circumstances.

This, then, is Mannheim's "ideal of an essentially human perspective"—the outlook of an employee. What makes the employee perspective valid is that given the goals of the employer, he must gain accurate knowledge about the social situation in order to get the job done. Within the historical limits provided by the values of his employer, the employee is motivated to find the truth of the situation. If he cannot, presumably he will be fired. This failure he can attribute to the historical invalidity of the boss' goals. If they are valid, he will find a way. If not, he will get a new boss. Moving from job to job will result in something like a synthesis, specifically a detached instrumentalist perspective. But while the employee's perspective focuses on the concrete and the particular, it does so at the expense of neglecting the choice of norms and goals. The employee becomes disengaged from value debates in order to become empirically engaged.

But no amount of effort from this perspective will end in Mannheim's goal of synthetic social knowledge. The result will be recipes. No amount of pyrotechnics from this position will accomplish more than to increase the prestige and power of those in charge, just as the pyrotechnics of the courtesan yield pleasure to her client, while gradually hardening her into a self-conscious tool. While Mannheim began with the important question "How is social knowledge possible?" he ends by outlining the ideology (and a successful ideology) of an intelligentsia for hire.

If we turn Mannheim's theory against his own formulations then we face difficult problems. If the goal of the sociology of knowledge is to develop a theory, in Mannheim's words, "concerning the significance of the non-theoretical conditioning factors in knowledge,"[52] then immediately we want to know to what sort of changes or successful distrustful actions such a theory would lead. If Mannheim's theory of the existential determination of ideas is correct in maintaining that social knowledge is limited by the position of the investigator, and if by position is meant the relationship to groups struggling for power, then the investigator who formulates the idea of a sociology of knowledge will be ignorant of his limitations and believe himself to be bias-free while he facilitates the rise to power of an affiliated group. Thus Mannheim's formulation leads one critic to argue that his theory is simply the ideological expression of the interests of the class of free-floating intellectuals."[53] This difficulty haunts all attempts to account for social knowledge and ignorance. For if we begin by trying to demonstrate that all men and women are conditioned to be socially ignorant and that their resistance to the social knowledge gained by escaping this conditioning is further evidence of their social ignorance, then any assertions that we may make as investigators of the situation have become unfalsifiable. We see many examples of this. The psychoanalyst claims that his critics reject his knowledge because of personality defects resulting in defensive maneuvers. B.F. Skinner claims that men reject behaviorism because it challenges their egotistical assumptions. Such positions not only preclude any test, but they also, according to Hartung, "destroy any possible rational basis for discussion of an issue, making it resolvable only through the use of physical force."[54] Thus the systemization of doubt accomplished by Mannheim's sociology of knowledge seems inevitably to lead to despair while the author himself never despairs but attempts to make the best of an impossible situation.

Epistemological Limits of Hierarchy

Another way to look at Mannheim's sociology of knowledge is to see it as an empirical description of the epistemological limits of hierarchical structures. The assumptions behind his theory correspond to the condition of hierarchical organizations. Hans Speier states the following necessary presuppositions of Mannheim's perspective:

1. Thinking is instrumental: in a technical form, how to achieve an end; in a promotive form, how to get an end adopted by people; or in a theoretical form, how to avoid any action.

2. Thinkers and actors are totally different roles and "the thinking individual identifies himself with certain needs of others who do not think and who want to act rather than to think."[55]

3. The basic needs of human beings are those pertaining to differential security, that is, economic need for gain, political need for power, social need for recognition.

4. Social action has as its objective a shift in the balance of security, that is, all social actions in the words of Speier, are distrustful.

5. "Only those ideas can ultimately be called true which are instrumental to the success of distrustful action."[56]

6. All distrustful actions are exempted from any normative or historical judgments because they are natural to the human animal. Speier argues that these propositions and the assumptions about social reality which underlie them reveal "a dogmatic unhistorical contention [resulting] . . . from a preoccupation with the differential insecurity of human nature."[57]

What is dogmatic and unhistoric about these propositions is the assumption that all social organizations are hierarchical and that all societies take the form of a plurality of hierarchies. Speier wants the adoption of a more relativistic position which would recognize that social actions differ from one social structure to another. In other language, the concern is not so much with the fact of the thinker's dependence on social context, but with the kind of a context on which the thinker is dependent. That is, does the context encourage or demand distortion or does it require the development of knowledge? Speier asserts that "the social order is never wholly reasonable," which I take to mean that in hierarchical social structures ideas are ideological. They are ideological in the sense that they go beyond the actual situation and, therefore, imply actions aimed at transcending some element of the structure. Speier points out, for example, that ideal reality does not contain the dualisms thinker-actor, theory-practice, abstract-concrete, which we find in class society. Thus ideological thinking both goes beyond the limits of those structured dualisms and obscures their reality. For Speier, the issue is how social investigators go beyond the interests of their group and their society to introduce new information to humanity. It is such men that we honor as the greatest thinkers, and not those who cater to the whims of their employers. Speier notes that in accounting for such men, Mannheim refers to their "social ambivalence." Speier argues that Mannheim's recognition of this quality indicates that the sociology of knowledge is limited in its ability to deal with philosophical thinking.

> "Socially ambivalent" thinking can always be found, even in times in which rhetorical and propagandistic thought dominates in quantity. "Socially ambivalent" thought disappears only with philosophical thought.[58]

The sociology of knowledge is a limited account to the extent that it cannot account for the ability of social investigators to become discoverers, innovators, and teachers of their fellow men. In fact, to achieve that accounting is what Mannheim himself was trying to do. We may see the sociology of knowledge as not merely the ideology of a free-floating intelligentsia for hire, but also as an attempt to depict an escape route from the informational limitations of hierarchical social structures. Its failure is due not to its intentions but to its inability to give an adequate account of the means by which existence determines thought, and of how to accurately impute a framework or viewpoint to a specific class or group. That is, it fails in the particular and concrete description of thinking in the social context while it has succeeded, of course, as general ideology of doubt, insecurity, and cynicism—an expression in Speier's words of "the professional self-hatred of the intellectuals."[59]

The Social Determination of Thought

The sociology of knowledge has failed most dramatically by its lack of a description of the means for the social determination of thought. Arthur Child, in an early survey of the literature, pointed out that such writers in the field as Max Scheler, Georg Lukács, and Ernest Grunwald, as well as Mannheim, had failed to develop any plausible theory of how social conditions produced or determined ideas in human minds.[60] Frank Hartung similarly argues that Mannheim "has developed no criteria by means of which a causal relation between thought and its existential basis can be recognized."[61] Child claims that the deficiency is due to the lack of any social theory of mind in the field. As he puts it, "only a theory that recognizes the role of the creative individual mind . . . can provide an adequate definition of the means of determination and a final justification, thereby, for the concept of existential determination itself."[62] The problem of the means of determination seems to be missed by most sociologists of knowledge because they assume the human mind to be passive and reactive. The notion that ideas are determined existentially owes its plausibility both to the assumed Lockean epistemology on which it is based and the truism that thought must be about something.

Further, there is no clear criterion in the sociology of knowledge for ascribing a given outlook or perspective to a particular class or political group. The problem arises from the notion of false consciousness introduced by Marx and maintained in this tradition. That is, we cannot construct the perspective of a given class by simply going out and taking a poll of opinions and ideas in that class. Throughout the literature of the sociology of knowledge, we find imputations that Marx's ideas are an expression of proletarian ideology even though he was a bourgeois intellectual; and that Proudhon's thought is petty-bourgeois, even though he was a proletarian. We must even understand that a member of the lesser nobility, like Lenin, could accurately express the outlook of the proletariat. Child comments:

> If there are proletarians whose thought is *not* proletarian and non-proletarians whose thought *is* proletarian, where, then, can one discover the criterion for proletarian thought—and for the thought, moreover, of every class and stratum and sector of society?[63]

Only Georg Lukács has taken up the problem in any serious way, according to Child. He summarizes Lukács's solution to the problem of imputations as: "proletarian ideology is what the proletariat would think if they knew enough to think it."[64]

Child comments:

> How is one to know *which* thoughts, feelings etc., are in point of fact, the ones rationally suited to a given class position? For this, after all, is Lukács' criterion of imputation. And the standard can be only the "ideology of the proletariat" itself. But thereby we enter a vicious circle, for it is rational suitability that determines the ideology of the proletariat, and it is the ideology of the proletariat that determines the rational suitability.[65]

Of course there is a way out, and that is to impute only those perspectives, ideas, value orientations, thought styles, and the like to classes and groups that have articulated them. Thus Marxism would be interpreted as the ideology of middle-class intellectuals. This imputation would provide us with some interesting insights, but the sociologists of knowledge would not go so far, for this empirical imputation would rob them of their ability to interpret and express the outlook of the various competing groups for which they might work. In the end, the sociologist of knowledge is not just a recorder or historian of ideas; he maintains the freedom to create ideas as commodities or weapons.

Conclusion

While these three approaches to the problems of social epistemology contain valuable insights and advice, they all fail to account in a plausible fashion for the possibility of social knowledge. Like Plato, each describes an extraordinary effort to be performed by someone more than human. This concept promotes cynicism and an antirational if not antiscientific approach to the study of human affairs. These thinkers— Bacon, Marx, and Mannheim—have described not a workmanlike or scientific endeavor but a heroic quest. Each has emphasized a particularly telling barrier to social knowledge—human cognitive limitations, institutional conditioning, and disintegrative potentials. Each approach implies that ignorance is functional in terms of social harmony and stability. Therefore each views social knowledge as dangerous, debilitating, and diabolical in the hands of others. If we can believe in the face of centuries of human experience that wisdom can be founded on pervasive ignorance and that supernatural dispensations are required to create knowledge, we can stop at this point. But if these paradoxical conclusions leave us unsatisfied, or if the vision of the heroic social investigator resembles all too closely the bloody specters of charismatic madmen, we must question the assumptions of these approaches to the problems of social epistemology.

3 Socialization Theories and Social Ignorance

> " . . . all governments, citadels, and armies are set up
> and organized as much against attack from the in-
> side as from the outside."
>
> —P. J. Proudhon

The concept of socialization is the philosopher's stone of political theorists, investigators, and reformers. Just as the philosopher's stone of the medieval alchemists promised to convert base materials to precious and perfect bodies, so the techniques of socialization promise to remake base human beings into perfect citizens. Both ideas have ignited the imagination of men and women, leading them to labor long and with unremitting failure to seek a magical solution to the problems posed by the supposed imperfections of matter and men. The labors of the alchemists laid the basis of the science of chemistry. The labors of those who seek to recast the social nature of the human species have continued to the present without scientific issue. But such failure may become our teacher and lead us to refound our investigations on different hypothetical rather than traditional dogmatic grounds. As the centuries of failure of the alchemist finally established the impossibility of a philosopher's stone, so the failure of social investigators can be interpreted as establishing the impossibility of socializing men and women to preformed values, opinions, and behavior.[1] The failure of recent investigators to demonstrate the supposed relations between child-raising practices and adult character, between teaching and moral development, or between political education and adult behavior can lead us to rethink our approach to the study of political and social phenomena. Thus the barren search may be producing the basic data of a new science.

The results of socialization investigations during this century (not to mention the countless failed attempts to "improve" humanity) indicate that people are not uniform replicas of an ideal citizen and perhaps cannot be molded into these. Or, to put it in fashionable language—political and social behavior cannot be either controlled or predicted in nontrivial ways by social institutions and behavioral techniques. This recognition does not mean the end of the quest for social science, as it seems to those who attempt the practice of science by mimicry. It means rather that social science requires a shift in perspective—a Copernican revolution, if you will—in which the goal of investigation aims at the prediction and control of organizational structures rather than of their human members. In this view political behavior is seen not as a support function, nor as a cause or an input effecting system stability or change—rather it is a complex output or result of system performance.

Most social investigators from Plato to the present have assumed that organizational success was dependent upon the effectiveness of social control. Further, it is frequently stated and usually assumed that social control can be exercised by either external techniques of surveillance and terror or by socialization leading to internalized surveillance and terror called conscience and guilt. The alternative view is that the ways in which people live their lives and perform their tasks are restricted by the fitness of the organizations in which they exist. By *fitness* we mean the extent to which an organization's structural and procedural design and practice facilitate the working functions of individuals. Learning to control organizations and to judge their fitness is a difficult task rather than a solution to problems of human misery. But so long as the task is not taken up, or is worked at only sporadically, that misery will surely increase.

But the concept of socialization remains to enchant us, for it prom-ises both to explain all human behavior and to mold and control such behavior to fit our ideas and institutional designs. Both results would relieve us of the arduous burden of science.

The first promise is the more vulgar attraction. Explanations based on socialization are the staple of the elementary survey course in social science. If a man stops for red lights, votes for Dwight Eisenhower, burns crosses at night, gives money to cancer research, attends church, and hates Germans, it is *because* he has been socialized to do so. No mystery here, only science, for if another man stops for green lights, votes for Adlai Stevenson, joins the anti-defamation league, smokes high-tar cigarettes, avoids church, and loves Germans, it is also *because* he has been socialized to do so. Socialization is a Cartesian concept in the worst sense—it explains everything and therefore nothing. If, like bourbon, prayer, or the late television movie, it helps get the social scientist through some cold lonely nights, so much the worse for it.

Further, the concept of socialization explains social ignorance with all its dogmatism and debilitating resistance to the best reform schemes of the social and political critic. The social reformer is always at pains to show why he is laughed at, ignored, or even punished for his efforts.

He or she who has discovered and described particular social evils and pointed to their causes must account for the apparent absence of rebellion or the failure to hear the call to revolution. Motivated as they often are by what is best in the species, at great effort and danger to their lives, reformers are pressed to conclude that their failures are due to some malevolent socializing enemy that has placed false ideas in the minds of the people.

Heroism aside, how are Americans to account for the lack of revolutionary fervor in the often deplored tyrannies of Soviet Russia or China? Is it possible that those hostile institutions do something of benefit to their citizenry? How are Russian and Chinese intellectuals, in turn, to account for the political stability of the decadent West? Could capitalists, in all their venality, actually perform some human services? The Cold War has done much to promote the idea of socialization as well as provide the funding for the burgeoning research in socialization techniques.

Socialization as Molding

The second promise, to mold human behavior, is older and is often coupled with idealistic aims of political reform and social revitalization. This aspect is implied by the word itself. "Socialize" is a relatively new term. The first citation by the *Oxford English Dictionary* is 1828 and the dictionary meaning is "to render social; to make fit for living in society." An article in the *Quarterly Review* of that year notes "The socializing and humanising effects of liberal commerce with other nations." In the nineteenth century, "socialization" usually referred to establishing something on a socialist basis, and we still talk about the socialization of medicine, industry, and other enterprises. But the technical meaning among social investigators is that of making the individual fit for society. While noting that theories of socialization are to be found as early as Plato, John Clausen writes that the first technical use of the term was by the American sociologist Edward Alsworth Ross.[2]

Ross, in his classic work, *Social Control,* was concerned with the need for the conscious design and maintenance of social order under the emerging conditions of twentieth-century society. The problem as he saw it was that modern social development was marked by a transformation of community into society, "that is, replacing living tissue with structures held together by rivets and screws."[3]

> To be "a kind husband, a devoted parent, and a good neighbor" no longer sums up the duty of man. As institutions multiply, it becomes as needful for us to respect them as to love one another. As social machinery gains in importance, the common welfare becomes more vulnerable.[4]

In his explorations of the various natural and invented techniques of social control, Ross raised many of the basic issues and themes with which the concept of socialization is concerned. First, Ross regarded the human species itself as consisting of individual nonsocial or antisocial animals which he likened to beasts that required taming. This taming, or "man-quelling" as he called it in his vigorous style, was best achieved in the youth of the animal, was permanent once accomplished, and was necessary to the development of a common conscience on which society was based. He used the term as follows:

> Men and women are socialized once and for all, but in time the socialized units die while new undisciplined persons keep swarming up on to the stage of action. The equilibrium achieved is perpetually disturbed by changes in the personnel of the group, and hence perpetually in need of being restored by the conscious, intelligent efforts of society.[5]

Ross further maintained that the danger of having to accomplish by artifice what had previously been done by natural group processes required not only the use of deception but of self-censorship by a social investigator.[6] For Ross declared that "One who sees clearly how he is controlled will henceforth be emancipated," and, "To betray the secrets of ascendency is to forearm the individual in his struggle with society."[7] Thus the risk of possibly "subverting all control that does not rest on force" descended on the social investigator, who must therefore be careful, according to Ross, to address himself to "those who administer the moral capital of society—to teachers, clergymen, editors, lawmakers, and judges who wield the instruments of control."

Paradoxes of Socialization

This brief account of Ross's work brings out the paradoxical nature of socialization as theory, as a subject of investigation, and as a perspective or approach to reforming and designing institutions. In the theory, socialization techniques, whatever their goals, require censorship and deception that in turn promote ignorance; therefore, theories of socialization are always theories about how to teach ignorance. In investigating socialization practices in a given society, the normal scientific canons of open and public inquiry with results based on an intersubjective consensus cannot be applied because such practices are subverted by disclosure. Finally, socialization in practice requires a unique and privileged perspective open only to the self-appointed. For if socialization techniques are successful in a given society, the social designer and investigator must be constrained by those practices in a way that makes them impossible to comprehend. Either the investigator must be exempt from the effects of socialization because of some extrahuman virtue or else socialization doesn't work as effectively as presumed.

Theories of socialization as molding contain the paradox that while the improvement of the species is the goal—improvement in terms of either moral development of the individual or the social development of the citizen—the means require some form of restriction of development. A striking example of this paradox is found in Plato's *Republic*. In Book II, Socrates maintains that the most hated state of the soul is a state of untruth or ignorance that is not recognized—that is, "the ignorance in the soul of the man who has been deceived."[8] As opposed to such "true lies" Socrates contrasts the "verbal lie." Verbal lies are useful, he tells us, "against one's enemies and those of one's so-called friends who, through madness or ignorance, are attempting to do something wrong" if the verbal lie will dissuade them from their harmful actions. Thus the censorship or manipulation of the Homeric myths is justified as medicinal or useful lying. Since Plato apparently considers the myths as lies in the first place, this is not so difficult to reconcile with his condemnation of the true lie. But in Book III, Socrates explicitly says that "it is fitting for the rulers, if for anyone, to use lies for the good of the city," while condemning the right of any citizen to lie to rulers.[9] Further, the Republic itself is founded on the "noble fiction" or caste-lie that the various classes are genetically determined to be superior or inferior.[10] Since the majority of the citizenry will have been lied to about their own nature, their past culture, and the nature of their rulers, and since poets and artists who seek new descriptions and expressive wisdom about the world are to be controlled or expelled, the citizens of the Republic will have been deceived, made ignorant, and thus put into a hateful state of soul.

We don't doubt Plato's ideals or his sincerity when he writes:

> Good education and upbringing, if preserved, will lead to men of a better nature, and these in turn, if they cling to their education, will improve with each generation both in other respects and also in their children just like other animals.[11]

But his deceptive socialization techniques undermine his goal. The men and women of Plato's Republic, whether guardians or producers, would not be wise (and therefore according to the Socratic if not the Platonic teaching, not virtuous) but systematically ignorant. This deceived ignorance is even more damaging to Plato's goals when we realize that he aimed at educating or socializing rulers primarily and believed that the character of the rulers determined the overall characteristics of the Republic and its citizenry.

Socialization-research findings cannot approach any ideal of objectivity since they must be about an unaware population and therefore are open to criticism and revision only by a select group of investigators and socializing agents. Both groups are probably uniformly biased in the direction of promoting the claims of socializing effectiveness and both are removed from sources of information that would reveal the failures and limitations of socialization. Indeed, as scientific canons are taken seriously in this area, findings indicate that socialization—as presently understood as a semipermanent cognitive or psychic molding— doesn't work. All social-science descriptions and explanations not based on widespread intersubjective criticism and consensus are suspect. For example, the more anthropologists learn about the extant preliterate societies the less reliable do the classic nonintersubjective accounts appear to be.[12] In socialization research, the closer to the subjects the investigator gets the weaker become the observed effects.[13]

The way in which people use dominant social and political formulas and beliefs in defensive and opportunistic ways is suprising given the supposed force of socialization. An intriguing example of some such ways is provided in Colin Turnbull's account of the adaptation of the Congo Pygmies. Deep in the Ituri Forest the BamButi have lived for perhaps 700 years or more as the ostensible slaves of more "civilized" villagers. When encamped near a village, the Pygmies participate in the rituals of the villagers' religion, submitting to rites of puberty, marriage, death, ownership, and the like. The Pygmies gain many days of feasting from this participation, but once back in the forest the newly declared man or bride reverts to other social behavior—the "man" sitting on his mother's lap, the "bride" abandoning her "husband." The strategy of the villagers in controlling "their" Pygmies is to indoctrinate and subject the Pygmies to the villagers' supernatural beliefs. As Turnbull puts it: "To the villagers these methods of social control are just as scientific and real as, say, political control through armed force."[14] The counterstrategy of the Pygmies is to separate their own cultural world from that of the villagers. They never celebrate or express their own beliefs around the villagers. Thus they gain economically from the largesse that accompanies the villagers' rites but also avoid coming under their supposedly internalized control. Indeed, Turnbull points out that the cunning Pygmies will often use the villagers' belief in evil spirits to their own advantage, as by claiming that foodstuffs or other things belonging to the villagers that they have consumed were "stolen" by "demons." Such explanations are hard for the villagers not to accept.

Turnbull summarizes the contest between the dominant villagers and the subordinate Pygmies as a standoff:

> The villagers seek to win the contest by domination; the Pygmies seek to perpetuate it by a kind of indigenous apartheid. Because the relation is one of mutual convenience rather than necessity,

it works with reasonable success in the economic realm. The villagers ascribe the success, however, to their spiritual domination; any breakdown they cannot correct they are content to leave to rectification by the supernatural, a formula that works within their own society. The Pygmies hold, on the other hand, that the forest looks after its own, a belief that is borne out by their daily experience. In the nature of the situation, each group is able to think it has succeeded, as indeed in its own eyes it has. The very separateness of the two worlds makes this dual solution possible.[15]

The villagers get the illusion of control; the Pygmies, as they say, get "to eat" or take economic advantage of the gullible villagers. Until Turnbull had the luck to encounter the Pygmies away from the villagers, anthropologists had taken the villagers' account of the situation as accurate. This misinterpretation is the danger of any social investigation that relies on the naiveté of its subjects. The trap lies in that the strategies for avoiding social control in the form of socialization are precisely exaggerated conformity, tendentious ignorance, and a dichotomization of the social world into "them" and "us." Insofar as the social scientists promote these strategies by avoiding intersubjective tests of validity, they contribute to the technical myths of domination. Statements and techniques that require some kind of secrecy, naiveté, or deception as the basis of their empirical validity or usefulness are suspect. They smack more of necromancy than science.

The privileged perspective required for applying socialization techniques involves positing an "unsocialized socializer." The existence of an "unsocialized socializer" inevitably undermines socialization as an explanation of social behavior accounting for more than a marginal variance since it can be avoided. If we take the position that past socialization has been weak or inconsistent in efficacy and therefore needs improvement, then to the extent that we improve socialization the possibility of further improvement of content or technique recedes. Successful socialization practices destroy the basis for either investigating those practices or altering them. Thus social reform based on the implied molding characteristic of socialization makes future reforms impossible. There is no place for a future Plato or Socrates in the Republic, none for a future Mao in a communist utopia, none for a Hobbes in the Leviathan, none for a new Skinner to emerge in a future Walden Two, and, as Marx noted, no possibility of his being a Marxist. Just as a successful explanation of socialization threatens to undermine its effectiveness, so successful socialization practices threaten their continued use as a means of social adaptation.

These paradoxes of socialization theory constitute only a formal or logical refutation and are not likely to persuade many of the necessity

of abandoning their underlying assumptions concerning human nature, learning, and social change. However, so long as those who cham-
pion the utility of socialization as an explanatory concept and/or a
strategy of either change or stability avoid confronting these paradoxes, their resulting statements are unfalsifiable because they rule out
possible conditions of counterevidence. When those conditions are admitted there is enough counterevidence to put doctrines of socialization
in doubt, if not to reject the formulation altogether. The dramatic
claims of socialization as both explanation and cure for the defects of
social and political design rely for their persuasiveness on these paradoxes as well as on lack of specific content. Avoiding the paradoxes or
supplying content drastically reduces the claims that can be made.

Research in Socialization

The research of several decades indicates that we do not know how to
develop moral character effectively, that we do not know how to educate our population into an active well-informed democratic citizenry.
Studies show little or no effect of conventional character and civic
education on the moral conduct and political behavior of children.[16]
Such education is indoctrination by omission, distortion, and prescription, teaching what is not to be thought, or said, or done. The sterility
of this approach can be grasped if we stop to imagine teaching driver
education in the same manner. Lawrence Kohlberg critically summarizes the last generation of research into the effectiveness of socialization as leading to widespread dissatisfaction with conventional theories
of social molding based on Freudian psychoanalysis, anthropological
culturology, and reinforcement (either Hullian or Skinnerian) learning
theory: "This dissatisfaction has arisen because the correlations found
in the studies have been low in magnitude and inconsistently replicated
from one study to the next. As a result, neither clear, practical, nor
theoretical conclusions can be drawn from the findings."[17]

We will now attempt to describe the basic theoretical approaches
underlying these studies, to locate the major issues involved in constructing a consistent theory of socialization, to point out the difficulties
of existing theories, and to review empirical findings.

There is no generally agreed upon framework for the analysis of
socialization.[18] Thus there is no organized body of findings or propositions. Definitions of socialization differ with the same author at different times as well as between authors and disciplines.[19] Sometimes socialization simply means social learning or the ways in which individuals
find out about their societies and how to "participate effectively in
social interaction."[20] That such learning goes on no one can deny.

People certainly learn something from the social institutions and political systems in which they live. But if we define the concept in this loose sense, then the problem remains of discovering, describing, and explaining how this learning takes place, what is its content, and what are its effects. But the great weakness of current theories and research is that most of the investigations to date consist of inventories of ideas, attitudes, values, and the like, that people possess at a given time, with the assumption that these are the result of socialization.[21] The assumption is, as Inkeles writes, that "every individual as we encounter him, is the outcome, the 'product' in a sense, of a given socialization process."[22] Thus socialization must be something real and efficacious since we continuously encounter its outcomes. This reasoning is circular in that it involves assuming the cause or process rather than investigating or demonstrating it.

Owing to the lack of a general framework, the evaluation of the evidence as to the presumed efficacy of socialization processes is difficult. Assumptions, definitions, and claims vary like the heads of Hydra and dismissing one on the basis of research findings seems to leave dozens of others to flourish. It is necessary, then, to try to systematize the propositions of current socialization theories even though this systematization may not please all those who work in this field. Socialization theories have lived too long on ambiguity and claims of "scientific infancy."

There are four major theoretical approaches to the description and investigation of socialization: Freudian-psychoanalytical, culture-personality, social-learning, and cognitive-developmental. The cognitive-developmental approach runs counter to the molding image of socialization and will be discussed separately and last. There are two minor approaches: the interactionist and the developmental. There is an eclectic approach derivative of the others called political socialization.

Each of the first three approaches stresses a particular assumption about the socialization process. While these assumptions are often utilized by other approaches they are not crucial to all. The assumptions which the respective approaches emphasize are (1) the primacy principle: that which is learned first is learned best, is unlikely to change, and will determine what is learned later in life; (2) the consensus principle: in order for societies to exist, motivational uniformity and cognitive conformity must be assured; (3) the passivity principle: the human brain is a passive receptacle or recorder of events and learning is a process of absorption; and finally an assumption important to the political socialization approach: (4) the structuring principle: that learned patterns of orientations (such as personality or a value system) structure or determine the learning of specific beliefs and attitudes. All of these assumptions are to be found in Plato and have been reiterated throughout the history of traditional Western political thought as well as ratified by behaviorists rebelling against that tradition.[23]

We will now take each approach in turn, first explicating the molding process it purports to describe and explain. Then we will attempt in turn to show (1) how the research findings fail to substantiate the claims made for the process and (2) that the major assumption of the approach is counterfactual. Then we will examine the cognitive-developmental approach as a guide to reorienting ourselves to political and moral education without recourse to indoctrinating ignorance or false hopes of reshaping human nature.

Psychoanalytic Theory of Socialization

Psychoanalysis as a therapeutic technique and an integrated theory of human behavior has both encouraged and reinforced the molding image of socialization. Psychoanalytic models of socialization in one vulgar form or another are the most well-known explanations of how such molding takes place. If every age has its illusion, this image of sculpting character by means of deliberate training in habits of defecation, eating, and sexual gratification is a candidate for the illusion of our epoch. Techniques of manipulating children and genitalia are a major concern of reformers, conservatives, and critics during our time.

We cannot in justice lay this folly entirely at the feet of Freud. It is easy to be tempted into an onslaught against Freudian thought on the basis of the destructive uses and misuses of psychoanalytic principles in modern education, child rearing, interpersonal relations, advertising, and social analysis. No one is alive in the United States, the nation that adopted Freud, who has not been assaulted or insulted by means of crude Freudian labeling. Many have had their relationships with their parents turned shallow and manipulative by the unseen child-rearing handbook that frightens parents out of spontaneity and guarantees them mechanical success.

The discounting use of Freudian and Marxian categories is a major barbarism of our time. Perhaps in an age of bureaucratization, when every authority is at once insecure in its knowledge and demanding in its need for ratification, every intellectual doctrine is doomed to be used as a tool for bullying and belittling the individual. However, this is not the place for a critical appraisal of Freud's theories and their impact on social and political thought. In fact, the point belabored in this volume that social ignorance is always a deliberate and never an accidental affair owes much to Freud's insights. What we must discuss is the interaction between the principles of psychoanalytic theories of development and the liberal preoccupation with education as a tool of government.

Freudian socialization theory is based on the insight that human behavior patterns are primarily learned rather than instinctually programmed. Freud wrote that "man is equipped with the most varied instinctual predispositions, the ultimate course of which is determined by the experiences of early childhood."[24] This implies the possibility, Freud speculated, that although most human beings were distinguished by their laziness and their slavery to irrational passion, improved socialization practices could lead to a civilization compatible with human need. He expressed this ideal this way:

> New generations, brought up kindly and taught to have a respect for reason, who have experienced the benefits of culture early in life, will have a different attitude towards it; they will feel it to be their very own possession, and they will be ready on its account to make the sacrifice in labour and instinctual renunciation that is necessary for its preservation. They will be able to do without coercion and will differ little from their leaders.[25]

Freud himself was skeptical of the ideal, and declared darkly that "the price of progress in civilization is paid in forfeiting happiness through the heightening of the sense of guilt."[26] Thus psychoanalytic theory comes near to the liberal doctrine of *tabula rasa* with its implication of human malleability and threat of incipient chaos.[27] It arouses our hopes and fears at the same time.

While the instincts of the infant are explosive and potentially destructive in their direct expression, they can be gratified in a variety of ways, according to psychoanalytic theory. Further, not only can they be directed at different objects in the world, but they can also be controlled in various ways allowing for delayed gratification or even forms of substitution. The infant is assumed to begin with a belief in omnipotence as if it is itself the world. Through disappointment and the direct intervention of adults the infant learns to differentiate between itself and objects in the world. Original tendencies of the organism were characterized by Freud as operating under the pleasure principle—that is, immediately seek pleasure and avoid pain. This principle is supposedly chaotic, leading to infinite variety in taste and value—an interpretation which parallels that of Hobbes and Locke[28] Interdiction of the pleasure principle by adults leads to a belief in their omnipotence, which the child tries to share by the delusion of introjection and identification. As differentiation of self-and-others and self-and-objects takes place, the pleasure principle is superseded by the reality principle. The reality principle simply means that the immediate regulation of pain and pleasure is made more complex and devious. The original gratifications are sought, but now the conditions of the outside world are taken into account. The reality principle is pleasure principle plus cunning and hypocrisy.

This cunning entails not only manipulation of others but also the manipulation of perceptions in the form of wishful fantasies. By projecting omnipotence onto parents and then introjecting their demands, the infant fantasizes a sharing of their power. This identification contributes further to the educability of the child. As Fenichel writes: "They [children] need supplies of affection so badly that they are ready to renounce other satisfactions if rewards of affection are promised or withdrawal of affection is threatened."[29] The young child's fears of punishment or loss of affection, however, do not result simply in compliance but rather in the child pretending he "feels 'bad' in situations where he actually feels 'good.' "[30] Thus the learning of delaying or redirecting gratification is accompanied by the learning of how to lie. Learning to dissimulate is the basis of morality, according to Ferenczi. Although compliance does not result from these processes, conscience does—"a constant watchman has been instituted in the mind." The end result of this complex process is an adult who not only knows right from wrong but desires to do right whatever his actual behavior and to avoid the discomforts that doing wrong brings in the form of guilt. While this adult is not quite the perfectly sculpted citizen that Plato thought might be obtained, he or she does promise a degree of stability and a predisposition for further educability by authority figures.

In this formulation the psychoanalytic exlanation of socialization seems to promise little to the reformer who would rework the stuff of human nature. Fenichel, for example, maintains that only a number of suggestions about child-rearing can be made for the purpose of avoiding later neuroses and the "effectiveness of such suggestions is very limited."[31] This is because such efforts are limited by social institutions and conditions. But what the family or the school cannot do alone the constella of institutions can accomplish: "Every mental phenomenon is explicable as a result of the interaction of biological structure and environmental influence. Social institutions act as determining environmental influences upon a given generation."[32] Thus what is taken away as a possibility of deliberate design is returned in the form of the contingencies of social and political history. But the claim of being the ultimate determinant is crucial.[33] Such determinism is a seduction for many. Coupled with the *tabula rasa* assumption, it again echoes the environmentalism of classical liberalism. The first political scientist to utilize psychoanalytic theory as a means of explaining behavior, Harold Lasswell, understood it just this way. He cynically concluded that "successful social adjustment consists in contracting the current diseases."[34]

Freud further contributed to his assimilation by liberal thinkers and reformers by his adoption of the primacy principle, which implies permanency and determinant character to the earliest learning. In turn, this principle implies that human behavior can be predicted and controlled in a simple fashion. Freud declared: "nothing once formed in the mind could ever perish . . . everything survives in some way or another and is capable under certain conditions of being brought to light again, as, for instance when regression extends back far enough."[35] This "conservation of the mind," as Freud calls it, means "it is a prominent feature of unconscious processes that they are indestructible."[36] Past stages in development persist, in Freud's view, and always can intrude or be utilized in the present, if indeed they do not predetermine how the individual will experience that present. For if all emotions and perceptions are somehow recorded by the mind, then it must be that the earlier ones will have a decisive influence over subsequent ones in the form of predispositions if not outright obsessions. Thus Freud concludes that "the experience of the first five years of childhood exerts a decisive influence in our life, one in which later events oppose in vain."[37] And again, the "little creature is often completed by the fourth or fifth year of life, and after that merely brings gradually to light what is already within him."[38] Passages like these imply the notion that the child is a kind of homunculus subjected to the traumas and unspeakable terrors of infancy, which in turn unfold in the course of later life like the plot of a Greek tragedy.[39] Since the age at which the most significant experiences of life take place is also the age of least capability for dealing with the world, the human psyche is demonically structured. Such statements by Freud and their elaboration by his followers and students seem to lay the burden of our discontents on the terrors of infancy.[40]

Freud sometimes expresses caution about the extent of "conservation of the mind" based on his clinical evidence. He notes that "perhaps we ought to be content with the assertion that what is past in the mind *can* survive and need not necessarily perish."[41] Pointing out our lack of evidence in this area, however, he concludes with the stronger statement that "it is more the rule than the exception for the past to survive in the mind." Freud's evidence concerning early mental life is based on the analysis of adult neurotics. Indeed, he claims that he seriously misunderstood the nature of this evidence initially. He believed that his patients who were suffering from hysterical symptoms had been sexually assaulted in their infancy because "they ascribed their symptoms to passive sexual experiences in early childhood . . . to seduction."[42] But Freud found these seductions to be highly improbable and indeed untrue. Having carefully traced the symptoms of the clinical present back through puberty to childhood, Freud found himself faced with a fantasy. He concluded that these fantasies of seduction were intended "to cover up the auto-erotic activity of early childhood." What he discovered from this experience was the fact of childhood sexuality—an element prominently denied in the social ignorance of his time. Later analyses and observation of children confirmed their sexual activity. Freud reasoned that infant sexuality led to traumatic occurrences in even commonplace instances because of the emotional and biological immaturity of children.

Freud's Questionable Evidence However important the public recognition of childhood sexuality which Freud promoted, his means of discovery and his evidence do not necessarily support the primacy principle. As Orlansky insists: "The reconstructions of infant experiences obtained from the analytic couch do not constitute empirical findings on the infantile situations."[43] Freud's own experience in such reconstructions suggests that it is a serious error to assume the validity of neurotic individuals' memories of infantile events. That there is a connection between such memories and the neurotic conflict I accept as demonstrated by Freud and other psychoanalysts. There is probably a connection between such memories and experiences of trauma. The psychoanalytic conception of neurotic traits as frozen, unalterable, and insatiable patterns of behavior implies that those response patterns which remain unaltered through life are necessarily subject to the "conservation of the mind."[44] To put it another way, "conservation of the mind" is one of the ways in which neurotic patterns manifest themselves in the form of symbolic and other fixations. Those experiences of childhood that later events oppose in vain are those traumatic events that become fixated in memory. Freud has generalized from this occurrence to state that all events of childhood are so fixated. As one author interprets him: "For Freud, the moral values internalized from parents persist relatively unchanged through life."[45] Maccoby argues that clinical evidence and the histories of deviants justify "our assuming at least a moderate degree of persistence in early learned values and modes of behavior."[46]

But even with this watered-down endorsement of the primacy principle, we find that such evidence and such histories justify no such thing. On the basis of psychoanalytic evidence the most we can say is: neurotic or pathological behavior patterns are characterized by their persistence, often persistence from an origin in infancy. Whether or not nonneurotic behavior shows such persistence (a persistence which later events oppose in vain, according to Freud) has not been demonstrated. Such a demonstration would be suprising and would undermine the definition of neurotic behavior. For if all behavior persists, or in other words is abnormally fixated, then what is to distinguish healthy patterns from pathological ones? Human beings would be a strange species indeed if they possessed no biological limits of health or if, as Freud believes, their social survival demands their individual pathological degeneration.

Further, the notion that recent or current experiences vainly oppose the fixations introduced in infancy is at least partly contradicted by the success of psychoanalysis in overcoming such fixations. Freud's motto "Where there is id, there shall be ego" makes no sense if the ego and its implied adaptability is only a narcissistic sham fronting for a demonic unfolding of infant nightmares. Of course the motto may be ambivalent and could imply to some a willful self-deception based on the recognition and acceptance of infantile fixations without any attempt to change them. Freud is never guilty, even in his most extreme formulations of the primacy principle, of maintaining that individual character can be consciously molded by appropriate parental techniques.[47] But that they can be molded is a common, even popular misinterpretation of psychoanalytic theory by Americans in particular. One frustrated psychoanalyst recounts that he was invited to talk to a group of American social scientists about the causes of Nazism in Germany. He offered several factors having to do with German culture, politics, economic patterns of industrialization, and the like. This approach was unacceptable, he was told:

> As a psychoanalyst I should point out how Nazism had developed from the German form of child rearing. I replied that I did not think that there was any such relationship; in fact, political opinion did not seem to me to be determined in early childhood at all. This view was not accepted and I was told that the way the German mother holds her baby must be different from that of mothers in democracies.[48]

This incident might be taken to indicate that some have accepted a parody of the psychoanalytic theory of socialization, but the interpretation is almost ordinary.[49] For it is difficult to keep in mind at once Freud's statements about the determining effects of the experiences of the first years of life and his insistence that adult behavior could not be predicted on the basis of infant history.

The primacy principle did not originate with Freud. Not only did Plato seem to accept it, but it was and is also a postulate of liberal environmentalism. As Ross wrote,

> The hackneyed metaphors; "potter's clay," "wax tablet," "bent twig," "tender osier," are so many ways of emphasizing the high suggestibility of childhood. The mark of the young mind is an absence of fixed habits, of stubborn volitions, or persistent ways

of acting. The staunch personality that can plough through counter-suggestions as tremorless as an ironclad in a flight of arrows we look for only in the adult. The child gradually builds it as a worm builds its worm-cast—out of material taken in from without.[50]

Perhaps like other reformers and rejected social innovators, Freud was only subject to wishful thinking. For the individual without habits, volitions, or persistent patterns of acting is the ideal audience for social and political philosophers. No wonder they prefer always to talk to youth or to those who are responsible for raising and educating youth and infants.

While some researchers more cautiously note that the primacy principle is a hypothesis, most research in socialization simply assumes it.[51] As a hypothesis it is unconfirmed; as an assumption it is unwarranted. The primacy principle is subject to serious objection on both theoretical and empirical grounds. Theoretically, the principle requires a human brain of enormous memory capacity. Empirically, the principle should result in a correlation of the value orientations of grown children and their parents, of child-rearing techniques and their personality traits, of adult political attitudes and parental political views. That the brain should have the information processing capacity required by the principle appears to unsubstantiated, if not impossible. The data on similarity and differences between parents and their grown children gives at best mixed and at worst negative support. Further, the persuasiveness of the idea may be due in fact to the limitations and distortions of human memory. We tend to remember those events of our infancy and those attitudes of our parents that are most similar to our present experience and viewpoint. While the evidence is not all in, nor is it conclusive, the primacy principle is a problematic assumption that requires replacement if our research on how people learn about their social contexts and develop moral judgment is to progress.

Child Rearing and Adult Character Roger Burton reports, "there are serious difficulties in demonstrating the relationships of child-rearing practices with later behavior."[52] Harold Orlansky reviewed empirical, experimental, and semi-experimental investigations in Western culture and other anthropological evidence on the relations between infant treatment and personality development. He found the evidence of these studies to be largely negative. Orlansky examined studies in the areas of nursing, mothering, sphincter training, bodily restraints, and frustration. The studies included specific parental practices: breast vs. bottle feeding, length of breast feeding, self-demand vs. scheduled feeding, weaning, timing of toilet training, swaddling, and the like. He

found no evidence associating supposedly favorable practices with se-
cure and unneurotic personalities. Some findings were contradictory,
some negative, and some methodologically suspect. For example, Orlansky reports that the data are too meager either to support or to
refute the thesis that early rigid bowel training results in anal character
structures.[53]

Anthropological studies and experimental evidence suggested that
the minimum needs of the infant are much less than current pediatri-
cian fads indicate.[54] Also, it is difficult if not impossible to characterize
the experience of infants as uniformly frustrating or satisfying. Indeed,
most descriptions of infant reactions in the first year of life have been,
according to Orlansky, "too much colored by a naive reading-in of
adult emotions into the infant which is comparable to the anthropo-
morphizing views of insect behavior once current among an earlier
generation of biologists."[55] That is, most descriptions of the infant's
feeling of omnipotence, of its rage when the breast is removed, of its
frustration when its arms are pinioned, and of its other reactions, are
the projected reactions of adults to the infant situation.[56]

Orlansky agrees that "early infantile frustration has a greater effect
on adult behavior than does later infantile frustration," and he
identifies this statement as the "firm logic behind the psychoanalytic
position."[57] But the real question, he argues, is whether experiences in
the first year of life structure personality so rigidly and firmly that
restructuring by later experience is unlikely. While Orlansky, indeed
everyone, seems to agree that in the first year of life incidents can occur
that are so devastating as to influence or shape future development, it
remains to be seen whether the experiences of ordinary infancy have
such affects. Some authors like Allport have maintained that the formation of dispositions in the first year of life are less stable than those
formed at subsequent ages.[58] Orlansky concludes:

> The rigidity of character structuring during the first year or two
> of life has been exaggerated by many authorities. . . . The events
> of childhood and later years are of great importance in reinforc-
> ing or changing the character structure tentatively formed dur-
> ing infancy.[59]

In summary, the Orlansky review indicates that the mechanical manipulation of infantile drives does not shape personality, at least not in
any simple recognizable way. If such shaping does take place, it has not
been demonstrated beyond the fact that traumatic occurrence—severe
deprivation of food, severe cruelty, or anything else of serious boiologi-
cal consequence—can effect later behavior related to the specific incidents. The primacy principle is placed in doubt by the lack of demonstration of importance of the first year of life experience. For if that

which is learned first is learned best, the first year of life should be the most crucial. The set or structuring that is supposed to take place at this time is undemonstrated. If, as Orlansky writes, "infantile indulgence does not necessarily produce a confident personality and if later gratification may offset earlier frustration, the range of 'potential' personality is, in any case, too large to be fruitfully delimited on the basis of present knowledge."[60]

Another attempt to establish the relation or nonrelation between infant care and personality was conducted by William Sewell.[61] Sewell's study was of 162 farm children aged 5 to 6. Mothers were interviewed concerning child-rearing practices such as breast or bottle feeding, nursing schedules, weaning, and bowel and bladder training. The children were given various personality tests. Sewell then attempted to test several null hypotheses concerning the relation of individual parental practices to personality traits of the children. Each hypothesis was a variation of the negative principle that personality characteristics would not vary significantly among children raised with different parental practices. On the basis of the evidence, Sewell could not dismiss any null hypothesis.[62] Further, by combining certain scores as a crude index of security/insecurity in rearing practices, he found that children reared in high-security environments did not differ significantly from those reared in low-security environments.

Kohlberg has criticized the usual socialization research that attempts to correlate child-rearing practices with individual differences in cross-sectional traits as a "metereological approach."[63] These naturalistic studies to date have done little or nothing to clarify theoretical issues, neither have they established the assumed relations between child care and adult character. Negative results, however, do not seem to slow down recurring fads of attempting to relate child-rearing antecedents to support of and participation in social movements as if some hidden key to the prediction of individual behavior might be gained. For example, Kohlberg charges that the studies of the antecedents of student activists in the 1960s contribute nothing to the understanding of personality development or socialization outside of American culture and they are of no sociological, political, or practical significance.[64] Indeed, what those ill-considered studies and many others in the area of "political socialization" do demonstrate is that there is a negative relation between the reported benevolent images of political institutions and leaders held by very young children and the political attitudes of unrelenting cynicism found among adolescents and adults.[65] As one writer comments on these "results" of socialization, "if this process is so effective why is it that we are experiencing widespread alienation and dissent from the basic assumptions of our political life?"[66]

The answers to that question by researchers in this field are remarkable in that they see no discrepancy between their findings and the assumed principles of socialization. Rather they reason that if the political images of childhood weren't so positive, the political cynicism of adulthood would be so great that a revolution would take place. Or they argue, as does Riccards, that the civic training of children in America is so idealistic as to promote the criticism and rejection of institutions and practices.[67] Few have entertained the possibility that the assumed principles of socialization might be wrong in whole or part in the light of such an astounding failure of results.

This is understandable since the "meteorological approach" makes no explicit link between the theory of socialization and research findings. But if we are to accept the theory and its principles, then there must be recognizable causal relations between specific socialization practices and adult behavior. Postulating gravity, we expect apples to fall down; if instead they float on the wind, we cannot attribute that result to gravity without making our theory vacuous. The fact that socialization researchers seldom hesitate to make reversals as well as ad hoc revisions in their hypothesis makes the challenging of socialization theories with negative findings difficult, if not impossible.[68]

In some areas there have been reported for decades high correlations between the attitudes and beliefs of parents and those of their children. Political party identification has been reported with correlations between .50 and .75. Unfortunately most studies of party identification have been based on recall, which is suspect.[69] If in fact political-party preference is significantly determined by parental attitudes, we would expect it to be an extremely stable attitude. Research in party preference in England has indicated that party allegiance undergoes considerably more change over time than was previously thought. In one year as many as 36 percent of a sample had switched parties and in one study over 15 years 40 percent of the sample failed to vote for the same party at three elections.[70]

In other value areas, a study by Aldous and Hill found continuity across three generations of the same family in several attitudes. The highest continuity was religious affiliation (64 percent); role specialization (34 percent); husband's occupation (32 percent); and educational level (20 percent).[71] However, the sample for this study was skewed in favor of Catholic, nonmobile, close-knit families, which the authors estimate make up less than 3 percent of the population. Thus the continuities are not impressive. They may suggest that the more formal and vacuous the attitude norm, as in religious or role preference, the greater the intergenerational continuity.

A study of intergenerational transmission of abstract values by Bengston produced negative results. In a study of 2,044 members of three-generation families in California, the author found that abstract values defined as "conceptions of desirable ends" were not transmitted as expected on the basis of the "socialization paradigm." His findings indicated that "neither cohort differences nor family similarity are factors which account for much of the variance in value-orientations between generations."[72] Therefore Bengston concluded that value orientations may be more influenced by developmental events, social positions, and idiosyncratic factors than parental attitudes. As he notes: "This is contrary to much of the previous literature in socialization theory and research. Perhaps these data suggest a need to take more seriously an 'undersocialized' view of the development of value orientations."[73]

Albert Reiss has pointed out that it has been possible in this century for the same individual to function successfully under the Weimar Republic, the Nazis, and the postwar German democracy.[74] If adult personality, character and civic values were as unflexibly determined as the primacy principle would predict, this versatility would not be possible. Reis concludes that the family is of little contemporary importance in the transmission of values and that only those values learned from parents that are reinforced by social and political institutions have any chance of surviving.

R. W. Connell surveyed studies done between 1930 and 1965 concerning the correspondence between parents' and children's political attitudes. Relying only on the studies that employed what seemed to him to be acceptable research methods, Connell found a lack of correspondence on attitudes toward war, communism, political involvement, prejudice, achievement, and family roles. He did find a strong relationship in political-party preferences but concluded that in other areas parental political opinions were largely irrelevant to their children.[75] Another major study of the relation between parental political values and those of their adolescent children showed only low to moderate correlations.[76]

I have not attempted here anything like a complete review of the evidence concerning the relations between infant care or infant training and personality or between parental and offspring values and attitudes. There is just not enough of the alchemist about me to wade through the literature. But more, if the primacy principle is correct, if no experiences are lost, if the first encounters between instinctual need and the available social means of satisfying them fatefully bends the twig, then the counterevidence cited here is not possible.[77] Perhaps the principle can be saved in a more precise, less global, and greatly restricted form. The negative and mixed results to date indicate only that the principle in its present form is an unwarranted, indeed false, assumption.

Does the Brain Forget Is the primacy principle within the realm of biological possibility? If we take the principle in the Freudian form as an implication of the conservation of the mind in which "nothing once formed in the mind could ever perish," we cannot deny the possibility. But we can assert that either the claims of the primacy principle must be reduced or it has not been established as probable. Neurophysiologists are divided on the issues as to whether or not there is "true forgetting" in the nervous system. Some psychologists like to extrapolate from limited evidence and declare:

> The brain functions as a high-fidelity recorder, putting on tape as it were, every experience from the time of birth, possibly even before birth.[78]

Other researchers in the area argue that the information-processing capacity of the brain is insufficient for the conservation of the mind to be possible. Warren S. McCulloch writes with some spleen:

> One of the cornerstones of Freud's delusion is the belief that we forget no single jot or tittle of what at any time has happened to us. By calculations that began naively with the senior Oliver Wendell Holmes and are today best handled by the physicist, von Forster, man's head would have to be the size of a small elephant to hold that.[79]

Perhaps the most judicious view of the problem is to note that "the basic proposition that no memory is ever completely lost is itself untestable."[80]

Those who hold that no memories are lost base their contention on evidence of remarkable recall encountered in hypnosis and on the findings of Wilder Penfield. During surgical operations on damaged brains, Penfield found that electrical charges applied directly to the brain produced "flash-backs."[81] Patients reported that they seemed to relive some past experience with great vividness. These experiences are almost halucinatory in their impact, "as though the stream of consciousness were flowing again as it did once in the past."[82] At the same time patients were aware of what was happening in the present. These experiences, called by Penfield "living through moments of past time," contain only those sensations of which the patient was aware in the historical past—that is, they are selective. But since they contain so much of seemingly irrelevant detail, Penfield concludes that they "argue for the existence of a permanent ganglionic recording of the stream of consciousness."[83]

Against Penfield's conclusions, Wooldridge argues that the evidence indicates only trivial past events can be recorded in the memory.[84] He hypothesizes that there may be particular causes for the recording of such seemingly unimportant events. His countertheory is supported by Baldwin, who found that "memories are never elicited by electrical stimulation unless the patient has a past history of epilepsy involving damaged tissue near the part of the brain where stimulation elicits the experiential recall."[85] Penfield's evidence seems similar to Freud's in that the brain appears to be capable of permanent recordings of memory under traumatic conditions. Thus such memories are not typical of brain functioning but represent instead malfunctions. Wooldridge concludes: "It seems likely that we record in our permanent storage only a small fraction of the events that we experience and, moreover, that we abstract and record only a tiny fraction of the originally present sensory data"[86]

Attempts to calculate the information-storage capacity of the brain seem to support Wooldridge's conclusion. For example, von Neumann (who thought, incidentally, that the nervous system had a memory that did not forget) calculated that a complete record of all sensory responses of a human organism plus the resultant electrical activity of the 10 billion brain cells for a lifetime of 60 years would require a memory with the information capacity of 2.8×10^{20} bits.[87] According to Wooldridge, this would require that *each* brain neuron have an equivalent of 30 billion on/off switches. This seems far beyond the range of possibility. Wooldridge recalculated the capacity, eliminating the recording of electrical activity, with resulting memory capacity of 6×10^{16} bits, which would require only 6 million on/off switches per neuron. But this smaller figure again does not seem to be within the range of possibility.[88] A smaller, more probable figure can be reached if we base our calculations on the fairly well-established human information-processing capacity of 25 bits per second. A lifetime would require, then, a memory capacity of 50 billion bits, which could be further reduced by limiting processing to a few hours per day. Such a capacity would require only 4 to 5 off/on switches per neuron, according to Wooldridge. Such a figure means, however, that very little of our experience would be recorded. J. Z. Young calculated the total inflow of information to the brain in a 50-year lifetime to approach a larger figure of 10^{15} bits. He adds, "There is no way of knowing how much of this is stored, certainly by no means all of it is."[89]

We cannot reject absolutely the primacy principle based on the idea that no memories are lost, given current information about the brain. We can, however, put the shoe on the other foot and point out that evidence for an information-storage capacity necessary to the principle has not been found. Further we can note that it would be an anomaly indeed if the information transmission and storage in the brain were not subject to Shannon's theorems and were therefore immune to noise and increasing entropy.[90] Strange things happen—but if we are to take them seriously they must be documented. We face daily seemingly extraordinary cases of memory lost and memories found. If, as von Neumann liked to assert, we know as little about memory as did the ancient Greeks, admission of that ignorance is in order.

Finally we must ask why a notion like the primacy principle seems so attractive in spite of the lack of evidence to support it? Why is it easy for most of us to recall a childhood incident or pattern of incidents to account for our present habits, failures, or strengths? When someone intones that the child is father to the man, why does that seem to explain so much human behavior? The answer, I think, lies not in how well we remember, but how poorly. As Ernest Schactel has put it, in his classic piece on childhood amnesia:

> Man perceives and remembers not as a camera reproduces on film the objects before its lens; the scope and quality of his perceptions and experiences as well as of their reproduction by memory are determined by his individual needs, fears, and interests.[91]

That is, our memories are determined by our present needs, not our past history. Remembering is affected by social convention, wishes, rationalization, and suggestion. It is perhaps easier to locate the cause of a current failure in the past of a childhood than in one's own present inadvertence, insensitivity, or ignorance. Convention once called for all to remember a "happy childhood" and to credit mothers and fathers with one's achievements. Current convention seems to operate in a contrary manner—in which my overeating, skirt chasing, boorishness, or the like, is explained in terms of my mother's ineptness instead of my own incapacities. Further, I can't do anything about my mother and the accidental but fatal traumas of my childhood except talk about them to qualified personnel at a rate of over $25 per hour. In either case memory is constrained by the conventional cliché.[92]

The rejection of the primacy principle does not entail a rejection of the scientific status of psychoanalytic theory. For I do not deny that childhood traumas can result in a fixation which interdicts subsequent learning or that analysis may help in such cases. I do deny "the lasting importance of seemingly trifling childhood experiences."[93] The brain is more complex than a tape recorder, more active and more subtle. If it were not, psychoanalysis could not achieve the results it does, nor could we theorize so grandly about the manner in which it works. It is just plain false to believe that all men and women are formed in personality and in moral and intellectual character by the age of five or so. People who are so formed get locked up, die, limp through life as best they can. Finally, those who argue for the impressionability of childhood and youth either have little direct knowledge of them or delude themselves. Nothing is more problematic or more likely to go wrong than the molding of infant habit. Because of their very lack of experience and knowledge, children are more conservative and more set in their daily ways than almost any adult. Their changes, when they come, are changes of growth and maturity. But seldom is it easy for a child to change its opinion just on the basis of new information.

Culture-Personality Theories of Socialization

Beginning in the 1920's and 1930's an unfortunate courtship and eventual marriage took place between psychoanalysis and cultural anthropology. This union produced a deformed interdisciplinary creature called culture-personality studies.[92] The research into what was called "national character," "basic personality type," or "modal personality" was directed at the question of what makes an American an American, an Englishman an Englishman, a Russian a Russian, and so on. To paraphrase Fromm, these social investigators wanted to know what makes individuals in various societies all *want* to do what they *have* to do.

The observations which motivated this research came from anthropology, which showed that an extraordinary motley of social institutions, values, and habits existed. Conditions that had been proclaimed unlivable by social thinkers and reformers turned out not only to be possible to endure but even to be appreciated and clung to in the face of "civilized" progress. But while human beings could express their humanity in a suprising variety of ways, they seemed to choose to do it in only one "culturally" defined way. The doctrine of cultural relativism was an attempt to recognize the integrity of the various cultures of the world while explicitly denying the feasibility of cultural experimentation. According to this doctrine you could not simply survey all the child-rearing practices in the world and choose the one you like best. Rather each culture and every item of behavior or attitude in it had to be understood as one system of interacting elements.[95] As Mead wrote, "the system of values involves in the end the whole culture."[96] This observed diversity and stability bolstered the idea that each culture exacted psychic costs for the regimentation it imposed on the potentialities of its members. Further, since this cost seemed to be born lightly and individuals not only would defend the practices and values of their own cultures but deny the defensibility or even the possibility of other cultures, massive cultural conditioning appeared to be at work.

This conditioning, since it involved obsessions and social ignorance, was not just a matter of learning.[97] Human plasticity plus social stability seemed to demand special mechanisms of definite molding in each society. Such molding would have to be somatic as well as cognitive.

Psychoanalytic socialization theory seemed to provide the mechanisms of conditioning that the anthropologists sought. The varied patterns of child-rearing which were observed were assumed to be responsible for the respective patterns of adult behavior and values. As adults train infants, according to this view, "they systematically though unconsciously establish in the infant's nervous system the basic grammar of their culture's pattern."[98] Thus as each newborn learned to live it simultaneously helped its culture to survive at a depth and with a tenacity that might withstand all but the greatest shocks. Therefore, redesigning of changing institutions not in accord with the "grammar" or "patterning" of the culture would be futile if not destructive. The changing of society required either a population of infants or total instruments for the remolding of men and women.

The results of cultural conditioning should cluster around characteristics of standard personality structure. For it was taken as an unquestioned assumption by the culture-personality school that human organizations required a consensus on "fundamental" attitudes, values, motivations, and the like. Accordingly, the function of socialization would be "the replication of uniformity," That is, the molding of a basic personality type.[99] The observed facts were that people cooperated with one another under an extensive range of social structures. This range seemed to rule out the possibility that this cooperation could be based on a fixed human nature. The assumed principle was that an inculcated set of common motives, meanings, and values could and would account for the cooperation.[100] Unfortunately the resulting research based on these facts and this assumption proved to be poor in both conceptualization and method.[101]

This poor quality was due more to the features of culture-personality theory itself than any lack of intellectual ability or rigor on the part of the rather distinguished group of investigators in this area. For once the consensus principle is assumed, then a consensus can and must be found. Once the consensus is assumed to be what Erikson calls an "instinctive" blueprint inscribed on the central nervous system of each individual, then it is a matter of ingenuity and imagination to describe it. There is no way, however, to check out, correct, or improve a given description. If two investigators each find a different consensus, there is no way to decide which is more or less correct. If an investigator's description of the consensus is wrong according to members of a given society, there is again no way to judge the conflicting claims because patterns of consensus are likely to be "unconsciously" held. If intervention based on a description of the consensus fails, the failure does not invalidate the description because covert as well as overt patterns are assumed to be at work.[102]

Failures of Basic Personality Research Culture-personality theory assumes what it must—but cannot—demonstrate. By assuming (a) the necessity of consensus and (b) the replication of that consensus in each individual, the theory is rendered unfalsifiable not by design but because the assumptions are false. That is, (1) there are no such things as a consensus on motivation, values, meanings in any society except as reifications of the constructs of investigators; and (2) there is no replication of such a consensus in the central nervous system of individuals or anywhere else. If (a) and (b) were true, it would be possible to isolate and describe the basic personality type in any society and to demonstrate the socialization processes that produced its features. Differing claims or hypotheses concerning either type or process could be evaluated on the basis of direct evidence. Instead, an intersubjective judgment about what is the basic consensus in a given society is not to be found.

Lindesmith and Strauss list several failings of culture-personality research.[103]

1. As noted in the last section, the assumed effects of infant experience of adult character are undemonstrated; instead, the literature in this area merely illustrates and documents assumed effects.

2. In order to salvage the doctrine of infant determination it is commonly asserted that if later experiences are the same as infant experiences, then the infant experiences will be determinant, but if not, not.

3. The explanations and description of this literature are distorted with adult fantasies and cultural assumptions. Skilled writers like Erikson wax poetic over the infant Indian's reactions to weaning and other experiences, in a manner that is as pernicious as it is persuasive.

4. No one can agree on what is fundamental about a given consensus or basic personality type. Investigators admit that persons change in adult life and that diversity is found in any society, but they argue that such changes and diversity are not "fundamental."

5. Since the primacy principle is assumed, the implication is that personality patterns of the basic social consensus cannot be taught directly.[104] More concretely, the same personality structures are claimed to result from different infant experiences and the same infant experiences are claimed to result in different personality structures.[105]

These difficulties are due, in part, to the assumption of what Anthony F. C. Wallace called the "microscopic metaphor." Each individual is assumed to be a smaller replica of the society's culture.[106] Representative of this approach is the work of Abram Kardiner and his associates. Kardiner subjected ethnological descriptions of various cultures to psychoanalysis, deducing from this a basic personality structure, or what we might call a model neurosis. Then child-rearing practices were investigated to see how the model personality was produced. According to this view, culture and social structures are products of the psychological needs, dispositions, and pathologies of individuals who have grown up in a certain pattern of child rearing. Or, as Kardiner wrote: "If we know how the basic personality is established we can make certain predictions about the institutions this personality is likely to invent."[107] Kardiner begins with certain universal human needs, emotions, and instincts which are suppressed in various ways by various child-rearing practices, resulting in various basic personalities and cultures.[108]

Once the persuasiveness of this kind of reasoning is understood to be a product of the microscopic metaphor, the descriptions of Kardiner and other researchers are not impressive. They cannot, in fact, give frequency characteristics of the basic personality they deduce from the ethnological material. That is, every individual appears to be a deviant and each individual description becomes an accounting for this deviancy, according to some presumed idiosyncrasy of developmental history.[109] It is easy to conclude that "basic personalities" are merely ideal types and do not exist in any given case.

An amusing and typical example of the failure of culture-personality theories of socialization is offered by Goldschmidt. He found that although most of the cultural traits of the Yurok-Hupa tribes of north-western California corresponded to those of the anal-erotic character described by Freud, the child-rearing practices focused no attention on sphincter training.[110] As Erikson reported, "In Yurok childhood, there seems to be no specific emphasis on feces or the anal zone"[111] This information would seem to be a clear refutation of the hypothesis that specific child-rearing disciplines produce personality types that in turn create institutions. Not so. The data from the Yurok-Hupa produced no embarrassment or reconsideration on the part of culture-personality partisans. Erikson simply reinterprets the data to confirm the theory by noting (1) that there are tensions in the society associated with eating and (2) the mouth, esophagus, stomach, and so on are attached to the anus. Thus if the mouth can be interpreted as an extension of the anus, the theory is saved.[112] Even those supporting the psychoanalytic theory of socialization have retreated from Freud's claims of sphincter training to the character traits of obstinancy, orderliness, and parsimony. Miller comments that Freud probably "overgeneralized" his conclusions about the relationship between sphincter training and anal-erotic character traits.[113] He concludes that the theory of anality needs modification. But given the failure to establish any association between the timing, severity, or style of toilet training with anal traits (which Miller notes), that modification would necessarily be a demolition.[114]

The demolition of the theory of anal character is a major blow to culture-personality theories of socialization. The traits of orderliness, compulsiveness, possessiveness, retentiveness, and the like, seem to be typical of Western capitalist society—indeed to be an almost complete catalogue of the Protestant ethic. If they are not produced by any standard infant discipline, the conclusion is that no such cultural, national, ethnic personality traits or types are so produced. The countertheory seems inescapable—that it is the institutions of capitalism with their emphasis on punctuality, saving, accumulation, which are the source of these traits.[115] But institutions, as we all know, do not determine adult character. Adults act with a willful stubbornness that can only be taken as determined so long as the determination is placed in the past. Otherwise we are faced with a situation in which institutions prescribe and reward certain habits, traits, behaviors, and the like, and people perform such insofar as they need those rewards. As Goldschmidt puts it, "the structural character of the society is one which rewards certain personality configurations so that they dominate the social scene and set the pattern."[116] Personality as we encounter it in the social world is not so much a product of child rearing as it is a response to institutional patterns. As such it is quite likely to exhibit a variety that evades any complete characterization, while it will show a pattern, a range, and a distribution that reflect the dominant institutional structures. Thus in a society like contemporary United States—where success is not well correlated with education, cognitive ability, genetics, or family social position—obstinancy and compulsiveness would seem to be adopted as personal characteristics more often than chance would allow, because in a game of chance those who plunge more often have better odds of winning.[117]

Anthony Wilden likes to remind us that when we use the labels *mankind, modern man,* or *human beings,* as in the sentence "Nowadays human beings are dreadfully wasteful of the earth's resources," we actually mean *industrial society.* That is, we attribute to human nature the characteristics of a historical social structure. Similarly, when we speak about German, American, or Chinese character we are actually talking about historical social structures, not genotypic personalities. As Wallace remarks, this looseness is all right for descriptive purposes when we want to compare one cultural group with another or when we want to speak compactly about our impressions of something as diverse and complex as a society or even a large institution. Indeed, we must at times speak this way and there are no problems so long as we do not take a figure of speech—a metonomy to be exact—for a statement of uniform replication. For we recognize the limits of our statements as soon as we must deal directly with one German, one American, or one Chinese. We find that each individual departs from the national or racial traits we have employed.

The business of national character and its production operates only at a distance and only if we are seduced by the assumption that social organization requires consensus. For the traits that we have picked seem to fit the consensus we seek. The microscopic metaphor has us by the imagination. If we recognize that we are attempting to make generalizations—needed and useful generalizations at that—about social structures, the matter becomes more reasonable. While we cannot see a social structure any more than we can unaided see an atom, we can treat the structure as an intervening variable. We can and do conjecture the structure of a society and the patterns of its institutions and proceed to test them in the course of living. Thus, while common personality types do not tumble endlessly out of the rocking cradle to create social structures, neither do structures produce uniform personalities. A variety of personality types with a great range of values, motivations, and cognitive patterns appears to be the empirical case in any society and such variety is probably necessary for the successful adaptability of a human organization. The motleyness of human character and perspective may be a product of a million years of selective pressure. It is therefore a strength of the species and a defect only to those reformers who are strong on intentions and weak on thought.

Consensus and Human Organization One of the most hallowed pieces of bunk in the attic of Western political thought is the consensus principle—the idea that social coordination and organization requires fundamental agreement on values and terms. Motivational and cognitive unity is a necessity of human society, the old saw runs, in complete disregard of the obvious diversity encountered in the real social world. The principle is defended from experience by the idea of "fundamental" or "basic." Thus the diversity we see is nonfundamental and the consensus we don't see but intuit or assume is, of course, fundamental. Since, as Carl Friedrich pointed out, no authors can agree on what is fundamental, the principle is immune to assault by counterevidence. Modern thinkers as different and antagonistic as Robert Dahl and Josef Stalin share the assumption of the consensus principle.[118] Reformers insist that motivational uniformity is prerequisite for an ideal society, at least.[119] These views imply the terrifying possibility that society can fall apart and scatter into chaos like helpless beads if the thread of consensus is broken, to borrow a metaphor from Wallace. Given this view, the source of human tragedy is the conflict of desires and cognitions between individuals who wish to learn, create, and otherwise develop their uniqueness and the society which sternly demands imitation, ritual, and the maintenance of "fundamental" orthodoxy for survival.[120]

Wallace argues that we must drop the consensus principle if we are to understand the processes of human organization. He argues that the assumption is empirically false and that it is an exact inversion of the social prerequisite of maximum human diversity.[121] Wallace cites the culture-personality studies as illustration of the empirical diversity found in even the simplest of human societies. Dahrendorf claims the empirical evidence concerning value consensus clearly contradicts the principle. Prothro and Grigg surveyed two random samples of voters in Ann Arbor, Michigan, and Tallahassee, Florida, concerning their degree of consensus on abstract democratic principles plus the concrete application of those principles. They found a degree of agreement from 94.7 to 98.0 percent on the abstract democratic principles. But they found something approaching "perfect discord" on over half of the statements dealing with applications of those principles. That is, whatever it is that the voters agreed on they could not agree on what it was, what it meant, or what difference it made. The authors conclude that their results offer no support for the consensus principle in its limited democratic form.[122] Whatever the claims, motivational unity cannot be a prerequisite of society.

Cognitive Diversity and Equivalent Meanings But what about a second element in the consensus principle—cognitive conformity? Even if people do not agree upon the same goals, isn't it necessary that they agree on the same labels and meanings for the furniture of the world? Wallace attempts to demonstrate both the formal and empirical possibility of human interaction based on cognitive diversity. Avoiding his mathematical notation, his first demonstration runs like this:

We often observe people in transactional situations of the sort in which A initiates, B responds, A consummates—in which mutual activities are carried to successful completion despite the fact that neither party to the transaction maps the exchange the same way. Thus transactions and transactional schemes are possible that are more complex than the cognitive map of any individual. All that is necessary for stable interaction, Wallace maintains, is that the cognitive maps be complementary, that is, broad, complex and organized enough to share *equivalent* meanings. Accordingly, "cognitive sharing is not *necessary* for stable social interaction."[123]

When we examine almost any human transaction we find both cognitive disconformity and successful interaction and we are hard pressed to understand or describe this combination, given our assumptions of conformity. When we successfully interact we tend to announce that there is an "understanding" or that we understand our compatriots. What the understanding is, is difficult to specify or difficult to believe when we state it baldly and simplistically. We learn almost daily that we do not understand others very well, nor do others understand us. Ordinarily this lack does not represent a problem. But if we become incapacitated in some way that limits our repertoire of available responses and therefore begin to act defensively, we demonstrate the "tendency of insecure persons to insist on the motivational identity of their friends, or their enemies."[124]

Equivalent cognitive content furnishes a sufficient measure of mutual predictability to make complex organizations possible. For example, two of us may talk about and interact with an object *x* which one of us defines as a "chair" and the other as a "Chinese Chippendale." Our definitions are not identical, but they are equivalent in the sense that when my "chair" burns, your "Chippendale" is destroyed. Thus, even though our respective maps designate or define *x* differently and these designations are coincident with our available responses (I may sit on the "chair" or use it for kindling, you may admire the "Chippendale" or display it as honorific evidence of taste), we can carry out numerous transactions involving *x* such as exchanging it, sharing it, and the like. You may not be able to understand my crassly utilitarian motives nor I to understand your impulses toward invidious consumption. Nevertheless, you may get a Chippendale and I may get some money for an ill-designed and worn-out chair.[125]

Wallace offers another kind of example:

> Consider a group of airmen at a defense airbase. At the sound of the claxon [Klaxon], they run to their aircraft, each taking an assigned seat, and commence the performance of their various highly specialized roles. There is one stimulus—the claxon—but its meaning, and the consequent responses, are different for each man. Nevertheless the meanings—and the responses—can be defined as equivalent because *whenever* the claxon sounds, each responds in the same way that he had before. It is this equivalence of meanings which makes possible that coordinated specialization of responses to standard stimuli which is achieved in culturally organized societies.[126]

If, as Wallace concludes, "to the extent that the meanings are equivalent, the group responses will be organized,"[127] how, then, do we maximize equivalence? The answer, of course, is that the more people know in the sense of being able to respond appropriately to a wide range of environmental and social variation, the more equivalence is available and thus the greater the possibilities not only of successful coordination but also of maximum organization.

A prerequisite of human society is a maximum diversity of cognitive structures. After noting that societies do, in fact, invariably contain a diversity of cognitive structures. Wallace writes:

> We now suggest that human societies may characteristically *re-*

quire the non-sharing of certain cognitive maps among participants in a variety of institutional arrangements. Many a social
sub-system simply will not "work" if all participants share common knowledge of the system.[128]

He goes on to indicate that this aspect of social life, which he calls "a
system of equivalent mutual expectancies," is recognized by social-contract theories, although Wallace maintains that the contract is implicit
and constantly changing.[129] However, we must seek to explain these
"social contracts" not in terms of any system of laws or institutions
which maintain them but in terms of the cognitive capacity of human
beings. Human beings do maintain such contracts by various means,
and the control techniques of hierarchy represent only a limited subset
of maintenance techniques. To the extent that complementarity of cognitive structures exists, such hierarchic techniques are not appropriate.
Rousseau seemed to grasp this incongruence in a vague way when he
proposed to make men dependent on nature rather than on other
men. However, he still sees the issue as one of control (by men, by
nature, or whatever) rather than one of increased responsiveness. It is
not as we become dependent on nature, but rather as we are able to
respond productively to nature, that social stability is achieved and
human freedom actualized. In this sense, we can understand Proudhon's epigram that " labor is the education of our freedom."

The problem of social-contract theories is what to do with cases of
deviance—those who simply disagree with the terms and/or content
of the contract and those who cannot meet its terms because of mental or psychological incapacity. Democratic social-contract theories face
the problem that while they insist on the right of the citizen to deviate, extreme deviation thwarts the democratic principle of contracts.
The problem of distinguishing between a valuable disagreement and a
disruptive deviance has been promoted to a paradox, according to
Friedrich:

> Democracy, based on the toleration of the view we hate, is possible
> only when there are no views of that kind; democracy, based on
> the ability to agree to disagree, is possible only when there are no
> disagreements serious enough to be dubbed fundamental.[130]

This paradox can be avoided if we drop the consensus principle,
which implies that deviance is a result of idiosyncratic cognitive structures.[131] For if mental derangement is simply a matter of unshared
meanings, values, and rules, we are all always treading the line of
madness. Against this view, Wallace argues that not diversity of cognitive content but cognitive deficiency and instability are the problem.
For example, he operationally defines a psychotic "as one who so frequently commits culturally defective acts as to lead his fellow or himself

to limit his participation in culturally organized society."[132] While the line between defective acts and deviant acts is certainly hard to draw, as clinicians like R. D. Laing have noted, we might assume that defective acts would be defined as those harmful to human life. Such acts are not the result of some regression to a nonsocialized primitive or infantile state, despite superficial resemblances. Their distinguishing mark is their extreme simplicity and barrenness.

For example, if a culturally defective person is threatened, the only choice available is panicked flight or murderous attack. A normal person would be one whose available repertoire of responses to threat would be sufficiently large to afford the choice of an action appropriate to the degree and kind of threat, such as stepping back, taking a defensive posture, or punching the threatener in the nose. According to Wallace, the restricted or incomplete aspects of defective acts are due to a drastically limited set of available predicates in the cognitive structures of psychotics. He calls this the "de-semanticization" of an individual's cognitive structure. Thus defective social acts are not due to a lack of reason in the sense of illogical or irrational thought. They are not due to a different, more primitive, less civilized, more infantile form of thought; but they are due to a lack of cognitive structure and content.[133]

A lack of predicates in an individual cognitive structure results in a lack of discrimination about objects and events in the world as well as the lack of ability to relate, in a complimentary fashion, to the discriminations of others. The "paleologic" presumably found operating among children, primitives, and psychotics is, accordingly, "the same old formal logic, operating . . . with a drastically limited range of predicates."[134] We may mistakenly assume that x and y are identical if they share a common predicate (or predicates) and if there are no other predicates for either of them available. Conditions under which maximum predicates, responses, and discriminations can be acquired thus become a central concern of any theory of human organization.

Organizing Diversity The goal of human institutions accordingly should be the "organization of diversity," rather than the "replication of uniformity," and this involves an approach radically different from that usually taken. Rather than the examination of uniformities, this approach requires an investigation of "the actual diversity of habits, of motives, of personalities, of customs which do, in fact, co-exist within the boundaries of any culturally organized society."[135] Research would center on the question of how various peoples do organize themselves despite the obvious failures and unreliability of socialization. Given this view, with its conception of culture as a continuously changing set of policies or fluctuating contracts, the human tragedy is seen as the lone-liness which may be caused by "the only partly bridgeable chasms of mutual ignorance."[136] In characterizing this outlook, Wallace directs the social investigator to the particularities of the situation, that is, to an examination of actual cognitive maps, or what he calls the "psychologi-cal reality," in contrast to the "structural reality" constructed by means of statistical or other kinds of generalization.[137] The relationship be-tween these two modes of description is complementary—we cannot describe both the way the social actors map the world and the way we map their collective actions at the same time.

A further implication of Wallace's approach is that culture or orga-nization is not something imposed on the human animal by environ-mental pressure, but rather that we must understand human beings as cultural beings. He maintains that culture—in the sense of a set of standardized models of equivalent mutual expectancies—is not a species-associated phenomenon. That is, the cultural nature of human beings has nothing to do with special attributes or dispensations.[138] According to Wallace the "capacity for learning is capacity for cul-ture."[139] What he calls the "degree of learned capacity" is composed of sensory discrimination, flexibility of action, reliability of memory, and semantic capabilities. Most important, the degree of learned capacity he describes as minimal for culture is not derived from some abstract model of man prior to society. Wallace proceeds by taking the fact of human cultures as given and deducing from that the minimal human capacity required for their production and maintenance. Specifically, human learned capacity differs from that of other animal species ac-cording to the "level of semantic capacity minimally adequate to the performance of the cognitive tasks required by known human cul-tures."[140] Thus culture is a product of human capacities and a created set of fulfillments of human needs. Or to put it in terms reminiscent of Marx, culture is natural to man.[141]

Wallace postulates that "organisms possessing cultural natures (and perhaps all organisms) act in such a way as to maximize the meaning-fulness of experience: They follow a Principle of Maximal Meaning."[142] This means that pleasure is associated "with maximal complexity and orderliness of the mazeway [cognitive structure—LDS] and . . . discom-fort with minimal complexity and order."[143] The Principle of Maximal Meaning implies quite different principles of coordination and social education than attempting to ensure motivational and cognitive unifor-mity.[144] As Friedrich wrote, "What binds a free people together is not an agreement on fundamentals, but a common way of acting in spite of disagreement on fundamentals."[145] Underlying all human cultures are "common modes of acting toward one another." As an anthropologist puts it, "There is no known human society in which men can kill, rape or rob at will, and there is no known society in which chidren and adults, at one time or another, and in one way or another have not experienced such desires."[146] But the statement is misleading and certainly does not lead to the conclusion that motivational uniformity must be achieved by socialization techniques lest a war of rape, killing, and robbery break out. In no primate society is killing, raping, or robbing at will permitted. Human beings are not unique in their proscriptions of species-threatening acts. As social critics have pointed out for centuries, what is unique to human experience is the sanctioning of rape, killing, and robbery characteristic of class society. Institutions are defended and preserved in the name of law and order that monopolizes such antisocial acts and perpetrates them as a means to the advancement of human culture and morality.[147] It is a short distance in the writing of the culture-personality school from an appreciation of culture to an understanding of culture as a disease that either must be destroyed, as Norman O. Brown implies, or maintained, as Freud, Lasswell, Lidz, and Kardiner hold.

The rejection of the consensus principle does mean the rejection of the idea of consensus itself. Men and women often work out agreements upon procedures, rules, perspectives, and even facts. How to facilitate the best agreement—that is, the most accurate, appropriate, useful agreement—is the issue to which social scientists should address themselves. What is reprehensible is the defense of just any agreement or deficient agreements as if rejection or replacement were a threat to social organization. As Friedrich noted, "All insistence upon agreement on fundamentals is basically related to the idea . . . that some persons know what is right."[148] Acceptance of the consensus principle dictates hierarchy as the only rational organizational form.

Much that is perplexing and contradictory about traditional political thought seems to be a product of assuming cognitive conformity to be a prerequisite of human organizations while recognizing the joys and utilities of cognitive diversity. While it is a tradition of hierarchy, it is also a tradition of freedom emphasizing both the abnormal fixation of human behavior and the audacious novelty of human action. By refusing to assume both hierarchy as the only viable social form and abnormally fixated routines as the behavioral norm, we can avoid many of the old perplexities and paradoxes. Hierarchy is only a technique of organization, sufficiently plausible to be adopted and, as we shall see, sufficiently damaging and frustrating to the human organism to make it difficult to change. For if man is culturally capable of sustaining and developing himself in spite of the disadvantages of his common class-structured societies, his inability to alter that condition to this time must be seen as a temporary and not a permanent deficiency. It goes without saying that the promotion of that deficiency as a conditioned subservience necessary to society is to be condemned as erroneous and deleterious to the life of the species.

Social-Learning Theories of Socialization

"Methinks the understanding is not much unlike a closet wholly shut from light, with only some little openings left, to let in external visible resemblances, or ideas of things without," wrote John Locke.[149] His metaphor of the mind as a closet into which things are forced conveys well the idea that "the understanding is merely passive" and that perception is "the inlet of all knowledge in our minds."[150] The assumption of this passivity principle (or "environmentalism" as it is sometimes called) is basic to social-learning or behaviorist theories of socialization. While the principle involves a crude bucket theory of mind as elaborated by researchers and reformists like B. F. Skinner, it also entails zoomorphism, or the insistence that there are no significant differences between human beings and other organisms.[151] In Skinner's formulation, the passivity principle is a dogma of scientific method. He insists that physics got nowhere until investigators quit looking for "causes" inside of objects, but rather gave up teleological explanations for statements of environmental contingencies. Earlier, Skinner liked to claim that "science insists that action is initiated by forces impinging upon the individual."[152] More recently he has ceased to speak oracularly and states only that "a scientific analysis of behavior must, I believe, assume that a person's behavior is controlled by his genetic and environmental histories rather than by the person himself as an initiating, creative agent."[153] While this statement is carefully identified as an assumption and just as carefully recognizes that persons contribute something even if only something genetic to behavior, it merely reiterates the passivity principle in a supposedly more tenable form.[154]

The point is that causes of behavior are to be sought in the events of the environment which can be observed and not in terms of the events of the mind which cannot. While Skinner's version of the passivity principle eschews introspection or "mentalism," it also rules out physiology. This point is important to understand because there is a strong degree of apriorism in Skinner's thought which leads to the sweat and shouts of battle whenever his theories of investigating behavior, of controlling behavior, and of reforming society are debated. If Skinner's assumptions and terminology are accepted, his conclusions follow. If instead they are taken as problematic, and if then evidence from neurophysiology, experiments outside the Skinnerian paradigm, and human-learning investigations are allowed, his conclusions are in doubt. Only if he can persuade us to look just at his evidence in his way does his work constitute the basis of a science of behavior. Otherwise he comes off as an ingenious experimenter and a half-baked moralist.[155]

Skinner's Metaphors The criticisms of Skinner have multiplied in recent years. A large number of them have seemed to talk past Skinner's doctrines to impugn his motives—because perhaps they operate from similar Lockean premises. I will present a schematic of Skinner's theory of learning and utilize the criticism of Noam Chomsky and others to show its limitations. Then I will review the findings of social-learning researchers whose work is based on variants of behaviorist learning theories to indicate their failure to illuminate the processes by which humans develop moral principles or learn values.

Skinner's experimental paradigm consists of the following elements: (1) a simplified, easily manipulated environment such as a box with one side or top open for observation; (2) a nonhuman animal that has been deprived of some biological need (such as food) moving freely within the confines of the box; (3) control by the experimenter of some device that rewards the animal by dispensing food pellets or making food bins available; (4) a device to record both the dispensing of food and some activity that can be mechanically recorded, such as pressing a bar or pecking a button.[156]

In a typical experiment, a starved animal is placed in the box for a period of time to "cool off." Animals typically dart frantically around the box trying to escape. Some critics claim the animals are learning the new environment during this stage but Skinner dismisses this as nonsense. After the animal learns that the jig is up and becomes placid, the observing experimenter decides what activity of the animal is to be increased in frequency or otherwise "shaped." The experimenter always begins with something the animal already does. Then the experimenter arranges a reward mechanism in such a way as to have an impact on the chosen activity. For example, a bar mechanism can be arranged so that when the animal presses the bar accidentally with any part of its body a food pellet is released. This arrangement eventually increases the frequency with which the bar will be pressed as the animal, in ordinary terms eschewed by Skinner, learns that "press bar" means "food."

In one ingenious experiment, Skinner placed a pigeon in a box in which the food dispenser was rigged to a clock to make food available on a basis unconnected to the activities of the animal. Six of eight pigeons were conditioned by such an arrangement to perform rapid "ritual" responses between food presentations.[157] Skinner concluded that this experiment demonstrated the development of superstition. "The bird behaves as if there were a causal relation between its behavior [whatever it happened to be doing when the food appeared—LDS] and the presentation of food, although such a relation is lacking."[158] In this case a response was conditioned but not selected by the experimenter.

After a particular response—bar pressing, button pecking, or whatever—is conditioned, a maintenance phase is sometimes used to make the conditioning more nearly permanent. While teaching a rat "bar pressing," reward is continuous—one press, one pellet, for example. But if the pellets cease at this point, the pressing will stop shortly. Skinner and others have demonstrated that if the rewarding is done intermittently, the bar pressing will continue long after food pellets cease to appear. That is, in the maintenance phase, a food pellet will drop only every third or fourth bar press, or some other pattern may be arranged. The scheduling of reward can become quite complex when the length of time between the animal's movement and the reward is also varied. This type of rewarding implies that irregular or unreliable rewarding is the best teacher, since Skinner and other behaviorists define learning in terms of the persistence of a response after reward has ceased.

In summary, the important features of these experiments are a controllable environment; the selection of an activity performed by a decorticate, deprived animal; a reward that occurs in temporal sequence to the selected activity; and an optional maintenance period in which the rate of reward is varied. With this simple but ingenious apparatus and method, Skinner has accomplished some amazing things, such as teaching pigeons to play ping-pong and guide air-to-surface missiles.[159] He has also described and explained in great detail and precision the special kind of conditioning that he calls operant—that is, conditioning by means of reward rather than punishment.

Skinner has developed an exacting technical terminology to describe his experiments. Food pellets and other stimuli are called reinforcements if and only if their availability is in a temporal relationship to a response of the animal or another stimulus and produces a change in the strength of response. Such strength of response is measured in terms of the rate of extinction after reinforcement has ceased. Thus in Skinner's paradigm, food pellets reinforce the bar-pressing response of a rat because the dispensing of pellets in a temporal sequence to the pressing of the bar strengthens that response. Varying the rate of reinforcement results in a schedule of reinforcement or particular pattern of sequential rewards.[160] This terminology is precise so long as the experimental situation we have outlined is maintained. However, Skinner employs his experimental paradigm figuratively as a metaphor to describe all learning of all organisms. When he does this his terminology raises serious problems. Chomsky argues that when these terms are used to describe human activites the result is either a false description if they are used in their narrow technical sense, or a series of vacuous statements if they are used metaphorically.[161]

In the experimental setting reinforcement has an exact meaning, but when Skinner tries to describe human behavior he uses the term "reinforcement" figuratively to refer to situations in which we would ordinarily say "he likes," "he wants," "he is satisfied," or something of the sort. Chomsky notes that Skinner must rely heavily on inexplicable notions like "self-reinforcement" to account for acquisition and use of language. Skinner writes that people can be reinforced though they emit no response, that the reinforcing stimuli may be imagined, or may even take place after the responding organism is dead, as in the case of an artist. In fact, we are able, within the Skinnerian terminology, to say that all behavior is controlled by environmental reinforcement only because we can figuratively label something real or imagined as the reinforcing stimulus—no matter what the response, and what the situation. When Skinner writes that "the laws of science are descriptions of contingencies of reinforcement" or that "teaching is the arrangement of contingencies of reinforcement under which students learn," we are at a loss to understand what is meant unless we detect the metaphorical use.[162] As Chomsky points out:

> A literal interpretation of Skinner's statements, where terminology is understood in something like the technical sense, yields obvious falsehood, and . . . a loose metaphorical interpretation does permit the translation of the familiar descriptive and evaluative vocabulary of ordinary discourse into Skinner's terms, of course with a loss of precision and clarity.[163]

Therefore Skinner can be understood as confusing "science with terminology."[164] The persuasiveness of Skinner's claim to laying the basis of a technology of behavior is based on the assumption of the passivity principle and the figurative but dogmatic adoption of a limited experimental terminology. If we assume the passivity of the brain and agree to label some feature of the environment a reinforcing stimulus every time we observe an action, we can explain all behavior.[165] Since there is never a dearth of at least imagined reinforcing stimuli in even the most denuded environment, there are no inexplicable actions. Unfortunately, such a theory is both *post hoc* and unfalsifiable. Demonstrations of effectiveness require either some approximation to Skinner's experimental paradigm—that is, dealing with subcorticate reactions, simplified environments, and the like, or simply post-hoc triviality. For anyone who has ever attempted to teach others or even to influence human behavior in any purposeful way, the scheme is hopelessly inadequate.[166] Using it, we can predict only the most trivial behavior, such as "I predict that you will wear some form of clothing to your next lecture." And such predictions work only until they fail—as when you walk into a lecture nude. Then, of course, that failure can be explained in terms of some other stimuli or merely taken as a statistically trivial instance, causing the prediction to be restated in probabilistic terms.

As a means of controlling behavior, learning theories based on the passivity principle, such as Skinner's operant conditioning, are at best parlor tricks and at worst grandiose frauds. Skinner proclaims that all the ways "of changing a man's mind reduce to manipulating his environment, verbal or otherwise."[167] For example, Skinner gives the following ways of evoking the verbal response "pencil": (1) say to the subject, "please say *pencil*"; (2) remove all pencils or writing instruments, hand the subject paper, and offer a reward for a picture of a cat; (3) have a tape recording playing, repeating the phrase "pen and . . . "; (4) put up signs saying "pencil"; or (5) place an oversized pencil in an unusual place. Given all these conditions, Skinner concludes that "it is highly probable that our subject will say 'pencil.'" He states proudly that "the available techniques are all illustrated in this sample."[168] From this and other examples, Chomsky for one concludes Skinner's claim that his theory permits the practical control of behavior is false.[169] While it is true that specific responses—gestures, words, eye-blinks, smiles, or the like— can be increased through operant conditioning, this manipulation hardly constitutes a "technology of behavior" any more than card tricks constitute a technology of telekinesis.

Achieving Robot Man Skinner must be given his due as the most articulate and imaginative spokesman of the passivity principle and its resulting behaviorism today. The popularity of his latest philosophical essay—*Beyond Freedom and Dignity*—is a reminder of the attractiveness of this position for reformers as well as for those threatened by the continuing failure of contemporary institutions. While the book itself is little more than a restatement of the psychology and political theories of Thomas Hobbes and John Locke, it seems to hold the promise of social order provided we are simplistic enough to treat men and women as robots. Skinner likes to proclaim that "no theory changes what it is a theory about."[170] That may be true of planets, rainbows, and stars but not of linguistic animals like man. The passivity principle teaches men to think about themselves and others as if they were robots and thereafter to design organizations for robots. As R. D. Laing has often pointed out, one of the best ways of controlling, or at least restricting, the behavior of another person is to tell that person what he or she *is*, not what he or she should be. Such attribution becomes even more definitive as a control device if the person is then placed in a context in which the attributed characteristics are the only ones permitted or encouraged. Skinner defines man as a simple response mechanism. He then places men (or animals in some cases) in experimental situations in which only mechanical responses are possible. Then he concludes that his theory and definition have been verified.

Skinner overlooks several problems. Complex organisms, like man, are capable of simple and low-order behavior when they are damaged or impaired, or when such behavior is appropriate. As Bertrand Russell remarked, even Sir Isaac Newton would have to learn his way through a maze much the same way a rat does. Men can behave like rats and pigeons, whereas the reverse is not true. To demonstrate, however elegantly, that a human organism can learn in the same manner as a decorticate animal tells us little about how such an organism does actually learn or is capable of learning.

A long list of socialization theorists and frustrated administrators from Plato to Frederick W. Taylor have sought to simplify human behavior in order to control it. Critics of this approach have noted that it means bypassing the cerebral cortex. Antiutopian authors have suggested mass lobotomies, language management, torture and punishment, and drugs as means to achieve this. It is perhaps Skinner's lasting and infamous achievement to demonstrate that the cortex can be inactivated functionally without pain and without resentment by impoverishing the context in which the human organism must act. The result is robot man in practice as well as in theory. While such total environmental manipulation is too costly to be of much danger—think of the expense required just to ensure that someone will say "pencil"—it does give us a clue toward the understanding of social ignorance. The human organism can be damaged and thus have its behavior simplified—this is the extent of the technology of behavior. It turns out to be a technology of destruction, an employment of all the age-old devices of domination with new scientistic labels. While Skinner fails as a scientist, he succeeds as an entrepreneur and as a politician. For if he can convince us that he is right, he will become right.

Skinner often denies the possibility of other modes of explanation with assertions that begin with "Science demands . . . , or "if we are to follow the lead of the physical sciences . . . , or similar preliminaries. Although he sometimes admits that his own assumption of the passivity principle is only a postulate whose validity must ultimately be decided by the success of investigations based upon it, such statements proclaim a metaphysical dogmatism that goes far in accounting for his own and his followers' rejection of experimental findings concerning latent learning, cognitive structures, maturation and development, and neurological functions. The metaphysics is a kind of inverted animism in which the "cause" of any action must be outside, rather than inside, the acting organism. If Skinner's assumptions are the only scientific ones, then only data based on them need be acknowledged. All other data are irrelevant—or worse, mere rationalization.

The passivity principle is more a political ploy or a hope than a scientific hypothesis. Indeed its resemblance to a hypothesis is based on the crude analogy with the antiteleological postulates of physics. The principle is a cornerstone of contemporary liberal and Marxist ideologies because it promises not only the reform but the perfectibility of human beings. This promise does not require wisdom or knowledge, but only the development of techniques of manipulation and an indomitable will. It is a Machiavellian-Leninist dream of a short cut to the improvement of politics. This dream that thinking can make it so—particularly thinking backed by the full apparatus of propaganda, terror, and indoctrination—is integral to contemporary political ideologies. Assuming the passivity principle gives the dream credibility by making it seem possible to achieve by "conquering the hearts and minds of the people."

The passivity principle means that social learning is a matter of the reception rules, perceptions, names, opinions, values, and the like, imposed by the socializing agent. The individual has only the choice of being socialized or of refusing. Refusal is antisocial and non- or poorly socialized individuals either are failures due to some genetic difficulties or are classed as deviants. In fact, refusal may be impossible within the framework of the theory, since deviance and delinquency have been attributed to delinquent socialization. The basic idea is that human beings are a pliable stuff that can be molded into a wide range of personalities tailored to fit socially determined roles.

Among alchemists were those who sought the philosopher's stone as a means of perfecting mankind and his world and those called "puffers," who merely labored to transform base metals into gold for their own personal enrichment.[171] Among researchers in socialization, those of the social-learning school are the puffers. They are assiduous in their experiments, laboring mightily with young children and college sophomores to demonstrate time and again the eternal principle that if you reward people for some action or attitude they will repeat it and if you punish them they will cease. Of course people will do this so long as they are in a situation controlled by an experimenter and/or don't know what is going on.

But despite all this wonderful success—hundreds of doctoral dissertations, thousands of articles, and much personal enrichment by means of the academic marketplace—the final goal of a socialized, dependable citizen eludes them. It does so not only because they have little or no image of what such a citizen would look like but also because they have yet to demonstrate a relationship between particular patterns of rewards/punishments and stable moral attitudes. Indeed their very success as "puffers" threatens to undermine altogether the very notion of "civic virtue" or "moral citizen." Like Hobbes, they are haunted by the idea that people will support only those political institutions, officials, and values that pay off and that such support is based on short memory and insatiable demand.

Research in Social Learning Maccoby remarks that "Social-learning theory has been the dominant point of view in socialization work for the past 25 years."[172] This point of view is wide enough to include those influenced by psychoanalysis but the common motif (in addition to acceptance of the passivity principle) is the attempt to translate traditional formulas of moral teaching into behaviorist terminology and to test them experimentally. The task is more difficult at the theoretical level than it may seem. There are two basic difficulties. First, as Bandura warns, "If social learning proceeded exclusively on the basis of rewarding and punishing consequences, most people would never survive the socialization process.[173] That is, if men and women had to learn their societies in the ways pigeons learn at the hands of Skinner, the probability of fatal mistakes as well as defective conditioning would be too high. For example, more often than not, theft and other forms of aggression are immediately and positively reinforced. Antitheft devices and discouragement merely make the reinforcement intermittent and are therefore likely to strengthen the thieving response. Indeed, our common notion of moral behavior as opposed to instrumental or self-interested behavior is that it is pursued for reasons other than reward. As Maccoby puts it, socialization for moral behavior "often involves substituting behavior which does not carry its own immediate reinforcement for behavior which does."[174] That relationship makes no sense. Either reward-punishment contingencies account for all human behavior or behaviorist theories of social learning are partial or wrong.

Social-learning investigators are little troubled by these difficulties. Rather the assumption is made that moral behavior can and must be accounted for by some reward-punishment scheme. Their investigations aim at finding out what kinds of negative or positive reinforcement and schedules of reinforcement produce stable, desirable behavior and under what circumstance identification with socializing agents will produce fast, reliable social learning without the pitfalls involved in reward-punishment schemes. Paradoxically, the goal is to produce behavior in the socialized subject that is impervious to further reinforcing stimuli.

In terms of finding out what kind of reinforcing stimuli and schedules of reinforcement produce something approaching moral behavior (that is, behavior not related to reinforcement), the results are confused or negative. Studies have attempted in vain to relate differences in conscience strength, measured in terms of resistance to temptation or guilt, to (1) early restraint or gratification of oral, anal, and sexual drives; (2) amount and method of discipline; and (3) parental attitudes. Surveying the results of these studies, Kohlberg concludes "that neither early parental handling of basic drives nor amount of various types of discipline have been found to directly correlate with moral attitudes or behavior"[175] That is, patterns of rewarding or punishing behavior in children have not been consistently related to unchanging patterns of conduct. Further, "no consistent relationships between resistance to temptation and guilt have emerged."[176] Punishment does not consistently produce guilt; indeed, "no positive or consistent relationship between earliness and amount of parental demands or training in good habits—obedience, caring for property, performing chores, neatness, or avoidance of cheating—and measures of children's obedience, responsibility, and honesty" have been found.[177] Likewise, Aronfreed observes that "no consistent association has been found between parental nurturance and various indices of the child's internalized control of its behavior."[178] What studies do show is that "direct training and physical types of punishment may be effective in producing short-run situational conformity"[179] However, various designs of reward and punishment patterns do not, according to Kohlberg, directly produce habits of moral character.

What these studies seem to show is that in a given situation, children will respond to specific rewards or punishments by conforming to standards of behavior, but that such responses do not carry over to other situations. That is, "The experimental studies of socialization are, in effect, cogent demonstrations of the irrelevance of early home reinforcement parameters for later behavior."[180] Or to put it differently, if schedules of positive or negative reinforcement were all that were available to produce moral behavior, there would be no moral behavior. Instead, there would be the spectacle of amoral boys and girls, men and women, doing whatever seemed to be immediately rewarding in the particular circumstance. The pioneering (1928–1930) experimental studies of Hartshorne and May, which concluded that moral behavior is situationally specific and unstable over time, have not been superseded in over 45 years of socialization research.[181] However much our Founding Fathers liked to declare that such amorality was the case and to describe the species as semimanageable knaves, it is completely inconsistent with the moral behavior that our civic ideals of honesty, loyalty, responsibility, courage, fraternity, and helpfulness entail. Thus the dream of the *tabula rasa* that allows us to write at will on the brains of infants turns out to be a moral nightmare—for the *tabula* gets erased from one situation to another. We are left then either to attempt to design totalitarian, if benign, societies with minutely regulated "free" choices, or simply terrorize the citizenry into crude conformity.

Problems of "Identification" The problems involved in the simple reward-punishment process of moral socialization are thought to be avoided by hypothesizing a second complementary channel of socialization called "identification" or "internalization." Identification is a process of learning "in which a person patterns his thoughts, feelings or actions after another person who serves as a model."[182] This process supposedly results in a stability of behavior that is independent of external contingencies of reinforcement.[183] "Internalized control" comes to be substituted through identification for control by social watchdogs. Instead of having to be taught how to behave correctly in various specific situations, the child by means of this second channel of socialization becomes able to anticipate the good behavior desired through mimicking the responses of a significant adult. Thus the necessary efficiency and stability missing from the reinforcement channel of socialization are restored.

But there are still problems. First, "identification" is difficult to measure and therefore the theory is hard if not impossible to test. For example, if identification is measured by the degree of similarity between the self-described behavior of the child and the description of parental behavior, the results are contaminated by the questions asked and may have little connection with actual behavior.[184] Research findings indicate that people show no greater similarity to their own parents than to randomly matched parental figures.[185] Bandura argues that behavioral similarities among same-sex peers can be attributed to identification processes but admits that locating "the sources of emulated behavior, however, is complicated by the fact that children are repeatedly exposed to multiple models, including teachers, other adults in the immediate neighborhood, peer companions, and a host of prestigeful models presented mainly through television and films."[186] That is, identification can only be assumed but not demonstrated.

Another way of measuring "identification" is by looking for hypothesized products of the process rather than by comparing children with their parents. The presence of certain outcomes, including sex-role behavior, mature behavior, resistance to temptation, and guilt reactions following rule breaking are taken as indices of successful identification. But the problem with studies of this sort is "that the myriad behaviors presumably generated by the single mediating process are not positively correlated to any appreciable degree."[187] It is hard then to believe there is a common source of the supposed modeling. These difficulties make it impossible to test the theory of social learning by means of identification by any "naturalistic" means. Strangely enough, the behavioral outcomes of the theory are the same as those of a theory that assumes that moral behavior is the result of a series of existential choices.[188]

The idea of identification was also an important element in psychoanalytic theories of socialization and its role there is similar to that which it performs in social-learning theories. For Freud's pleasure principle cannot result in moral attitudes or behavior, therefore he suppposed that it was infant identification with parents which caused conscience. The difficulties with Freudian identification, however, are identical with those just reviewed. Further, the psychoanalytic explanation of how and why identification takes place cannot account for all the obvious identifications with adults that take place as children grow up. American boys, to take one group, typically emulate sports stars, as well as comic-book heroes and television personalities; but according to psychoanalytically oriented theories of identification:

> In order to get a boy to emulate a baseball player such as Mickey Mantle, it would be necessary for the youngster to develop an intense attachment to the brawny model, who would then withhold affectional responsiveness, thereby motivating the child to incorporate the modeled stylistic behavior. Or the athletic youngster would have to develop strong incestuous desires toward Mrs. Mantle, hostile rivalrous feelings toward the baseball slugger, and as a way of reducing anxieties generated by his libidinal feelings and the anticipated threat of castration, the boy would begin to swat home runs.[189]

The patent absurdity of this, coupled with the negative results concerning the similarities of children and their parental models, has led to a reduction of the idea of identification to one of observation learning. That is, identification is understood as selective imitative behavior determined by various incentives. The research focus has thereby been limited, in good behaviorist tradition, to understanding what contingencies of reinforcement produce effective identification in the form of internalized controls.

A simplified experimental paradigm of such research looks like this. A group of children observe the behavior of adults such as expressions of aggression. The adults' behavior is thereupon reinforced negatively or positively, immediately or sluggishly, strongly or weakly ad infinitum as the permutations of all these possibilities are exhausted in different experimental designs. Then the imitative or modeling behavior of the subjects is observed and measured. The results are not surprising. When observed behavior is punished or is indicated as painful or distasteful by verbal and other cues, it is unlikely to be imitated.[190] Further, when the imitative behavior itself is positively reinforced it is more likely to persist.[191] The converse also has been demonstrated.[192] Finally, since much imitative behavior persists when no immediate reinforcing stimuli are found, "It is assumed that . . . behavioral similarity per se acquired secondary reinforcing properties."[193] Or more simply put, "monkey see, monkey do."

The implication of these experimental findings, according to Bandura, is that while traditional theories of identification assumed intimacy as a prerequisite, stressed the decisive unilateral role of parents, downgraded the role of peers, siblings, and nonfamily adults, and implied that social organizations were not sources of moral conduct, actually "a broad range of modeling influences, both actual and symbolized, must be incorporated in a comprehensive theory of behavior transmission."[184] The ball game is over. We can assume again that socialization has taken place by means of identification and/or contingencies of reinforcement; but we cannot know who or what was identified with nor can we specify the reinforcing stimuli. Children can apparently pick and choose as they please whom to model as well as decide what is reinforcing.[195] To account for their eventual moral character or lack of it in this way may be of some comfort to parents, teachers, clergy, community leaders, and people of like status, since it gets everybody off the hook. But declaring bankruptcy, whether moral or intellectual, is a costly and disquieting way to avoid failure.

Bandura emphasizes that reinforcement contingencies prescribed by social and political institutions account in large part for social behavior and he agrees with Reiss's criticism of assuming the family as the major socializing agency. But he argues that social and political systems cannot account for the varieties of social behavior actually found and that therefore parents can complicate "behavioral transmission" by inducing defiance, avoidance, and deviant responses.[196] If the social-learning theory of socialization was unfalsifiable before Bandura's revisions, it is nothing more than hyperbole after. If persons conform to social expectations of moral behavior, it is due to social institutions; if they do not, it is due to the family. Of course, no outcomes can be predicted but all can be explained after the fact.

Problems of Internalization The lack of generality in moral behavior, as indicated by the findings that low correlations exist between "various aspects of honesty, between moral knowledge and honest behavior, between tendency to criticize and tendency to repair damage, between guilt and resistance to temptation," and so on, not only undermines psychoanalytic theories of identification, but is also a challenge to so-cial-learning theory.[197] If moral behavior is due to conditioned anxiety resulting in "internalized" control, then such anxiety must generalize to a wide variety of situations that should result in correlations of moral attitudes and behavior. Aronfreed maintains that socialization has a "remarkable consequence" of increasing the child's behavioral stability independent of external events, culminating in its control of its own behavior through "internal monitors."[198] But he admits that such internal control has not been found to be related consistently to the care or treatment of infants, to training procedures, or parental nurturance.[199] It seems fair, then, that since no data exist for such internalized control except that children and adults often choose to do one thing or another on grounds that do not involve reinforcement, the transference of the "control" of behavior from outside to inside should be rejected altogether.

"Internalized control," whatever it may be, implies something like a behaviorist demon inside the person, rewarding and punishing acts or attitudes. Perhaps we should refer to this demon as each person's "skin-ner." However, this innovation seems no advance over traditional con-cepts of conscience and virtue and just as obfuscating as Freud's super-ego. The research of the social-learning "puffers" leads to the rejection of the passivity principle. As Bandura concludes, "Observers do not function as passive video-tape recorders which register indiscriminately and store symbolic representations of all modeling stimuli encountered in everyday life."[200] But if the savages of infancy and childhood can choose—if they can even interpret punishment as positive reinforce-ment—then they are not molded, determined, or controlled in their development.[201] Influenced, restricted, sometimes damaged, often con-fused—all this yes, but the moving hand that writes on the *tabula* of the mind is an autonomous one—perhaps even an intentional, self-created one as the phenomenologists insist. Just as the puffers seemed to have done the most for the foundation of chemistry, perhaps the behaviorist and social-learning researchers have done the most for a new founda-tion for the social sciences, for they have shown that even the most elaborate processes of rewards and punishments ultimately fail to ac-count for moral behavior. Unfortunately their demonstration can also be interpreted after the style of the theological positivists to mean that moral behavior does not exist, cannot be taught, and should not be sought.

Political Socialization

Research in political socialization is an eclectic affair long on assumptions, confidence, and sheer number of studies, but short on evidential support for its ambitious claims and until recently devoid of theoretical coherence. Political-socialization theory being an eclectic enterprise, its assumptions are shared in part with other approaches. The three major assumptions, according to David Marsh, are (1) adult political opinions are largely the end product of socialization processes; (2) adult political behavior is shaped significantly by the attitudes learned during childhood; and (3) individual adult political opinions and behavior have an important impact on the operation, particularly the stability, of government.[202] Searing, Swartz, and Lind present a similar trio. They list the assumptions as (1) the primacy principle—"the belief that early political learning is relatively enduring";[203] (2) the structuring principle—the belief "that the learning of specific attitudes toward policies, leaders, and events is structured by basic political orientations";[204] and (3) the relevance principle—"issue beliefs are related to demands and supports, which in turn affect system outputs and persistence."[205] The third assumption, as Marsh points out, is "the most grandiose and the least precise. This assumption avoids so many complex sociological questions that one wonders why so few authors have stood back to consider it and its implications."[206]

But the relevance principle is the key to the whole enterprise. For the major claim of this research is that the study of how people acquire their political values will pay off in an increased ability to predict and control political stability and change. So dogmatically held is this claim that the major devastating finding of the research—that the political attitudes of preadolescents are antithetical to those of adults—has been understood as supporting it. Richard Niemi writes, "If indeed the earliest learned attitudes have a significant spill over into later life, idealization of political authority by children is a potent explanatory variable in seeking to understand support for the government."[207] But the research indicates that the earliest learned political attitudes *do not* spill over into later life.[208] Adult political attitudes are predominantly cynical as opposed to the political idealization of children; therefore we can only conclude that such idealization is an impotent explanatory variable.

Like the sexual braggadocio of the neighborhood vamp or stud, the claims of political-socialization theorists and researchers about the impact of inculcated attitudes on political-system persistence are hard to verify. After all, there have been no revolutions in American government for some time; and in some countries of Europe and Asia there have been massive political changes. If we can attribute all this to the success or failure of political-socialization practices, we may not actually be able to foresee or control the course of political events but at least we can sleep better. Indeed, these claims are little different from those of traditional political thinkers in terms of the efficacy claimed for the "molding" of people, but they are different in terms of content. This quotation from Dawson and Prewitt will give the flavor and intensity of the claims:

> Political socialization is a molding force. Man is fairly plastic. The very notion of social self, from which is drawn the idea of a political self, implies this. It is true that in the overwhelming number of cases social institutions are geared to producing citizens who more or less replicate their predecessors. In this sense political socialization is conservative. But there is nothing inherent in the process to make it so. The powerful molding possibilities in political socialization can be adapted to radical and total alterations as well—if not as easily as they have been adapted to incremental changes and protection of the social order.[209]

One of the earliest criticisms of this research was that it had a conservative bias.[210] Dawson and Prewitt deny this criticism and cite two examples of "radical and total alterations" in political values—the enslavement and transport of West Africans to America, and the incarcerations of racial and political deviants in Nazi concentration camps. They conclude: "The lessons of American slavery and German concentration camps are an important corrective to any tendency to impute conservatism as a necessary component of political socialization,"[211] for these examples show that severe dislocation results in "extensive personality and cultural alterations." These remarkable assertions reveal the overconfidence and simplicity of current theory. Perhaps even more disturbing is the underlying cynicism. It is not that human values or preferences are considered all equally valid. Rather all are equally invalid.[212]

Definitions of "political socialization" as a subject matter of research reflect the eclecticism of the enterprise as well as the unthinking bombast of its theoretical claims.[213] In general it means nearly any study having to do with attitudes toward government, public policy, authority, and ideology. Usually it means the study of the political attitudes of children and youth. Research in this area has increased in popularity in the 1960s and 1970s primarily, I think, because the development of reliable socialization techniques seems to provide relief for today's harassed statesman and his political-science advisers who find it more and more difficult to accomplish goals and point with pride to a definite record of performance. Fred Greenstein, among others, has claimed that improved socialization techniques would lead to a decrease in policing.[215]

Dawson and Prewitt echo his view.

Of all the mechanisms which might induce obligation, political socialization is the cheapest and most efficient . . . compliance based on the feeling that obedience is "good" or "appropriate" is cheap. When authorities can depend on such a mechanism, they can direct their resources and energies toward other goals.[215]

I understand these authors to be saying that political socialization is a possible and superior substitute for government effectiveness. A citizenry might base allegiance on the performance of government. Indeed, that seems to be the meaning of the slogan "popular sovereignty," and a key notion of classical liberal democracy. Since ineffective governments would fall if such a critical citizenry existed, this assessment of performance seems to threaten stability. According to this increasingly popular view, elites are the source of political stability and the discontented masses are the sources of costly and precipitous change. The masses must be made to be—or perhaps already are—uncritical and passive, in order that elites may become creative.

The Political Relevance of Socialization Jack Dennis identifies Easton as the major formulator and proponent of what he calls the hypothesis of "the system relevance of political socialization."[216] Given this hypothesis (or rather this assumption of the relevance principle), Dennis concludes, "The major goal of political socialization . . . is to generate diffuse support." Diffuse support is defined as encouraging the sentiments of legitimacy and compliance.[217] The question remains, according to Dennis, of how important political socialization is in generating such support. As he points out there are other ways of doing this: "Alternative means for maintaining support could be overt, continuing use of force, the meeting of political demands efficiently . . . or broad structural changes in the system to cope with major stress from the environment.[218] But the basic assumption of system relevance, indeed, of the proposition that all political systems engage in some program of socialization aimed at generating diffuse support in maturing children and youth, have yet to be theoretically elaborated or empirically tested.[219]

The attachment to the relevance principle is due to the contemporary haunting sense of political failure. Evaluated in terms of the actual impact of government policies on the lives of the citizenry, modern government appears to be as ineffective as a crumbling dynasty of ancient history. The classical notion that government's role is to insure the good life, to provide the social and natural resources for the pursuit of happiness, is more and more unbelievable. The modern sense of government gives it only the duties of supervising stability and muting conflict. The popularity of socialization theory in academic, journalistic, and political circles is an admission of the bankruptcy of the ideal of an efficient *and* democratic government. But it is also a way of interpreting the disturbing data from voting studies that reveal the political arena as being a largely projective screen for the personal whims, phobias, and obsessions of the occasional voter who does not simply follow in his parents' footsteps.

Such data could be interpreted as being a sign that political decisions in United States society are no longer crucial or related to the day-to-day conditions of life. That is, apathetic and irrational voters may indicate that the traditional political units of city, state, and nation are not congruent with the actual decision-making units. I think it likely that such units are the bureaucracies of corporations, of public agencies, and of educational institutions. However, the voting data are largely interpreted as indicating that the mass of people are simply incapable of participating in significant decisions. Thus governments persist in spite of failure, candidates are more likely to be elected who use the adman's appeal, and cultural and civic values must be constantly protected from irruptions of irrationality. Numerous modern social thinkers have seen the political world of the Western democracies in just this way. From Mosca and Pareto on they have argued for the development of a scientific manipulation of behavior without recognizing the paradox that this entails.[220]

In current political socialization theory we find the ideal of a science of politics wedded to a retreat from politics. This combination is the target of most critics. Traditional socialization theory did concern itself with goals as well as means. Classical theorists in this tradition did attempt to restrict or eliminate politics—in the sense of questioning and deciding upon certain institutional arrangements—by focusing exclusively on politics as ruling or by attempting to design political structures which would produce definitive arrangements. But their historical juxtaposition in textbooks has produced an image of a highly self-conscious dialogue about the ends of political arrangements and the welfare of the species. Scholars steeped in this tradition find the present technical approach misleading and pernicious. James Steintrager writes:

> We need clear and precise statements about what mankind's goal is or ought to be, about what the goal of behavioralism is, about what control or manipulation might mean. The time is past when intelligent men can ritualistically reassert their faith in the democratic process or assume that things will work out either because history means inevitable progress or because of a hidden crypto-teleological faith that the nature of man, once liberated by science, will prove to be gentle and decent. Of course no decent person opposes mankind or anything that will help mankind. Hence the decent person will not oppose science. But we

need to know what decency is and how it may come to pass that decent men may govern the behavioral processes. The success of science demands that we escape the peculiar prejudice of our scientific culture which obscures these questions or tells us that we cannot answer them.[221]

Steintrager correctly detects the obscuring of certain basic political questions in the contemporary approach to socialization. But the classical approach was also deficient, obscuring the questions of human epistemology upon which any socialization theory must be based.

Modern research in the fields of anthropology, sociology, and experimental psychology, as we have seen, is useful in that it indicates that the assumptions underlying the relevance principle of political scientists are false. The strength of the relevance principle—apart from the false hopes that it engenders—is due to the assumed truth of the consensus principle and the passivity principle. If motivational and cognitive consensus are necessary to society and if the citizens' minds, as Hobbes wrote, "are like clean paper, fit to receive whatsoever by Publique Authority shall be imprinted in them," then the molding processes of political socialization must be universal in any functioning political system.[222] But if those principles are not true, then the relevance of socialization practices cannot be established by any new debates about higher ends or goals. The assumed relevance of political socialization is a dead issue insofar as it might serve to guide our actions, our educational practices, or our investigations of the world.[223] Theories of political socialization live on only as sets of names for all the unexplained variance in our investigations and for the ignorance entailed by our traditional political and social wisdom.

The Structuring Principle The primacy principle we have dealt with previously, and we need note only, after Marsh, that "the political socialization literature, in common with the general socialization literature does not set out, or attempt to set out the conditions under which attitudes learnt during childhood will shape behavior"[224] Searing and his colleagues argue that the structuring principle is just as crucial to the justification of the study of children's political attitudes, for if orientations are not systematically related to adult behavior and opinions on specific political issues, then there is no reason for political scientists to investigate them.[225] The structuring principle holds that certain basic frameworks or orientations—like personality, or like identification with a particular political party, ideology, social class, interest group, or ethnic community—will determine or structure the learning of specific issue beliefs. If we ask someone his or her opinions about the expanded use of nuclear energy for the generation of electric power, the answer should be related to or shaped by more basic orientations. Republicans, conservatives, authoritarians, Italians, and others in the universe should show some consistent tendency to take one side or the other.

Searing and his co-authors point out that political-party affiliation is the paradigm of how political orientations order or coherently organize issue beliefs.[226] Voting studies have shown that party identification accounts for some variance in foreign and domestic political opinions.

> Indeed the structuring principle seems to have been introduced to socialization theory by projecting such party identification findings to cover basic political orientations in general. Thus party identification is said to function as an organizing cognitive structure. It provides cues for evaluating new emergent issues. Most issues involve matters which are complex and distant from the ordinary citizen's perspective. These ambiguities are resolved by adopting the party's position rather than struggling with each issue on its own merits.

Some earlier sources of the structuring principle in the American political tradition are the economic determinism of the Founding Fathers[227] and the psychologism introduced by Harold Lasswell in the late 1920s, which argued that political opinions were primarily determined by personality.[228] Both of these assumptions have been largely discredited.[229] Members of the working class, for example, are not consistently radical or even anticapital. Communists and fascists are not consistently neurotic, sexually repressed, or psychopathic.[230] The quest for a way of developing "democratic" personality as opposed to an "authoritarian" one has been barren.

Searing and his colleagues, in their test of the structuring principle, found that very few and only weak relations could be found between political orientations and issue beliefs. They conclude that: (1) socialization orientations are not related to political attitudes; (2) party identification is not strongly related to issue beliefs; and (3) political orientations are no more related to issue beliefs than the discredited personality factors.[231] Their findings are similar to Philip Converse's analysis of the Survey Research Center's data that resulted from asking the same people about their attitudes toward political issues over a six-year period. Converse writes that only thirteen out of twenty respondents were consistently on the same side of an issue even in successive interrogations. [232] Other studies over the years have, as Marsh notes, indicated that "very few individuals have the type of complex political belief system which might support and underpin stable political attitudes."[233]

The instability of most political attitudes and the lack of demonstrated relations between political orientations and issue beliefs is paralleled by the inconsistency between attitudes and behavior. Beginning with Lapier's 1934 study, which showed inconsistency between verbal statement and the treatment of Chinese customers in restaurants and hotels, the relation between an individual's verbally reported attitudes and overt behavior has time and again been found weak.[234] Wicker's review of these studies forced him to conclude that "predictions of overt behavior can be made more accurately from a knowledge of the situation than from a knowledge of individual differences."[235] Attitudes-behavior inconsistency seems to be the final blow to the structuring principle. With its demise goes the last of the basic assumptions of political socialization theory and research.[236]

Failures of Political Socialization   Political-socialization research has been a major field of work in political science since the late 1950's. Early researchers found that children idealize political figures to an astonishing degree. According to them, young children are very early "politicized," learning that there are authorities over and above their parents. These authorities are initially "personalized" in terms of individual men— usually the president and the local policeman. Further, these individuals are "idealized" as wise and benevolent. Later children learn to identify the processes and structures of government, such as legal procedures and the Congress, and thus their conceptions of politics are "institutionalized." Finally, as children mature they become increasingly cynical about the political system and its actors.[237]

It is not clear from the findings that children learn to idealize political figures at all. It seems more likely that small children assume that all adults are wise and benevolent unless proven otherwise. Thus "idealization" of authority figures is more in the nature of a null hypothesis on the part of the child. For example, there is a lack of significant differences between the views of ethnic minority and majority children concerning the wisdom and benevolence of authorities. Hess and Torney note that working-class children "idealize" political authority more than do middle-class children.[238] This observation makes sense if we understand such "idealization" as an absence of political learning—that is, the less politics is discussed in the home or the more politically apathetic the parents, the less the political learning; and therefore political authorities are the more assumed to be like parental authorities. In the more politically active middle-class home or in the case where political events such as the Vietnam war, labor struggles, or the Watergate scandal penetrate the home, political cynicism emerges sooner. These statements are only alternative hypotheses to account for anomalous results such as the high rate of cynicism among some Appalachian children, and the apparent drop in the level of political support among children in the 1960s.[239]

Since children's idealization of political figures and institutions is fervently believed to be important to the maintenance of political stability, the inculcating of such idealization is therefore part of any strategy of stabilization. But if we are correct in understanding that such idealization is in fact an indication of political ignorance, then what is being advocated is the old cynical notion that ignorance insures stability. Niemi argues that an objective presentation of the political system to young children will lead to a weakening of support and the increasing likelihood of change.[240] Further elaboration of this theme would indicate that the most stable political system would be one whose citizens were most ignorant and most childlike in their political beliefs and activities. It does no good to argue that whether one views such a situation positively or negatively depends solely on attitudes toward stability or change. Much more is at stake. For institutions to maintain and enforce a state of political infantilism would require pervasive biological damage leading to mass pathologies and impairment of performance. Perhaps this outcome is the most we can expect from political-socialization techniques.

While Hess and Torney state that "the public school appears to be the most important and effective instrument of political socialization in the United States," this conclusion has been subjected to the criticism that no links have been established between the changes of political attitudes in students and what is taught in the classroom.[241] Indeed, some studies show that there is no connection—particularly between college political science courses and increased student political interest.[242] Prewitt and Okello-Oculi conclude after studying the socializing effects of education in new nations: "However attractive programmed political education might appear on paper, the political and administrative realities caution us not to expect significant results."[243]

Coupled with findings which indicate that mass media are more capable of reinforcing previously formed attitudes than of changing them and that early political attitudes are poor predictors of current behavior,[245] this conclusion indicates that theories of political socialization, however persuasive they have come to seem to us, have little evidence to support their claims.

I detect a flagging of enthusiasm among researchers and theorists in this area. As long ago as 1956 Herbert Hyman commented:

> What a strange imbalance we find today! Political behavior is seen as determined by all sorts of motivational and emotional factors operating through complicated psychodynamic processes. Certainly such behavior is full of purpose and direction, but it is guided if only imperfectly, by reason, knowledge, judgment, intelligence. Men are urged to certain ends by the way the political scene in which they act is perceived and given meaning. Some cognitive map accompanies their movements towards their ends.

The role of the cognitive processes must be reinstated as a necessary counterbalance to distorted analysis of political behavior.[246] But in political science the imbalance remains. As Steintrager remarks, "Every effort is made to shy away from an explanation that would indicate that reason, however understood and however inadequate, enters into the choice of goals or shapes attitudes."[247] When studies are labeled with the term "political behavior," it is still likely that you will learn more about weaning practices and other sources of childhood trauma rather than something about the way men and women actually perceive and act in deciding or not deciding upon institutional arrangements.[248] To get at this latter realm of behavior requires the discarding of political-socialization theory, both modern and classical. The next priority, as Hyman wrote more than ten years ago, is the development of a theory of social learning formulated in terms of perceptual and cognitive processes.

Cognitive-Developmental Theory of Socialization

Socialization theories as both studies and frameworks for understanding problems of social epistemology are attractive. Some of this attractiveness is trivial. For example, when we argue after Mannheim that consciousness is determined by social life, we may be only asserting a truism. If Sartre is correct in arguing that "consciousness is always consciousness of something," then in any social situation consciousness must be consciousness of that situation. In other words, knowing is always determined to some extent by the object known. But, of course, "determined" here seems an inappropriate word. That we cannot know more at a given time than the object or objects we are knowing or have known is both true and trivial. Most statements about the social determination of ideas can be reduced to this.

Socialization theories have more than this going for them.[249] The idea that there is some connection between what people know about the world and the social structure in which they live seems obvious. Anthropologists have demonstrated time and again that men and women in different societies and cultures in some way see the world differently. Further, many social structures involve social ignorance of the kind Malinowski described in the Trobriand example. When members of one society encounter another society they are often appalled by such ignorance. Indeed, social structures seem to foster not only ignorance but also harmful behavior. And finally we encounter, again and again in human history, persistence of social operations and outlooks long after their usefulness has been exhausted.

We may say then that socialization theories get their most serious support from the recognition of the problems of social ignorance with which they attempt to deal. Social structures fail and fall. Men and women fail to escape from or to change social situations that are inimical to human life. The most dramatic example of this failure is that of the German concentration camp. In order for 9,000,000 people to be eliminated without disrupting the German war effort, those victims had to become accomplices in their own destruction. That so many of them did become so seems to be testimony to the premises of socialization theories. But that many of them did not become accomplices and rather managed to revolt, even to temporarily defeat their oppressors under the most extreme circumstances, represents a falsifying instance. That men and women patiently and apathetically suffer devastating social practices is a fact of human history. But that they often overtly and continuously covertly resist such practices is also a fact.

The approach to social ignorance which we have called socialization theories represents, at best, a way of talking about, but hardly a way of acting upon, these problems. It is primarily a *post hoc* theory. We are perplexed at both the accepting passivity and the denying recalcitrance of the species. We are not sure when and where such responses are likely to occur. Thus this approach does not lead to the development of social science. Nor does it aid us in attempting the project of adapting social structures to meet the needs of the human species. At best, it addresses itself to real and crucial problems, but it responds to these problems in a purely symbolic way.

I have not spoken of the ingenuity and frequent care which researchers have put into the studies of socialization processes in the last forty years. Indeed, I have reviewed probably less than a quarter of the mountainous literature on the subject. I am both impressed and dismayed at what I have read. Impressed with the methodological sophistication that has developed over the years and that provokes me by its results to reject the age-old conviction that social wisdom and civic virtue can be shaped by the will of reformers. I am dismayed by the blindness that prevails to the massive failure of theories of socialization. This failure, we have seen, exists at the levels both of formal inconsistency and of empirical findings. The theories contain hidden paradoxes that call upon our faith to make them work as explanations. The findings falsify the expectations of the theories.

But there is further a frightening failure of those who hold and support the theories to confront their political and social implications. Theories that understand social knowledge in terms of uniformity of thought, that understand social ethics in terms of conformity of actions are of little use in an age of large, propagandizing, and amoral political and social institutions. To paraphrase Anthony Burgess, once you have human beings believing that doing what they are told is good because they get rewarded for it instead of punished, then ethics no longer exists. The state can tell its citizens that it is good to exterminate another nation or race. Indeed, that is what states do in the twentieth century.[250] Such theories of socialization are pernicious at a time when the need for the advancement of social knowledge and the improvement of moral judgment is acute. Just as wisdom cannot be produced by getting everyone to think alike (objectivity by means of epistemological terror), so morality cannot be produced by getting everyone to act alike. While those banal goals may not be possible, the destruction of the human capacity for social investigation and experimentation and for ethical discourse and judgment is possible. With that destruction goes the species.

New Assumptions Given the problems with traditional theories of socialization, it makes sense to approach the issues with alternative or counter assumptions. Suppose we assume, instead of the primacy principle, that experience of childhood only rarely has major impact on the intellectual and moral capacities of adults. And instead of the consensus principle, let us assume that a viable human organization requires a maximum diversity of cognitions and value judgments. And rather than take the brain to be a passive instrument, let us assume that it is an active, seeking organ, one that probes experience with endless intentional questions. Finally, let us give up the search for an explanatory demon of personality, ideology, innate preferences, or whatever, and attempt to understand human judgment as the result of sophisticated processes of conceptualization and evaluation. With these alternative assumptions, what would the processes of socialization look like? Fortunately we have a detailed picture.

The cognitive-developmental theory of socialization is based on the pioneering work of Jean Piaget and the further elaboration and modifications of Lawrence Kohlberg.[251] The first assumption of this approach "is that basic mental structure is the result of an interaction between certain organismic structuring tendencies and the structure of the outside world, rather than reflecting either one directly."[252] The mind therefore is not something passive as the social-learning theorist would have it, nor is it innately patterned as the pure developmental theory assumes. The theory provides for rationally achieved adult values different from those inculcated in childhood.[253] It rejects the notion that moral development can be measured by degree of conformity to group norms. It understands morality not as a set of opinions, preferences, or attitudes but as a rule system or a logic guiding the course of action.[254]

Kohlberg lists eight assumptions of the cognitive-developmental theory, the most important of which are the following: (1) development or maturation involves transformations of cognitive structure which cannot be explained by contiguity, repetition, or reinforcement; (2) the development of such cognitive structures is the result of interaction between the structure of the organism and the structure of the environment; (3) these cognitive structures are schemata or rules of action; (4) affective and cognitive development represent different perspectives and contexts of structural change rather than distinct realms; (5) social cognition always involves role-taking or the awareness that the other is like the self and is related to the self in a system of complementary expectations.[255] A further important idea is that of stages of development or "the transformations of simple early cognitive structures as these are applied to (or assimilate) the external world" and are subsequently restructured[256]

Moral judgments, in this view, are universal, inclusive, consistent evaluations of courses of action grounded on objective grounds.[257] Piaget writes:

> For conduct to be characterized as moral there must be something more than an outward agreement between its content and that of the commonly accepted rules: it is also requisite that the mind should tend towards morality as an autonomous good and should itself be capable of appreciating the value of the rules that are proposed to it.[258]

Moral conduct is thus the result of individual decision in a specific situation.[259] Moral rules or principles function analogously to the hypotheses of the physical scientists. They are believed as "social laws or realities just as physical principles are felt to define physical laws or realities."[260] Once moral judgments are understood in this way it is obvious that the conduct of children is not moral. While the child can obey its parents and other adults it does not have the cognitive capacity to formulate such judgments. Indeed, it is an important point of the cognitive-developmental theory of socialization that only a limited degree of moral education is possible in the parent-child context. The autonomy and reciprocity necessary to moral judgment can be learned only in a context of equality. As Piaget writes, "In order to really socialize the child, cooperation is necessary for it alone will succeeed in delivering him from the mystic power of the world of the adult."[261] Or as Kohlberg has it, the development of moral judgment requires extensive "role-taking" opportunities.[262] An important implication of this requirement is that moral development is not accomplished at the cost of intellectual or emotional immaturity. Finally, the cognitive-developmental theory views moral development and growth as a normal occurrence. The lack of such development must be accounted for by frustrating factors.

Stages of Moral Development The idea that social development—or the maturation of moral judgment—is dependent upon cognitive growth is supported empirically by the fact that children's intelligence "has a greater number of social-behavior correlates than any other observed aspect of personality."[263] Kohlberg argues that the predictive power of the intelligence quotient is due to the fact that the faster the cognitive development the faster the rate of maturation of social conduct and moral judgment. The cognitive component in the development of moral judgment has two aspects, according to Kohlberg.[264] One aspect of the development of moral judgment has to do with knowledge of group norms and conventional standards of behavior. The child must learn what the rules are. The second aspect of this development is in terms of cognitive structure or forms. Examples of such forms are conceptions of justice, reciprocity, and equality. The conception of reciprocity depends upon the awareness of logical reciprocity—as, if A is B's brother, then B is A's brother or sister. Such awareness develops around ages six and seven, according to Piaget.[265] Another cognitive form essential to the development of moral judgment is intentionality—discriminating between what the actor intended to do and the actual outcome of the action. Piaget maintains that such discrimination depends upon more general cognitive differentiation between subject and object, physical and mental, and the like.[266] Thus moral development will have both cultural and class content (the conventional standards) and cognitive forms (the concepts of relations and differentiation). The learning of both depend upon the growth of the child and the quality of its environment.

Piaget's early investigations consisted of questioning children concerning their comprehension of the rules of games—asking them to evaluate the behavior of others depicted in hypothetical stories and probing their understanding of responsibility and fairness. From these queries emerged a pattern of development of increased autonomy, complexity, and subtlety of moral judgment. Younger children tended to understand rules as ready-made and imposed by adults and to regard any act of obedience as good and any act of disobedience as bad regardless of the content.[267] Similarly, younger children regard justice as "what is commanded by the adult."[268] Older children not only master the rules of a game but also take an interest in the legislation of such rules, the anticipation of how they apply to future cases and their codification."[269] Likewise older children develop a sense of equality which demands distributive justice and equity based on age, ability, motivation, previous actions, and the like.[270]

For example, one of Piaget's associates queried 167 children concerning the following story:

There was a big boy in school once who was beating a smaller boy. The little one couldn't hit back because he wasn't strong enough. So one day during the recreation he hid the big boy's apple and roll in an old cupboard. What do you think of that?[271]

The conduct of the younger boy can be judged either as naughty or as justified retribution. He was judged right in paying back his larger antagonist in the following proportions according to age:

Age	Percentage Justifying Retribution
6	19
7	33
8	63
9	72
10	87
11	91
12	95

Piaget argues that these statistics show an increasing sense of reciprocity with age. Younger children condemn the smaller boy's actions as bad because they violate the rule forbidding stealing or taking what belongs to others. Older children argue that evil should be repaid with evil or at least some degree of balance between the antagonists maintained. When the question: "If anyone punches you, what do you do?" was asked following the story, the results were similar. Younger children were more likely to judge hitting back to be naughty, while older children were more likely to maintain that blows should be returned.[272]

Kohlberg investigated further in this area and came up with six stages of moral judgment divided into three levels as presented in Table I. These stages form a sequential series. That is, one is not free to choose stage 6 or a principled orientation to moral judgment without having passed through stages 1, 2, 3, 4, and 5. According to Kohlberg, higher stages displace lower stages by reintegrating their content in a more complex structure. [273] Thus the higher the stage, the more differentiated and the more integrated.

Kohlberg's stages were defined in terms of free responses to ten hypothetical moral dilemmas, coded under 25 aspects of moral judgment.[274] Stages do not depend upon a right answer (since true dilemmas are employed) but on the manner in which the subject reasons out

Table I
Classification of Moral Judgment
into Levels and Stages of Development

Levels	Basis of Moral Judgment	Stages of Development
I	Moral value resides in external, quasi-physical happenings, in bad acts, or in quasi-physical needs rather than in persons and standards.	*Stage 1: Obedience and punishment orientation.* Egocentric deference to superior power or prestige, or a trouble-avoiding set. Objective responsibility. *Stage 2: Naively egoistic orientation.* Right action is that instrumentally satisfying the self's needs and occasionally others'. Awareness of relativism of value to each actor's needs and perspective. Naive egalitarianism and orientation to exchange and reciprocity.
II	Moral value resides in performing good or right roles, in maintaining the conventional order and the expectancies of others.	*Stage 3: Good-boy or good-girl orientation.* Orientation to approval and to pleasing and helping others. Conformity to stereotypical images of majority or natural role behavior, and judgment by intentions. *Stage 4: Authority and social-order-maintaining orientation.* Orientation to "doing duty" and to showing respect for authority and maintaining the given social order for its own sake. Regard for earned expectations of others.
III	Moral value resides in conformity by the self to shared or shareable standards, rights, or duties.	*Stage 5: Contractual legalistic orientation.* Recognition of an arbitrary element or starting point in rules or expectations for the sake of agreement. Duty defined in terms of contract, general avoidance of violation of the will or rights of others, and majority will and welfare. *Stage 6: Conscience or principle orientation.* Orientation not only to actually ordained social rules but to principles of choice involving appeal to logical universality and consistency. Orientation to conscience as a directing agent and to mutual respect and trust.

Source: Lawrence Kohlberg, "Moral and Religious Education and the Public Schools: A Developmental View," in T. Sizer, ed., *Religion and Public Education* (Boston: Houghton Mifflin, 1967), p. 171.

his or her response. These six stages represent a refinement of Piaget's two stages—heteronomous and autonomous. Kohlberg and his associates have tested the stages in a wide range of cultures, social classes, and sex groups.[275] The findings generally support the developmental model. Stage 4, a conventional-authoritarian orientation, is the dominant level of most adults according to the findings. Kohlberg argues that if his sequences are an accurate description of structural development, then it must be demonstrated that persons at stages 5 and 6 have gone through stage 4, while persons at stage 4 have not gone through stages 5 and 6.[276] Otherwise it could be argued that his stages are arbitrary or that they merely represent the way different age groups are handled by socializing agents.

Since each stage of moral judgment integrates and replaces previous material and is not simply additive, Guttman scaling of the use of the stages in free response is rejected by Kohlberg. But he employs such scaling when using measures of the comprehension of each stage. The findings indicate, in general, that subjects can correctly comprehend all stages below or at their own level, show some comprehension of stages just above their own, and a little or no comprehension at levels two or more stages above their own.[277] While the pattern of actual use of stages is not cumulative, such patterns generally indicate that approximately half of a child's moral judgments will fit a single stage with the remainder distributed in a decreasing fashion around this. Kohlberg summarizes: "An individual's response profile, then, typically represents a pattern composed of the dominant stage he is in, a stage he is leaving but still uses somewhat, and a stage he is moving into but which has not yet crystallized."[278] He concludes that each person has a preference for using the highest stage he can produce. Further, Kohlberg's investigations indicate high consistency of stage use across varying situations. The correlations run from .31 to .75 with the median .51.[279] He argues that a "general first moral level factor" (that is, the developmental stage of moral judgment) accounts for most of the covariance from situation to situation.[280]

Kohlberg presents evidence to support his contention that his six stages represent a cognitive-developmental sequence produced by the interaction of the cognitive capacity of the human organism with its social environment. His evidence indicates that stages change regularly with age, that there is a general moral factor consistent across situations, that the frequency of use of a given stage is more highly correlated with frequencies in adjacent stages than frequencies in distant stages, and that it is easier to shift a child one stage higher than to produce any other sort of shift in moral judgment.[281] We cannot, of course, take it that he has proven his case once and for all. But his decades of work have produced supporting evidence that requires the cognitive-developmental theory of socialization to be taken seriously as a counterhypothesis to traditional explanations.[282]

Prerequisites of Moral Development Given the Piaget-Kohlberg formulation, how do we account for an Adolf Eichmann, who by Kohlberg's own analysis operates at the first and second (pre-moral) stages of development?[283] We can ask, "If the stages are a natural development, why doesn't everyone reach stage 6?" Kohlberg has two kinds of explanations for this objection. The first is the concept of cognitive regression and the second is the idea of the social or experiential prerequisites of development.

It is Kohlberg's view that "cultural teaching and experience can speed up or slow down development but it cannot change its order or sequence."[284] For example, as the child matures it learns to differentiate between the status of dreams and reality. Recognizing (1) that dreams are not real, children proceed sequentially to learn that (2) dreams are invisible to others; (3) dreams come from inside the person; (4) dreams go on inside the person; (5) dreams are not material in substance, and (6) dreams are self-caused.[285] This sequence of stages begins around age five in American children and is completed by age seven. However, some cultures proclaim the reality of dreams. While studying moral development among the aboriginal Atayal of Taiwan, Kohlberg found that younger members of the tribe showed the same developmental patterns as American boys toward a subjective concept of the dream despite the fact that Atayal culture rejects the idea. But at age eleven, Atayal boys begin to score lower on the scale of the dream concept than younger children. Kohlberg hypothesized that at this age the youths became aware of the cultural doctrine of the external origin of dreams and that the awareness induces a regression to more infantile conceptions.[286] He labels such phenomena regressions because they represent more than a simple change in content. The conflict between the cognitive development of the child and the ideology of the culture promotes further complications and a more general disorientation.[287] Experimental studies by Langer which are cited by Kohlberg indicate that some forms of cognitive conflict lead to further development and some to regression. The specification of such conflicts is taken by Kohlberg to be an eventual goal of cognitive-developmental theory.

If Kohlberg is correct in this concept of cognitive regression, then we would not expect an adult like Eichmann to be necessarily "mentally ill" or psychologically disturbed but we would expect him to suffer cognitive limitations, that is, to have difficulty in reasoning clearly about the world and to be in doubt about his own perceptions. The observed superficiality and banality of Eichmann's thought fits the model well.[289] Attempting to teach morality as conformity to group norms would have the effect of promoting cognitive regression. Indeed, the lamented decline in both the intellectual skills and moral acumen of American students may be related to the teaching of morality according to traditional socialization theories. According to these theories it is dangerous to teach children to be critical of political and social institutions—to teach them, in effect, to reason autonomously on moral questions. But the cost of avoiding such "dangers" is not only a decline in the level of moral discourse and behavior but a more general decline in the level of cognitive ability. Thus, as Jacques Ellul has declared, the important effect of propaganda is not so much a uniformity of attitude and action but disorientation and loss of contact with reality.[290]

Piaget claims that "cooperation alone leads to autonomy."[291] Kohlberg has elaborated on this to argue that social stimulation in the form of role-taking experiences is necessary to moral development. He claims that "social-cultural influences on cognitive-structural aspects of social development may be best conceived in terms of variations in amount, kind, and structure of role-taking opportunities."[292] The child begins with empathy—that does not have to be taught. But according to Kohlberg, social motives are neither instinctive nor are they learned through reward and punishment experiences leading to increased anxiety. Rather, the self and its capacity for autonomous judgment is born out of a social or, more exactly, a sharing process—the learning to take the role of the other and to comprehend the probable impact of actions on that other. This learning requires both opportunities to participate in various roles plus the cognitive capacity to assess situations and conceptualize their relevant components.[293] By participation, Kohlberg means both sheer interaction and responsibilities in decision making.

For Kohlberg, moral maturity is "the capacity to make decisions, judgments which are moral (that is, based on internal principles) and to act in accordance with such judgments."[294] This conception of moral maturity is unfortunately class biased. Indeed, Kohlberg argues, that middle-class children, because of their increased occasions to make decisions, to take responsibilities, and to direct the activities of others, have greater opportunities for role taking and therefore have accelerated rates of moral development and are more likely to reach higher stages of moral judgment.[295] For this argument to be the case we would have to believe his assertion that leadership roles require more sensitivity to the perspectives of others. Kohlberg argues, "The group leader must role-take all the subordinate's roles and be aware of their relations to one another, while the subordinate is only required to take the role of the leader."[296]

But the opposite argument can be cogently made: Leadership roles, because of the control of resources associated with them, elicit obsequious and defensive behavior that (1) makes role taking less relevant and (2) denies the leaders sufficient cues to understand the roles of subordinates. Homans, for example, maintains that a cost of leadership is isolation. He writes, "A leader . . . is dangerous; his followers will have some reason to avoid him, especially when they may do so legitimately."[297] Students of organization likewise report the isolation of administrative roles.[298] The lack of accurate feedback involved in such roles, because subordinates are motivated to disguise what is going on, promotes autistic attitudes.[299] Kohlberg seems innocent of such observations. While he notes that the research of Brim suggests that the effect of role taking is more pronounced for those in inferior roles, he dismisses the findings as applicable only to dyads.[300]

Problems of Moral Formalism Moral maturity involves more than acts and judgments consistent with internal principles. That formalistic approach, usually associated with Immanuel Kant, ignores the impact of the actions and judgments on others. Formalistic morality based on the idea that principles must be certain and that action is merely the fullfillment of duty is a class and cultural phenomenon. Deliberately ignoring or subordinating the impact of so-called moral actions is the mark of administrative and bureaucratic morality. The quality of moral judgment depends, as Kohlberg often recognizes, upon the individual's ability to conceptualize a given situation in terms of (a) its significant elements or features, (b) the relations between those elements, (c) a working model of the situation based on (a) and (b) that can generate accurate estimates of probable outcomes, and (d) a sense of what outcomes are better or worse for human life.

None of the above conceptualizations or hypothetical explanations is easily constructed. They require both cognitive capacities, such as logic and verbal ability, and social skills based on the experience of trial and error. Indeed, moral judgment is a complex skill. The fact that we regard the unyielding application of principles as something higher than a skill represents a class bias that takes "skill" to mean mechanical repetition and "judgment" to mean deciding which *a priori* rule applies.[301]

Moral judgment, like any skill, cannot be learned from books. Verbal and logical abilities can be improved through formal learning, as well as the knowledge of the content of social and political values and rules. These facts are only part of the story. According to Piaget's genetic approach to cognitive development, two basic kinds of activity are involved in the acquisition of knowledge. The first activity is labeled logicomathematical, being the processes of bringing together, discriminating, ordering, counting, and the like; and the second activity is physical exploration and information extraction. "It is thus acting in the external world that, according to Piaget, the child elaborates a more and more adequate knowledge of reality. It is precisely the successive forms of his activity in the course of his development that determines his modes of thought.[302] The divorce of these two types of activity represents a blockage of moral development.[303]

Facts and Values The point about blockage is often obscured by the arguments of logical positivists and logical empiricists who claim that facts and values are radically different and that scientific inquiry must be concerned only with facts. These assertions perform two different functions. First, they validate the scientists' claims (vis-à-vis social and private institutions) to intellectual freedom. Second, they also enable the scientist to work in the service of any particular values and to ignore or even prevent any reasoned inquiry and criticism of such values. The persuasiveness of these assertions (apart from the kind of bolstering assumptions and arguments we have just examined) lies in the logical demonstrations that facts are distinct from values. But demonstration of such a distinction does not imply the conclusion that human reason and science are concerned only with facts.

It is possible to take up a position of "critical dualism" or "critical conventionalism" like that of Karl Popper. Popper emphasizes that decisions, norms, or values cannot be reduced to factual statements or cannot be derived from a set of statements of facts without declaring values to be nonrational. Standards of human social conduct are not to be found in the regularities and facts of nature. "Critical dualism merely asserts that norms and normative laws *can* be made and changed by man. . . . Norms are man-made in the sense that we must blame nobody but ourselves for them: neither nature or God."[304] But Popper emphasizes that values are not simply arbitrary, for all their conventionality. He argues that men construct symphonies, calculi, and plays, as well as institutions, and that it does not follow that any one symphony or institution is as good as another.[305] There is no suggestion, however, that judging social norms is analogous to judging paintings. Implicit in all of Popper's writings on the "open society" is the idea that social norms must be judged against the criterion of human development in the direction of the increasing autonomy of action and judgment necessary to the scientific enterprise. His critical dualism points out that values and norms cannot be derived from the observed facts of nature. That they cannot no more makes such values incapable of systematic analysis and judgment than it does scientific hypotheses. For such hypotheses or theoretical statements likewise cannot be derived logically from individual factual observations, according to Popper.

Eugene Meehan notes that both the problem of induction and the problem of the fact/value relationship "refer strictly to a logical disjunction between different kinds of propositions."[306] This disjunction has been interpreted in many ways since Hume pointed it out, but Meehan notes that there is no implication in the logical argument that facts and values or particular cases and generalized statements have no relationship to one another. While the logical links are missing, strategies are available to connect the different types of propositions. One of these strategies for overcoming the problem of induction was developed by Popper. The fallibilistic strategy maintains that while we cannot argue from the truth of singular statements to the truth of theories, we can test theories by deducing singular statements from them and finding out if the statements are true according to experience. This is a simplistic account of Popper's position, but the important point is that "there can be no ultimate statements in science."[307] That is, all scientific theories are problematic; while theories can be found to be false, no theory can ever obtain the status of certainty on the basis of any number of confirming observations. While we can improve our theories on the basis of criticism, constructing competitive theories and testing in practice, we can never deduce theoretical certainty from experience. There are no formal reasons why we cannot adopt the same strategy for the improvement of social values that Meehan has suggested, for value judgments, like scientific theories, can be found to be true or false, better or worse.

In terms of classical Western political theory, the problem of moral development has been misunderstood as a clash between reason and passion. This misunderstanding is based partly on the recognition that both our physical theories of the world and our moral principles are and must be to some extent independent of the environmental stimuli. Wishful thinking and doing what titillates lead to disaster. While a Galileo may be forced to publicly recant his views on cosmology, he cannot be made to see the world "correctly." Likewise, we recognize that people often act in accordance with moral principles even though it may cost and pain them. But this independence is not due to a restriction of responses. For example, George Klein notes the general assumption that motivations based on organic needs or drives distort or impair accurate perception. He argues that such needs, in fact, inform and improve our perceptions. Were there some sort of nonmotivated organism without needs but only responses to environmental stimuli, a very complex environment would lead to overload or to arbitrary filtering. The needs of an animal provide a directedness to its actions and perceptions. At the same time there must be a cognitive structure connecting the satisfaction of such needs with the relevant features of the environment. Klein states, "If a given result is to be achieved, behavior must be provided not only with a motor but with a steering wheel and a map—which cognitive attitudes supply."[308]

Similarly, Meehan has argued that without a purpose to our research there are no means of establishing criteria for deciding, say, what features of a situation are significant or trivial. Further, without the testing in use of our theories to achieve those purposes, we cannot assess the reliability of our cognitive models. Meehan notes:

> Organized human experience, or human knowledge, is a structure suspended in mid-air, a pattern open in every direction, and relentless pursuit leads invariably to an endless regression. The patterns of relations that men create derive their strength from their relation to other patterns, from the results achieved by using them in particular situations, and not from the strength of their moorings.[309]

Both our physical knowledge and our social knowledge are intentional, hypothetical, and practical. To remove one of these elements is to stunt the human capacity to know. Thus, as we sometimes understand that dogmatism and science are incompatible, so we must recognize that the same is true of dogmatism and ethics. But conversely, as we understand that knowledge of the physical world is impossible without theoretical frameworks and tenacious expectations, so is social knowledge impossible without moral judgment. The autonomy of human knowledge is a delicate affair that depends upon our attention both to human needs and to environmental facts. For as Klein states, "By being responsive to drive aims and to reality alike, thought and behavior achieve paradoxically a certain freedom from both masters."[310]

Conclusion

I have tried to show that the findings of more than forty years of research in socialization processes falsify the loose set of theoretical propositions and assumptions that have directed them. There are no known reliable techniques for the molding of human character or the inculcation of civic virtue. This negation represents a challenge to our conventional wisdom about how human organizations work and how social knowledge is produced. The Piaget-Kohlberg cognitive-developmental approach helps us account for the findings that show no or little relation between techniques of child rearing and adult character; between parental values and the values of their children; between behaviors in different social settings; *and* between personality and political orientations and opinions on specific issues. At the same time their approach raises serious issues about the design and practice of both political education and social investigation.

Kohlberg declares that "all social knowledge implies an act of sharing, of taking the view point of another self or group of selves."[311]To approach the problem of social knowledge from the traditional elitist perspective thus leads to various forms of obscurantism and dogmatics, however humanely motivated the social investigator. For if sharing is to be avoided for fear of contamination, the viewpoints of others will be seen only as forms of ignorance. Hierarchical structures based on such fear are designed with numerous devices to thwart role taking and reciprocity or to make them unnecessary. The means of escaping ignorance thus becomes another means of perpetuating it. Resulting plans of political education in civic virtues turn out to be schemes for conditioned passivity.

The goal of political education is not the inculcation of correct or timeless values and moral principles; it is rather the clarification of the processes by which such values and principles are conceived, are applied, and eventually are modified. The teacher's or parent's own values and moral judgments play an important role in such clarification. By articulating such values, by defending them with coherent argument, by working out their implications in hypothetical situations, by applying them as rules of action and by modifying them in the light of experience, the teacher and parent provide a paradigm of civic virtue. Poorly thought-out values and principles result merely in failed morality, while well-constructed ones lead to an improvement of our social knowledge and practice even as they fail in specific elements. We can reinterpret the Socratic dictum that knowledge is virtue as meaning neither that knowing you know nothing is the humble approach to the good life or that knowing the eternal verities is the basis of good citizenship. Knowledge is virtue in the sense that our ability to construct complex, reliable explanations of the social world is basic to judging what makes a difference to human life and to achieving that which contributes to the improved quality of life.

4   Patterns of Cognitive Deprivation

> . . . we are driving our chidren mad more effectively
> than we are genuinely educating them. Perhaps it is
> our way of educating them that is driving them mad.
> —R. D. Laing

Proudhon once declared, "Knowledge is poison to the slave." His epigram gives us a sense of the paradoxical situation we are exploring. For how can it be that knowledge or information could harm a human being? That it does so under some circumstances is well known. Ronald Sampson states: "When you have never lived otherwise than in fetters, you are not able to recognize the fetters for what they are. You learn to adjust your wants to the goad in order to preserve the precious illusion of freedom."[1] But the case of the slave or dominated person is really not so clear. Certainly knowledge of fetters would increase the probability of successful escape. Also there must be some knowledge of the fetters lest the subordinate forget his or her place and be destroyed. Knowledge may be poison in the slave's situation, but only some knowledge, and the reasons are not to be found solely in the context. It is the impact of the context on the human organism that is crucial.

Avoiding Catastrophe

The physician Kurt Goldstein offers a possible answer to our question. According to him, knowledge is poison when having it requires an impossible response of an incapacitated individual. His answer is based on observations of brain-damaged World War 1 veterans in Germany. His patients behaved in ways that avoided confrontation with their disabilities; such confrontation would lead to catastrophic situations involving uncontrollable anxiety. The experience of a catastrophic situation induces a total incapacity to respond normally for some time afterward. Patients defended themselves against catastrophic situatons—when they were called upon to perform beyond their limited capacities—by the following devices: (1) by avoiding dangerous situations and seeking situations of minimal irritating stimuli; (2) by maintaining a state of general apathy, refusing to respond to most or all stimuli; (3) by busy work, successfully completing the tasks within their capabilities; (4) by meticulously ordering the objects and activities of their lives: and (5) by fleeing from all relatively unstructured situations.[2] These procedures correspond to the negative attributes of human social behavior cited by traditional political thinkers from Plato to Pareto. Severely incapacitated human beings behave like the dupes of social ignorance and their strategies of survival read like a catalogue of the failures of human nature.

This kind of defense suggests that slavery itself does not cause people to avoid knowledge. The relationship is more complex. Knowledge is avoided when human beings are incapacitated. Thus it is the damage to the organism caused by slavery or domination that is the source of robot behavior and the decision, as Wilhelm Stekel has it, not to want to know certain features of the situation. For example, Goldstein writes that his patients became more anxious as their conditions improved and conversely adjusted better the more severe their disability. A totally blind veteran adjusted easily to his limitation by restricting his movements; restricting his aspirations to move or accomplish tasks; and studiously ignoring the fact of his blindness in conversation and apparently in thought. This patient's injury improved and he regained partial sight. Goldstein comments on the case:

> . . . then he became upset; he sought to orientate himself by means of sight, but owing to its imperfection succeeded badly. He was thus well adapted to his world when he had been blind. Now for the first time, he spoke of something's not being right with his vision, and this previously quite contented man dropped into a state of depression. "What's to become of me if I can't see?" he would cry.[3]

The more damage the organism sustains the more completely is the fact of damage denied and compensated for by defensive reactions. Goldstein summarizes the process by noting that "the adjustment is made in proportion to the severity of the defect. When the latter completely blocks any essential activity, the readjustment becomes much better than in cases of lesser disturbances."[4]

It is hard not to admire the biological utility of the human organism's defenses of retreat, apathy, and anesthesia. However, these defenses may well be politically dangerous and hamper social development. That is, these processes of individual survival might work toward collective destruction. For if men are the makers of their own social structures and if such structures because of faulty design are damaging to their members, then the first adaptive maneuver is likely to be a restriction of life in the form of limited aspirations, increased apathy, and a censored awareness of the damaging features of the structure. Thus a situation that requires a high degree of critical awareness in order to correct the structural error through change and development is likely to result instead in compensatory reactions.[5] Or worse, original design faults may be intensified to increase anesthesia and reduce the possibilities of confronting catastrophic situations. This process of accommodation to damaging social contexts fits the historical record more closely than Marx's optimistic and simplistic belief that increased suffering leads to increased revolutionary activity. It is also more useful for the understanding of political behavior than are current explanations which argue that mass apathy indicates a high level of well-being and satisfaction among citizens. I conclude that the image of man as a passive robot with a blotter brain is based on the empirical features of certain pathological conditions. While claims of determining the content of thought and behavior have not been sustained, the subservience and acquiescence supposedly resulting from socialization can be understood as symptomatic of widespread organic damage.

The Abstract Attitude

But what kind of damage are we talking about? Certainly it is nothing so simple as being blind or crippled. The bulk of Goldstein's patients had suffered some form of brain damage. Although they appeared to be normal under most circumstances, they all lacked what he called "an attitude to the abstract." Under this general "lack" he grouped the following deficiencies: (1) inability to imagine objects not present; (2) inability to account to one's self for one's actions and thoughts; (3) inability to separate the ego from the world; (4) lack of freedom.[6] Such patients could not complete any task that required other than concrete behavior governed by specific stimuli. They could not, for example, recognize the geometrical figure of a square. But if the drawing of the square were altered to resemble a concrete object like a house or a window, it was then easily recognized. Patients also could not act out simple but abstract tasks such as drinking an imaginary glass of water. Also they could not understand simple stories that did not relate to their immediate environment. Lack of the ability to assume an abstract attitude leads, according to Goldstein, to an absence of initiative, impairment of voluntary activities, the inability to shift from one topic to another or one situation to another, and finally an inability to make choices.[7]

Goldstein's diagnosis is based on his idea that there are two basic types of human behavior and that these require two kinds of attitudes. He defines the two types of behavior with the warning that his distinction is easy to misunderstand.

In "concrete" performances a reaction is determined directly by a stimulus, is awakened by all that the individual perceives. The individual's procedure is somewhat passive, as if it were not he who had the initiative. In "abstract" performances an action is not determined directly and immediately by a stimulus configuration but by the account of the situation which the individual gives to himself. The performance is thus more a primary action than a mere reaction, and it is a totally different way of coming to terms with the outside world. The individual has to consider the situation from various aspects, pick out the aspect which is essential, and act in a way appropriate to the whole situation.[8] But Goldstein goes on to caution that "abstraction represents . . . a preparation for activity" and that it is therefore more correct "to speak of an attitude toward the abstract."[9] Action of any sort always involves a concrete attitude, however, and the distinction between the two kinds of behavior has to do with the attitude that precedes action. "In the concrete situation action is set going directly by the stimuli; in the situation involving the abstract, action is begun after preperation which has to do with a consideration of the whole situation."[10] Goldstein argues that normal concrete actions are dependent on the abstract attitude which comes into evidence if the normal course of behavior is disturbed by some changed feature of the environment. The source of his patients' behavior was the lack of a necessary element of normal behavior, which meant that their actions were totally dependent on the environmental stimuli. Their actions, I take it, would resemble simple reflexes. However, the simplicity of such reflexes would be evident only if a change or alteration in the action were necessary. Goldstein concludes that in normal behavior people alternate between abstract and concrete attitudes according to the requirements of their situation and the task at hand. But if either attitude becomes dominant, inappropriate behavior will result.[11]

Ignoring the symmetry he has constructed, Goldstein concentrates his attention on the pathological state he calls lack of the abstract. He suggests that such a lack might occur on a mass scale under the following circumstances: First, in a given society the habits, customs, and institutions that guide human behavior for some reason "attain a certain emancipation from their original meaning."[12] If the relation between routine and the needs of human life becomes tenuous or nonexistent, an abnormal condition results. The consequences of this condition are anxieties produced by the expeience of catastrophic situations in which socially given routines fail to solve actual problems or achieve

needed results. Goldstein believes that if the occurrence of such catastrophic situations is frequent and extensive enough, the resulting confusion may result in some form of minority domination. Minority
domination would mean that one group would rule, reserving the abstract attitude to itself, while the majority would obey and live lives
restricted to concrete behavior. The resulting elite/mass society would
be one in which most people's behavior would be like that of Goldstein's patients. According to him, the mass man "behaves like a man
with an injured brain; he lacks . . . the attitude toward the abstract,
losing himself in activities determined by concrete demands."[13]

The Pathology of the Abstract

The scenario is plausible in the light of recent history, but there are
certain problems. Why should the habits, customs, and institutions become emancipated, or more accurately, separated, from their original
meaning?[14] It is not clear that they should automatically do so. Goldstein's explanation fails here because he has failed to investigate what
we might call the pathology of the abstract. His failure is symptomatic
of the one-sided and class-ridden viewpoint of much contemporary
social science. For that reason, it is important to understand. First, what
do I mean by pathology of the abstract? Take the following description
by Pierre Janet of persons who cannot act concretely:

> They can ordinarily comport themselves like other people, chat-
> ter or complain of their disabilities to intimate friends; but di-
> rectly action becomes important and by consequence involves the
> manipulation of reality, they cease to be able to do anything and
> tend to withdraw more and more from their avocation, the
> struggle with other people, external living and social relation-
> ships. Indeed their lives are highly specialized and utterly mean-
> ingless—without active relationship either to things or to
> people . . . such minor interests as they retain are always given to
> those matters that are farthest from material actuality: some-
> times they are psychologists: before all things philosophy is the
> object of their devotion; they become terrible metaphysicians.
> The spectacle of these unfortunates makes one ask sadly
> whether philosophical speculation is no more than a malady of
> the human mind.[15]

According to Elton Mayo, the outstanding characteristic of such persons is their lack of practical skill in communication, cooperation, experimentation, and making things. Mayo argues that modern educational structures, particularly at the university level, produce people
lacking in what he calls social skills. This lack is particularly the case, he
insists, of the way in which social scientists are trained. As he writes:

"The so-called social sciences encourage students to talk endlessly about alleged social problems. They do not seem to equip students with a single social skill that is usable in ordinary situations. . . . [The student] . . . learns from books, spending endless hours in libraries; he considers ancient formulae, uncontrolled by the steady development of experimental skill; the equivalent of the clinic, or indeed of the laboratory is still to seek."[16] The pathology of the abstract occurs, then, when men and women are denied or deny themselves access to direct knowledge-of-acquaintance with the social and productive processes. Mayo considers this lack of active experience in diverse and developmental situations to be a product of faulty educational design, although there are obvious class biases operating which he does not consider. He suggests instead that this lack is a product of urbanization and industrialization and does not attempt to understand the total process by which it comes about.

Richard Sennett offers a more promising clue to the understanding of the process leading to a pathology of the abstract when he notes that revolutionaries, reformers, and social planners tend to purify their experience "by having the dissonances interpreted as less real than the consonances with what is known."[17] In these cases it seems to be the roles—whether revolutionary, reformer, or planner—that demand such purification of experience. The social investigator who assumes all, one, or any combination of these roles (or seeks to serve others in these roles) tends also to purify experience by postulating simple robot men and denying dissonant perceptions. This tendency is due to what Popper refers to as the "complementary" relation of knowledge and power. That is, the roles mentioned require both—power, to coerce obedience; and knowledge of human needs and the requirements of a satisfactory collective life. Having power entails the ability to suppress criticism, but such ability makes it likely that others' important dissatisfactions will not be voiced and therefore that needed basic information will not be available. We have seen, for example, that the social investigator, in these roles, in trying to account for people's resistance to his wisdom, usually ends by making it impossible for his theories about society to be falsified. An unfalsifiable theory, however, is not capable of producing information. The result is social myths—elaborate thought structures constructed out of a minimal number of crude assumptions about human life. Karl Popper summarizes the point by noting that the "holistic planner" does not understand that:

> It is easy to centralize power but impossible to centralize all that knowledge which is distributed over many individual minds, and whose centralization would be necessary for the wise wielding of centralized power. But this fact has far-reaching consequences.

Unable to ascertain what is in the minds of so many individuals, he must try to simplify his problems by eliminating individual differences: he must try to control and stereotype interests and beliefs by education and propaganda.[18]

The revolutionary, reformer, social planner—indeed any social investigator who understands that the purpose of social science is the improvement of the quality of human life—must actively interfere with and change the procedures and patterns of social life. Such actions will be met with reactions varying from enthusiastic approval through voiced criticisms to outright rejection. It seems that attention to criticism would impair implementation; thus the temptation is to "suppress unreasonable criticism," according to Popper, in the name of revolution, progress, and science. The better the original idea of change the more unreasonable will criticism seem, and the more likely will be the suppression of resistance to the change. But once unreasonable criticism is actively suppressed (rather than, say, refuted by results, arguments, or analysis), reasonable criticism will invariably be subdued. No matter what the intentions, all criticism will become suppressed once any kind of criticism is suppressed.

In such a situation, expressions of satisfaction become suspect to the degree to which criticism is punished. If expressions of criticism are subdued and expressions of satisfaction are exaggerated, then measuring the impact of any given change on the quality of life becomes impossible. As Popper notes, "It will be difficult to ascertain the facts, i.e., the repercussions of the plan on the individual citizen; and without these facts scientific criticism is impossible."[19] This impossibility does not prove that revolutions, reforms, social engineering, and social science are destructive or impossible. But it does indicate that political power is not an effective means of improving human life. Men may seek power for whatever reasons, but the hope that power will promote needed change, provide freedom, increase knowledge, or help the species is empty, however well-intentioned the seeking. Political and social power may be the means to many things, but better conditions of existence are not among them.

The pathology of the abstract consists of imposing symbolic definitions onto the world rather than using the symbols to investigate the occurence and relationships of phenomena. The imposing can be done in several ways: (1) by constructing ideal categories and concepts of the world; (2) by constructing unfalsifiable theories of the world; and (3) by adopting a stance of absolute relativism in which one concept, definition, or theory is as good as another. Each of these are ways of preventing the modification of frames of reference in the light of experience. Thus, the individual involved in the pathology of the abstract lacks freedom in much the same sense that the individual encapsulated in the concrete does. (See the discussion a few pages on, of the Head versus the Hand.) Just as people lacking an attitude to the abstract cannot carry out certain operations requiring a change in their frame of reference, so people involved in the pathology of the abstract cannot carry out operations requiring the implementation and subsequent modification of a frame of reference. While abstract men or women may chatter more, fancy more, and argue more, their daily activities do not appear to be different from those of Goldstein's patients in terms of the frozen patterns of their behavior. Both are passive but in different ways. Hamlet beguiles us with his talk, but until his belated activities of the last act he avoids the catastrophic situation involved in confronting his mother and uncle in their guilt. He responds to events with a stereotyped madness which appears almost cunning. Shakespeare depicts the pathology of the abstract in many characters—the poetic but impotent Richard II; Ulysses, the ineffectual rhetorician of political order; and Prospero, whose fanciful schemes must be implemented by the concrete and deformed Caliban. In each of them, the lack of freedom, and more importantly the lack of knowledge, is nearly disguised by the incessant talk and speculation.

To purify experience is then to become deliberately ignorant. Because the social investigator does not have the requisite knowledge to design human organizations, he seeks the power to impose his poor concoctions. Thus, most of his effort is spent defending his use and need for power on the basis of absolutist definitions of human nature. Human nature must, therefore, remain as much a mystery to him as physiological paternity is to the Trobriander. The traditional social investigator knows human nature completely, so for him it is necessarily simple, passive, and devoid of anything but the most formal characteristics.

Judging the Human Species

The goal of most political thinkers, whether traditional or organizational, has been to devise a political structure more effective than its individual human parts. My goal is to try to conceive of an organizational form approaching the effectiveness of its human parts. This is not just a whim or even a judgment on my part. The very act of judging the qualities of the human species by a member of that species is falacious, however persuasive. Of course, we may have an opinion about mankind or even a passionate love or hatred for the species. But no objective evaluation is possible, or, rather, any evaluation is necessarily tendentious. The ordinary clichés of judgment, such as "men seek always for power" or "men act only in their own self-interest," are, upon examination, circular in form and quite unfalsifiable. Other more virulent judgments concerning the inherent laziness, stubbornness, and irrationality of mankind are little more than statements of individual frustration and disappointment.

For an animal whose major means of adaptation is the making and using of tools, to be inherently lazy is an astounding paradox of evolution. It is like discovering that lions are actually vegetarians. Likewise, as we contemplate an animal whose major means of social coordination is a communication process that requires almost continuous learning, for such an animal to be inherently stubborn, systematically in error, and irrational is unbelievable. If either judgment were true we would not be here, or at least we would be a far different sort of creature capable of survival only in lush climates and in very small social units.

The opposite sort of judgments—that man is inherently "good" or "altruistic," or "peaceable," or the like—are equally fallacious. These judgments carry qualifications that account for all the counter evidence of "badness," "selfishness," and "aggression" as due to evil social, economic, and political systems. But these same qualifications make the assertions unfalsifiable. For the "state of nature" or "healthy environment" in which this remarkable creature is to be found is always a theoretical, not an empirical, condition of the human qualities claimed. Basically these claims of man's theoretically good qualities are means of pointing out his empirically bad qualities. With flatterers like this, mankind is scarcely in need of any detractors. When a man describes the inherent wickedness of man, it is usually in the defense of some scheme of domination and exploitation. When a man celebrates man's natural goodness, it is usually the prelude to some plan of improvement involving coercion and self-denial. All judgments of this kind can be used as and are nearly always meant to be justifications of political actions and political structures. The resulting political actions always involve restricting and molding human existence, and the resulting political structures are always hierarchic.

Man's eminent biological success—measured in range of habitation, multiplicity of life styles, and size of population—cannot be accounted for if traditional judgments of the species are valid. And the issue is not whether this success has made man happy. The problems of contemporary survival and successful adaptation are necessarily different from those of the past. Between the species and the environment there is a continuous interaction creating new problems that may or may not be solvable. Thus the ultimate success of man is unknowable. However, such a success will not consist of a problem-free world, for that is little more than a fantasy of tired bureaucrats. That man should be recognized for the remarkable achievements of his past by no means requires either a blindness to present difficulties or a mindless optimism about the future. Man has survived, and he has propagated. He might have done the former better or more easily, and he certainly must exercise discretion in the latter.

The judgment of man by men would be only a matter of spleen and nonsense were it not for the political consequences of such assertions. When judged, the species is necessarily measured against a subjective standard of habit and desire (I wish men were more —— or less ——) or against an "objective" standard of organizational conformity. Subjective standards are more easily recognized and are, therefore, not troublesome, while organizational standards are more often assumed and unrecognized. However much the details of these standards differ throughout history and across the earth's extent, they share a common form—men are commanded and required to act in simple, routine ways without failure, hesitation, question, or resistance and with minimal rewards. Men must live up to certain rules. Men must learn automatically to repeat certain correct actions. Men must curb their appetites and, indeed, learn to master the demands of their bodies. Failure is called error; hesitation is weakness; questions are heresy; resistance is sin; and desire is greed. Given the imposition of an abstract schema on the complex human responses to an equally complex and fluctuating environment, the species is necessarily judged error-prone, weak, contentious, rebellious, and selfish. In turn, this evaluation of man's potentials is used to justify the obvious biological costs of the hierarchies that produce the evaluation in the first place. If men were not ignorant, lazy, irrational, or the like, rulers would not be needed.

To begin the construction of a scientific framework of political thought we must first reverse this bias. Sanity demands our allegiance to human survival at the highest possible level. Man, the species, is neither good nor evil, wonderful nor wicked, for men, the members of that species. The species is. We are members. And, as Nietzsche points out, we are the species that introduces values into the universe. These are human values. They are based on human need and human satisfaction. The highest values are those rooted in our own physiological structure. They cannot be used to judge humanity itself. Men exist and their existence is the standard from which all evaluations on this earth are made. In short, men—their capacities and their needs—are the basic facts of social science. Man's survival is the criterion for judging not only conduct but conceptualization. Organizations, whether societies or institutions, are important tools of human adaptation. As tools they fail or succeed (or, more exactly, succeeed at greater or less cost) and they must be continuously evaluated. But their failure, when they fail, cannot be deemed the fault of man's nature. Organizations must be judged on the basis of how they enhance or damage the life of the human organism. To invert that relationship is like prescribing surgery for the hand in order to make it fit the clumsy limitations of a poorly designed hammer.

Karl Deutsch observed:

> To my mind it is of tremenduous fundamental importance, for the understanding of processes in human society, to realize that human society consists of putting together relatively simple, large feedback cycles by means of fantastically complicated components. For society is primitive compared to the resources and arrangements of re-combinations available to the individual for short times.[20]

He went on to argue that we should try to devise organizational patterns that utilize individual complexity, rather than try to simplify the possibilities of behavior generated by the human brain to fit the "big simple social nets which get a priority."[21] Deutsch's observation and his program are important, but they remain little more than pious wishes if we do not understand why the social investigator opts for the simplistic organizational form of hierarchy over the complex possibilities of human life. The relationship between the social investigator and the social system is dangerous and often vicious and thus more than an epistemological issue. Or rather, the relationship illuminates the crucial political nature of epistemological issues. For by postulating principles of human nature, rather than investigating what that nature might be, the social investigator defends or designs pathogenic structures that divide the workers of the hand from those of the head, and subordinate both to the administration of abstract principles.

The Head versus the Hand

This division is a source of much human passivity, for both kinds of worker tend to be less capable of defending themselves as they are confronted with the unacceptable alternative of their deformed counterparts. The worker of the hand tends to lose, or rather to deny, his freedom by becoming encapsulated in the concrete. He aids this process because he wishes to avoid the obvious limits of a life governed by the pathologies of the abstract. He sees the worker of the head as a being of words and formulas, ignorant and helpless, yet dangerous because of his lack of respect for materials and life. For the worker of the hand, theoretical thought becomes something to be avoided because it is not only likely to get you into trouble on the job and make you vulnerable and incompetent, but likely also to corrupt. Such corruption may proceed until you are not a mere servant but an agent in manipulating the servility of others. A society with many members who despise theory, logic, symbols, and imagination is sick. This sickness is all too evident to those of us who work with our heads. But what of the converse?

The worker of the head tends to deny his freedom by means of the pathology of the abstract. Again, he aids this process because he wishes to avoid the situation of a life encapsulated in the concrete. He sees the worker of the hand as a being with automatic reflexes helplessly manipulated by anyone who can gain control over environmental stimuli and yet all the more dangerous because of the hand worker's willingness to serve any master and his lack of respect for the ideals of an aesthetic and well-examined existence. For the worker of the head, the material world becomes something to be avoided because it evokes helpless longings for effective action and undermines faith in the principles, formulas, and ideal goals of civilization. The worker of the head is afraid of succumbing to a world of crude hedonism since his ignorance of the world of material production limits his awareness of the nonsymbolic aspects of life to simple but long-denied bodily needs. W. R. Lethaby declares that "society becomes diseased in direct ratio to its neglect and contempt of labour."[22] This pathology is not so obvious to those of us who work with our heads, for manual labor is what we are continuously escaping.

Bureaupathic Responses

Victor Thompson describes another set of dichotomous responses to the simplistic feedback loops of bureaucracies. He labels these responses *bureaupathic* and *bureautic*. They result, he maintains, from the inability of individuals to adjust to certain necessary qualities of modern organizations, namely routinization, attachment to subgoals, impersonality, categorization, resistance to change, and preoccupation with hierarchical relations. That is, he does not examine "bureaupathology" as concerning how bureaucratic organizations are pathogenic, but rather as concerning the way that personal needs lead to exaggeration and exploitation of characteristic organizational qualities. Thompson assumes, as do nearly all social investigators, that any sickness to be found is generated solely by the frailties of human beings. Bureaupathic behavior is characterized by excessive aloofness, ritualistic attachment to routines and procedures, deep resistance to change, petty insistence on prerogatives of authority, and excessive concern with status.[23] Its main source is the inadequacy of the individual and his resulting insecurity. As Thompson puts it:

This pathological behavior starts with a need on the part of the person in an authority position to control those subordinate to himself. . . . While the need to control arises in large part from personal insecurity in the superior, it has conceptual sources as well.[24] The conceptual sources are traditional beliefs that there is only one best, or scientific, way to do things and that the discovery and implementation of this way is the task of all those in authority roles. That is, the administrator's drive for the control of subordinate behavior has the same conceptual source as the social investigator's. Both conceive their task as that of constructing certainty under prevailing conditions of chaos. They want to discover basic principles and deduce operations and formulas that can be imposed and enacted with minimal thought and no deviation. However, Thompson notes that the conceptual sources are hardly compelling and that personal insecurity is more important as a motivation.

If we understand that the personal insecurity is fear of the catastrophic situation which would result if the inadequate knowledge of the administrator or investigator were confronted with the need to provide an actual conceptual framework for social adaptation, then Thompson's point is well taken. He notes that a major source of insecurity is the increasing conflict between knowledge and power in bureaucratic organizations. "The intellectual, problem-solving content of executive positions is being increasingly diverted to specialists, leaving hierarchical rights (and duties) as the principal components of executive posts."[25] The administrator commands those he does not understand and yet the traditional source of his superiority is greater information and wisdom. Presumably a nonbureaupathic response to this situation would be to deny or ignore the anxiety. This attitude would supposedly result in rational bureaucratic behavior that is different only in degree from that of the bureaupath. The difference is that the exaggerated behavior of the bureaupath is more self-indulgent. While the bureaucrat administers the situation by means of abstract rules and categories, the bureaupath exploits the situation to satisfy compensatory "personal needs" for security, order, deference, and status.

The bureaupathic executive might well be seen as a superbureaucrat instead of as a self-indulgent deviant. For the exaggerated insistence that these individuals put on adherence to the rules, procedure, deference patterns, and traditions of bureaucracy may result from taking the organization seriously. That is, bureaupaths actually believe that desired results obtain from an unvarying implementation of formulas. The bureaupath's pathology is that of the abstract. What a healthy bureaucrat might look like would be an individual who could simultaneously believe in abstract categories and formulas while being responsive to the concrete complexity of details and processes. Schematically this combination might seem possible, and indeed it is achieved to some degree by many men and women. But it is not a true synthesis, and the outward signs of its achievement may be apathy, addiction, or the development of techniques of handling excess anxiety by means of disciplines such as Yoga and Zen Buddhism. The classic philosophy of "healthy" bureaucrats is Stoicism, and the self-denial and resignation we find there are evidence not of an integrated but of an impoverished existence.[26]

Bureautic Responses

Bureautic responses are characterized by Thompson as being "rather extreme cases of resistance to bureaucracy."[27] According to him, this resistance, while having some basis in the frustrations of normal bureaucratic operations, is basically due to a failure of maturation. The bureautic, who resists all interrogation, has low powers of abstractions, needs to personalize, fears bureaucracy, is suspicious and nearly paranoid, lives only for the present, and is insensitive to the needs of others. For him, Thompson writes, "the organization is a great battleground." He indicates that the bureautic's basic problem is incomplete or defective socialization; the bureautic fails to grow up. This immaturity is most evident, according to Thompson, in the bureautic's general inability to abstract. Thus, he is incapable of taking on the roles of others in imagination or practice, incapable of understanding the meaning and necessity of general categories and laws, and incapable of deferring gratification. "The bureautic's inability to abstract or generalize makes it impossible for him to understand why an exception cannot be made in his case." Thompson has little sympathy with the bureautic response and seems to understand it much less than he understands the bureaupathic. He notes that it occurs most often in the clients of a bureaucracy. His description seems to resemble closely that of Goldstein's brain-damaged veterans. The bureautic is continuously threatened with the catastrophic confrontation of his own rigid and concrete behavior with the complex and abstract demands of the bureaucracy. His incapacities are not the result of socialization but of the encapsulated situation of the subordinate worker. If for "the client" we read "class" in Thompson's description, then we can understand bureautic people as the working-class clientele of the administrating bureaucracy.

Public Languages and Formal Languages

Thompson's distinctions are almost ones of style. To choose either of the two repetitive and frozen behavior patterns (bureaupathic or bureautic) is impossible except on quite accidental grounds of birth, education, and whimsy. In fact, a British sociologist, Basil Bernstein, has differentiated the linguistic styles of social classes in terms that parallel those of Goldstein, Janet, and Thompson. Bernstein began his research, in the 1950s, concerned to discover the influence of the working-class environment on cognition. More specifically he was puzzled, like others, that although the educational system of Great Britain was reformed to promote those of superior ability regardless of wealth or class, universities remained largely populated by students of middle- and upper-class origins. This distribution was even more puzzling since test samples of nonverbal intelligence showed that the distribution of intelligence in the working and middle classes was approximately the same. Skewed differences did show up on verbal intelligence tests. Bernstein discovered that children from different class backgrounds spoke predominately different kinds of language. He called the dominate linguistic form of the working class a "public language" and that of the middle class a "formal language."[28] These languages differed not so much in vocabulary as in structure and syntax.

Bernstein described the public language of the working class as being expressed in concrete, descriptive, emotive, and tangible symbolism. The syntax was simple and logic was little developed, feelings were largely expressed through accompanying gestures and intonations, and statements contained few personal qualifications. The public language indicated a sensitivity toward the content of objects, and Bernstein reasoned that it was an indication of a less developed cognitive differentiation on the part of its working-class users.

The formal language of the middle class Bernstein described as being expressed in abstract, general, and discursive symbolism. The syntax was elaborate and the logic advanced, feelings were expressed through the patterned arrangement of words rather than through gestures, and statements were rich in personal qualifications. This formal language indicated a sensitivity to the relationship between objects. It was oriented toward the expression of structure. He summarized his distinction in this way:

> The typical, dominant speech mode of the middle-class is one where speech becomes an object of special perceptual activity and a "theoretical attitude" is developed towards the structural possibilities of sentence organization. This speech mode facilitates the verbal elaboration of subjective intent, sensitivity to the implications of separateness and difference, and points to the possibilities inherent in a complex conceptual hierarchy for the organization of experience.
>   . . . This is not the case for members of the lower working-

class. The latter are *limited* to a form of language use, which, although allowing for a vast range of possibilities, provides a speech form which discourages the speaker from verbally elaborating subjective intent and progressively orients the user to descriptive, rather than abstract concepts.[29]

To paraphrase Bernstein in the simplest manner, a public language emphasizes things rather than processes and structures, while a formal language emphasizes processes and structures rather than things.[30] He states that middle-class children do have access to the use of public language as well as formal language, but that working-class children do not have such an option.

In his later work the distinction between the two languages appears to stem from their implicit attitudes toward authority. The public language of the working class is a language of resistance in which individual differences are minimized, social solidarity is stressed, rules are expressed in categoric statements, and meanings are implicit. Bernstein argues that these qualities block certain kinds of learning and facilitate others. For example, users of a public language understand and respond to authority as the result of an inferior-superior social relationship and not as the outcome of an impartial administration of general laws. "Reasons" for having to behave a certain way are not given or expected. Thus any deviancy is a direct challenge to the individual authority. Bernstein concludes:

> The frequency of, and dependency upon, the categoric statement in a *public* language reinforces the personal at the expense of the logical, limits the range of behavior and learning, and conditions types of reactions and sensitivity towards authority.[31]

Thus public-language users would learn or understand Thrasymachus' argument that justice is whatever is in the interest of the stronger much more easily than they would grasp Socrates' abstract notion. This linguistic form expresses and fosters a low-level conceptualization, which the author characterizes as "an orientation to a low order of causality, a disinterest in processes, a preference to be aroused by and respond to that which is immediately given rather than to the implications of a matrix of relationships." This minimal conceptualization, he suggests, "partly conditions the intensity and extent of curiosity." It is in fact a form of secrecy. The meaning of public-language statements is understood only by those who share the context of the speaker. As Bernstein puts it, "It fosters a form of social relationship where meaning is implicit, where what is not said, when it is not said and, paradoxically, how it is not said, form strategic orienting cues."

In later work, Bernstein becomes more general and renames his two speech systems. "Public language" becomes "restricted code" and "formal language" becomes "elaborated code." A restricted code (which can be limited in terms of either structure or vocabulary) occurs, according to Bernstein, in closed communities like prisons, combat units of the armed service, criminal subcultures, children's peer groups, and married couples of long standing. What all of these communities have in common is not only their shared identifications, as Bernstein notes, but also their subordinate context. These communities exist dependent upon larger formal units to which they are subordinate in theory. Bernstein argues that "restricted codes can be considered status-oriented speech systems." And while he adds that "the codes reinforce the form of the social relation, by limiting the verbal signaling of personal difference," he fails to see that restricted codes thus limit the ability of those in superior positions to understand and therefore direct subordinate behavior.[32] A restricted code not only limits the learning of its users but presents outsiders with an image of faceless solidarity, conformity, ignorance, and deference. Bernstein observes that "a restricted code is available to *all* members of society as the social conditions which generate it are universal."[33] The "all" should be qualified by the phrase "who perform subordinate roles." The dichotomy of language systems is finally, in Bernstein's words, "the old polarity of *gemeinschaft* and *gesellschaft* in another guise."[34]

Likewise, an elaborated code can be understood as a structure of secrecy facilitating certain kinds of learning and perception while blocking others. Users of a formal language or elaborated code perceive authority as based on some kind of reasoned principles. Thus they expect reasons for commands or treatment they receive, whether or not such "reasons" actually motivated the command or whether or not the personal treatment is specifically intended. Bernstein does not discuss this expectation, but it seems an obvious blind spot promoted by formal language. Users of this language expect every event to have a clearly recognizable cause and every individual case to be subsumable under a general law. When whimsical, irrational, or unintended events occur, such people must use all their ingenuity to explain them or lapse into superstition. An order from the boss will likely be taken by restricted-code users as nothing more than the boss' nutty notion, whether or not it was occasioned by situational determinants. Likewise, an order from the boss will likely be taken by elaborated-code users as an initiative determined by the boss' superior information and understanding of the rules, whether or not it was occasioned by his ulcer or by a recent tiff with his wife. The point is that the actions of those in authority are neither always self-serving nor always the objective administration of principles. Indeed, most actions are a mixture. Both codes lead to distorted perceptions of such actions.

Bernstein concludes: "Clearly one code is not better than another; each possesses its own aesthetic, its own possibilities."[35] Elsewhere he notes:

> A *public* language contains its own aesthetic; a simplicity and directness of expression, emotionally virile, pithy and powerful; and a metaphorical range of considerable force and appropriateness. . . . It is a language which symbolizes a tradition and a form of social relationship in which the individual is treated as an end, not as a means to a further end. To simply substitute a *formal* language (which is not necessarily a logical, impersonal, emotionally eviscerated language) is to cut off the individual from his traditional relationships and perhaps alienate him from them.[36]

But while the two codes or languages cannot be ranked, Bernstein notes that they are valued differently. In contemporary class society, he maintains, middle-class children learn to use both codes, as we have noted. A child possessed only of a restricted code will not get far in the educational system. Thus the open educational system tends to perpetuate and even to legitimize *class differences.*[37]

The ideal would seem to be to make both codes available to every member of society. But this ideal is as mechanical as that of the happy bureaucrat. While both codes may have their aesthetic qualities, both also restrict and distort social perceptions. Combining two sets of systematic distortions does not necessarily result in a corrected view in the way that the optician's lenses correct for astigmatism. Personalizing impersonal rules or impersonalizing personal preferences does not help our understanding. We see both codes used by politicians to take credit for certain outcomes while avoiding the responsibility for others. For example, the President may present himself to the public using either code to take credit for a drop in food prices while disclaiming responsibility for, say, the outbreak of war. There is a shift in codes in these cases and Bernstein's description is useful in gauging what sort of images public figures are trying to project. There is nothing to be gained by having everyone learn both codes except that it would make everyone available for administrative roles. Since such roles are necessarily minority ones, Bernstein's suggestion is largely a hopeless sentiment.

Bernstein writes that "the semantic function of a language is the social structure."[38] We cannot then change the social structure by changing language. For, while the author maintains that it is legitimate to infer social and psychological behavior from language, he notes that language is a product of such behavior. As he puts it, "What one is doing is simply looking at the social structure through a particular institution, the institution of language." He adds that the importance of the approach is "that it may throw some light on how the social structure becomes part of individual experience and inasmuch as this is done, it illuminates the relationship between sociology and psychology." This matter deserves more attention than we can give it here. What is most significant is that both codes distort by selection, that is, by taking one or a few aspects of a situation or a phenomenon and treating the part as the whole. Such selection further distorts those aspects selected. For example, to take human love as the driving force of the universe gives a false notion not only of physical reality but also of human love. Selected elements—logical, personal, nonverbal, conceptual, and the like—become aggrandized and therefore falsified. Calling our attention to the importance of logic is one thing; claiming that logic is the key to efficacious action and correct understanding is another. The same is true of social solidarity, nonverbal communication, concrete awareness, and the like. We can forgive any distortion by saying, "Thank God it was brought so forcefully to our attention." While forgiving is presumably decent and human, such a reason is without merit. What usually dazzles us in these cases is the simplification and resulting magical solution offered by such distortions. The proposition that we might solve all through love of justice or honesty is both appealing and impossible to test. Bernstein's codes are means by which we may be selectively aware of our situation. But the necessity of such selectivity is based on an organic need for protective ignorance. Goldstein's blind patient never spoke of his blindness. We may infer that users of restricted and elaborated codes are likewise avoiding the social aspect of their lives which is most threatening to them.

The Productive Attitude

We have explored the characteristics of two types of attitude—the abstract and the concrete—in terms of the behavior patterns, roles, and codes appropriate to each. This exploration indicates that healthy human activities require more than Goldstein's "alternation" between these attitudes, since both represent not only a partial relationship to reality but an attempted exclusiveness that entails a denial of certain features of the context. As we have seen, neither attitude by itself can ensure an adequate level of human survival, and yet both make that claim. Thus the relationship between these attitudes is symbiotic. A person who chooses to live in terms of an abstract attitude requires people who are capable of the concrete activities of production and maintenance. He also must repress awareness of his own concrete behavior. For, as Goldstein points out, all concrete behavior takes place within a frame of reference or selected context conceived abstractly and all behavior is at the same time concrete. No one can escape the concrete any more than anyone can escape the abstract. The choosing and living of one or the other of these attitudes thus represents a loss of autonomy.

Autonomy we can define as the ability to respond directly and immediately to a stimulus configuration that has been and is being constructed out of aspects of the situation which are appropriate to the actor's needs. The responses of an autonomous human being are not mechanically repetitive, but differ in a range of subtle adjustments that are too minute to be verbalized and can be known only by direct experience. The stimulus configuration, or frame of reference, of an autonomous human being is not a simple frozen structure of certainty but rather a fluid, complex pattern of rich detail and precision. The key to this concept, as I understand it, is the fact that it is not a summation of partial attitudes, but a different kind of attitude resulting in different behavior requiring different social and political roles and different codes. I call this attitude the productive or creative attitude, and I believe we all experience it to some extent in the necessary productive activities found in all but the most pathological of lives. It is not an ideal state for which we should strive; it is rather a state of biological health which we should protect and nurture. The productive attitude is a basic characteristic of the animal that has successfully adapted to the enormous ecological range of the human species and whose very anatomy is formed by the creative activity of toolmaking and the manufacture of environments.[39] The suppression, denial, and distortion of the productive attitude with resulting loss of autonomy is damaging to the human being. This damage is basic and biological, as can be seen by the symptomatic defense mechanisms that accompany it.[40] That is, cognitive deprivation caused by role restrictions and impoverished organizational networks is damaging in two ways. First, it reduces the capacity of the individual to respond appropriately and to choose appropriate response patterns. Second, it requires a set of defenses that drastically restrict the perceptions, motility, aspirations, and actions of the individual. It is the second set of results that we most often observe and attribute to the nature of the human animal. But when we observe such behavior, we are watching an animal that has been "functionally decerebralized," to use Ludwig von Bertalanffy's phrase.

Autonomy requires both skill and conceptualization, though it is perhaps false to separate the two abilities. Goldstein states that productive actions must be imbedded in an abstract set. Again, this dichotomous way of describing the situation probably has more to do with the social circumstances under which we live than with the features of productive activity. However, these kinds of description are probably the best we can do given present-day experience. Just as the Trobrianders manage to procreate without acknowledging or understanding the nature of physiological paternity, so we manage to feed, house, protect, decorate, describe, and maintain ourselves without acknowledging or understanding the productive process. Clear conceptualization here would require a change in our practices and our institutions as well as in our vocabularies.

Cognitive Postulates

Thus we must start with the rather limited notion of an "abstract set" or "stimulus configuration." While some behaviorists, like Skinner, consider such a notion mentalistic, others, like E. C. Tolman and Harry F. Harlow, have argued that an account of any animal behavior of a complicated sort requires the use of models involving variables intervening between environmental stimulus and organic response. Tolman argued, "Behavior qua behavior exhibits not only purpose but also cognitive postulation as to the nature of the environment for mediating and supporting the purposes."[41] Among cognitive postulations, Tolman includes the following elements: (1) postulations of discrimination features, or the preselection of kinds of stimuli to be responded to; (2) postulations of manipulation features, or what kinds of physical supports are required of the environment; and (3) postulations of relative positions and orders, among the first two features, of what kinds of patterns (gestalten) are anticipated. These basic cognitive postulations are inferred by Tolman from the behavior of rats in experimental situations such as maze running. He argues that they are prerequisites for what we call consciousness. Consciousness for him is a unique type of postulation in which the results of an act or a series of acts are anticipated in such a way that a choice can be made whether or not to carry out that act or actions.

> [Consciousness] . . . is a *representation* of results so that the latter can themselves become determiners for or against the act which leads to them. If these represented results are "good," the impulse toward this act can thereby momentarily and suddenly be reinforced; if "bad" it can be weakened. Wherever there is a sudden drop in the learning curve, then there is consciousness. For only by representation of its results (through memory or imagination) could acts hitherto infrequent become thus suddenly and consistently frequent.[42]

By utilizing cognitive postulates, the organism can make shifts from one set of responses to another. Tolman writes, "To make an adjustment to an act is to achieve a representation (based, of course, upon what has happened on previous occasions when this act or similar ones have actually been performed) of the probable stimulus results to be expected from the act."

Tolman's notion of cognitive postulates seems to refer to the same phenomena that Harlow calls "learning sets, Krech "hypothesis," Bateson "deutero-learning," and that experimental psychologists and clinicians label variously to designate the apparent requisites of productive behavior. For our purposes it is sufficient to see that all of these concepts enable us to talk about learning as an active process. The organism brings to the situation a set of skilled responses—and, in the case of more complex organisms ranging from say rats to primates, the organism also possesses the ability to project or map out possible patterns of actions and consequences such that results can be anticipated and present activity modified in the light of such anticipations.

As Tolman emphasizes, this inference is no "mentalistic" theory. Cognitive postulations are inferred strictly from the behavior of the organism. We theorize that the organism must organize its perceptions in a certain pattern or according to a certain map in order to behave the way we observe. If we follow Tolman and like-minded experimental psychologists, we can continue to submit our theories of cognitive structures to a series of experimental tests. Thus we are by no means talking about operations available only through immediate introspection by the organism itself. What we have done is to hypothesize that there is no simple one-to-one determination betweeen the stimuli of the environment and the responses of the organism. Rather the pattern of the relationship is more like one in which the organism initially acts upon the external world in crude ways that are further elaborated through experience until we observe patterns of increasing differentiation of response and recognition. This model given, learning consists of acting on or reacting to variances of physical stimulation that were not recognized in the past.

Bateson records an interesting example of this process. A female porpoise was trained to accept her trainer's whistle and accompanying food as a secondary reinforcement. Each time the porpoise was brought into the training tank she was rewarded only for a conspicuously different piece of behavior. Old tricks from previous trials were not rewarded. Thus each trial began with the porpoise being "wrong," giving the old response that this time did not elicit a reward. After fourteen sessions of this kind, which upset the porpoise considerably, Bateson reports that she showed great excitement and during the fifteenth session put on an elaborate show of new responses which included four actions never before observed in porpoise behavior. The porpoise finally caught on or learned to recognize the training situation as one requiring novel behavior.[43]

What sorts of contingencies would stop or inhibit this sort of learning? Obviously an unchanging and uniform environment would make it impossible. That human organisms are little suited to such contexts is evidenced by the results of sensory-deprivation experiments.[44] But what sorts of conditions produce the familiar image of a changing environment and resistant robot-like humans apparently doomed by the change?

Cognitive Maps

In his article "Cognitive Maps in Rats and Men," Tolman explored some of these restricting conditions in an experimental setting. Here he substituted the concept of cognitive maps for his earlier cognitive postulations. A cognitive map represents a set of criteria about the nature of the experiential world that enables the organism to discriminate among various stimuli and to select those to which it will respond. Tolman writes:

> The brain . . . is far more like a map control room then it is like an "old fashion" telephone exchange. The stimuli which are allowed in are not connected by just simple one-to-one switches to the outgoing responses. Rather, the incoming impulses are usually worked over and elaborated in the central control room into a tentative, cognitive-like map of the environment. And it is this tentative map, indicating routes and paths and environmental relationships, which finally determines what responses, if any, the animal will finally release.[45]

The important feature of this new formulation of Tolman's is that it allows us to distinguish between narrow strip maps and broad comprehensive maps. That is, there are different kinds of maps with different implications for the animal's learning patterns. Tolman's experiments indicate that the narrower the cognitive map the less able the animal (in this experiment, a rat) is to deal with changes in the environment. Either kind of map can be accurate and lead to successful results. However, the narrower the original cognitive map, the less useful it is in the case of new problems. Contrarywise, the wider and more comprehensive the cognitive map, the more adequately it will serve under changed circumstances. Of course, it must be kept in mind here that Tolman is discussing the cognitive postulations of rats running through mazes. While it is relatively easy for him to distinguish between narrow and broad maps, when we use the concept to describe human cognitive structures the discriminations are not so easy. A narrow cognitive map seems, however, to correspond to the kind of cognitive structure possessed by Goldstein's brain-damaged patients.

A narrow strip map is so designated by Tolman because in his experiments with rat maze-running it was established that animals which learned under certain conditions behaved as if they comprehended only the mazeway which led to food. Other rats under certain conditions learned not only the mazeway but also "a wider comprehensive map to the effect that food was located in such and such a direction in the room."[46] Thus Tolman's original use of spatial terms to describe the two types of cognitive structures was justified on the basis of his evidence. But the distinction is much more complex. When applied to human cognitive structures, these terms are metaphorical. Narrow cognitive maps take in less of the world in the sense of fewer discriminated features. That is, one might have a highly abstract, general, and cosmopolitan view of the world which, due to its paucity of detail, would be as "narrow" as, say, a highly detailed view of Gum Stump and environs. Narrow maps have fewer names, fewer predicates, and are dogmatic.

A narrow map may be highly developed in terms of rhetoric, with an elaborate and extensive vocabulary. It may be rich in synonyms, for example, and hide an impoverished stock of names or recognized features of the environment. Likewise a lack of predicates is often signaled by an abundant vocabulary necessary for explaining a complex world with a few distinguishable characteristics. The dogmatism of a narrow map is due, however, not so much to any inherent psychological tendencies on the part of the individual as to the need to defend against the possibility of a catastrophic situation. Dogmatism, rigidity, intolerance, and the like, are the result of a narrow map, not the cause. That is, a narrow map is lacking in information, in terms both of the degree of the map's organization relative to the environment and of the map's utility for detecting environmental variance. It represents an inferior adaptation or a basic incapacity. This incapacity must be handled in much the same way that Goldstein's patients dealt with their disabilities. Much experience must therefore be disregarded or discounted or else the entire cognitive structure would come into doubt.

Individuals with narrow maps apparently learn through conversions, moving from one narrow dogmatic view of the world to another and another as the exigencies of life demand attention. Learning by conversion is perhaps more evident in the political world today than the religious. It works in the narrowest pragmatic sense, but at great individual and social costs. Philip Slater has commented on an American thought pattern that he calls the Toilet Assumption—"The notion that unwanted matter, unwanted difficulties, unwanted complexities, and obstacles will disappear if they are removed from our immediate field of vision."[47] Such removal can become drastic and destructive. Although the possessor of a narrow cognitive map is defending himself against a world with which he cannot cope primarily because of his lack of knowledge, he is dangerous, or potentially so, since the maintenance of such a map logically demands a cleansing and simplification of the world about him.

Character Armor

The destructiveness inherent in narrow maps is directed first against the individual, since certain perceptions, thoughts, experiences, and the like, must be distorted. A narrow map results in various degrees of numbness and psychosomatic disorders. The brilliant but erratic student of Freud, Wilhelm Reich, described such numbness as "character armor":

> The character consists in a chronic alteration of the ego which one might describe as a rigidity. It is the basis of the becoming chronic of a person's characteristic mode of reaction. Its meaning is the protection of the ego against external and internal dangers. As a protection mechanism which has become chronic it can rightly be called an *armor*. This armor inevitably means a reduction of the total psychic mobility.[48]

Reich characteristically maintained that "character armor developed as the chronic result of the conflict between the instinctual demands and the frustrating outer world."[49] This formulation suggests again that the individual is a passive victim rather than active participant in the process of repression that Reich describes.

Despite this oversimplification and Reich's resulting idea that sexual denial is the central, if not the only, cause of character armoring, he does point out the aggression generated in dampening or censoring biological reactions to the environment. This aggression is directed against the individual's own biological system. Further, this aggression is directed against the environment, both social and physical, which is rank with improper stimuli and temptations. While armoring may be successful, according to Reich, for the time being, "it means at the same time, a more or less far-reaching insulation against stimuli from the outside and against further influences of education."[50] This inability to learn from experience is what stands out as the most prevalent indication of narrowed cognitive maps. The biological costs of such an inability are great and should be more thoroughly investigated.

Broad Cognitive Maps

What are the characteristics of a broad cognitive map? To begin, Tolman's designation of the opposite of a narrow strip map as a broad comprehensive map is unfortunate. It seems to indicate that there are simply more things in the broad map. There are more of some things, as we shall see, but a broad map is not somehow bigger. The ideal, then, is not a map that contains everything. A comprehensive map in any absolute sense would be isomorphic with the environment and of no use to the organism. No organism responds to all stimuli either at the same time or even over time. For economic reasons there must be a selection. In fact, stimuli are partially constructed by the organism on the basis of responses available. Once we recognize this, however, it makes no sense then to argue that strip maps are necessary or to ruminate on the terrible consequences of possessing total information or knowing everything. Ignorance is never a virtue despite the occurrence in social-science literature of statements like the following: "Ignorance must be viewed not simply as a passive or dysfunctional condition, but as an active and often positive element in operating structures and relations."[51] That we must choose what we want to know and how we want to know is clear. To talk about such choices in terms of the "functions of ignorance" is perverse. A broad cognitive map is not an alternative means of being ignorant, but an alternative means to knowledge.

Let us take our metaphor further. Suppose we are going on a trip and want a map of the area. What sort of characteristic would we demand of such a map? We want it to be relevant, reliable, precise, complex, and novel. A relevant map is one that is meaningful to us, that is selective on the range of our possible actions. There must be some places on the map that correspond to where we are and to where we can get to. The map may be complete in all other requirements but obviously does us little good if it does not aid in our choice of possible activities.

Relevance is difficult to discuss these days, but the reason is that the irrelevance of cognitive structures requires the defensive patterns of behavior with which we have by now become familiar. Through their proud irrelevance, many academics contribute to the formation of strip maps. Graham Wallas became dissatisfied with abstract political philosophy because it was not relevant to daily political action. He saw that political decisions came to be made on a rule-of-thumb basis by those possessing training in this area. He cites the example of a chief official of the British Colonial Office in the nineteenth century, who was also a professor of political economy at Oxford. Wallas wrote: "Because [Herman] Merivale saw that the political philosophy which his teachers studied in their closets was inadequate, and because he had nothing to substitute for it, he frankly abandoned any attempt at valid thought on so difficult a question as the relation of the white colonies to the rest of the British Empire."[52] An elaborate but irrelevant cognitive map is a narrow map limiting the individual's ability to choose stimuli and develop responses.

A reliable map is, of course, a necessity if we are to base our actions on it. It must be accurate. This requirement is well recognized and demands little comment. We should note, however, that accuracy is a relative measurement and thus we must continuously test our map in practice and modify it in the light of our results. A reliable map is therefore a flexible map, that is, one that can be altered in many ways without disturbing its overall intelligibility. Our metaphor limits us here because any printed map would become unusable if we were to note new details on it. A broad cognitive map must be "written" on in some way quite different from the way we would write on a sheet of paper.

A precise map is one that supplies many elements of evidence. For example, we would want our map to be to scale. Without scale and the resulting elements of evidence which a scale map supplies, it would be very difficult to get to any particular objective or to discover any unreliability in the map. We might drive along and learn to be satisfied with wherever we ended up, but our consultations of the map would be largely ritualistic. The more exacting the scale—say yards and feet are represented as well as miles—the more likely we can plan our movements according to the map's directions and again the more likely we are to discover any discrepancy. Thus precision of detail is necessary to maintain the reliability of the map. Similarly, we would want our map to be complex—to possess many structural levels or units of dimensionality. A topographical map, for example, tells us not only distances but terrain. A complex map might have dimensions or structural levels of distance, topography, vegetation, and geological formation. Each additonal dimension would aid us in making more appropriate choices of routes, given our energy resources and our goals, and under certain circumstances would help in choosing destinations.

Finally, we require novelty of our map. It must tell us something about the area we are to traverse that we do not already know; otherwise we are merely wasting our time. A completely redundant map would be no aid to improving our performance. While novelty is a clear criterion for purchasing a map to go on a trip, it is not clear what a novel cognitive map would be. Perhaps it is clearer to conceive of a broad cognitive map as improbable or unlikely in relation to the environment. If we take a state of high entropy or maximum uniformity as the most probable state of any system, then in contrast we desire a cognitive map of minimum entropy or maximum organization. Such a map would be characterized as one of maximum information. "Information" is used here in Warren Weaver's sense as "a measure of your freedom of choice when you select a message."[53] The maximizing of information would thus entail a sizable repertory of names and discriminating predicates.

A broad cognitive map would make possible a large range of messages, many of which would, of course, be factually false at any given time. In contrast, a narrow cognitive map limits the range of possible messages, and thus at any given moment in time the possible false messages generated are fewer. However, over time, the broad map would generate a greater number of reliable messages and the narrow map would generate a greater number of unreliable messages. In fact, this is another way of talking about fallibility. A narrow map tends to be unfalsifiable in consequence of its logical organization, or its lack of discrimination. Thus it does not generate correcting information. The certainty of a narrow map ends in the chaos of a total breakdown and conversion. The uncertainty of a broad map results in the continuous generation of information leading to restructuring and recoding in the light of current needs and available opportunities. Warren S. McCulloch expresses this complex notion this way:

> We pay for certainty by forgoing information that fails to agree with other information. No machine man ever made uses so many parallel channels or demands so much coincidence as his own brain, and none is so likely to go right. Similarly, our hypotheses should be so improbable logically that, if they are instanced, they are probable empirically.[54]

I hope this brief introduction to the range of issues involved here will lead to the development of a better and more precise vocabulary for discussing the quality of human knowledge and attempting to find out how to improve that quality.[55] So long as knowledge is understood as a purely quantitative problem, we will continue to worship ignorance as a welcomed escape from information overload.

Causes of Strip Maps

Tolman's experimental findings concerning the conditions likely to produce the formation of strip maps instead of broad ones is pertinent here and a useful introduction to the problems in this area. According to him, strip maps are caused by (1) brain damage, as we would expect; (2) an inadequate array of cues—that is, a disguised or confusing environment; (3) overrepetition in original training; and (4) overmotivation or too strongly frustrating conditions during training. We seem to have found here a common ground among the brain-damaged patients, slaves, and dominated individuals. All three possess strip maps of their environment. The slave and the dominated individual have such maps because one or any combination of the conditions 2, 3, and 4 are present in their lives. The narrower their maps the more their responses seem either to be tied concretely to the immediate stimuli of the environment or to be removed from environmental context. In short, the narrower the map the more pathological is the behavior. We can functionally decerebralize the human being—damage his brain, or hers—by (a) deliberately and continuously lying or impoverishing the context; (b) by bombarding him or her with repetitive and extensive propaganda; and (c) by relative deprivation or frustration of that person's needs or wants. These operations are typical of all hierarchical organizations and all class societies based on such institutions.

The cognitive model of human learning has been adopted by some socialization theorists. They argue that all cognitive structures are inherently conservative. Leon Festinger maintains that when an individual encounters information contradictory to his cognitive expectations he will experience dissonance. Dissonance can be caused by being in disagreement with other people, by having to choose between alternatives, by acting contrary to one's beliefs, and by experiencing negative or disruptive outcomes of prescribed courses of action. If the organism learns from experience, then dissonance in each of these cases would likely be reduced by changes in cognitive maps and by trying new activities. For example, an individual could modify his cognitive map, take account of the new information, and alter his activities in congruence with that information. Festinger has shown, through a series of experiments on both human beings and rats, that often the organism will not learn but will use other means of dissonance reduction. Festinger hypothesizes:

> If an organism continues to engage in an activity while possessing information that, considered alone, would lead it to discontinue the activity, it would develop some extra attraction for the activity or its consequences in order to give itself additional justification for continuing to engage in the behavior.[56]

Or put somewhat differently:

> Very often persons find themselves in a position where they must endure some unpleasant situation. The cognition that a person has that the situation is or will be unpleasant is dissonant with his cognition that he must endure it. One way in which he can reduce this dissonance is by convincing himself that the situation is not as unpleasant as it first appeared.[57]

Festinger thus uses cognitive theory to account for a large range of nonadaptive human behavior. His studies seem to indicate that people and rats will go to great lengths to avoid altering their cognitive maps. Like Goldstein's patients, many of Festinger's experimental subjects seemed to be able to delude themselves all the more the greater the discomfort or suffering they underwent. In applying his theory to rats, for example, Lawrence and Festinger found that nonreward, delay of reward, and increase of effort in a learning situation "indirectly created attractions or incentives in the situation." According to the authors, "They do this by creating dissonance in the animal, thus leading it to discover additional satisfactions."[58] When faced with cognitive inconsistency, humans may respond in various ways.

William J. McGuire lists the following ways of resolving cognitive inconsistencies: (1) stopping thought or repressing the matter; (2) "bolstering," or submergence of the inconsistency in a larger body of consistencies; (3) "differentiating," or distinguishing between more important and less important parts of a belief that is involved in inconsistency and showing that only the less important part is inconsistent; (4) transcendence or reconciling of inconsistency at some higher level of synthesis; (5) changing the object about which an opinion is held rather than changing the inconsistent opinion; (6) devaluating peers whose views are inconsistent with one's own or changing one's views; (7) devaluating the task which causes the inconsistency; and (8) bearing and making a virtue out of inconsistency.[59] In short, cognitive inconsistency—which means, after all, only the encounter with unexpected and therefore informative variance—can result in anything from learning or changes in cognitive maps to outright avoidance.

Cognitive Consistency

Dissonance theory and other theories of cognitive consistency assume a motivational drive for consistency. Such a drive would seem to indicate that incongruous perceptions and nonsupportive information would be avoided in order to preserve maximum consistency. That is, the simplest way to maintain consistency would be to refuse to learn. Freedman and Sears reviewed the extensive literature on avoidance of dissonant information and concluded: "Clearly experimental evidence does not demonstrate that there is a general psychological tendency to avoid nonsupportive and to seek out supportive information."[60] Of further embarrassment to dissonance theory are the findings that under some conditions information that results in cognitive inconsistency is preferred to information that would promote consistency.[61] Jerome Singer suggests that a "homeostatic" regulation of inconsistency may occur, which would mean that some inconsistency would be sought, particularly if a state of maximum consistency has been attained. A homeostatic model indicates that inconsistency would be sought for its own sake and not as a means to consistency or "as a vehicle for achieving pleasant instrumental outcomes."[62] For example, "the homeostatic assumption would produce the prediction that, with respect to consistency between expectations and outcomes of experiments, outcomes that are mildly counterintuitive when contrasted with expectancies should be preferred to outcomes that are widely discrepant from expectations."[63]

Another group of investigators, whose approaches to the problem are labeled "complexity theories" by McGuire, have an entirely different notion of motivational drives. McGuire argues that the organism that they assume is romantic and unlike the classic organism that opted for stability, redundancy, familiarity, confirmation, and avoidance of the new. He notes:

> Complexity theory's romantic organism works on a quite different economy. It has a stimulus hunger, an exploratory drive, a need curiosity. It takes pleasure in the unexpected, at least in intermediate levels of unpredictability. It wants to experience everything; it shows alternation behavior; it finds novelty rewarding.[64]

Despite their assumption of a drive for cognitive consistency, investigators are forced time and again to admit that "having inconsistency may be adaptive under certain conditions."[65] We conclude that, depending on the context and the cognitive map involved, individuals will sometimes seek novelty or information that is inconsistent with expectations and will sometimes avoid novelty and deny inconsistent information. There does not exist enough evidence to derive a motivation for cognitive consistency and its resulting cognitive conservatism. Novelty is often attractive as well as disturbing in the sense that other beliefs or even "facts" are made doubtful by its recognition. If the organism is intact and the environment tolerable, learning will take place.[66]

Many of the data generated by experiments in cognitive dissonance show some of the means by which men and animals avoid catastrophic situations. We find in this literature examples of organisms finding new reasons to love their situations when the means and opportunity to change them are not available. We also see people, when confronted with contradicting information, bolstering their images of reality by seeking confirming information, by relating only to like-minded associates, or even by extensive proselytizing. But Festinger's critics have pointed out that all of these findings can be accounted for without postulating an "aversive motivational drive toward consistency."[67] I conclude that such behavior patterns are due to functional decerebralization resulting from narrowed strip maps. Theories of cognitive consistency merely substitute cognitive tyranny for the environmental tyranny of the radical behaviorist. Both result in the image of the passive robot. While one model appears idealistic and the other materialistic, their predications about the course of human behavior are nearly identical and their prescriptions in terms of education and promoting social knowledge call for similar techniques of conditioning, censorship, and conformity.

Conclusion

Feyerabend states, "Epistemology, or the structure of the knowledge we accept, is grounded upon an ethical decision."[68] Herbert Marcuse declares, "Epistemology is in itself ethics and ethics is epistemology."[69] Both statements emphasize the relationship between conceptions of the possibility of social knowledge and possibilities of social interaction. Closed societies generate narrow maps and "closed" minds. Open societies provide the conditions for the constructuion of broad maps and "open" minds. But the decision to choose an open or closed society—or more exactly, a nonhierarchical or a hierarchical institution—is not a "mere value judgment." For to exist with a narrow cognitive map of whatever style is for a human organism to exist as a cripple. In the midst of an epidemic, it makes no sense to reevaluate the diseased state as normal because its occurrence is of high statistical frequency. Nor does it make sense to talk about decisions to be in favor of one state or another. The preference for disease is not rational, nor can it be defended on biological grounds.

At this point we must be blunt and say that to opt for pervasive states of human disease is a decision in favor of death over life. We cannot tolerate such a decision as anything more than a symptom of a diseased state. Please note that I am not making the claim that those who disagree with my perspective in general or in detail are sick. I am saying that a decision for death and disease is irrational. I presume we all seek health and that the basic issues are those of establishing criteria of human health and health-producing contexts and institutions. As A. T. W. Simeons put it, "If [man] wants to free himself of the threat of psychosomatic suicide, he will sooner or later have to perform the painful operation of allowing new insights to criticize what he has hitherto considered the acme of his wisdom."[70]

5   The Functions
of
Theory in Knowing

> What is needed is the development of a methodology which allows for, and perhaps even demands, the use of our imagination.
> —P. K. Feyerabend

Active Learning

If knowing is something we do instead of something that happens to us, then knowledge is something we make, not something waiting to be discovered. Learning, then, is not looking or absorbing, but is a complex process of formulating solutions to the problems created by the confrontation of organic needs with the conditions of the environment. According to David Krech, "Learning consists of changing from one systematic, generalized, purposive way of behaving to another and another until the problem is solved."[1] The content of knowledge is not anything like a filmed or taped recording of environmental objects and events encountered by the organism. Baconian cleansing and polishing of the mind, even in the more modern form of logical positivism and logical empiricism, do not lead to wisdom.

Indeed, we have come to the point where we must declare that we cannot and do not learn by simply wandering humbly about with our eyes bulging, nostrils flaring, and skin tingling. We must emphasize this obvious point just as men at the beginning of the modern era had to assert emphatically the equally commonplace idea that we cannot learn by simply reading books and citing hallowed authorities.

J. Z. Young writes:

> Many of our affairs are conducted on the assumption that our sense organs provide us with an accurate record, independent of ourselves. What we are now beginning to realize is that much of this is an illusion; that we have to learn to see the world as we do.[2]

To emphasize this last point, Young offers the example of the congenitally blind who can be restored to sight with surgery. After recovery from the operation the patient opens his eyes to see

> only a spinning mass of light and colours. He proves to be quite unable to pick out objects by sight, to recognize what they are, or to name them. He has no conception of a space with objects in it, although he knows all about objects and their names by touch. "Of course," you will say, "he must take a little time to learn to recognize them by sight." Not a *little* time, but a very, very long time, in fact, years. His brain has not been trained in the rules of seeing. We are not conscious that there are any such rules; we think that we see, as we say, "naturally." But we have in fact learned a whole set of rules during childhood.[3]

These rules constitute, Young continues, "a way of life—a way of seeing, talking, and behaving, which we rely on for the satisfaction of our needs."[4] Other experiments indicate that human infants do have an innate capacity to perceive form, but it must be developed through experiences.[5] Riesen's experiments with chimpanzees raised in darkness points to a similar conclusion.

> The prompt visual learning so characteristic of the normal adult primate is thus not an innate capacity, independent of visual experience, but requires a long apprenticeship in the use of the eyes.[6]

The "rules" of seeing are revealed by various optical illusions that depend for their effectiveness on disguising a set of visual cues to closely resemble a different spatial situation. A classical example is the Ames room (after Adelbert Ames, Jr.), in which figures appear to be gigantic or lilliputian rather than close or distant. Demonstrations of this sort indicate that

> perception is a functional affair based on action, experience and probability. The thing perceived is an inseparable part of the function of perceiving, which in turn includes all aspects of the total process of living. This view differs from the old rival theories: the thing perceived is neither just a figment of the mind nor an innately determined absolute revelation of a reality postulated to exist apart from the perceiving organism. Object and percept are part and parcel of the same thing.[7]

In the case of these constructed illusions, experience in the form of trying to touch objects or otherwise perceive them leads to a correct spatial perception based on an altered set of assumptions or rules congruent with the abnormal situation. Ittelson and Kilpatrick hypothesize that in visual perception "the subject relates to the stimulus pattern a complex probability-like integration of his past experience with such patterns."[8] Thus, "the world each of us knows is a world created in large measure from our experience in dealing with the environment."[9]

Neither our experience nor that of any animal is lived in a haphazard or "trial and error" manner. David Krech found that the apparent randomness of rat maze learning was due to the fact that mazes were so constructed that any consistent right-hand or left-hand orientation on the part of the learning animal would lead to correct choices on an average of 50 percent of the time. Thus systematic responses by the learning animal showed up statistically as pure chance when the animal's error curve was plotted. Corrected for this, Krech's results indicated "that the animal is from the very first behaving in a *unified, systematic* manner,"[10] and that the learning process contains little haphazard behavior. Krech summarizes his view of the learning process this way:

> The animal, in adjusting to a change in his environment (learning), goes about it in an orderly, systematic manner. To the animal any new situation is not a confused, meaningless conglomeration of sensory impressions to which he makes confused, meaningless, uncoordinated, and unrelated responses. The animal is not altogether a victim of his immediate environment in the sense that each specific reaction is the result of a specific, momentarily-acting stimulus. He brings to each new situation a whole history of experiences. These experiences the animal is ready to apply. *From the very beginning,* perhaps, the animal goes about solving his problems in a straightforward, comprehensive manner wherein each response is not to be considered as a *Ding an sich* but as a meaningful part of his total behavior. The animal, in executing a series of movements which we call "perfect," "errorless," "learned," "integrated," is not doing something which has arisen from a series of "imperfect," "unintegrated," "chance," responses. He is now merely running through a different set of integrated responses, which series of integrated responses were preceded by other just as integrated responses.[11]

Krech labels such responses "hypotheses." The term *hypotheses* is chosen because it carries with it the following characteristics: systematic behavior; purposive behavior; abstract behavior; and behavior not dependent upon the immediate environment for performance.[12]

Each of these perceptions undermines the assumptions of naive empiricism and passive human organism that it implies. We see that learning can take place when the organism undertakes initiatory activity within the environment. In some animals, this initiatory activity may range from instinctive responses to loose patterns of exploratory behavior. In the human animal, initiatory activity is often of symbolic or verbal form, and more independent of the immediate environment. Such initiatory activity we will call abstract. In human beings, learning begins with behavioral postulates that range from crude general sets of habits somewhat like those of Krech's rats to the systematic, purposive, and articulated conceptual framework of a modern scientist. Behavioral postulates most basically are a patterned set of anticipatory responses which can be quite simple, or a hypothesis; more complex, or an explanation; extended in complexity and application, or a paradigm; and inclusive, or an image. The actual set of postulates which we infer from observation of activities we will call the individual's cognitive map. Actual statements of the map will be designated theories, whether they be simple hypotheses, complex paradigms, or inclusive images.

Learning consists of increasing the organism's repertoire of responses, which can be understood as an enrichment of the organism's cognitive map, possibly resulting in new postulates. While a response may be simply added to the given repertoire, alterations in the cognitive map are organizational, and the resulting postulates may be quite different from and in conflict with those of the past. Put another way, the addition of certain responses such as skills precludes the possibility of adding other responses. As a result, a cognitive map will become more specific (more discriminatory), more complex, and more reliable in terms of particular aspects of the environment. The final cognitive map will be unique to the organism's responses and discriminations and to the particular features of the lived environment. Learning is thus a process of differentiation. James J. Gibson and Eleanor J. Gibson offer this description:

> We learn to perceive in this sense: that percepts change over time by progressive elaboration of qualities, features, and dimensions of variation; that perceptual experience even at the outset consists of a world, not of sensation, and that the world gets more and more properties as the objects in it get more distinctive: finally, that the phenomenal properties and the phenomenal objects correspond to physical properties and physical objects in the environment *whenever learning is successful.* In this theory perception gets richer in differential responses, not in images. It is progressively in greater correspondence with stimulation and not in less. Instead of becoming more imaginary it becomes more discriminating. Perceptual learning then, consists of responding to variables of physical stimulation not previously responded to.[13]

Further, learning is an organizing process. It does not result simply in an increased repertoire of habits but in an increased capacity to adapt to environmental changes. Learning, according to Harry Harlow, results in the formation of sets:

> The learning of primary importance to the primates, at least, is the formation of learning sets; it is the *learning how to learn efficiently* in the situations the animal frequently encounters. This

learning to learn transforms the organism from a creature that adapts to a changing environment by trial and error to one that adapts by seeming hypothesis and insight.[14]

Learning does not result either in a welter of images, concepts, and memories decorating each percept with a profusion of associations, nor in a series of forced automatic reflex responses to specific stimuli. Learning is not a process of simply accumulating ideas or reflexes. It is a process of increasing the organism's capacity to adapt through greater differentiation of the cognitive map. The resulting complex, precise, and reliable map is inferred from the flexible and rich repertoire of actions available to the organism.

An intriguing paper by D. M. McKay is most useful in clarifying the distinction between conceiving the act of knowing as a passive reception and the act of knowing as an active response. McKay speculates on the design of an intelligent automaton "required to react within its field of activity as if it knew the current state of that field."[15] Such an automaton would require some form of physical representation inside the mechanism. This could be obtained in two ways. In the first, the final symbolic representation of the environment would be "a kind of filtrate of the input signal."[16] In the second, the input would not simply be coded or symbolized, but would "stimulate an 'imitative' internal response-mechanism, designed to adapt its activity to match or counterbalance internally what is received" through sensory devices.[17] That is, the second automaton would continually modify its internal representational activities to match the incoming signals.[18] Further:

> In the first the conceptual framework is predesigned, and "thinking," if such we call it, is confined to its categories. In the second the conceptual framework evolves to match the stationary statistical features of the world, and new hypotheses—in the form of tentative organizing routines—are always being framed.
>
> If, moreover, the abstractive system is allowed to include in its data the activity (at various levels) of its own organizing routines, we have the possibility of symbolic activity representing in effect metalinguistic concepts. It is difficult to set any limits to the types of conceptual activity that are thus within the scope of an automaton on this principle.[19]

McKay continues his exercise by noting that "the operational equivalent of an event of perception in the second case is the framing of a satisfactory internal matching-response."[20] He concludes:

> An automaton designed on statistical principles, which can evolve an internal organizing routine to respond adaptively to regularities of its sensory input, is capable in principle of developing its own symbols for concepts of any order of abstraction, including metalinguistic concepts, without prior instruction. Any

resemblance between such an automaton as described and the human brain is scarcely coincidental, but is logically inadmissable as evidence.[21]

McKay's final automaton is capable both of abstraction and of creating theories. In other words, it is capable of the kind of learning that we are attempting to describe and differentiate from, say, receiving instructions and acquiring reflexes. That human beings do receive instructions and do acquire conditioned reflexes is not to be denied. Nor is the experimental and clinical work of men investigating these kinds of learning to be ignored—men such as I. P. Pavlov, Sigmund Freud, and B. F. Skinner. However, to attempt to reduce the active kind of learning we are here describing to a stimulus-response process of any kind is to distort and even ignore much of our knowledge of human behavior and human capacities. Reductionist behaviorism ignores Harlow's principle that "the results from the investigation of simple behavior may be very informative about even simpler behavior but very seldom are they informative about behavior of greater complexity."[22] As we shall see later, there is reason to believe that the human brain works along principles like those of McKay's machine.

Theory and Knowledge

Theory is a prerequisite of knowledge and the quality of our theorizing is one of the determining factors in the quality (or degree of differentiation, responsiveness, and productivity) of our knowledge. The preceding experimental studies, psychological theories, and cybernetic speculations can be summarized this way. Or we can turn to the enterprise of scientific knowing and find that many scientists and philosophers of science emphasize the necessary role of theory in the process of discovery. As N. R. Hanson states it:

> Physical theories provide patterns within which data appear intelligible. They constitute a "conceptual Gestalt." A theory is not pieced together from observed phenomena; it is rather what makes it possible to observe phenomena as being of a certain sort, and as related to other phenomena.[23]

Feyerabend characteristically makes a more extreme statement:

> It is conceptual possibilities we must investigate when we want to understand science or knowledge in general, and not "facts," "results of observation," and the like.[24]

Unfortunately the necessity of theory in the quest for knowledge has become a mechanical dogma. The fault lies with philosophers of the logical positivist school who seem to promise instant science if only researchers would formulate theories, deduce hypotheses, and rigorously test them. Where the theories come from is of no interest so long as they are formally stated in an exact language with a precise syntax.[25] In the social sciences this view has become popular because the testing of any and all trivial propositions can be justified as advancing science. Such testing of trivialities has been called by Muzafer Sherif a "technician's sport" that merely apes the supposed activities of physical scientists.[26] Doing science by analogy may be productive of professional papers but is unlikely to further knowledge, for what we learn from the testing of theories is no better or worse than the significance, novelty, and relevance of the theory at stake. The mechanical testing of anything we might imagine to be the case is busywork at best and at worst is a means of defrauding the National Science Foundation.

A theory, as we have noted, is a symbolic articulation of cognitive maps at various levels of abstraction and specificity, that is, a hypothesis, an explanation, a paradigm, or an image. A theory is a part (a verbal part) of the human being's organized response to self-selected stimuli in the environment. The other parts are skills in the form of appropriate muscular movements and the neural patterning we have labeled cognitive maps. Theories are written or spoken. Skills are demonstrated in action. Both are open to immediate inspection, but as we have noted, cognitive maps are inferred, being based on our analysis of stated theories and demonstrated skills. The three elements—verbal (or symbolic) statements about objects and relationships, muscular skills (both productive and social), and neurophysiological patterns of recorded experience—constitute what I will call knowledge. A theory, then, is something which human beings create. Theorizing is an activity, although a verbal activity. Like any action, theorizing has an impact on the individual's cognitive map, thus possibly increasing the range of available responses and, therefore, the range of potential perceptions. This is the meaning in Hanson's statement that "seeing is a 'theory-laden' undertaking. Observation of x is shaped by prior knowledge of x."[27] A good theory enables us not only to see the world in new ways but also to see the world better, that is, in a more organized and differentiated manner.

The form of a theory is a set of concepts related by a consistent body of rules. More simply, a theory is a statement in which names are related with regularity. Thus even declaratory sentences and questions are theories, although of such a low level of abstraction and so specific that we seldom consider them as such. A theory can be thought of as analogous to a light in the darkness. It illuminates certain features of the world, making them amenable to human consideration and use. These features are there whether or not the light falls on them, but in the dark they are more likely to be bumped into with possibly harmful results than foreseen or searched out. Some theories are dim, others brilliant, some crepuscular like moonlight, others focused tightly like searchlights, and some are so ill-aimed or irrelevant that they reveal nearly as little as no light at all.

By being able to state our cognitive postulates in verbal or other symbolic forms, our species is more capable of working directly on the organization of our cognitive maps. This capacity helps to free us from a total dependency on the contingencies of environmental events for the development of knowledge. Such articulation also makes social or cooperative learning possible on an immense scale. By further modeling our inventory of available responses, it enables us to strategically select our future experiences.

Intelligibility The functions of theory are three: intelligibility; prediction; and discovery. Theories make the fragmented world of immediate experience intelligible (or meaningful) by naming phenomena. As the archeologist V. Gordon Childe writes:

> Naming a thing objectifies it and asserts its existence. Whatever is named exists for the society that names it and uses the word. "To exist" is here used operationally. The last assertion may be restated as follows: Members of the society that name a thing and use the symbol will take account of the named thing in their actions and will adjust their behavior to it.[28]

Theories fulfill the function of intelligibility by serving as a vocabulary of public discourse. More complex cognitive patterns arise in the members of a community as they are able to articulate their own postulates and describe their actions, motives, and goals.[29] The resulting communal vocabulary makes possible collective action based on complementary activities and viewpoints, rather than on mass conformity of movement, as is the case of herding animals, or on genetic specialization, as is the case of social insects.

For human beings the world becomes intelligible as it is labeled and described, and many theories are no more than "a set of pigeon holes, a filing cabinet in which facts can accumulate."[30] A labeled world appears to be an explained world. Thus the least abstract and the most specific of theories are languages, and when utilized as explanations such languages constitute mythologies.

Theories state more or less approximate models of the physical patterns of events and objects in the world. Of course, we cannot step back and make a neat comparison between our theories and the real world, for it is the constitution of what is real that is at stake. This difficulty has led many thinkers to claim, as Meehan does, that "the universe in which man lives is created by man and not discovered."[31] Such a view is mistaken or at least overstated. Much of the human universe is created and certainly human knowledge is a product of the species. But such knowledge is intentional and purposive knowledge of something, and we can say a good deal about what that something is. That human knowledge is problematic does not mean that the universe is problematic. We create our knowledge of the universe, not the universe itself. This distinction means that the goal of our theories is not just an accurate and parsimonious picture of reality, but the formulation of problems and their solutions which are significant in terms of human life. As Popper states it:

> We do not merely want truth—we want more truth and new truth. We are not content with "twice two equals four," even though it is true: we do not resort to reciting the multiplication table if we are faced with a difficult problem in topology or in physics. Mere truth is not enough; what we look for are *answers to our problems.*
>
> Only if it is an answer to a problem—a difficult, a fertile problem, a problem of some depth—does a truth, or conjecture about the truth, become relevant to science.[32]

This seems to be the point that Meehan wishes to make also. For he asserts that "what is most needed is a set of procedures of inquiry that will force attention to serious omissions or discrepancies and an orientation to testing that can produce suitable modifications in existing practice."[33] The knowledge that we seek is practical and hence historical and context-bound. Its quality or truth is reflected in the quality of human life. We can summarize our position with Popper's statement that "science starts from problems, and not from observations."[34]

Prediction Jurgen Ruesch notes:

> The scientist has to rely upon theory, because only few events are accessible to direct observation or measurement. The majority of processes in nature or within the human being himself are either so slow or so fast that they escape perception.[35]

A theory, then, is a conjectured pattern of objects and events, goals and procedures. If a theory is not to be trivial, it is conjectured in terms of the possibility of action. This conjectured pattern is improved in terms of its complexity and precisions through social collaboration based on the articulation of a wide range of cognitive postulates. Childe insists:

> Patterns are not perceived, their abstract outlines have to be discovered. Perception is a private affair; the discovery of general outlines of patterns contained therein is the result of social cooperation and it is society that objectifies the categories thus discovered.[36]

This function of theory we normally call "prediction," meaning that stable patterns persisting through time have been discovered and described in such form that plans, operations, and other actions can be based on them. A successfully predictive theory says crudely: "Do this, and get that result." Success discloses only that the pattern designated falls within the limits of reality, not that it exhausts reality or that it is isomorphic with reality.

This relation of prediction to reality can be illustrated by the following anecdote demonstrating the fallacy of affirming the consequence. I found the basic outlines of the story in a news item in the *San Francisco Chronicle* several years ago. I have elaborated it as a teaching aid.

> A young speeding motorcyclist in Los Angeles struck the side of a moving car. The motorcycle was demolished and the car badly damaged. The rider, Miggs, suffered only minor scratches. He explained the event this way: "I wasn't killed, because I'm invulnerable." His friends scoffed. Miggs replied that he would test his theory. "I'll walk into a moving car. I predict the car will be damaged and I will not be hurt." The young man carried out his test with witnesses present. As a result a car was damaged and Miggs again escaped injury. But still many of his friends were not convinced, while others had to admit the plausibility of his theory, which had now sustained two successful experimental tests. The scoffers so upset poor Miggs, raising doubts about his methodology and experimental design, that he was forced to attempt a third test. "I'll stand on the tracks in front of the 6:30 Southern Pacific fast freight. I predict a major train wreck and no damage to myself." The test was duly carried out and so was Miggs. His prediction failed, and for all thinking men, his theory was proven wrong.

This story illustrates the notion that theories are never verified, but if rightly constructed and sufficiently tested, will ultimately be falsified and subsequently replaced by another or other theories. There is no such thing as a certain theory except insofar as a theory is emptied of empirical content. Theories are always partial and, in an absolute sense, wrong.

Thus Childe maintains that our theories must always be partial because: (1) The limited symbol-processing capacity of the human brain and human organizations requires that information be coded at a high level of abstraction. (2) Change is ubiquitous in the environment and many events occur and phenomena exist beyond the human sensory capacity; specifically, some things, like electrons, are too small; some events are too fast or are drawn out over many human generations; and some features of the environment are too fine to be discriminated. (3) And the patterns of relationships in the physical environment are more complex than is our neural capacity for modeling them.[37]

It is somewhat misleading to state that theories have a predictive function. The goal of scientific knowledge is not to be able to specify or predict anything or everything that is going to happen in the future. That goal implies something we do not and probably cannot know—that the universe is deterministic. Further, as a goal it does not provide us with a practical criterion for judging the worth of our theories, since complete prediction entails total knowledge of all past events and relationships. We can labor in vain for years with poor theoretical constructs like those of the Skinnerian school of behaviorism, ignoring (or rather excusing) our failures to specify stable patterns suitable as a basis for action on the grounds that we do not yet have total information. This excuse is the same as claiming that we will know (or predict) the future when we will know it.

However, as a means of pretesting our theory, we may wish to see whether it can predict occurrences in the controlled conditions of the laboratory. But we can test only restricted or even trivial parts of our theory under these conditions where something like "total" information is available to us. Successful laboratory predictions (requiring, of course, extensive formalization and rigor) indicate that our theories are a reasonably sound basis for action.[38] Whether or not they actually are sound requires testing them in practice and being willing to modify them or adopt alternative theories if they partially or wholly fail to furnish helpful results. When we claim that a theory is predictive we usually mean that it has stood up under laboratory testing and may therefore be a likely model of some actual pattern of events in the universe.[39] If it were not for the extensive use of predictability as a criterion for scientific theories, I would suggest our stating more accurately that our theories are best constructed to reveal stable patterns of events, relationships, and phenomena.

Discovery "Every physicist forced to observe his data as in an oculist's office finds himself in a special, unusual situation. He is obliged to forget what he knows and to watch events like a child,"[40] writes N. R. Hanson. His remark points to the third function of theory—to provide us with a schema of investigation that leads us to look in places and for things which are not immediately available to our senses and which often require the construction of special apparatus.

Theories lead to discoveries, provided we take them seriously enough to plan our actions upon them and are sensitive to their failures. When formulated rigorously with great precision of detail, theories also enable us to detect minute variances in the environment and thus lead us to increase our range of perceptual discrimination—that is, to see more and to see in finer detail. We can conceive of this aspect of theories as sets of expectations (or more simply, sets of questions) which, when successful, lead to the discovery of new entities like the positron or new objects like the planet Uranus (to cite classic examples), and when unsuccessful, lead to more accurate and reliable models of the environment.

Uses and Abuses of Theory The old story about the four blind men who encountered an elephant can be employed as an illustration of the uses and misuses of theory in achieving knowledge. The four men encountered the elephant from four different positions or perspectives. The first man, running his hands along the elephant's trunk and being told that he was touching an elephant, said, "elephants must be very like large snakes." "No," replied the second blind man who encountered a leg, "an elephant is like a tree." "Oh no," enjoined the third, who had run into the elephant's side, "this animal is much more like a wall." "You are all wrong," declared the last man, who had grasped the elephant's tail. "Elephants are much like ropes." Their situation is like the human species vis-à-vis the physical environment, or like modern man vis-à-vis the complex societies and institutions within which he lives. That is, the objects of our knowledge are more extensive and complex than our sensory apparatus.

Just as the blind men can feel only a specific part of the elephant at any one time or place, so we encounter our social and physical environment in bits and pieces. Upon our encountering something new and disturbing, like the elephant for the blind men of the story, we interpret our immediate data in the light of past experience. Initially we use a metaphorical language—x, the unknown, is like y, the known—to describe what we have encountered, just as the blind men do. But having come at the object from different positions and experiences, our perceptions will differ according to our perspectives. But each perspective is quite reasonable (even if somewhat random, as in our example) because it is part of one's history or life and, therefore, is at least partially valid or one would not have survived.

Given our perspectives and our initial metaphorical descriptions, the next step is to communicate our findings. This is important precisely because of the limitations of our senses and our perspectives. The worst thing we can do at this point is to attempt to hammer out a consensus. For example, the first and last blind men might agree that an elephant is a snakelike animal, thick and muscular in places but thinning out at one end, and thereby override the others. The result is an erroneous conception of elephants and a loss of valuable data.

It is better to assume that everyone is both somewhat correct and somewhat in error, that is, since no two perceptions of the object are identical, take them to be complementary—equivalent or different aspects of the same phenomenon. The blind men could test this assumption by exchanging places and discovering that when number 1 stands here the elephant is like a snake, but when number 1 stands in number 2's spot the elephant is like a tree, and so on. Having ascertained the equivalency/complementarity of their descriptions, the blind men would now have some idea of the complexity and extent of the object "elephant," and a vocabulary (albeit not a very precise or exacting one) with which to discuss it among themselves. They could venture further to make and test predictions like "If an elephant is like a snake, then if I feel along this portion long enough I will encounter a small triangular head." This pretesting and reformulation of the model of the elephant might proceed until the men were mutually satisfied that they knew enough about elephants to act on or with them. This conclusion, of course, would lead to series of discoveries involving the blind men's new ability to get places not previously available to them.

The story is intended only as an illustration, not as a methodological formula. It makes the point that even though theories which are initially a bit silly can still be useful and even indispensable to cooperative efforts at creating knowledge. Although each blind man, in time, might gather sufficient data to construct a reasonable notion of elephants and their behavior, the process would be long and treacherous. Cooperative knowing is faster and more accurate. And cooperative knowing demands theoretical articulation. At many points in the story false theories, errors, dogma, and myth might result. There is no methodological guarantee of reliable knowledge, but having some idea (or model) of the process in which we are involved would seem to help our efforts.[41]

The inexhaustibility of environmental detail and pattern is something that we most often ignore or take for granted. Such inexhaustibility does not mean that the physical world is unknowable or unordered, but only that its range of variance and complexity of structure is greater than our sensory and neural capacities. That four blind men will attain only a very imperfect picture of the elephant does not mean that the elephant is essentially an ambiguous or imperfect sort of animal. All human knowledge is partial. Partiality implies not that the search for truth is futile, only that it is endless. Truth—accurate, detailed, and relevant knowledge—is a product of continuous learning. The image of truth as a fixed set of eternal and immutable laws, like the theorems of Euclid's geometry, has its source in the need for the restriction and management of knowledge required by hierarchical social forms. The concept of absolute truth represents an abstract description of the ideal conceptual structures of hierarchical organizations, because it implies the end of learning.

Theorizing as a Bad Habit The recognition that theory is a prerequisite of knowledge seems to lead to fears of chaotic relativism and demands for cognitive hegemony. While the freedom to observe and experiment is given nearly universal recognition, it is usually accompanied by severe limitations on theorizing. Theorizing is recognized as fun and pleasurable, but we are warned that, like masturbation, it should be resorted to only on special occasions (if at all) and is likely to lead to insanity or idiocy if we indulge too often. The belief is that if unfettered theorizing were permitted, we would be drowned in speculations and none of these would have sufficient plausibility to induce anyone to go about the task of pretesting and application. Examples offered of this phenomenon are the self-serving and self-fulfilling theories human beings devise to rationalize neurotic incapacities—ranging from the elaborate constructs of paranoia to the conspiracy theories of everyday prejudices and fixations.[42]

Such personal dogmas are not the result of uninhibited theorizing, but of what Anthony Wallace describes as "de-semantication," or impoverishment of cognitive maps. Lacking sufficient predicates and the means or capacity to learn more predicates, the individual is forced to construct quite abstruse and elaborate compensatory fantasies to account for his or her experiences as well as to defend truncated postulates. Such compensatory fantasies are, of necessity, arbitrary and completely relative. Any one story that defends ignorance is as likely or unlikely as another. The distinguishing features of these theories are their extreme reductionism, their unfalsifiability, and their lack of productivity in the sense of leading to new responses and new discriminations. They often conform to scientistic criteria of theoretical adequacy in that they exhibit an economy of premises, logical consistency, empirical adequacy, certainty, and capacity to predict. Indeed, this resemblance has led some psychologists to conclude that the scientific enterprise, at least in its scientistic form, is pathological.[43] Herbert Feigl writes:

> Radical empiricism has a good deal to do with the wish for intellectual security, i.e., with the desire to restrict one's extrapolations to the domain in which they have been thoroughly tested; it also has a good deal to do with the fear of the invisible and intangible. Hypothesis-phobia has often been a personality trait of positivists—that is why they are such *negativists!* The theoreticians on the other hand do not mind living dangerously. This seems commendable as long as they keep their theories open to revision. Fixation on theories is of course a frequent weakness. But rivalry, competition, and fierce criticism are the order of the day and help in the avoidance of dogmatism.[44]

The Struggle for Intelligibility By making a sharp distinction between the "context of discovery" and the "context of justification," one makes the act of theorizing a mysterious, dangerous, and somehow contextless enterprise. The issue is not theory vs. observation, or rationalism vs. empiricism, nor some other dichotomous war. At stake is the understanding that the formulation of theories is a major part of the scientific enterprise. Creating theory is as important as testing theory. Anyone can sit around thinking up theories, just as anyone can peer endlessly at the world. But the construction of theories that are useful to knowledge is a quite different matter. While Hanson rejects the notion that theories are arrived at through Baconian induction, he also argues that "physicists do not start from hypotheses; they start from data."[45] And he adds:

> The initial suggestion of an hypothesis is very often a reasonable affair. It is not so often affected by intuition, insight, hunches, or other imponderables as biographers or scientists suggest. Disciples of the H-D (hypothetical-deductive) account often dismiss the dawning of an hypothesis as being of psychological interest only, or else claim it to be the province solely of genius and not of logic. They are wrong. If establishing an hypothesis through its predictions has a logic, so has the conceiving of an hypothesis.[46]

Hanson calls the search for hypotheses "the struggle for intelligibility" and maintains that C. S. Peirce's notion of "abduction" or "retroduction" is an accurate model of theory building.[47] According to Peirce, from the occurrence of certain facts an inference is made in the form, "If hypothesis A were true, then the surprising or puzzling fact C would be a matter of course." The hypothesis explains or makes a reasonable statement of pattern, including the puzzling or troublesome facts, and therefore gives some indication that it might be true. The hypothesis is entertained only as a possibility, or as Peirce has it, an interrogation.[48] The choice of possible hypotheses is not at all haphazard. According to Peirce, "The best hypothesis . . . is the one which can be the most readily refuted if it is false. This far outweighs the trifling merit of being likely."[49] But adds in another essay:

> It is the simpler hypothesis in the sense of the more facile and natural, the one that instinct suggests, that must be preferred, for the reason that, unless man has a natural bent in accordance with nature's, he has no chance of understanding nature at all.[50]

These two statements might be interpreted as contradictions, but I do not think that interpretation does justice to Peirce's meaning. In his view, the best hypothesis is one that both goes against common sense (or as Feyerabend puts it, is counterintuitive) and is compatable with the experience of the individual. This canon can be better understood if we recall that the source of all theory is our cognitive maps.

The Practical Basis of Theory

We may adopt and adapt an already articulated theory from another field of inquiry, or we may playfully combine and recombine previous articulations and concepts of our own. Even in these cases, however, the patterns of concepts and relationships are rooted in human activity. Many scientists, philosophers, and historians have recognized this human root in one way or another. Benjamin Farrington states this point:

> Science, whatever be its ultimate developments, has its origin in techniques, in arts and crafts, in the various activities by which man keeps soul and body together. Its source is experience, its aim practical, its only test that it works. Science arises in contact with things, it is dependent on the evidence of the senses, and, however far it seems to move from them, must always come back to them. It requires logic and the elaboration of theory, but its strictest logic and choicest theory must be proven in practice. Science in the practical sense is the necessary basis for abstract and speculative science.[51]

Farrington describes periods in the history of technology when theory was "wholly merged in the operations," because of the sharp class division between those with manual and those with literate skills. Theory "wholly merged in the operations" I take to mean theory not articulated by the practioners. For the practitioners of certain skills must have the requisite cognitive postulates in order to produce reasonably satisfactory results, and if these postulates—these theories—are not articulated we must infer them. The sources of the most successful theories in the physical sciences have been the patterns imbedded in productive and largely industrial techniques, as was acknowledged by Galileo, Newton, and Bacon, among others. Agreed, human skills entail much more than machine building and tending, resource extraction, chemistry, and the movement of mass, and more than measurement of spaces and financial accounting. But these skills have thus far been the primary source of scientific theories.

While the patterns of social techniques do inform man's notions of nature, knowledge, and organization, social theory remains largely merged in day-to-day operations. The verbal articulation of social techniques under conditions of hierarchical institutions and relationships of domination is dangerous. For both subordinates and superiors depend for their survival upon their counterpart's ignorance of such techniques. How we manage to evade the noxious demands of our superiors and how our superiors manage to keep us at bay are the essential secrets of our social system.[52] This concealment makes it inviting to look elsewhere for models.[53] Because of the success of the physical sciences, modern social thought has been based on mechanical, geometrical, and mathematical models. The resulting theories have been poor, as we all know.

Despite the fact that nearly any theory is better than none at all, where and how we get our theories is more important than we realize. For example, if we wish to know about matter and energy, industrial techniques are an appropriate and historically successful source of hypotheses and models. When we try to know the solar system, the techniques of surveying, navigation, and measurement have been appropriate. Historians of science often cite examples from the development of cosmologies to illustrate the use of imaginative and fanciful theories in contributing to human knowledge. They point out that Copernicus' heliocentric theory owed much to his neo-Platonic beliefs and cite similar instances in which ideology or mysticism has influenced or inspired successful cosmological theories in the cases of Kepler, Galileo, Newton, and Einstein.[54] Cosmologies probably represent special cases and the focus on them in most histories of science is misleading. After all, the moon or stars do not suffer if our theoretical models of their movements are wrong. But when we theorize about the species and its social institutions, erroneous findings can be devastating.

Plausible Fictions Farrington calls attention to a different tradition of theorizing exemplified by the teachings of the Hippocratic school of medicine.[55] For example, the Hippocratic tract "Tradition in Medicine" begins.

> In all previous attempts to speak or to write about medicine, the authors have introduced certain arbitrary suppositions into their arguments, and have reduced the causes of death and maladies that affect mankind to a narrow compass. They have supposed that there are but one or two causes; heat or cold, moisture, dryness or anything else they may fancy. From many considerations their mistake is obvious.[56]

The author objects to basing science on arbitrary postulates, and to narrowing the range of acceptable causes. He further objects to philosophizing in an area in which sound results were regularly attained and were desperately needed by the sick patients. As he writes, fancy and startling new hypotheses are not admissible in the study of medicine but are appropriate for "dealing with invisible or problematic substances." Another tract in the same tradition specifying rules for theorizing is quoted by Farrington:

> One must attend in medical practice not primarily to plausible theories, but to experience combined with reason. Now I approve of theorizing if it lays its foundation in incident, and deduces its conclusions in accordance with phenomena. . . . But if it

begins, not from clear impression, but from a plausible fiction, it often induces a grievous and troublesome condition. All who act so are lost in a blind alley.[27]

The author of "Tradition in Medicine" castigates the "new method" in science, which begins with the suppositions of hypotheses or plausible fictions. The fad of the intellectual world at the time (the fifth century B.C.) was the doctrine of elements, that everything consisted of hot, cold, dry, and moist principles in various combinations. Earth was cold and dry; air, hot and wet; fire, hot and dry; and so on.[58] As this fashionable doctrine was applied to medicine it supposed that a sick man was one who was under attack by a harmful principle—hot, cold, wet, or dry—and that the right way to cure was to apply the opposite principle—hot to cold, wet to dry, and the like. But reducing a science to principles would destroy its ability to achieve results, according to the author. "It would be useless to bid a sick man to 'take something hot.' He would immediately ask 'what?' Whereupon the doctor must either talk some technical gibberish or take refuge in some known solid substance."[59] But the hot "something" may have a variety of different affects that harm or even kill the patient. Thus it is the specifics of the situation that are important and not the "principles."

Modern social investigators who utilize the "principles" of general systems theory, behaviorism, or of some borrowed mechanical or biological analogy represent a similar instance of trying to found science on "plausible fictions."[60] It is easy enough for a political scientist to prescribe "growth" for a political system but the ordinary citizen is liable to ask the impertinent question, "Grow what?"[61] It may sound enlightening to discuss "inputs" and "outputs," "stimuli" and "responses," or the like, but just as in the ancient example, further questions as to what is meant often result in technical gibberish or traditional platitudes. In the Hippocratic tradition, theorizing is something that must be done with skill, care, and attention to the concrete situation. It is not an activity for the armchair or the library.[62]

Theory as Negation The Hippocratic rules of theorizing contrast with the alternative view that theorizing is somehow an independent, arbitrary, mysterious, astonishing, and negative act. From Socrates to Marcuse and Feyerabend, through Descartes and Hobbes, there exists a tradition that understands the first steps of theorizing to be a negation of the situation—or as Hobbes put it, a "feigning of the world to be annihilated."[63] Sartre, for one, refers to the theoretical capacities of human beings as their "nothingness." Within this tradition have developed many strictures against theorizing too often and too extensively, even as the creative but explosive nature of theory is extolled. Only the few may dare such antics. To theorize on the basis of a few postulates or a plausible fiction, as the Greek physicians noted bitterly, is to ignore the arts, the techniques, the cunning of the species. And yet these mundane activities represent an important aspect of human knowledge and important clues to the limits and features of reality. To despise them deliberately is to render theorizing a hit-or-miss activity. Theorizing in a closet, as Hobbes described it, is an activity in which madmen, morons, children, and geniuses have an equal chance to contribute to human knowledge. Just as we understand that to labor without theory (or without verbal articulation of our cognitive postulates) is to commit ourselves to the contingencies of the environment, so to theorize remote from the arts and techniques of labor is to commit ourselves to a kind of epistemological roulette. The fact that—given time and many trials—something may come of such activities no more affirms their value than the occurrence of rain validates our prayers and dances.

Many contemporary strictures on theorizing—(1) that resort to theorizing is appropriate only when an accepted theory has drastically failed; (2) that the best theories are mathematical or geometrical in form; (3) that theories based on mechanical models are superior; (4) that theories must be immediately statable in a form that makes measurement and pretesting possible; (5) that theories must be empirical, meaning congruent with common sense and social institutions; and (6) that theories should be as abstract, objective, and esoteric as possible—result in restricting verbal articulation of cognitive maps.

Theory and Action In the social sciences this restriction has meant an effective divorce of theory and action. People act on a day-to-day basis on their cognitive postulates without the opportunity to increase their knowledge of social techniques and practices through cooperative learning, by asserting and testing the occurence of patterns of events, phenomena, or relationships, or by adopting a schema of investigation leading to discoveries of things not previously noticed or expected. There is a discrepancy between our social techniques and our social theories. Further, when we need to develop new techniques we are at a loss how to proceed and must fall back on chiliastic modes of action that come dangerously near the level of trial and error.

Having labeled parts of our cognitive maps personal, spiritual, irrational, judgmental, passionate, prejudicial, or simply value-laden, and having excluded these from realistic, rational, or scientific consideration, we are not likely to produce many useful or relevant theories in the social sciences. Contemporary political theorists, for the most part, either study the classic theories of the past, adapt models from other areas of inquiry, or play imaginatively with whatever concepts are at hand. The data with which the political theorist should start is that of human life—all areas of it. Not only the ordinary data, but the painful, the problematic, the surprising, the astonishing, and the puzzling data also must be used. Not only the practices of ruling but the defensive patterns with which ruling is necessarily resisted must also be attended to.[64] The continuous contradiction that our rules, ethics, and constitutions exhibit against the actual occurrence of events is, as Marx held, a strategic starting point.

In our present United States political system, too often the dishonest succeed over the honest, the stupid win over the smart, and the poor and misdirected policies seem to drive out those better conceived. To say this means making value judgments, of course. Without value judgments the struggle for intelligibility would simply not occur in the social and political realm. In a social science without value judgments, all that is needed is the continous re-formation of our language to coincide with actualities. We can define "honest," "smart," "well-conceived," so that they apply only to those men or policies which do, in fact, get elected, appointed, or implemented in the given political system. We can call this language manipulation "empirical theory." In this case, "political education" comes to mean "learning to be cheerfully stupid, righteously corrupt, and committed to misdirection."

Such learning is painful and perhaps impossible. It means learning to dissociate ourselves from our actions. We are dismayed at our stupidity, ashamed of our corruption, and uninterested in our politics. To be otherwise would mean insanity. Thus, we act out our private scripts. In so doing we come to deeply distrust theorizing, at least in any practical sense, since it would require us to take our roles seriously and confront their maddening contradictions. But if we consider that lack of theory or poor theory is part of the problem, we may begin to move out of our difficulties.

Theorizing is action and must be judged as any other activity is judged, that is, according to its success or failure in contributing in specific ways to the quality of human life. As Young puts it, "The better our words and symbols become the better we live."[65] Conversely, if we neglect and even distrust our words and symbols, the worse we live. Theory and practice are two aspects of the essential human process of knowing. To divorce them, to attempt one without the other, or to attempt to subordinate one to the other, ends in a loss of capacity to know.[66] Feyerabend writes:

> Experience arises *together with* theoretical assumptions, *not* before them, and . . . an experience without theories is just as uncomprehended as is (allegedly) a theory without experience: eliminate part of the theoretical knowledge of a sensing subject and

you have a person who is completely disoriented, incapable of carrying out the simplest action. Eliminate further knowledge and his sensory world (his "observation language") will start disintegrating; even colors and other simple sensations will disappear until he is in a stage more primitive than a small child.[67]

Social Theory and Social Life Having grasped the practical and instrinsic nature of theory, we must realize that how we make our theories is a matter that cannot be left to chance. Hanson has argued for the study of the logic of discovery or "the way in which scientists sometimes reason their way towards hypothesis" as a legitimate area of conceptual inquiry.[68] It does us no good to understand how to justify theories if the theories we have at hand are irrelevant, absurd, trivial, or otherwise useless in the enterprise of improving action. Marx presented the outlines of the problem in his "Twelve Theses on Feuerbach." He reasoned that an empirical materialism which neglects theory for passive observation gives rise to abstract idealism. Knowing is reduced to either thinking or observing, but is not deemed a practical activity involving the survival and evolution of men. Thesis VIII reads:

All social life is essentially *practical.* All the mysteries which lead theory towards mysticism find their rational solution in human practice and in the comprehension of this practice.[69]

In short, the context of discovery for social theory is social life itself and any workmanlike verbal articulation of the postulates involved in the practices of society can lead to improvements, fertile experiments, and significant change.[70]

Ignorance is a political issue. Ignorance, mystical theory, and human-damaging social practices go together. Social structures that encourage ignorance inevitably come into conflict with the enterprise of knowing. Gunnar Myrdal states:

The hypothesis is that we almost never face a random lack of knowlege. Ignorance, like knowledge, is purposefully directed. An emotional load of valuation conflicts presses for rationalization, creating blindness at some spots, stimulating an urge for knowledge at others and, in general, causing conceptions of reality to deviate from truth in determined directions.[71]

To note that ignorance is purposeful and even functional in certain social structures is not to imply conspiracies of diabolical intent. The maintenance of ignorance is a high, noble, and even moral calling requiring the ascetic denial of the human experiences of social and productive skills. At its best, it requires Plato's philosopher-king. It is nearly always done in the name of wisdom, truth, or objectivity. For, if we deny, in the name of some extrahuman absolute, the essential human sense activity involved in knowledge, knowing becomes the manipulation of ignorance. Elaborate, difficult explanations must be devised to account for the world in terms of a set of drastically limited predicates derived from an economical number of plausible fictions.

But if we admit human ingenuity as well as fallibility, and adopt the principle of explicitly stating our value premises, how we achieved them, and what evidence we have for holding them, we can move toward social knowledge in the sense of more effective and accurate conceptual structures.[72] Then we can cease, as Marx puts it, the interpretation of the world and begin to change it.

Plato's epistemology can be understood as the insistence that without theory there is no knowledge (at least, no deliberate or comprehensive knowledge but only bits and pieces of data disclosed by parochial experience, which he calls opinion). It can be thus understood without adopting his extreme position of maintaining that theory is knowledge. The understanding is difficult to convey, if not impossible, if the practical context of knowing is ignored. Farrington argues that Plato's idealism was the product of a society whose productive activities were becoming increasingly dominated by slavery. Greek society came to despise labor because it was done in the context of degraded human conditions. Work was done by slaves, with slaves, or in competition with slaves. From Plato's time on, the practical context of work seemed shameful and miserable to most political philosophers. Thus Aristotle's conclusion that those who work with their hands could not function as citizens. In our time the workman's situation—be the work material or symbolic—has declined to a similar context of degradation. Work has been degraded by its subordination to the demands of poorly engineered, skill-displacing machines and the codified routines of bureaucratic megamachines. The practical context of work and life has become shameful and miserable. More and more we ignore and despise the practical and productive context of knowledge and move toward idealism. The significance of theory is recognized today as it was in Plato's time. But this significance is joined once again with authoritarian claims.

6   Theory and Dogma

> No content can be grasped without a formal frame
> and . . . any frame, however useful it has hitherto
> proved, may be found to be too narrow to compre-
> hend new experience.
>
> —Niels Bohr

Political Causes and Political Theory

"Fundamental doubt is the father of knowledge," writes Max Weber.[1] Yet we often view such doubt as a painful and dangerous state of mind. With fundamental doubt—the doubting of everything which Descartes prescribed—comes the metaphysical fear of a world devoid of meaning. As soon as anything seems possible, it becomes necessary to establish limits or certainty. Put differently, with the recognition of theoretical possibilities comes the danger of metaphysical speculation. Thus, while nearly all political philosophers begin by doubting existing ideas and practices, they immediately prescribe new certainties and condemn new doubt. Doubt and certainty, imagination and inhibition, seem to go together in man's quest for knowledge. C. Judson Herrick notes that "doubt is the parent of thought" and almost immediately concludes that "intelligence begins with inhibition" and that "thinking in even its highest efficiency consists very largely in the inhibition of irrelevancies."[2] It is not clear whether this description of the process of creating knowledge or learning as a dialectic of doubt and certainty is an accurate model of neurophysiological operations, or the reflection of pathological procedures.[3]

As Wilhelm Stekel notes, doubt and certainty are the polar states of compulsion neurosis. "The doubter seeks *one* static point in the multitude of changing worlds, he seeks *some* kind of faith. . . . The Dogma is the end of doubt."[4] Basic to the compulsion neurosis is a conflict between instinct and prescribed behavior. The individual has the choice of denying his own biological needs or running the risk of social punishment. Stekel therefore maintains that "fundamentally, every doubt is a doubt of oneself." And he further points out that "the doubter is not an unbeliever. As long as he is doubting he is contending with a belief.

He is not a nihilist or a negativist. He is a positive individual engaged in a fight with negative values."[5] Paradoxically, the source of doubt is certainty, that is, closed social structures, their prohibitions of action and thought and their accompanying closed conceptual structures. The failure of practice initiates learning, at least under some conditions. Our knowledge is revealed as partial, faulty, or irrelevant, and we begin the search for information. Thus we learn by adding to, discarding, or reorganizing our skills, our cognitive postulates, and our symbolic statements of pattern that constitute our knowledge of the world. Ideally, this knowledge should be fluid and changing, that is, based upon a broad, complex, and exacting cognitive map. Often it is quite the opposite, tending to be narrow, absolute, and dogmatic. When knowledge is thus frozen and errors continuously suppressed, our cognitive maps become, metaphorically, more brittle and fragile, more in need of defense than of development. Then failure becomes disastrous as the distance between the patterns of knowledge and the data of experience increases until the very possibility of human knowledge seems to be at stake. We talk then of the failure of reason, but not of the failure of theories, premises, plans, procedures, or images of reality. At such times in history men have found it necessary to labor not simply toward correcting, adjusting, or adding to knowledge, but toward creating fundamental knowledge itself. As the old assumed patterns necessary to the detection of environmental variance come to be too problematic to be useful, new certainties seem required in order that learning may proceed, that failure may once again become a means to development rather than a threat of impending catastrophe.

Political Theory and Political Order At such times, during deep crisis and breakdown, the creation of knowledge, the production of theory, and the construction of certainties appear to be identical tasks. These are the usual contexts of production of heroic political theories. Thus theorizing is often seen by both practitioners and audience as an almost superhuman act of creating political knowledge and imposing that knowledge as a cognitive hegemony onto the chaotic world of social dissolution. Sheldon Wolin writes:

> The intimate relation between crisis and theory is the result not only of the theorist's belief that the world is deeply flawed but of his strategic sense that crisis, and its accompaniments of institutional collapse and *the breakdown of authority, affords an opportunity for a theory to reorder the world.*[6] (my emphasis)

But theories do not and cannot order or reorder the world. People order, or rather construct and reconstruct, political institutions. With any task of construction, a theory is a useful, even necessary, guide to such activities. But, being only guides, theories are subject to revision as they are tested in practice. To the extent that we attempt to make a theory "reorder the world" we must represss, annul, and deny reality. Only by an unbounded faith in the omnipotence of thought can such an enterprise be undertaken. Thus it is that the theorizing activity seems to many critics to be a retreat from the world.

The great traditional political theories from Plato through Machiavelli and Hobbes to Marx have been creative responses to massive political failures. Each thinker in his way has seen himself as the discoverer of new knowledge and new certainties in a world where the very capacity to know and to exist seemed to be at stake. While each man failed to construct something totally new, each articulated the experience of his own time of madness, and each added new patterns and new visions of political reality that led in the hands of others to the construction of new institutions and new certainties.

The actions of the political theorist, the reformer, the revolutionary, and even the innovative scientist have been interpreted as pathological substitutes for more rational developmental activites. For example, Goldstein writes:

> Uncertainty and anxiety force the individual into abnormal activities (i.e., substitute phenomena) or into neurosis or suicide. Substitute phenomena reveal their abnormal character, their origin in the abnormal isolation produced by anxiety, by their abnormal stress on *partial* aspects of human action or nature, and by their compulsiveness, their lack of freedom and relationship to reality, to life. Their true nature is sometimes misunderstood because they may have a high value in themselves, as, for example, when they consist in religious beliefs, in valuable scientific ideas, in sacrificing oneself for political reasons.[7]

The difficulty is that the abnormal activities or substitute phenomena—in the thought of men and women who view their task as saving, defending, founding, or in some profound way changing the political world—do in fact contribute to development. While we acknowledge and even appreciate the contribution, it is worthwhile to explore the possibility that development is better served by less heroic activites.

For example, Wolin interprets the activities of the political theorist as those of creating and defending political order. According to him, the political philosopher "must reconstruct a shattered world of meanings and their accompanying institutional expressions; he must in short fashion a political cosmos out of political chaos."[8] This mandate captures well the self-image of most great political thinkers in Western tradition as well as a sense of the identified nature of the theoretical task. But note that the willingness of political theorists to subordinate other values to that of order seems parallel to the compulsive sense of orderliness Goldstein found in patients who had undergone impairment of the ability to make meaningful changes in their environment.[9]

This abnormal stress on the particular aspect of human action that political order represents does not imply that individual theorists were neurotic or brain-damaged. That is not the point. Such theorists have articulated the pressing need for order in the absence of a social and institutional capability for creative or developmental adaptation. Their extreme sensitivity to institutional and social failure, their hope for better political arrangements, and their concern for order are linked. Further, there is a striking parallel between the pathological learning of an individual whom we label neurotic and the pathological learning of social organizations that attempt internal structural and procedural rearrangements in order to avoid environmental hazards.[10] The political theorist participates in this pathology to the extent that he tells us not to see or respond to certain aspects of the environment because of the fatal results he foresees. That is, to the degree that the theorist advocates social ignorance—even as he makes important criticisms of existing arrangements and useful suggestions for improvements—to that degree he is an agent of pathological learning.

Entropy and Permanent Revolution While it is true that no human organization can respond effectively to all aspects of its environment in any finite period of time, it is also true that no human agent can foresee those aspects that can be safely ignored over time on the basis of present conditions. As Proudhon expressed it:

> Be sure of this: no one on earth is capable, as Saint-Simon and Fourier have pretended, of drawing up a system, complete in all its parts, which needs nothing but to be put in motion. That is the most damnable lie that could be presented to mankind.[11]

Wolin writes that "the subject-matter of political philosophy has consisted in a large measure of the attempt to render politics compatible with the requirement of order." He continues:

> Although conditions of extreme political disorganization lend an added urgency to the quest for order, the political theorist writing for less heroic times has also ranked order as a fundamental problem of his subject-matter. No political theorist has ever advocated a disordered society, and no political theorist has ever proposed permanent revolution as a way of life.[12]

This passage has haunted me for many years. First, because it seems to me to capture the concerns and perspectives of the dominant political thinkers in the Western tradition if we exclude anarchists such as Antiphon, Proudhon, or Kropotkin. Second, because I believe that all these thinkers have badly misunderstood the nature of political order in consequence of factors that influence and mold the theoretical impulse in times of social catastrophe. There are three such factors: widespread institutional failures; the breakdown of political and social discourse; and the isolation of the theorist. Each of these is related to the others. The breakdown of discourse is produced by institutional failure. This combination results in a divergence between experience and official vocabularies, making it difficult for institutions to work properly. In turn, the theorist's isolation stems both from his distrust of institutions that are not effective and from the lack of social dialogues.

Though theorists have lived and worked in less troubled times, the factors associated with political failure have molded the traditional picture of the theorist and his task. Despite the weight of this tradition, I believe that what political thinkers from Plato to Marx have been advocating and describing is maximum social entropy with consequent inadvertent disorder and chaos. They have done this precisely because they failed to propose permanent revolution as a way of life. "Entropy" is a difficult concept but it has advantages over the even more difficult concept "order." For example, order is relative whereas degree of entropy can be measured.[13] A craftsman's order might be a philosopher's chaos, but we can establish, in theory, the entropy of the craftsman's or philosopher's working systems without such comparisons. Statistically, maximum entropy is maximum probability, that is, absence of novelty, change, differentiation, distinctions, and the like.[14] In political thinking we can conceive of maximum entropy in the terms of Ellul:

> Entropy, which is . . . a state of maximum disorder, is at the same time the state of greatest homogeneity; when all parties are homogeneous, there is no longer any exchange, and entropy will prevail.[15]

For example, let us compare the disorderliness of three groups of people. One group (Figure a) is organized hierarchically along the lines of Plato's Republic. There are three roles.

(Figure a)

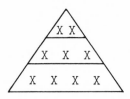

In this group there are nine members distributed over the three roles.

(*Figure b*)

```
X  X  X
X  X  X
X  X  X
```

Another group (Figure b) is organized in a square pattern, with the nine members distributed over nine roles.

(*Figure c*)

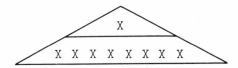

A third group (Figure c) is organized so that the nine members are distributed over two roles. Which of these groups is the most orderly?

Many people would pick the groups in Figures a and c, as these best approximate hierarchical forms. But in terms of entropy, Figure c is the most disorderly, Figure a is next, and Figure b is the most organized. This ranking is the case not only in the formal terms of probabilities but also in terms of homogeneity. Figures a and c represent organizational structures requiring and producing homogeneous behavior. Both require high degrees of cognitive conformity to ensure that common roles are recognized and accepted in common compliance. Figure b is the least entropic, that is, the least probable. Each of its nine members is assigned to a unique role. Such an organization would require not only cognitive diversity but in addition cognitive complexity of a high degree to enable its members to coordinate their activities successfully.

Such organizations might be called egalitarian if we understand by that term that all members are not equal in sameness but equally unique. For example, Morton Fried defines egalitarian society this way:

> It is one in which there are as many positions of prestige in any given sex-age grade as there are persons capable of filling them. If within a certain kin group or territory there are four big men, strong, alert, keen hunters, then there will be four "strong men"; if there are six, or three, or one, so it is.[16]

Obviously this discussion has introduced only the bare outline of the problems involved in conceiving of organizations of low social entropy.

How the roles in them are developed has not been discussed, nor how they are connected, nor how they interact. These aspects must be left for a work of substantial size in itself. The point to be made here is that alternate modes of political analysis and political theory can be developed aiming at the ideal of permanent revolution. What stands in the way of this development is not only the technical and conceptual difficulties involved but also a vast political mythology that reinforces the narrow and erroneous outlook of the past.

For example, a primary political myth asserts that human beings, for various reasons, promote chaos if not controlled, wherefore men and women must be restrained by massive and unitary control systems—whether republican, tyrannical, or mass-based. The truth in the myth is that human beings have a great capacity to struggle against social entropy by striving for differentiation, autonomy, and excellence of workmanship at the same time that they seek to extend and elaborate the networks of social interaction and communication. This struggle can be seen as a promotion of chaos only within the simplistic terms of hierarchical organizational form. So long as we accept that form as necessary and universal and so long as we further base our notions of political order on its accompanying myths, we promote social entropy.

Organizations are the tools of collective action required for the continuing survival and development of the species. They are also human products. As produced tools, they must be evaluated as means and never as ends in themselves. Cooperation is so fundamentally a human capability and need that we can postulate that there will always be some form of organization, some set of social and political relationships, wherever there are surviving members of the species. Social organization may vary in size, complexity, effectiveness, or form, but it is ubiquitous in human affairs. Like the water which so totally immerses the fish as to be unnoticeable, social order is so continuously present that we are numb to its existence, often mistaken in its recognition, and incapable of grasping it in a holistic vision.

The question for human beings is never whether to prefer order over chaos but to decide what kind of order is to be utilized. Debates over appropriate kinds of order and organization have been regularly conducted in terms of my "order" against your "chaos." It is exactly such terms and such outlooks that do produce chaos in the form of social entropy. The human task is to teach others, continuously, the patterns of your own order while learning to understand and appreciate the orders of others. To insist upon the homogeneity generated equally by each doing his or her own thing or by everyone doing the same thing increases entropy. For about the only nondestructive things possible to isolated human beings are the simplest sorts of biological functions, just as the only things possible for everyone to do together are exactly the same kind of functions. Whether a member of a herd or a hermit, persons in situations of social entropy lose their individuality. Such a loss is inimical to both personal and species life.

If the maintenance or defense of order is taken as one of the primary goals of human organizations, and the articulation of such maintenance as a major task of political theory, then the requirements of human health are inevitably distorted, denied, and mystified in the practice of political philosophy. The preoccupation with a purely political order—almost invariably hierarchical—leads to the subordination of human life under a formal and alien ideal. Whether this preoccupation be expressed in terms of a resistance to change, or by a servile adjustment to environmental changes, it promotes political entropy.

I do not charge that classical political theory is some kind of conspiracy against life, only that it has erred in understanding the nature of its theoretical and political tasks. But those errors are such that they have made it difficult to elaborate, criticize, and correct those tasks. Each epochal thinker has been cranky with his predecessors and impressed with his own insight. Progressive descriptions of political problems and solutions to them have not emerged, as a host of unsympathetic critics like to point out. Certainly political theory is not to be abandoned as a human enterprise, nor is the tradition to be despised. But we must not try only to find those basic and pervasive errors in assumptions and perspective that have blocked development, we must work also to understand the particular difficulties which we face in trying to correct them. To charge that political theory has gone wrong because it has not advocated, understood, or investigated the possibilities of permanent revolution is one thing; but to understand why it went wrong, and stayed wrong, despite the efforts of some of the greatest minds of the species, is quite another. This phenomenon demands our intelligence and enthusiasm to explicate and understand. Otherwise we fall into intellectual terrorism—hateful of the past, self-righteous about the present, and incapable of the humility necessary to achieve knowledge.

Thomas Kuhn's Theory of the Development of Scientific Knowledge

It is fashionable in the field of political science to contrast the achievements of the natural sciences with the lack of progress in developing social knowledge. To glean the secret of scientific progress is a popular endeavor. Most such effort has had limited success, since it is the form (rather than the substance) of scientific endeavor—as expressed in the logical expression of experiments, research designs, and mathematical laws—that tends to get picked up from the writings of philosophers of science or of scientists turned philosophers.

Political and social scientists attempting to imitate "natural science" methods are much like the primitive tribesmen of Melanesia. Invaded with the full technological regalia of the industrialized nations during two world wars, the Melanesian culture of the South Pacific was devastated. Many responded to this by forming movements of social revitalization called "cargo cults." The faith of the cargo cultist is that if the last remnants of their old culture are repudiated and if proper facilities are prepared, their ancestors who have mistakenly bestowed their magical wares on the white man will land by plane and ship with cargo. The cultists painfully construct crude replicas of airfields, wharves, factories, radio transmitters, and the like, in the hope that their ancestors will bring them the cargo of manufactured goods and foodstuffs that they have seen pour forth from the transport ships and airplanes of their invaders. Time and again crops are destroyed, houses burned, ritual obscenities committed, and the cargo awaited in vain. With each failure faith seems to grow stronger that if only more people believed, believed more strongly, prepared more extensively, and cut themselves off totally from the old ways, their prayers for cargo would be answered.[17]

Astounded by the successes both real and imagined of the natural sciences, many social scientists in general and "behavioral" political scientists in particular behave much like Melanesian cultists. In their striving to catch up, to make the study of society and politics scientific, they form millenarian sects to destroy and desecrate the practices of the prescientific past and to act out what they imagine to be the method of science. This program can take the form of either crude data collection or premature formalization. Political scientists often ape the language and forms of the natural sciences in the belief that if their faith is strong enough, their repudiation of the past complete enough, their performance of the rituals of scientific method exacting enough, then accurate and detailed knowledge of the world will result. Failure to achieve such knowledge results in renewed calls for more commitment and more extreme measures of repudiation and faith.

But just as Melanesians through chiliastic rituals learn new techniques of collective action and organization, often leading to self-conscious efforts at political independence, so the forays of political scientists into the realm of the philosophy of science have caused the discipline to become more self-conscious of its epistemological basis and the need for the development of an autonomous methodology.

For over a decade the writings of Thomas Kuhn describing conceptual progress in the natural sciences in terms of periodicity have been important to discussions of the need for an order demanding cognitive conformity and motivational homogeneity so that the development of knowledge may take place. If he is correct, then my interpretation of the lack of achievement in the history of political thought is wrong and my advocacy of permanent revolution as prerequisite to social knowledge is mistaken. For those reasons I must analyze his argument in some detail.

Kuhn describes the source of his thesis this way:

> "To the extent that the book [*The Structure of Scientific Revolutions*] portrays scientific development as a succession of tradition-bound periods punctuated by non-cumulative breaks, its theses are undoubtedly of wide applicability. But they should be, for they are borrowed from other fields. Historians of literature, of music, of the arts, of political development, and of many other human activities have long described their subjects in the same way. Periodization in terms of revolutionary breaks in style, taste, and institutional structure have long been their standard tools. If I have been original with respect to concepts like these, it has mainly been by applying them to the sciences, fields which had been widely thought to develop in a different way."[18]

In turn, Wolin has amended Kuhn's idea of periodicity and his concept of paradigm as a means to analyze the activity of political theorizing and its relation to political development. This reciprocation closes the circle, for Kuhn's ideas are derived from the notion that cognitive hegemony is a prerequisite of political and social organization and from the resulting need to account for cognitive change and institutional development by means of a theory of periodicity. First, the political community is understood as requiring cognitive hegemony which periodically breaks down, allowing change. Second, the scientific community is treated as if it were a political community. Finally, the political community is treated as if it were Kuhn's scientific community. The result is a reinforcement of the false idea that social organization requires conceptual and behavioral conformity and that social change requires destruction.[19]

Kuhn's thesis is plausible on the face of it because he conforms to and confirms some of the cherished myths of hierarchical organizations and class society. He does this by defusing scientific knowledge and scientific practice as a basis for attacking traditional political dogmatism. For if knowledge is the result of creative imagination, experimentation, and open criticism, as Popper and others have claimed, then organizations that repress such activities are antithetical to human understanding. It is no accident that Popper is the enemy of Plato and Kuhn at once, for both thinkers are asserting that it is power that produces knowledge. While Kuhn's thesis may be attractive in general because of its familiarity, it founders in detail because it shares all the paradoxes, the leaps of faith, and the ambiguity of the outlook that ignorance is the source of knowledge. I will try to describe these problems, to account for the plausibility of this model of scientific revolutions, and even to appreciate some of Kuhn's insights into the nature of knowledge production under conditions of cognitive hegemony.

Dogma and Science Kuhn's book, describing the development of science as a succession of cognitive hegemonies, each ended by revolution and the foundation of a new orthodoxy, has been widely discussed and very influential in the social sciences. The book contains enough ambiguity to allow varying interpretations. It is in the first place an attack on certain principles of logical positivism and logical empiricism. Kuhn stated this in a discussion of the first published form of his theory:

> The view of science to which my paper objects holds that the true scientist, in the absence of sufficient information, draws no conclusions at all. I have maintained . . . that there is no such option. Unless he is to abandon research entirely, the practitioner of a mature science must commit himself to a set of concepts that additional information may cause him to replace. They are as much a part of his professional tool kit as are his laboratory instruments.[20]

In short, the logical positivists' dictum that scientific statements can be made only about phenomena already observed "forbids the scientist to rely upon a theory in his own research whenever that research enters an area or seeks a degree of precision for which past practice with the theory offers no precedent."[21] Most simply then, Kuhn is reiterating the need for cognitive presuppositions and theory in the enterprise of creating scientific knowledge.[22] At this point, Kuhn is in company with dissenting philosophers of science like Herbert Feigl, Karl Popper, N. R. Hanson, Stephen Toulmin, and P. K. Feyerabend, who reject inductivist interpretations of science and also reject Pierre Duhem's restricted notion of physical theory as a logical summary and classification of experimental findings.[23]

The traditional account of the history of science is of an accumulation of facts and their logical and mathematical expressions. Duhem argues that the physical sciences progress in the following manner:

> The experimenter constantly brings to light facts hitherto unsuspected and formulates new laws, and the theorist constantly makes it possible to store up these acquisitions by imagining more condensed representations, more economical systems. The development of physics incites a continual struggle between "nature that does not tire of providing" and reason that does not wish "to tire of conceiving."[24]

In contrast, Kuhn's view is that science has progressed but is not in any sense cumulative. The rigor, specificity, inclusiveness, and experimental success of scientific theories has improved, according to him. But while many others have made this same argument and concluded therefore that critical and imaginative theory construction was an important part of the scientific enterprise, Kuhn's point is that science progresses by means of commitment to a particular cognitive structure.[25] As Feyerabend notes, Kuhn "defends not only the use of theoretical assumptions, but the exclusive choice of one particular set of ideas, the monomaniac concern with only one single point of view."[26] Toulmin argues that Kuhn has mistaken a logical point, the necessity of preconceived ideas for investigation, with a sociological point, the collective commitment of a community of scientists to a specific dogma.[27] In the give-and-take of criticism and revision of his theory, in which Kuhn has been involved since the mid-1960s, he has been quite consistent in asserting that it is the "community structure of science" which is the clue to progress. He maintains that "the explanation [of scientific progress] must, in the final analysis, be psychological. It must, that is, be a description of a value system, an ideology, together with an analysis of the institutions through which that system is transmitted and enforced."[28] Further, the notion of commitment and conformity have also remained central to his understanding of science. Commitment and criticism are, of course, contradictory, and Kuhn holds that "it is precisely the abandonment of critical discourse that marks the transition to a science. Once a field has made that transition, critical discourse recurs only at moments of crisis when the bases of the field are again in jeopardy."[29]

Kuhn is the most successful apologist for dogmatism. But what makes him successful is that he is not simply an apologist. He is not defending any particular scientific dogma. Nor is he arguing that any dogma is a good or useful thing. His work has been interpreted, particularly by social scientists, to mean that a discipline can become scientific by adopting a particular set of postulates as a cognitive hegemony. Kuhn belatedly repudiated this interpretation.

> I claim no therapy to assist the transformation of a proto-science to a science, nor do I suppose that anything of the sort is to be had. If, as Feyerabend suggests, some social scientists take from me the view that they can improve the status of their field by first legislating agreement on fundamentals and then turning to puzzle solving, they are badly misconstruing my point.[30]

His apology focuses on innovation and the self-correcting operations of the scientific community. He is willing to take on the complexities of the situation of scientific knowing as he sees it, and this willingness results in a number of valid insights, but also in an ambiguity that easily allows, if not encourages, misconstruing. Kuhn throughout stresses the dual nature of the scientific enterprise, that "though successful research demands a deep commitment to the *status quo,* innovation remains at the heart of the enterprise."[31] He has most forcefully emphasized the paradox that "science is both dogmatic and devoted to discovery."[32] In the view of A. Rupert Hall, Kuhn is trying to answer the question: "How is the intellectual freedom which is essential to originality in science to be reconciled with the necessity of adhering to a certain code, to established themes and recognized practices?"[33] This attempt puts Kuhn in the tradition of a long line of liberal thinkers who have tried to reconcile the freedom of the individual with the commitment to consensus on which the democratic state supposedly rests.

His answer to the paradox is quite complex. Kuhn argues that precisely because of the community commitment to what he calls a paradigm (initially defined as "an accepted model or pattern"), failures in the accepted way of viewing things will accumulate in sufficient force to bring the conceptual structure and practices of the community into question. At these times (and apparently at these times only), it is legitimate to search for and propose new theories and new practices. This way of addressing the question is in contrast to the more "radical" tradition of, say, a Jefferson or a Popper, who proposed a commitment to periodic revolutions as a solution. Kuhn also rejects the moderate pluralist-bargaining solution, regarding a proliferation of competing theories and methods as a sign of an immature science. He also declines to limit theorizing by applying the canons of a strict empiricism which holds that a highly confirmed theory "must be retained until it is refuted, or at least until some new facts indicate its limitations."[34]

Kuhn's "commitment to a paradigm" involves what he calls "arbitrary elements" and is not simply a commitment to a set of rules or highly confirmed theories.[35] It is a pretheoretical commitment—that is, it is a commitment to a set of cognitive postulates that are only partly articulated in theoretical statements and rules, but that also include educational models and practical procedures. This commitment results in a "drastically restricted vision," which in turn leads to "a knowledge and understanding of esoteric detail that could not have been achieved in any other way." Thus the "one great virtue to commitment to paradigms is that it frees scientists to engage themselves in tiny puzzles."[36] Normal science or normal research, which is possible because of this commitment, consists of puzzle solving which "seems like the effort to assemble a Chinese cube whose finished outline is known from the start."[37] That is, problems are taken up that are known in advance to be solvable and whose solution is known, at least in outline. This activity might lead to stagnation, Kuhn admits, but he insists that it is doomed to fail.

> Normal science often suppresses fundamental novelties because they are necessarily subversive of its basic commitments. Nevertheless, so long as those commitments retain an element of the arbitrary, the very nature of normal research ensures that novelty shall not be suppressed for very long.[38]

Apparently the element of the arbitrary is crucial to puzzle-solving failure. By becoming a true believer in one cognitive mapping of reality (for partly arbitrary reasons) and attempting "to force nature into the preformed and relatively inflexible box that the paradigm supplies,"[39] the inquirer will experience persistent and detailed failure and a crisis of faith will result. The crisis, in turn, will result in a revolutionary period of extraordinary research, theory proliferation, and philosophical controversy until the community closes ranks around a new cognitive hegemony. John Watkins summarizes Kuhn's view of the scientific community "as an essentially closed society, intermittently shaken by collective nervous breakdowns followed by restored mental unison."[40] Rather than limiting reason to leave room for faith, as Kant supposed was necessary, Kuhn proposes to lift all limits on faith in order to achieve reason.

The Concept of Paradigm Three elements in Kuhn's theory-description require further analysis to fully understand why he believes that dogma can lead to conceptual progress. These are his concepts of paradigms, of normal science, and of cognitive revolutions. Many readers of Kuhn have gone astray by their mistaken assumption that his concept "paradigm" means the same thing as "conceptual structure," "scientific theory," "master philosophy," "intellectual framework," or "world view." This difficulty is largely due to his loose and ambiguous use of the term.[41] Margaret Masterman claims that Kuhn uses " 'paradigm' in not less than twenty-one different senses"—ranging from a myth through a scientific achievement, a standard illustration, a gestalt figure, and a set of political institutions to an organizing principle which can govern perceptions and a new way of seeing.[42] However, from the first sketch of his theory Kuhn has repeatedly insisted that paradigm is more than an articulation of theory or method. He defines a paradigm as "in the first place, a fundamental scientific achievement and one which includes both a theory and some exemplary applications to the results of experiment and observation."[43] Further it is an "open-ended achievement" and an "accepted achievement," in the sense that a group of scientists attempt to "extend and exploit it in a number of ways." He points out that other terms, such as *"theory"* or *"intellectual framework or rules,"* would require an explicit statement, and contends that such statements are not available in the scientific community, nor are they possible. What can be discovered, he argues, is "the particular model achievements from which, at any given time, the members of a scientific specialty learn to practice their trade."[44]

Kuhn's insistence on the role of concrete achievements and actual practice, rather than abstract theory in the process of scientific innovation, is his original contribution to the philosophy of science, according to Masterman.[45] In his "Postscript" of 1969, Kuhn put more stress on this concreteness. He first redefines "paradigm" in a circular manner, thus: "A paradigm is what the members of a scientific community share, *and* conversely, a scientific community consists of men who share a paradigm."[46] He further re-labels this shared thing a "disciplinary matrix" consisting of (1) symbolic generalizations; (2) shared beliefs in particular models; (3) shared values concerning the nature of truth, reliability, and the like, such as norms for good predictions and good theories as well as notions of the relations of science to society; and (4) shared exemplars or concrete problem solutions found in both the educational situation and the experimental laboratory.[47] His stress is now on what he calls, after Polyani, the "tacit knowledge" of scientific practice, or "knowledge embedded in shared exemplars."[48] He now seems to be trying to describe what Farrington called "theory wholly merged in the operations," what we labeled "nonarticulated theory," and what, of course, Tolman first designated as "cognitive postulates."

Kuhn's emphasis on the particular learning-by-doing-exemplary-problems pedagogy of the physical scientists is solidly within the pragmatic tradition. Hugh Dalziel Duncan writes:

> Even in our society the most abstract and theoretical percepts of the chemist or the physicist can be understood only through acquaintance with the processes of chemistry and physics as they are carried out in the laboratory. There is no science whose conceptual forms are not derived ultimately from the practical handling of matter.[49]

That is a succinct statement of Kuhn's major, although not entirely new, contribution to the philosophy of science. In order to account for the occurrence of innovation in the midst of dogmatic conviction, he has to further retreat from the idealistic conception of science proposed by the logical positivists and empiricists. While his analysis points in the direction of paying attention to what scientists actually do, his original concept of "paradigm" and "paradigm commitment" seems to fade in importance or explanatory power.

Kuhn's notion of pretheoretical (that is, nonarticulated) premises on the part of the scientific community is parallel to Tolman's idea of cognitive postulates on the part of individual learning animals. Both are inferences after the fact from behavior. Both the professional community and the learning animal behave *as if* they assumed reality to consist of such and such objects related in certain lawful ways. Thus, at the basis of our most abstract conceptualizations of space, time, ontology, and the like, we find physiological processes in the case of the individual animal and productive processes in the case of a community. Our abstractions are rooted in the daily patterns of existence produced by the interaction of the biological needs and capacities of our species and the resources and processes of the environment. They do not come out of thin air, nor are they products of pure thought or mind. Kuhn does well to recall this basic fact to our attention. For when we ignore or obscure the material processes of our abstraction we lose the route to the improvement of our knowledge.

A paradigm is thus an intervening variable like Tolman's cognitive map. It is something we infer from what a scientific community actually does, but its status is somewhat different from that of Tolman's concept. In theory, at least, an individual's cognitive map should be identical with the stored information of the central nervous system. But it is likely that paradigms represent what Anthony Wallace calls "structural reality," that is, "a world of meanings, as applied to a given society or individual, which is real to the ethnographer, but . . . is not necessarily the world which constitutes the mazeway of any individual or individuals."[50] A paradigm is thus either an observer's reconstruction of the collective postulates of a community or an inverted and idealistic representation of the practices and context of the community's operations. Insofar as a paradigm is shared in the first instance it must be articulated in symbolic forms. Only if it is in such a form does talking about paradigm commitment seem to make any sense. Otherwise this commitment simply means being a member of the professional community. Paradigms in either sense do not make things happen or cause progress, stagnation, process, or anything else. They are rather the results of human actions, communications, and social processes.

Kuhn maintains that paradigms comprise something which accounts for scientific progress and procedures. He writes:

> Having isolated a particular community of specialists . . . one may usefully ask: what do its members share that accounts for the relative fullness of their professional communication and the relative unanimity of their professional judgments? To that question my text licenses the answer, a paradigm or set of paradigms.[51]

While he now considers that answer too simple, his newer term "disciplinary matrix" is not much better than, say, "extrasensory perception," "telepathy," or any other term that would convey Kuhn's *a priori* conviction that dogmatism and the replication of uniformity are a necessary prerequisite of communication and cooperation. Such an approach is a result of what Popper calls the "myth of the framework."

> Kuhn suggests that the rationality of science presupposes the acceptance of a common framework. He suggests that rationality *depends* upon something like a common language and a common set of assumptions. He suggests that rational discussion and rational criticism is only possible if we have agreed on fundamentals.[52]

Despite the emphasis that Kuhn and his supporters place on an "empirical description of what scientists actually do," he has assumed that they must do some things like sharing a common cognitive map of reality and also sharing a commitment to that map resulting in an imperative set of assumptions, rules, methods, and practices. Further, he assumes that somehow all this must result in better knowledge. He does not seriously consider the alternative possibility that it is cognitive complementarity, with its resulting fluid conceptual structures and practical arrangements, that is at the basis of scientific cooperation and progress. Nor does he consider that the dogmatism he finds among scientists is a barrier to the development of knowledge, rather than an impetus. It is obvious that he does not consider such an alternative as possible, wherefore he has not in his researches looked for any of the examples or facts that might support it. In this attitude he is consistent, for his commitment to his own theory allows him to disregard troublesome phenomena that do not fit it. What he thus does not consider is the clue to his failure.

The Concept of Normal Science Kuhn characterizes normal science as puzzle solving. His model for puzzle-solving operations consists of exemplars found in textbooks of science. By "exemplar" he means "the concrete problem-solutions that students encounter from the start of their scientific education, whether in laboratories, on examinations, or at the ends of chapters in science texts."[53] The major feature of scientific education is the exclusive use of textbooks which "exhibit . . . concrete problem-solutions that the profession has come to accept as paradigms, and they ask the student, either with a pencil and paper or in the laboratory, to solve for himself problems closely modeled in method and substance upon those through which the text has led him."[54] The sort of learning produced by this procedure he calls "finger exercises." Kuhn concludes that "scientific education remains a relatively dogmatic initiation into a pre-established problem-solving tradition that the student is neither invited nor equipped to evaluate."[55] These problems are puzzles in the sense that the answers are known beforehand and can be looked up in the "paradigm" so to speak. Kuhn is adamant that this is an empirical description of what scientists actually do.

> For a scientist, the solution of a difficult conceptual or instrumental puzzle is a principal goal. His success in that endeavour is rewarded through recognition by other members of his professional group and by them alone. The practical merit of his solution is at best a secondary value, and the approval of men outside the specialist group is a negative value or none at all. These values, which do much to dictate the form of normal science, are also significant at times when a choice must be made between theories. A man trained as a puzzle-solver will wish to preserve as much as possible of the prior puzzle-solutions obtained by his group, and he will also wish to maximize the number of puzzles that can be solved.[56]

Nothing new is expected from this conduct. Indeed, novelty in the form of anomalies that arise when puzzles fail to be solved properly is to be avoided. The "enterprise seems an attempt to force nature into the preformed and relatively inflexible box that the paradigm supplies."[57] Normal science is dull, pedestrian, and yet highly detailed and precise.

Kuhn's point in this description is to deny that scientists test and criticize their theories as other philosophers of science claim. Rather, the extreme faith and commitment of scientists in their theories leads to their building exceptional and often expensive apparatus, laboring long and hard on tedious details, and learning to experience failure usually as personal shortcomings, not as reflections on the conceptual tools with which they are working. Kuhn admits, "If the normal puzzle-solving activity were altogether successful the development of science could lead to no fundamental innovations at all."[58] For normal science consists in the larger sense of the operations of applying, articulating, and maintaining the paradigm. There can be a succession of paradigms only if there is failure.

Normal science is highly resistant to change, according to Kuhn. The scientists ignore ordinary failures. They ignore anomalies or unexpected occurrences. Their failure to solve one set of puzzles prods them to look for another, more profitable, set. Only massive, community-wide failures lead to the kind of research that results in proposing new theories and methods and the demonstration of new exemplars. This resistance is highly important in Kuhn's view. He argues that there are always counterinstances available to attack any theory, that there are always anomalies, and always grounds to doubt the coincidence of the limits of scientific knowledge with the limits of reality. Kuhn states that "every problem that normal science sees as a puzzle can be seen, from another viewpoint, as a counterinstance and thus as a source of crisis."[59] The fit between any paradigm and reality is so poor that it guarantees failure, to be sure, but also embarrassment. This might lead one either to abandon a good theory before all of its possibilities have been exhausted, or to abandon the scientific enterprise. Resistance produced by community rigidity and commitment supposedly guarantees efficient exploitation of a scientific theory through tenacity, makes possible the discrimination between productive and nonessential failures, and keeps individual scientists from succumbing to the "essential tension" of research and throwing in the towel. If science were a critical procedure, it would quickly destroy itself, for "the rejection of science in favor of another occupation is . . . the only sort of paradigm rejection to which counterinstances by themselves can lead."[60] It is easy to see how some have read Kuhn's work as an indictment of science.

The principle of tenaciously defending theories is not unique to Kuhn among philosophers of science. Again, he is different because he rejects the notion of continuously testing theories and because he advocates the tenacious defense of a cognitive hegemony. But here again, his best point is that concrete relevant practice is the source of productive theory and that such practice is a result of taking theories seriously enough to try them out extensively. But puzzle-solving practice results in puzzle-solving paradigms, and Kuhn plainly never stops to consider that other sorts of paradigms might be more productive of knowledge. He wants to make the point that accepted theories must be replaced by more acceptable theories and not simply rejected. Kuhn states, "Once it has achieved the status of paradigm, a scientific theory is declared invalid only if an alternative candidate is available to take its place."[61] Paradigm commitment or dogmatism means for him that theories will be replaced and not discarded and that new theories will emerge from concrete operations. Thus such a commitment is pragmatic. Dogmatism, fixation, faith, or whatever we call it, works.

The difficulty with such a crude pragmatism is this: The fact that some process or organization "works" does not tell us how it works, whether some alternative might not work better, or whether the observed results are produced by some other processes of which we are unaware. Kuhn's notion that we obtain brilliant progress in the sciences by means of a commitment to mediocrity and orthodoxy is similar to the sometime social-science dictum that stability, efficiency, and development result from bureaucratic conformity and routinization. His account of orthodox scientific practice leading to revolution and change is much like Crozier's picture of bureaucratic organizations staggering from one crisis to another.[62]

The Army-Ant Theory of Organization Kuhn wants to show that, given the commitments of the scientific community, progress will occur, no matter what. That is, it is not dependent in any way on the scientists' understanding of what they are about or on their collective or individual capabilities. The notion that routinization produces innovation, that mindlessness results in insight, or that ignorance is the means to knowledge is based on what I call the army-ant theory of organization. The case is plainly the contrary: that routines inevitably fail, that mindlessness leads always to catastrophe, or that ignorance engenders crisis. Failure, catastrophe, and crisis are often overcome by the brave and creative efforts of men and women. To locate the causes of such efforts in disaster is the essence of the army-ant theory. Such a theory is the logical outcome of the image of robot man and bucket epistemology. No doubt it is an account of human and organizational development. But it is so homiletic and so much a projection of wishful thinking that it is not at all useful as a model on which to base action or understanding.

Let us take a closer look at the living example with which we can grasp the basic failures of this outlook. Army ants are found in the tropical forests of South America, Africa, and Asia in colonies of 100,000 to 150,000 individuals. They live by systematic pillage of their environment, periodically marching out in columns that devour nearly everything in their path. Observers have noted the similarity between the ants' progress, as they move across the jungle floor, and a human military expedition. The ant column wheels to flank, surround, and devour prey like well-drilled cavalry. Naturalists have tended to grant this ant great reasoning ability, and many have been most enthusiastic about army-ant organizational characteristics. What is most strange about the collective behavior of the army ant is that apparently it is a result of far more intelligence and learning ability than any individual can demonstrate. T. C. Schneirla points out that ants have little sensory acuity, learn only by rote, and generally are highly stereotyped in their behavior. He notes that "the individual ant, as a matter of fact, is ill-equipped for advance learning."[63] The actual nature of the ants' extremely simple organizational processes and limited adaptive ability is revealed by an occasional catastrophe. If an ant column encounters a large expanse of flat regular topography such as an asphalt road or an airfield, it will circle back on itself and form a mill. The ants then march in a circle until death. The seemingly complex and purposive behavior of the ant column is revealed by such a catastrophe as incapable of major adaptation.

Schneirla comments: "How the essentially uncomplicated repertory of the individual ant contrives, when ants act in concert, to yield the exceedingly complex behavior of the tribe is one of the most intricate paradoxes in nature."[64] The army-ant organizational paradox is analogous to Kuhn's paradox of the individual dogmatism and communal innovation in the scientific community. The riddle of the army ant has been solved. What holds the colony together is trophallaxis, the continuous exchange of chemical substances. Basically the reproductive cycle governs a colony's behavior. Maturing cocoons and newly hatched ants excite the tribe. The hyperactive new ants turn the colony into a churning throng. As individuals spill out of this throng, their chemical trail is followed by others. At the periphery, the ants try to scramble back but are pushed forward by the relentless mass. The chemical trail laid down by the reluctant advance of the ants at the head of the column is strictly adhered to by the mass. Once the trail is laid the ants swarm forward. Schneirla found that the field operations of the army ant more nearly approximate the principles of hydraulics than those of military science. The flanking and envelopment of prey observed is a result of the continuous efforts of the advanced ants to return to the swarm plus accidents of terrain and the attraction of booty. The ants bivouac at night in living "nests" composed of the ants themselves. At daylight the churning begins and a column spills out again. This nomadic behavior continues for about 17 days until the larvae mature into the pupal state, thereby exerting a "quieting influence" on the ants that handle the cocoons. The tribe then goes into permanent encampment for 20 days. During this time the queen ant produces many thousands of eggs. As the eggs hatch into larvae and new worker ants emerge from cocoons, the rhythm of activity reaches a crescendo, resulting in another cycle of nomadic foraging.

Explanations of the ants' behavior based on reasonable notions, like exhaustion of food supply or more questionable ideas of the "mental powers" of ants or their organizational genius, have been logical but mistaken. As Schneirla notes; "The whole complex process is carried out by individuals which do not themselves originate the basic motivations of their behavior."[65] The stereotyped responses of the ants to the reproduction cycle, trophallaxis, and the accidents of terrain produce the seemingly complex and goal-directed behavior of the tribe. In a sense, the army ant is completely inner-motivated and thus dependent on the environment. "In the diversity of its natural habitat, the stereotyped army ant is presented with innumerable possibilities for variation in its activity. The jungle terrain, with its random layout of roots and vines, leaves and stones, liberates the ant from its propensity to destroy itself and diverts it into highly adaptive patterns of behavior," comments Schneirla.[66] Thus what is basically a self-destroying set of habits is adaptive, provided randomness is supplied by the environment.

In an intriguing paper, Von Neumann has tried to demonstrate formally how such a result can happen. He argues that in principle an organism (or organization) can be built more reliable than its individual parts, if it can sustain the cost of multiplexing communication channels (or extensive redundancy of channels) and if *randomness* of stimulus can be maintained.[67] In the ants' case the redundancy of communication is provided by trophallaxis, or the continuous exchange of chemicals, and the randomness is supplied by the irregular terrain of the jungle. Without randomness such an organization tends to amplify errors, Von Neumann notes.[68]

Many human organizations appear to be based on the principles of army-ant organization. Fixated and abortive behavior patterns fostered by hierarchies are often celebrated as "homeostasis" or "tendencies toward equilibrium." The anthropologist Jules Henry suggests that what we call homeostasis in the social sciences is merely a resistance to change and innovation at the expense of efficacy and human survival. Social institutions, according to Henry, condition a certain readiness to respond which becomes obsolete or even destructive when environmental conditions change. Therefore development is discontinuous and problematic. Henry concludes, "The beautiful expression of the American soldier, 'snafu,' more closely approximates social reality than any theory of social homeostasis."[69] Because, he maintains, "every change, every provision that is made in society provides for malaise in the future and does not provide for balance."[70] Thus social disorder, "snafu," chaos, crisis, and revolution are a necessary element of survival for any army-ant type of organization.

But it is not the inability to learn or the resistance to change which ensures the survival of an army-ant type of organization. Rather what ensures survival is the ability of that organization's members to *not* learn dogmas and to resist routines. If it were not for this ability, such organizations would survive only in favorable environments. The dangers to human organizations are the lethal twin stereotypes of coding in communication and routines in action—or, more simply, myths and rituals. Schneirla writes: "When human societies begin to march in circular columns, the cause is to be found in the strait-jacket influence of the man-made social institutions which foster such behavior."[71]

Kuhn's theory boils down to little more than a faith in the occurrence of enough environmental or other variations to prevent human emulation of the army ant suicide mill. When we note, however, that the practice of normal science is designed to suppress novelty or the detection of environmental variation, it is hard to be as optimistic as he is. Science has in the past stagnated for long periods of human history. There is nothing in Kuhn's analysis to suggest that it is not entering such a stage of decline at the present time. The lesson of the army ant is that any relatively closed system operating in accordance with a finite set of internal principles may appear to develop and learn so long as environmental variation prevents the completion of those operations. As K. W. Lashley has noted, and Wallace emphasized, the mere lack of discrimination in the response of an organism or organization may give its behavior a false appearance of generalization and abstraction. Myth is always more complex than theory, for it must account for everything with a minimal set of predicates. The generation of larger numbers of journals, articles, books, graduate schools, and symposia may be only the outward signs of suicidal milling on the part of the scientific community.[72]

The Concept of Scientific Revolutions Revolutions are extraordinary occurrences in the history of science, according to Kuhn, but they are the periods when scientists become critical, generate hypotheses, and develop the ingenious experiments that we all think of when we consider the romance of science. During these heroic periods, "Scientists see new and different things when looking with familiar instruments in places they have looked before. It is . . . as if the professional community has been suddenly transported to another planet."[73] In attempting to describe such periods of extraordinary science, Kuhn falls back on these and other visual metaphors.

The conversion from one paradigm to another is characterized as "a relatively sudden and unstructured event like the gestalt switch."[74] Not only do scientists come to see differently, but they also see different things. There is a change in the facts as well as in the theories which account for the facts. If such a period is heroic, it is also a mystery. Kuhn's description of sudden conversions and his denial of any completely logical or rational criteria for abandoning one paradigm for another has left him open to charges of irrationalism.

All this is to be expected. Having falsely abstracted routine and innovation, Kuhn is at a loss how to recombine them in a productive process. Contextless innovation is a mystery called genius or talent, and is caused by accident, fate, or personal demons. Likewise the drudgery of mindless puzzle solving seems humanly impossible. Both these incredible activities require extraordinary human beings, obsessed with either a fixed idea or a fixed routine that nothing can alter. Kuhn's account of extraordinary science is a magical one of intuitions and lightning flashes. Kuhn claims that his lack of detailed description of what scientists actually do in revolutionary periods is due to the fact that such revolutions are "invisible" in terms of official history. Science textbooks, he says, are written in 1984 style—the past is restored after each revolution as if present scientific practice were the goal toward which all scientists had been working.[75]

The revolutionary break for Kuhn is absolute. There is no linear or cumulative development of scientific knowledge. Paradigms are incommensurable, like religions.[76] Thus Kuhn writes:

> Just because it is a transition between incommensurables, the transition between competing paradigms cannot be made a step at a time, forced by logic and neutral experience. Like the gestalt switch, it must occur all at once (though not necessarily in an instant) or not at all.[77]

The switch involves personal psychology, outside influences, professional pressures, and other things.[78] It is in periods of extraordinary science that "elements of arbitrariness," Kuhn suggests, become so important to scientific progress. This "arbitrariness," like the randomness of the army ants' environment, keeps the closed scientific community from ossification. The injection of irrational beliefs, such as the Pythagorean mysticism that seems to have influenced most physical scientists since Copernicus, personal whims, and fancies serve to shake things up and cause new ways of seeing. It is perhaps this arbitrariness, rather than any failure of puzzle solving, that is the key to the avoidance of closure.

Partial Systems and Rules of Faith   The ambiguity throughout Kuhn—celebrating the detailed and mundane rationality of normal science and insisting on the need for the magical conversions of revolutionary science—is a kind of epistemological dishonesty which the novelist Herman Broch maintained is typical of any partial system of thought. By a partial system, Broch meant one that systematically ignored features of the social and physical reality, especially the results of its own practice, characterized, as he phrased it, "by that uncanny, I might almost say that metaphysical, lack of consideration for consequences."[79] Kuhn's paradigmatic science and the army ant troops are such systems. All of the criteria for judging good work, for testing hypotheses, for abandoning lines of thought, are internal community standards supplied by a given paradigm, according to Kuhn's account. Thus he too is forced to "take refuge in an alliance with the irrational."[80]

Partial systems or half-way revolutions are typical of the style of thinking of the modern age, according to Broch. Their apparent advantage is that they allow the development of quite definite formulas that facilitate and simplify decisions. Since they are partial they can be closed and therefore built up axiomatically. Such systems are built on a "single and exclusive concentration on a single value system" which give them an "ascetic severity." Accordingly, all rules may be reduced to logic or what Broch calls "ruthless" logic, which causes the "immolation of all sensory content."[81] This "unleashing" of logic is typical of the disintegration of Western civilization into numerous partial, single-value systems and their practicing communities all competing for the reins of tyranny as Madisonian factions. Kuhn's contribution is to remind us that the practice of modern science, as a ruthless dehumanized logic and a closed community, is no exception. All partial systems of thought and the hierarchical professional communities that adopt them require the separation of appearance and reality, the divorce of facts and values, and the denial of accountability for either reality or values. Reality is insisted upon as a nonhuman foundation of knowledge. Values are denied as the subject of rational inquiry. Thus partial systems are immune to outside judgment and interference and retain privileged elements of irrationality and arbitrariness.[82]

That the same dogmatic scheme might be utilized by the sciences in their struggle for autonomy against political and institutional obscurantism is at first glance surprising. It might be supposed, because of the emphasis in the natural sciences on the hypothetical spirit, experimentalism, and criticism, that arbitrary faith would play little part in their conceptual schemes.[83] Feyerabend assures us that this supposition is not the case.[84] He argues that dogmatism results when we seek autonomy for critical inquiry by means of appeal to a nonhuman or suprahuman foundation for knowledge. For a decision to found knowledge on any absolute basis—a basis, that is, which is immune to the criticism of men and women—results in a closed community of inquiry. Such communities are characterized by features of (1) true-believer psychology; (2) indoctrination through discounting of the novices' previous experience and the parceling of knowledge into pieces acquired at successive stages of apostleship accompanied by tests and threats; and (3) guiding principles of validity which are logically vacuous. These characteristics result, according to Feyerabend, because any epistemology not human-based requires a fundamental rule of faith and its accompanying institutional enforcement.

Such rules of faith take the form of statements like: "Biblical scriptures are the revealed word of God," "Experience is the basic test of knowledge," or "Science is the facts." But such rules of faith are logically vacuous—that is, no meaningful statements can be derived from them. The rule does not tell us what is valid scripture and what is a forgery, a copyist's mistake, or even a lie slipped in by the devil. Likewise, the empiricist's rule that all true assertions must be in accord with experience doesn't tell us what experiences or whose experiences are to be taken as legitimate and what experiences are to be understood as delusions, projections, false consciousness, mere appearance, etc. Testing assertions as simple as "all swans are white" turns out to require some tough decisions about categories and their application, not to mention the ability to distinguish between facts and opinions, observations and dreams, theories and obsessions, and like disparities. While such rules of faith are logically vacuous, Feyerabend notes that they are psychologically reinforcing of whatever already existing set of propositions we wish to defend. We need only argue that such propositions are based on the rule of faith and dismiss counterevidence because it is counter. According to Feyerabend, "The very vacuity of the rule makes it a most valuable means in the defense of ideas one wants to preserve," because it enables us to get on to the more important task of propaganda.[85]

It is the rule of faith involved in the philosophical reconstruction and defense of the natural sciences that promotes the lamented and disturbing revolt against scientific political and social inquiry, not any ideological or passionate longing for mysticism or metaphysics. For this rule allows and even promotes the discounting of observations and experience that run counter to accepted ideas. Further, it makes any sort of rational discussion of differences impossible. Scientific knowledge, like politics, it seems, comes out of the barrel of a gun or at least out of the recommendations of a tenure committee.

Kuhn not only describes the dogmatism that results from the defensive posture of a closed professional community committed to a partial system of thought, but he further maintains that this dogmatism accounts for the intellectual success of the enterprise. In consequence he must divide the scientific enterprise into daily conformity and periodic revolt, but he will not even allow scientific revolutions to be understood in terms of Popper's notion of critical science. Kuhn begins in agreement with Broch's description of partial systems of thought, insisting that scientists too must have their faith, albeit a faith in a "disciplinary matrix," or else they would have no standards for judging failure and success. What is different about Kuhn is not this commonplace dedication to "irrational inspiration" as a foundation but his insistence on what Broch labeled the "irreducible residue of the irrational" involved in altering that foundation.

Perceptual Fixation and Novelty Kuhn denies that extraordinary science consists of conjectures and refutations—of a rational process of proposing, testing, and criticizing theories until one is adopted by the community for detailed work. Thus he writes:

> The criteria with which scientists determine the validity of an articulation or an application of existing theory are not by themselves sufficient to determine the choice between competing the-

ories. . . . [Popper] has sought to solve the problem of theory
choice during revolutions by logical criteria that are applicable in
full only when a theory can already be presupposed.[86]
To fully understand Kuhn's stance here we must go back to his early
writings on the great scientific revolution he has fully studied—the
Copernican revolution. There he gives this initial description of paradigm breakdown and change:

> [This] . . . is the logical structure of a scientific revolution. A
> conceptual scheme believed because it is economical, fruitful,
> and cosmologically satisfying, finally leads to results that are in-
> compatible with observation; belief must then be surrendered
> and a new theory adopted; after this the process starts again. It
> is a useful outline, because the incompatibility of theory and
> observation is the ultimate source of every revolution in the sci-
> ences. But historically the process of revolution is never, and
> could not possibly be, so simple as the logical outline indicates.
> As we have already begun to discover, observation is never *abso-
> lutely* incompatible with a conceptual scheme.[89]

That is, in the case he is dealing with it was not clear to astronomers
that the Ptolemaic system was incompatible with observation. Indeed, it
yielded more accurate predictions than did Copernicus' new theory. Or
as Kuhn comments later, Galileo's law of falling bodies does not represent experience better than Aristotle's; rather, "it goes behind the
superficial regularity disclosed by the senses to a more essential, but
hidden aspect of motion."[88] Noting that if Galileo had ever performed
the experiment with the two cannonballs from the tower of Pisa, the
results would have been compatible with Aristotle's theory but not with
his own, Kuhn writes: "Galileo himself got the law not from observation, but by a chain of logical arguments."[89] From examples like these
Kuhn reaches this conclusion:

> Innovations in a science need not be responses to novelties
> within the science at all. No fundamental astronomical discovery,
> no new set of astromomical observations, persuaded Copernicus
> of ancient astronomy's inadequacy or of the necessity for
> change. Until half a century after Copernicus' death no poten-
> tially revolutionary changes occurred in the data available to
> astronomers. Any possible understanding of the Revolution's
> timing and of the factors that called it forth must, therefore, be
> sought principally outside of astronomy, within the larger intel-
> lectual milieu inhabited by astronomy's practitioners.[90]

Thus Copernicus' revolution resulted from the general ferment and
turbulence of the Renaissance, since "change in one field decreases the
hold of stereotypes in others."[91] In Kuhn's view what saves science
from ossification is not variation in the physical environment, but upheaval in the social environment. The element of arbitrariness is a

social and political element—something like an accident of history. But Kuhn appears now not to have given us any explanation or description of changes in conceptual structures at all. He has only labeled such changes "revolutions" and "extraordinary science." "Miracles," "divine intervention," or any other label would tell us just as much. As Toulmin notes, "By dubbing a change 'revolutionary,' we do not escape responsibility for explaining the 'occasions on which and the processes by which' it came about."[92] Kuhn does not conceive of the possibility that science progresses only to the extent that it is open to the problems of the productive processes of society and the needs of human survival. Behind his "element of arbitrariness" lies the struggle of adaptive evolution. But, as far as it goes, his description of the necessity of irrational motivation and action to overcome the dogmatism of a closed autonomous professional community is possibly accurate.

Kuhn suggests that his model of dogma-crisis-revolution-dogma is also applicable to the learning of the individual. This model then seems to be the source of his skepticism about the efficacy of mere observation as leading to any serious challenge of accepted theory. Kuhn cites an experiment by Bruner and Postman on the perception of incongruity, which "provides a wonderfully simple and cogent schema for the process of scientific discovery."[93] That is, "Novelty emerges only with difficulty, manifested by resistance against a background provided by expectation."[94] A careful reading of Bruner and Postman's paper does not substantiate this conclusion.[95] Their experiment was simple. They exposed five different playing cards to 28 Harvard and Radcliffe students. Some of the cards were anomalous or trick, for instance, a black three of hearts, a black four of diamonds, or a red two of spades. The experimenters found that the recognition threshold for the trick cards was four times as high as for normal cards. Subjects reacted to the trick cards by dominance, or denying their incongruity; by compromise, for instance, saying, "a purple three of hearts"; by suffering disruption, for instance, saying, "I do not know what's going on"; and finally, over time, by recognizing and identifying the incongruity.[96] Dominance, or denial, was the most frequent response, occurring in 27 of the 28 cases. More than half of the subjects suffered a disruption before final recognition. The authors' theorize:

> Given a stimulus input of certain characteristics, directive processes in the organism operate to organize the perceptual field in such a way as to maximize percepts relevant to current needs and expectations and to minimize percepts inimical to such needs and expectations.[97]

They call this response "the construction-defense balance in perception." Although the authors predict that an organism will ward off the perception of the unexpected for as long as possible, they admit, "It is either a very sick organism, an overly motivated one, or one deprived of the opportunity to 'try and check' which will not give up an expectancy in the face of a contradictory environment."[98]

What they overlook in their experiment is the fact that their subjects have a drastically reduced ability to "try and check." When one expectancy fails, it must be replaced by another, as Kuhn so clearly points out. Not just any other expectancy will do; it must be a plausible and useful alternative. That is, recognition of incongruity is resisted if such a recognition does not make sense. I submit that it does not make sense to assume that someone would fool with playing-card colors. Only those with some acquaintance with the habits of experimental psychologists would be likely to conceive of this possibility.

The experiment is analogous to the situation of Kuhn's puzzle-solving scientist because in each case the abstract or theoretical attitude is repressed or inhibited. In the case of Bruner and Postman's subjects, the theory that card deck conventions have been tampered with is not plausible, not congruent with ordinary expectations of human behavior. A paranoid, however, might immediately detect the trick cards because he suspects that people are capable of doing anything to confuse or humiliate him. Such a level of suspicion is dysfunctional to maintain. An incongruity that requires bizarre postulates (like those of paranoia) for recognition is not a fair basis on which to construct a theory of perception or scientific discovery. Kuhn's ordinary scientist, however, has learned not to theorize rather than to simply expect that his perceptions will be wrong. Novelty does not emerge with such difficulty for those who are looking for it. That is what makes "normal" scientists deem the search for novelty so dangerous—it is usually successful and destructive of dogma. Those who can conceive of reasonable and different sets of expectations with relative ease—those who are not dogmatically committed to a given way of seeing the world—are likely to recognize facts that are embarrassing to current stereotypes.

Postman and Bruner speculate that the greatest barrier to the recognition of novelty is the tendency to fixate perceptual hypotheses with minimal confirmation. Under stress, they note, perceptual recklessness and fixation is likely.[99] This explanation makes more sense than Kuhn's interpretation of perceptual inertia. It is hard to understand the evolutionary survival of any organism that is reluctant to recognize novelty.

N. R. F. Maier et al. noted some years ago that psychologists failed to differentiate between fixation in learning and fixation in abnormal behavior.[100] In learning a response, fixation refers to the animal's repeated ability to give the correct response to the stimulus. If reward ceases, the response ceases. If, however, animals are rewarded intermittently, the response lasts long after the reward stops.[101] This behavior has led some to theorize about schedules of reinforcement, implying paradoxically that the best reward is a punishment. Maier's experiment produced abnormal fixation by means of frustration. Rats were forced to jump from a stand to either of two doors, one of which opened to allow access to food and one of which remained closed, causing the rats to fall to a net below. When the level of frustration was high enough— that is, when no rational strategy was rewarded—for example, the rats adopted a fixated response of jumping either to the right or left (or at symbols on the doors) no matter what. This fixation persisted even when a winning strategy again became possible and the rats had learned to discriminate the right answer. Maier and his colleagues concluded that "continued failure causes the animal to 'give up' and when this point is reached the mastery of a new problem no longer takes place. Instead the animal has formed an adjustment which is a fixed mode of behaving."[102] In short, "frustration causes a . . . habit to become fixated."[103] They go on to make explicit the differentiation of kinds of fixation that they consider to be crucial.

> If we suppose that frustration may lead to fixation, this fixation may be of a qualitatively different nature than that produced by learning. In the sense that such fixations are not the ordinary ones produced by learning they may be called abnormal fixations. Frustrations also lead to other forms of behavior which have been called abnormal . . . and it therefore seems justified to so classify these fixations. Case histories of neurotic people contain much evidence of persistence of unsuccessful modes of behavior and when these arise through frustration they are readily classified as belonging to the abnormal.[104]

I conclude that Kuhn has used a model which applies more appropriately to a context promoting abnormal fixation of expectations than to a context of ordinary learning or scientific discovery. If there are problems of conceptual inertia and perceptual denial in the scientific community, then I suggest that their cause lies in the structure of that community rather than simply in human psychology. Indeed, if the community is designed, as Kuhn maintains, to perpetuate cognitive hegemony, abnormally fixated or "dogmatic" behavior on the part of its members is to be expected.

The Dogmatism/Innovation Puzzle

Kuhn's thesis, I hope I have shown, is slippery. Reconciling dogmatism and innovation, certainty and novelty, domination and freedom, and similar oppositions, might be seen as the perennial puzzle of the social sciences. But the puzzle's source is not just the basic theistic and authoritarian structure of Western political and philosophical thought, to which Popper has called attention.[105] The most important sources of the puzzle are the dogmatic, certain, and domineering structures of hierarchical social and political institutions that scientists must live in—and must continuously subvert and periodically adapt in order that they meet the minimal needs of human life. Toulmin characterizes Kuhn's solution to the puzzle in the case of the scientific enterprise as the discovery that "narrow-mindedness itself can be expedient for the development of science."[106] Kuhn's ambiguous solution thus entails proper obeisance to dogma in order to get on with the necessary innovation, doubt, and resistance required by progress. The solution is at least as old as Hobbes and it is a cruel one. What is cruel about it is that the individuals who are forced to cheat—that is, innovate, doubt, and resist—are always liable to prosecution and punishment for unscientific or antisocial behavior even as they are potential heroes. They must live under conditions of terror, forced by the demands of social and physical reality to break the rules and likewise, for the sake of their social survival, forced to honor the rules. This conflict requires severe distortions of perception, as well as creating conditions of profound self-hatred. With this solution life continues certainly but at a hectic pace, in a limited depth, and with a muted variety.

Kuhn notes that any puzzle can also be interpreted as a counterinstance to an accepted theory. The puzzle of how innovation occurs in a context of dogmatism appears to me to be such a counterinstance. Its paradoxical formulation and the lack of a satisfactory solution or explanation, including Kuhn's attempt, suggests the necessity of constructing a new set of assumptions about creativity and social organization.

Paradigms as Exemplars Of the two meanings of paradigm which Kuhn has endorsed—the sociological, or set of habits, and the pragmatic, or exemplary achievement—he emphasizes the second sense as the deeper of the two. Both point to the concrete practices of a scientific community over theoretical or conceptual rules, methods, or frameworks. It is not conceptual structures at all that Kuhn stresses but what he calls "components of knowledge tacitly embedded in shared examples."[107] The evidences for the set of habits of a scientific community are to be found in current textbooks in the form of problems and their solutions. The evidences for the exemplary achievements are actual artifacts, discoveries, experiments, and the like, that, in the words of Masterman, are used analogically. She argues that paradigms are constructed, not adopted. Each science in her view starts with a trick.

A known construct, an artifact, becomes a "research vehicle," and at the same moment, if successful, it becomes a paradigm, by being used to apply to new material, and in a non-obvious way. It thus has two kinds of concreteness, not one: the concreteness which it brought through being a "picture" of A, and *the second concreteness which it has now acquired through becoming applied to B.* This second kind of concreteness is the kind which the hypothetico-deductive view of science tries to account for; but the first, in the hypothetico-deductive view, is not accounted for at all.[108]

That is, models, theories, deductive systems, ways of seeing, and the like, emerge from successful practice. A solution, device, or technique in one area is successfully applied again in another area, thus reinforcing the notion that imbedded in these practices are patterns useful for explaining the structure of reality. This proposition fits in with Peirce's and Hanson's insistence that scientific knowledge proceeds by means of abduction, not induction or hypothetico-deduction, and that inquiry begins with problematic practice and troublesome facts, not just with theory. It also parallels Farrington's notion of theory merged in operations and his emphasis on technical and productive processes as the source of scientific theory. Masterman's interpretation of Kuhn parallels Theophrastus' dictum that "we must, in general, proceed by making reference to the crafts and drawing analogies between natural and artificial processes."[109] Even though Kuhn insists that he introduced the concept *paradigm* "to underscore the dependence of scientific research upon concrete examples,"[110] he ignores the industrial and technological sources of abstract scientific knowledge.

Puzzle Solving and Human Need What Kuhn calls puzzle solving is historically, at least, a good deal more than that. As Farrington notes, the earliest exemplars employed by the Ionian physical scientists were techniques of production. "They were observers of nature whose eyes had been quickened, whose attention directed, and whose selection of phenomena to be observed had been conditioned, by familiarity with a certain range of techniques."[111] Such techniques not only worked as laboratory tricks but were also successful practical operations, changing, expanding, and sustaining human life.

The more recent example of Louis Pasteur reveals the shallowness of Kuhn's notion of puzzle solving. The "puzzles" in Pasteur's work (which enabled him to lay the theoretical basis for modern microbiology, immunology, and biochemistry) included: why different forms of tartaric acid behaved differently toward polarized light; the creation of life; the source of contaminants in industrial alcohol fermentation; spontaneous generation; the spoilage of wine, beer, and vinegar; the improvement of the quality of French beer; the prevention and cure of anthrax and hydrophobia, and more of the like.[112] Notice that these range from esoteric laboratory problems, through grand speculation, to practical questions of industry. Pasteur was self-conscious about problem choice. Against those who argue for the complete autonomy of scientific research developing according to its own internal logic, producing discoveries by accident or "serendipity," Pasteur argued, "Chance favors only the prepared mind." His biographer René Dubos adds, "The mind must be prepared by scientific training and technical proficiency but also by the awareness of social needs."[113]

Science and Industry The debt science owes the productive skill and technological developments of mankind is not often acknowledged. Dubos maintains that, contrary to the myth that science causes techno-logical advance, "the fundamental changes in the ways of life and in the human environment that have occurred throughout history have not resulted from the application of theoretical knowledge."[114] While Du-bos emphasizes the impact of the far-ranging experimentation of pre-history and "historical accidents and social forces" on the development of human knowledge and science, he does not explicitly acknowledge the processes of social production as the impetus of scientific progress. Most notably, Marx has made the connection. But his own economistic investigations of the productive process and its effect on human knowledge is crude and unsatisfactory after a brilliant beginning in the *Economic and Philosophical Manuscripts of 1844.* There he criticizes the separation of the natural sciences and the productive processes this way:

> Industry is the actual historical relationship of nature, and thus of natural science, to man. If industry is conceived as the esoteric manifestation of the essential human faculties, the human es-sence of nature and the natural essence of man can also be understood. Natural science will then abandon its abstract mate-rialist, or rather idealist, orientation, and will become the basis of a *human* science, just as it has already become—though in alien-ated form—the basis of actual human life. One basis for life and another for science is *a priori* a falsehood. . . . Science is only genuine science when it proceeds from sense experience, in the two forms of *sense perception* and *sensuous* need; i.e., only when it proceeds from nature. . . . Natural science will one day incorpo-rate the science of man, just as the science of man will incorpo-rate natural science; there will be a *single* science.[115]

I understand Marx to mean in this passage that just as religion repre-sents the abstracted and inverted conception of human affective and sociable life, so does idealist science represent the inverted conception of human reflective experimental and productive life. To rephrase

Marx, man makes science, science does not make man.[116] Or, more specifically, science derives from the patterns merged in the operations that produce the sustenance of human life—industry is thus the basis of science, not science the basis of industry. If the scientific knowledge of our day were lost, the human species could create it again, provided our productive facilities and skills were not destroyed. Conversely, the loss of productive skill on the part of a large part or all of the species would mean the end of science. Many would disagree with me on this point, of course. The argument is quite old, going back to Plato and Aristotle, who worked hard to divorce knowledge from the context of productive life.

Farrington writes that in early Greek thought, science was a way of doing something. Later, Plato insisted that it was a way of knowing. Since Plato insisted that there be no practical test of knowledge, this approach made science come to mean "talking consistently." While Farrington notes that historians are still debating the degree to which industrial handicrafts had passed to the hands of slaves by Plato's time, it is clear in the writings of both Plato and Aristotle that manual work was considered degrading. Thus the science they described was one for those who did not engage directly in manual work or techniques of production. Farrington concludes: "Their science consisted in being able to give the right answers to any questions that might be asked. The rightness of the answer mainly depended on its logical consistency."[117] Kuhn's addition to the controversy is that he manages to avoid the pitfalls of the pure idealist position with its questionable claims of cumulative, increasingly quantitative, and concise logical laws of the structure of reality, while maintaining the need for the relative insulation and autonomy of the scientific community. Kuhn's description is a prescription for the continued alienation of scientific investigation from the problems of human survival except in those random ways in which these problems slip into the concerns of the community. The way they must get in is not through statements of concern or values on the part of scientists: they must come in camouflaged as new artifacts, achievements, and techniques.

Kuhn's Contribution Kuhn is correct in emphasizing the implications of the relationships of theoretical abstractions to productive processes. First, there is an abstract pattern (or patterns); imbedded in the exemplar activity, this pattern is never fully articulated, nor is it in theory possible to fully articulate. The pattern is learned first as a set of cognitive postulates. In this way the postulates or assumptions of the natural sciences are learned by the student in the course of laboratory practice. They can be learned only in such practice, for in actually carrying out the operations or utilizing the exemplar as a model the individual gets exposed to the full range of nonverbal information available. No textbook, or lecture, or explanation can substitute for this experience. It is important to note that each person must learn the pattern—that is, create an appropriate response to the operation or model.

Kuhn is wrong in viewing this process as an imposition of a cognitive structure on the student of science. He points out in several places that individual scientists differ in their interpretations of paradigms. It would be clearer to say that individual scientists create different but complementary patterns from the same examples. It is this difference that is crucial for the progress of knowledge. But this diversity becomes useful only if it can be articulated.

Tacit Theory Tacit theory in the form of cognitive postulates derived from concrete practice is tyrannical. Bertolt Brecht wrote of the "tyranny of familiarity," referring to the social and political postulates imbedded in the routines and experience of everyday life. Tacit dogma in the scientific community, as in the political community, is found in the form of unexamined and uncritical practice, not in the form of theoretical orthodoxy. What explicit dogma there is is the dogma that restricts and/or demeans attempts at theory articulation. This dogma has several forms. Its most blatant statement is Newton's admonition not to make hypotheses. More recently, there is the logical positivist rule of theory conservation which states that alternative theories should not be created or considered unless current theory has failed in some crucial way. Finally there is Kuhn's version, which states that "logical articulation is not a value for its own sake, but is to be undertaken only when and to the extent that circumstances demand it."[118] The result of adherence to this dogma is that changes in cognitive structures take place behind our backs, so to speak—that is, uncritically and unconsciously.

The suppression of theory articulation renders practice resistant to criticism and to change. Judith Merkle has noted this pattern in the development of organizational structures and their ideologies in American society. Americans do not theorize. Instead, as she puts it, "American organization [in industry] has tended to be built around machines or machine-like practices carried out by hand."[119] An implicit theory is adopted and implemented, but without being recognized. The pattern is: adoption of a new technique or piece of machinery; reorganization to meet the demands of this innovation and to get increased production out of it; final result, a self-validating organizational structure. As Merkle writes:

> In such systems, it is actually the operating hardware that "proves" its organizational validity, rather than a "theoretical"

study of results. Such "concrete" proof set before practical men tends to encourage them to apply the accompanying organizational "principles" to other situations, creating a tendency toward a sort of linear explanation of machine-based organizational systems that stops not at some point of decreasing efficiency or logical inapplicability, but only when it meets insupportable obstacles.[120]

Among Merkle's examples are the assembly line (adopted from the disassembly operations of the meat-packing industry), Frederick Taylor's invention of high-speed steel cutting, and the computer. In each case, adoption of a practice results in organizational changes that appear to be demanded or simply common sense, but that in turn involve far-reaching theoretical specifications of human nature, efficiency, work, rationality, and the like. Such specifications, or rather implications, in their nonarticulated form are unquestioned and unquestionable. Critics are forced to take on what is seemingly a totalistic world view and thus are easily dismissed as utopians or neo-Luddites.

Theory Suppression and Crisis The final result of restricting theory articulation is the mystification of human activities. Current scientific methods, or industrial organizations, take on the appearance of necessities or eternal principles to be adopted by or imposed on a recalcitrant humanity. Inhibited articulation, resulting in unreflective practice, appears as a cognitive hegemony. This is an inversion fatal alike to the defender and the critic of society. For the result of this procedure is crisis, as Kuhn emphasizes. Neither fully aware of the postulates involved in the models or techniques employed, nor possessing any reasonable theoretical alternatives, humans who experience anomalies or failures are forced into denial, compromise, or breakdown. The new paradigm in the form of a successful technique will be adopted in an enthusiastic manner, for it represents a release from confusion and intolerable anxiety. Such confusion in the form of self-doubt, doubts about the efficacy of reason, and other forms, becomes the experiential basis for the fear of change, criticism, and theorizing. Suppression of theory creates cognitive crisis. In turn, cognitive crises produce dogmatic theory whose efficacy relies on the suppression of alternative theory. Kuhn comes close to accurately describing this process, but he implies that it is somehow demanded of, and not chosen by, a community, a society, or even a species. Once the suppression of theoretical articulation is adopted, periodicity results. Kuhn's argument is not only circular, it is viciously so.

Puzzle Solving as Mindless "If there are revolutions, then there must be normal science," writes Kuhn in answer to Popper's and Feyerabend's criticisms.[121] Thus he emphasizes that the heart of the scientific enterprise is patient and painstaking laboratory work. But he goes on to describe that work as mindless puzzle solving. He further contributes to the romanticization and glorification of "revolutionary" theoretical innovations much as his critics do. This controversy appears to be a variation on an old theme of administrative mythology—that manual work is slavery and that mental work is creative. This attitude further implies that men who wish to make things or make science must become slaves of some kind, while those who wish to make theoretical innovations must become irrelevant masters. But Kuhn's account of scientific change contains the seeds of a different interpretation based on the recognition that, as Childe argues, "Creation is not making something out of nothing, but refashioning what already is . . . creation . . . is at once 'free' and 'determined.' "[122] For the heart of innovation lies in painstaking work and being steeped in the details, nuances, and minute variations of what A. D. Ritchie calls "haptic" experience, or first-hand knowledge of events, objects, and processes.[123] That is why the laboratory, not cognitive consensus, is the key to scientific maturation.

Reproductive and Productive Thinking Maier has argued that problem solving involves changes or restructuring of past experience in many instances, rather than simply reapplying that experience to new situations.[124] The first kind of problem solving he calls productive thinking; the second kind, reproductive thinking. We do not distinguish between the two, Maier maintains. By insisting on conformity to past successful operations, we encourage reproductive thinking but inhibit the productive kind. Likewise, to repudiate the past results is an inhibition of reproductive thinking. Maier found that subjects who had the greatest opportunity for modifying their experiences to solve experimental problems were ones operating in a context where pertinent elements were perceptually present.[125]

Kuhn's puzzle solving would result in what Duncker calls functional fixation, or the inhibition of finding new uses for previously used objects and procedures.[126] What is required in problem solving is rather the availability of a wide range of functions for the objects and procedures at hand.[127] Duncker writes that "what is really done in any solution of problems consists in formulating the problem more productively." And he adds:

> The final form of a solution is typically attained by way of mediating phases of the process, of which each one, in retrospect, possesses the character of a solution, and, in prospect, that of a problem.[128]

Merely realizing that something does not work, according to Duncker, "can lead only to some variation of the old method," while the recognition of *why* it does not work results in a variation that corrects the defect.[129]

Ordinary science is not likely to be the functionally fixated procedure that Kuhn describes, although there may be ordinary scientists who are limited in their imagination, inhibited by the context of their work, or improperly trained. The laboratory work of the scientists is more likely to be productive problem solving involving minute but continuous reorganization of past experience. Although I am not well versed in the history of science, I suggest that investigation would show that the best "ordinary" science is quite revolutionary.[130] The problem is that it is necessary to be in the situation to grasp the daily and minute variation that over time leads to startling results. The results are not easily accounted for without knowledge of the process. Their explanation seems to require the notion of revolution. As Feyerabend writes:

> Revolutions, then, are the outward manifestation of a change of the normal component that cannot be accounted for in any reasonable fashion. They are substance for anecdote though they magnify and make visible the more rational elements of science, thus teaching us what science *could* be if there were more reasonable people around.[131]

Thus, the important lesson in Kuhn's attempt to account for scientific progress is that to romanticize and glorify revolutions, emphasizing the discontinuity and nonrational elements they involve, results in a demeaning of actual productive work. Ordinary science appears dull and nonproductive compared to the dramatic change of revolution. While this appearance fits our preconceptions of the stagnation and revolutionary upheavals required by hierarchical organizations, it does not illuminate the process of human creativity. Revolution is a myth demanded by ignorance and distaste for detailed labor. Mindless puzzle solving is a myth demanded by the misunderstanding and worship of the extraordinary science of revolution.

Conclusion

Dogmatism is not a necessary fact of intellectual coordination, and it is vicious as a regulatory principle. When we find cognitive hegemony it is either an artifact of an investigation that assumes *a priori* the necessity of cognitive consensus and then proceeds to construct one, or an expression of an actually imposed symbolic code limiting what can be communicated through official channels. Such a code may be enforced by control of communication channels and media based on a monopoly of resources—time, energy, tools, people. Only in this latter case does cognitive hegemony "cause" anything and then what it does is to severely limit individual articulation of theory. Creativity is driven underground under this limitation. Kuhn's description of contemporary science may be accurate, and therefore a study of the organization of science is important.[132] For if Trigant Burrow is correct in asserting that "basically, experiment is more native to man than tradition. Man is by nature the forager, the hunter and the digger,"[133] then when we find evidence of dogmatism we need to look for the elements of the social context which are suppressing experimentation.

7   The Image-Conditioned Animal

> Altering frames of reference are a prerequisite to
> scientific progress. Not what we look *at* only, but
> what we look *from* is decisive in determining what we
> shall see.
>
> —Trigant Burrow

Suppose we consider that we are dealing not with defective animals but
with sick or struggling ones. A surviving defective species would be
inconsistent with the theory of natural selection, whereas a diseased
species, or one in the throes of an adaptive struggle, presents no such
anomaly. If the latter situation were the case, it might easily (though
wrongly) appear that the species is inherently incapable, because in fact
its survival would require some kind of accommodation to or overcoming of inadequacies. We would be witnessing a biological drama in
which a species is involved in re-creating itself. Errors in selecting goals
and means of life would abound, but the possibility of discovering
better goals and more effective means through experimentation would
be present. This more optimistic view of the human struggle for social
knowledge and adaptation marks the remarkable work of the American social biologist Trigant Burrow.

Thus far we have examined the forms of the attempts of Western
political thinkers to account for the apparent ubiquity of social ignorance and the near impossibility of social knowledge. I have argued
that these attempts were in vain since they require us to believe that
social knowledge is at once possible and impossible—possible to the
chosen few and their elite pupils and impossible to the necessarily
ignorant many. But the resulting hierarchical division of society into
those who think abstractly and those who labor concretely under the
others' direction, I maintain, has the consequence of systematically disturbing and distorting human perceptions. The goals and values of
society become arbitrary, and morality beyond conformity impossible.
Further, the failure to create a viable project of social science in more

than three thousand years of effort indicates that it is time to shift our frame of reference and consider that what is at issue is just our traditional way of formulating the problems of social knowledge.

Perhaps we have been studying and treating symptoms while overlooking the disease. For our most hallowed social wisdom is mythical in structure and no guide to effective adaptation. Our wisest of political theorists start from the premise that they are dealing with defective creatures. But if deficiencies are assumed and ascribed to all, then investigation of actual human capabilities is frustrated. Further, defective creatures require hierarchical organizations for their care and direction. Such organizations must be based on sound knowledge of human nature. The image of socialized man that these organizations require in order to establish their legitimacy installs unthinking patterns of action for reward and punishment as the norms of behavior. The teaching and enforcement of this norm renders human judgment defective, and a robotized being is inadvertently achieved. Accounting for human knowledge therefore necessitates a recourse to heroes and periodic revolutions—even as such heroes and revolutions appear to be impossible according to the various theories of dogmatic or robotized humankind.

The Catalogue of Symptoms

To summarize traditional accounts of social ignorance, we find a human condition described in this way: Human beings are inherently defective.[1] In order that they may survive as a species, they must overcome their defects (lazinesss, selfishness, and irrationality) by learning a series of noble lies which, in effect, deny those defects. These "lies" are not necessarily verbal, but are embodied in daily routines of speech, interaction, and work patterned by institutionalized definitions and prohibitions. These criteria make human beings sick with respect to their natural, though defined as defective, characteristics. That is, they are taught to deny their bodily needs and their perceptions, while aspiring to become imaginary ideal creatures.

This denial is a neurosis at best, a psychosis at worst. For the organism perforce adapts to its environment and to environmental changes by withdrawal and dissociation. Such adaptation is called, variously, transcendence, law and order, or living according to principles. The noble disease then is "healthy" insofar as large numbers of people are subject to a particular form of it. So long as there is a consensus about behavior patterns, repressions, fantasies, compensations, and outrage, the disease becomes health. In turn, deviations from this consensual illness in the form of eccentric individual neurosis are treated, condemned, or punished, since deviations represent a real threat to the existence of social organization by adumbrating possible complete cognitive disintegration. The weakness of the consensual diagnosis of disease is that it is arbitrary, and recognition of this fact may result in anarchy. Notice that we have come full circle: defective organisms require arbitrary and false behavioral and cognitive hegemonies which, in turn, produce defective organisms. The pronouncement and defense of this description in various guises represents what Alvin Gouldner has called the "mortician" role of the social scientist—the dedicated burying of all human hopes for an improved quality of life.[2]

An Altered Frame of Reference

How can we be sure that we are dealing with a catalogue of symptoms rather than with an actual description of the disease? There are several indications (including the inability of social investigators to include their own behavior and viewpoint within the pathological context they are attempting to describe), the most important of which is the lack of any ideas of how to prevent or cure the disease. Trigant Burrow suggested that our knowledge of social illness is at the same level as our past medical knowledge in the days when a diagnosis consisted of statements like "He is sick of a fever."[3] Such a statement allows treatment in the form of symptomatic relief, but it tells us nothing about prevention or cure. According to Burrow, it is a "surface observation" of symptomatic manifestations or external indices of a diseased state. Diagnosis of the disease, prerequisite to treatment, requires an altered frame of reference; one that allows us to see in depth, inside the organism. He sums up this process in this way.

> Objective inquiry involves an intra-organic alteration in ourselves. It means not only that we see what is inside but that we have become newly equipped, inside-seeing persons. *It means that by virtue of a premise which presupposes depth and dimension we have not only acquired a facility for taking account of the internal process at which we look but that also there has automatically come about an alteration in the internal basis from which we look at it.* Thus, in respect to a diseased organ or part, medicine has steadily progressed to a fundamentally altered frame of reference in the interpretation of the phenomenon or process observed by it.[4]

Social investigation has revealed only symptoms or surface indices of human biological disturbances because of its dimensionless perspective which results from the mistaken belief that the investigator can become free of the context he seeks to understand. The major aspect of the altered frame of reference which Burrow proposes is that it is self-inclusive. He argued that this altered perspective in the sphere of social investigation was analogous to Einstein's altered perspective in the sphere of physical investigation. For him, the most significant aspect of relativity was "its surrender of a position of unquestionable fixity or absolutism."[5] Burrow concluded early in his attempts to go beyond symptomatology that

> the inadequacy of our present mental system of evaluations is its failure to include in its envisagement the basis upon which we evaluate. On the contrary, a basis of relativity possesses the distinctive significance that it includes its own process within its own envisagement.[6]

As we shall see, the adoption of a self-inclusive viewpoint alters drastically the social-science enterprise, not by eschewing objectivity, but by offering a practical means toward achieving it. Burrow's contribution to social knowledge is so important and so much neglected that it is worthwhile to trace the path which leads to his conception of an altered framework of investigation as well as to summarize his overall perspective and achievements.

The Social Neurosis

Burrow began his career as a psychiatrist. During the early wrangles among Freud, Jung, and Adler, Burrow refused to take sides, arguing that their views were complementary rather than contradictory.[7] Freud's emphasis on physiology and biology was what most impressed him. Burrow's psychoanalytic papers contain a running criticism of what was to become Freudian dogma. Hans Syz summarizes the major concepts developed at this time as follows: (1) that there is a preconscious or precognitive stage of human existence exemplified in the infant's identification with the mother, in contrast to the predominant notion of infantile power-seeking; (2) that obsessive sexual strivings and other neurotic behavior patterns result from the imposition of cognition and objectification onto the primary preconscious; and (3) that neurosis is a general and social phenomenon, not merely an individual occurrence.[8] These themes were all elaborated in his later work, but what is essential to our discussion is Burrow's development of the argument that individual psychotherapy dealt only with symptoms and that so-called normality was merely a popular form of neurosis. Burrow's views changed when a student and analytic subject, Clarence Shields, challenged him to exchange roles. Shields charged that Burrow's interpretations were autocratic and arbitrary, but when the roles were reversed (reluctantly on the part of the analyst) Burrow in turn found Shield's behavior and ideas to be autocratic and arbitrary. Out of the confrontation of these two men developed what Burrow called "group analysis" or "the laboratory method in psychoanalysis." Based on these initial clinical explorations he concluded:

The standards of behavior of the community and those of the neurotic do not differ essentially. That is, the community does not impose on the neurotic, as a sort of alien, a distasteful censorship which blocks his "biological trends." Analysis of community reactions indicated that society, too, is the victim of compulsive drives toward self-satisfaction. Indeed, the behavior of the community as a whole is guided by standards as shifting and arbitrary as those of the neurotic.[9]

Normality as Pathological

The mental state labeled "normality" had three essential characteristics, according to Burrow. First, normal standards of dress, morality, behavior, and the like, were completely arbitrary and based on esoteric premises. Second, the underlying motivation of "normalcy" was identical for the isolated psychoneurotic as well as for the socially adapted and for the successful as well as for the failure. And third, normality as a mental state was unchallengeable by reason or criticism. In short, normality "possesses the credibility of a superstition and hence is by common consent immune to the scientific tests of actuality."[10]

Burrow broke with Freud's ideas on the issue of the "social neurosis," as he came to call it. For example, he rejected Freud's notion of a restless and obsessively acquisitive sexual urge, but argued instead that man was primarily nonsexual in the sense of not being inherently driven to the satisfaction of certain physical sensations for their own sake. Both the sexual urges of the individual and the interdicting repressions of normal society were symptoms of deeper conflicts and represssions, and, in fact, were mutually reinforcing. Repression for Burrow was "a disorder of the common social mind."[11] Thus he argued:

> Normality too, then, is neurotic. Normality too has its repressions and its substitutions, its secret symbols and equivocations. The difference is that as normality possesses the warrant of the institutionalized and current, it enjoys the protection of consensus.[12]

To a degree, Burrow's observations on the social neurosis have become commonplace, at least to the extent that people talk of "society being sick." But he never sought to defend or in any way justify the fact of social neurosis or to offer any palliatives or cures. Instead, he argued that we must develop laboratory techniques to observe, to describe, and to analyze social institutions and social values.[13] Burrow described his method as a "practical laboratory of psychoanalysis in which a consensual agreement concerning the subjective material has rendered possible an exact observation of individual deflections precisely as the laboratory of structural biology has made possible the scientific observation of structural divergences from a commonly accepted phyletic norm."[14] What he sought to establish through his group method was no less than a biological standard of health and knowledge, resulting in an objective science of psychiatry. He predicted that resistance to such a course would be great and that the effort would therefore be painful and difficult.

Social scientists often responded to Burrow's idea of a laboratory method by asking him for a verbal description of events which he observed by this means. But such descriptions from outside the processes of social interaction and expressed in verbal symbols were exactly what he was trying to avoid. As he put it, "It is one thing . . . to shift the affect from one idea to another, and it is quite another thing to divorce completely the *sphere* of the affect from the *sphere* of the idea."[15] Burrow was seeking the causes of the willingness of human beings to sacrifice themselves and their fellows for symbols and ideas. He had no intention of substituting one set of affective symbols, or images as he called them, for another.[16]

Neurosis and Repression of Social Instincts

To understand Burrow's insistence on a method that allowed a direct observation of organic reactions we must take account of his conception of neurosis. He agreed with Freud that "neurosis represents the thwarted expression of the life of the individual," and that the result was the production of fantasy substitutes that separate the neurotic individual from his social and physical environment.[17] But Burrow was not satisfied with Freud's formulation of the aetiology of the neurosis. Freud wrote that neurosis was an expression of the rebellion of the instincts (or id) against reality or, in other words, of the unwillingness of the instincts to be adapted to necessity.[18] For Freud, the neurosis was "the outcome of a repression which has miscarried."[19] Burrow asked, "What is the source of repression?" That is, he turned Freud's explanation around, seeing the neurosis not as caused by rebellious instincts but as caused by a repressive social environment—an environment that in turn was repressed. Thus, while the locus of pathology is the individual according to Freudian theory, it is both the social and physical environment of the species' evolution according to Burrow. An individual's neurotic disturbance is due to a universal disturbance of the species. Specifically, both disturbances are due to the repression of human social instincts. Burrow wrote: "It is the illusion of our differentiation that is the essence of the neurosis. It is the fallacy of our personal separateness that is the meaning of our societal discord."[20]

The Biology of Conflict

Burrow explained the origin of this separateness in the following way. The child originally learns to evaluate the environment in terms of its biological reactions. Like other animals, human beings are well equipped with an "internal proprioceptive sense of the right and accurate adjustment."[21] But this sense is interdicted by parental claims of good and bad. Many statements of the goodness or badness of such and such behavior are dishonest statements about what is convenient for, or in conformity with, their own wishes. Burrow charges:

> What the adult arbiter of the child really has up his sleeve is the child's conformity to *him* and *his* convenience. Accordingly, the parent or guardian lays down the proposition that a good little boy does not destroy costly bric-a-brac or that only a bad little girl plays in the mud with her nice clean rompers on. Both these postulates are utterly false as every sponsor for them knows. But that is not the point. The point is that such statements are incomparably adapted to the ends of adult commodity. The truer rendering of the proposition in either instance would be to the effect that the misdemeanor in question would occasion inconvenience or chagrin to the parent.[22]

Burrow's conclusion was that the conflict thus incurred—through the parental conditioning of an image of right and wrong that interdicts the organic responses of the child—lies at the root of the pathologies of the species. An arbitrary, imposed response without factual basis comes to be substituted for the reactions of the organism. Burrow stressed, "It is the insidious intimation of benefit or of harm inherent in the tabooed act itself that is the pernicious instance."[23] That is, it is not the interceding of the parent that is harmful, but rather the parents' dishonest statements about features of the environment or behavior patterns as being inherently "good" or "bad" independent of any biological evaluation. Based on this explanation, Burrow could later redefine neurosis as

> the unconscious but universal instilling into the human offspring of a wishful, non-objective sense of right or fitting behavior rather than a biological and objective sense of discrimination between what is fitting and not fitting.[24]

Burrow's argument at this point appears to be a new version of the perennial nature/convention controversy in political thought. But his position is novel. He does not argue that conventions are good and nature bad, or vice versa. He does maintain that the imposition of conventions that are arbitrary and falsely presented makes it impossible for the human organism to respond effectively to the "natural" environment. That is, Burrow does not hold that certain behavior patterns are natural and therefore good, but that, given conditions of universal neurosis, we rarely see or experience natural behavior patterns and do not recognize them when we do.[25]

In our terms, Burrow's findings and interpretation indicate that attempts at socialization and the enforcement of cognitive hegemony result in internal physiological conflicts which render human beings inept, both in their sensations and their reason. Thus he declared that "in the organismic sense, we are none of us thinking clearly because we are none of us feeling clearly."[26] Again he refuses to take sides in the ancient war over passion versus reason, but offers the startling indictment that "normality is but the collective dream-state of man's waking life."[27] Our educational practices of teaching each generation what is good and bad—based upon our collective or individual sense of decency, or "conscience," or "beliefs"—produces, not simply conformity, but what Hans Syz labels "autistic image dependence," which combines outward obedience with private advantage.[28]

Burrow's analysis of normal socialization practices leads him to an indictment of morality:

> Thus man's "morality" is, in my view, nothing else than an expression of the neurosis of the race. It is a complex of symptoms representing the hysterical compensations of society that are precisely analogous to the compensative reactions manifested in the hysteria of the individual. As "morality" is essentially the pain of the neurotic due to an intuitive sense of his inadequacy to the demands of his own code of behavior, so morality expresses equally the pain of the social organism because of its ineptitude to meet the requirements of the generic social codes.[29]

By insisting on an absolutist consensus, immune from counterevidence or criticism, we get arbitrary images manipulated by isolated individuals for their own advantage. The imposition of conventional morality results in a Hobbesian world of all warring against all for personal advantage and autistic absolutism.[30]

The Social Image

Socialization produces not social knowledge, but social ignorance in the form Burrow called the "social image." In the paper in which he introduced the term, he began from a materialistic base. "Thinking is a biological process," Burrow wrote. "Its manifestation is a function of the social organism. Thought and action are coterminous and the measure of consciousness is its productivity."[31] But if thinking is a biological process, how can it become harmful to the individual or society? Why is thinking not self-adjusting in, say, the way walking is, or seeing, or grasping? Because, Burrow insists, we have become preoccupied as a race with our own images. Therefore, "we unconsciously substitute the private satisfaction of arbitrary social images for the largest interests of the race as measured by its activities as a concerted functional unit."[32] This, then, is the key to his notion of the "social neurosis": "the social image is prompted . . . by the same tendency to substitution, symbolism, and indirection which through Freud we have found to underlie the dream."[33] The social image is a group or "syndicate" form of mental imagery and the author offers the following examples: " 'the church,' fashion, property, the absolute, democracy, insanity, 'The North and the South,' civilization, caste, money, equal rights and so forth."[34]

Burrow's notion of a common conceptual structure or social image possessed by a society seems to be identical with that of many authors.[35] The features of the social image that everyone seems to agree to are: (1) It is expressed in symbols (mostly verbal) and their accompanying emotional affects; (2) it is often implicit and always incompletely articulated in linguistic form; (3) it is systematically instilled in each generation through various agencies of socialization and education; (4) it is an ordering device, ensuring common meanings and responses by means of stereotypical metaphors, models, myths, or other symbolic devices; (5) it is most difficult to recognize as something other than reality or experience; (6) it is impossible to test or evaluate, as well as difficult to question; (7) it is anonymously authored; and (8) its absence would mean idiocy or insanity.

While Burrow's account agrees with this inventory, what the other authors see as a necessity of social life he sees as a symptom of fundamental derangement in the species. As he noted, "Vicarious images, however much they may enjoy the protection of social convention, are still vicarious images. However general their acceptance by the current and institutionalized mind they are none the less impediments to consciousness and growth."[36] All agree that men and women live in "second-hand worlds," as C. Wright Mills put it, and most argue that the second-hand is the only kind of a world that human beings can live in.[37]

Burrow defines the social image as

> the individual's mental picture or idea along with the superstitious feeling, emotion or affect attaching to it as this affectively toned idea is related to the ideas of other persons from the point of view of this wholly superficial "right" or "wrong" appearance; that is, from the point of view of the individual's advantage or disadvantage in respect to the opinions or social images of others.[38]

While others note the collective nature of the social image, he emphasizes its subjective, or rather autistic, basis and the subsequent results of this. The social image represents a superficial and obsessive view that involves inevitable social conflict, an authoritarian perspective, interference with biological processes, and interorganismic tensions. The persuasiveness of the social image is dependent upon the transference or "replacement of the object as directly related to the organism as a whole by a mental picture as first imparted by the individuals who inculcated in us this symbol—or image—association."[39] That is, the authoritativeness of the image is based upon our necessary adaptation to the superiority of the parental figure which presented and enforced it upon us.

This transference produces two premises concerning reality. The first is that thought or ideas determine behavior. Burrow refers to this as "the notion . . . that intellectual ideas and concepts are effective determinants of an organism's behavior, that they are biologically dynamic."[40] He notes that "belief in the efficacious agency of the idea is universal."[41] This first premise implies that human beings can be controlled and even drastically changed by controlling or changing their ideas about the world, an implication that leads to the intense efforts to manipulate the opinions or images of men so typical of our age. Burrow denies that such a directional relationship exists. As he puts it:

> Whether in individual or nation, it is not one's thinking that determines his pattern of reaction, but one's pattern of reaction that determines his thinking. If in man's symbolic usages he has unknowingly employed affects or deviate feelings instead of feelings that are consistent with his organism's primary relation to the environment and to others, symbolic interpretations are of no avail.[42]

The belief in ideational determination is a symptom of deranged relations of the organism to the environment and to the realm of symbolic expression.

The Isolated Individual

The second premise implied by the transferred authority of the social image is the primary reality of the isolated individual. The parent teaches the child by assuming that he or she is a separate entity seeking his or her own advantage. Thus the child learns to behave properly, not through recognition of any biological criterion but instead because a reward will be forthcoming if the behavior meets the parental criterion of "good," or a punishment if it is judged to be "bad." To make sense of such a situation the child must assume the separateness of his own ego and the novel nature of his own advantage. He learns to conform outwardly for entirely personal advantage, that is, for the avoidance of punishment as well as for the opportunity to utilize the same means of manipulation defensively against the parent and eventually against members of the species who have become "others." The result is a "subjective fallacy," as Burrow called it, or the failure to recognize the underlying biological unity of the species. Just as he repudiates the assumption that ideas determine behavior, Burrow emphatically denies the notion of the isolated individual as a unit of analysis:

> Man is not an individual. He is a societal organism. An analysis, whether individual or collective, that is based upon differentiations assumed to rest upon legitimate scientific ground rests in fact upon very transient social artifices and lacks the support of a true biological basis. Man's analysis as an element means his isolation as an element. And his isolation is an essential affront to an organic group principle of consciousness.[43]

Symbolic conditioning, that is, connecting some pain or pleasure to the occurrence of a sign, requires an illusion of separateness. The resulting illusory entity Burrow called the " 'I'-persona."[44]

The combined premises of ideational determinism and isolated individual result in a bidimensional image of reality consisting of the individual ego and its advantage. There is a world of all-powerful symbols manipulated by autistic, self-centered organisms. This perspective, Burrow tells us, is superficial and unreal because it represents a mere conceptual construction of life substituting for the experimental process of life itself. That is, this "personalistic delineation" of reality represents, in Burrow's words, "a system of absolutism, preclusive of data existing outside its own autogenously circumscribed principle."[45] Since "the autistically oriented cognitive function tends to adhere to and to reinforce the limited, self-centered perspective which it was supposed to observe and evaluate," the perceptions of men and women are distorted, at least in those aspects where recognitions of events or situations would require a re-evaluation of individual images or personas presented to the world.[46] Not only do this distortion and absolutism mean that social science is not possible under these conditions, but they also imply the inevitability of destructive social conflict.

The allegiance of the isolated individual to a given social image is based on securing his own advantage. Those with other images are enemies. That is, personalistic allegiance demands social conformity. Burrow declares: "The symbolically separate individual requires that the organisms of others as well as of himself shall act or 'behave' in a manner that represents the surrogate of harmony as expressed socially under the symbol 'right' or 'good.' "[47] But the resulting harmony is ersatz, punitive, and precarious. Deviations are not mistakes or even new points of view, they are attacks upon the social existence of the species.

Further, dissenters are necessary, since a species-wide agreement would make the good/evil distinction meaningless and therefore useless as a means of obtaining autistic advantage. Given the fixed and absolutist perspective of the social image, "the advocates of a system are necessarily the unconscious adversaries of that system."[48] In other words, there is no advantage to being a "good" democrat unless fascists or other heretics exist. Further, Burrow seems to be saying that social images are defense mechanisms on a social scale like the reveries, fixated ideas, and dreams of the neurotic person. Therefore the "social substantive 'I' " becomes fanatically attached to a given symbol such as communism, capitalism, or Christianity, to the degree that it must defend itself against opposite impulses.

Burrow repeatedly states that it does no good to demonstrate the error of such attachments, since they result from a general species disturbance. As defense mechanisms, social images are unstable because they are means for dealing with symptoms only and not with the underlying disturbance. As the inadequacy of one attachment is revealed through its decreasing ability to afford relief, its opposite becomes more attractive. Acts of conversion are the most intense "peak" experiences, giving maximum symptomatic relief. Over time, a person utilizing such a form of adaptation tends to become indifferent to all social images or utilizes them in increasingly heavy and frequent doses like a heroin addict. The social results are periodic waves of crime that evoke what Burrow calls "destructive waves of virtue."[49]

Thus, beneath the outward conformity of collective allegiances to social images, conflict exists always, irreconcilable and destructive. Socialization, or the practice of conditioning symbolic affects, results in a haunting possibility of complete dissociation or madness. Or, put somewhat differently, the attempt to create a political order on the basis of common names, as Hobbes expressed it, results in a subjective state of total warfare, as each " 'I'-persona" interprets these names quite differently.[50] Burrow sums up the situation:

> The observation of social groups has made it apparent that, in respect to man's subjective interpretations, there is lacking a unanimity of accord in the images or symbols possessing a supposedly common meaning. Not only this, but, like the manifest symptom or dream-image of the neurotic patient, this outer unanimity of agreement is found to serve merely as a diplomatic code or gesture beneath which each individual reserves the right to an interpretation that rests entirely upon his private feeling with respect to it.[51]

A system of social reflexes such as a goverment or a corporation rests then on the "cluster-reactions" of subjective presuppositions which "possess all the fatality of chemical combinations."[52] Underlying each system of social agreement is a conspiracy of autistic individuals who agree only as a means of having their absolute autonomy ratified by others.

> Our economic, religious and political views, then would seem to rest not upon the covenants of an accepted ethic with respect to one another, but upon quite proprietary and posessive claims, which being private and covetous, rest upon subjective pre-possessions that are completely lacking in objective authority. It would appear that there is no economic system, that what we call our economic system is really a proprietary system.[53]

Beneath the mechanical consensus of our Hobbesian society there lurks in each of us an ambitious prince who continuously manipulates appearances (after the advice of Machiavelli) in a futile attempt to subjugate, all the while actually serving each other in maintaining the illusion of individualism.[54]

The Autocratic Perspective

Our private princes, so to speak, are autocratic in their autonomy and thus incapable of learning about the social world except in the limited sense of learning how to calculate consequences in order to preserve their spurious advantage. As Burrow wrote: "An unchallenged autonomy, as viewed objectively, is of the essence of dogma and fundamentalism."[55] That is, the "I"-persona maintains what Burrow called an "unconscious absolute," rigid and autocratic in perspective.[56] The judgments reached from such a perspective are necessarily fixed and obsessive and therefore unreliable because they cannot be modified in the light of experience. Burrow asserts that "each of us maintains opinions merely by virtue of the assumed criterion of his own personal judgment."[57] As the popular expression has it, "I know what I like." Any conscious change of liking, any growth or development, would mean a surrender of individual autonomy and an admission of inferiority. Further, the criterion of absolute judgments is always comparative, as Burrow points out, and therefore creates the specter of the heretical enemy both without and within. Thus, "when the individual judges from a frame of reference that is comparative or fixed, he necessarily judges fixedly."[58] Since "the substantive 'I' represents a sort of walled-in principality of artificial and symbolic affects,"[59] its judgments are esoteric, bizarre, and unrealistic. This quality is often quite evident when we listen to others, and such observations are the empirical basis for the previously mentioned "myth of the framework," that is, the notion that individual judgments can themselves be judged only in terms of some cluster reaction or collective mythology.

The autocratic perspective of the "I"-persona results in a scarcely concealed authoritarianism in human interaction. This result is significant not only in terms of the hierarchical social structures which are based upon it but, more important to Burrow, such a perspective makes social science and social knowledge impossible. By excluding the "unconscious absolute" of our own perceptions from analysis when we, as social investigators, try to describe social and political reality, we find ourselves not only accused of utilizing intellectual means to carry out "distrustful acts" (seeking to add to our own power or detract from the power of others) but also guilty of just that—however inadvertent or unconscious such a purpose may be. This is revealed in much of the critical rhetoric of the social sciences, whether we utilize standards of methodological, ethical, or stylistic correctness in judging the work of others.

Burrow notes, "Telling other people what one presumes to believe they ought to know is the very keelson of our religious, political, educational, and psychiatric systems."[60] Our social as well as our intellectual roles are divided into two categories—positions of autocratic and projective control over others (administrator, parent, teacher, boss, therapist) and positions of reciprocal subservience (subordinate, child, student, employee, patient). Instead of learning, we go through various situations of "transference," being conditioned or conditioning in turn, depending upon the roles we are enacting. Thus, the goal of social science becomes not knowledge, but rather "the prediction and control of behavior."

Burrow's attempt to alter the perspective of the social investigator from an exclusive to an inclusive principle is a prerequisite of a new social-science enterprise. Burrow notes that "medicine . . . became a science when the symptoms of the individual ceased to be the focus of interest and when interest became focused instead upon the pathological germ or cause of definite alterations of tissue and their characteristic symptoms." However, in the social sciences today, "only the symptoms of the individual afford concrete material for the study of the causes of an existing disorder."[61] The authoritarian perspective of the "I"-persona is manifested in the social sciences in the form of various demands for "objectivity." But the objectivity achieved is always subject to exposure as biased by others also claiming "objectivity." What this "objectivity" actually amounts to is a last-ditch attempt to defend the autocratic perspective by refusing to take account of the actions and reactions of the social investigator in making and reporting observations. We never know what the investigator is thinking, feeling, or doing, or if we do we are not allowed to consider such things in evaluating his research.

Distortion of Symbolic Processes

The reflexes of the social image interfere with and suppress the biological processes of the human organism. In reacting to affectively conditioned images, the individual must restrict biological responses or at best translate them into symbolic expressions which are projected onto the environment. If we note that in conditioning an animal we must restrict the animal's responses and limit or control the available stimuli, then Burrow's point becomes clear. Accompanying the conditioned response is a physiological state of inhibition. Man's symbolic behavior, Burrow stresses, is miniature in comparison to the overall response of the organism to its environment. He notes, "It is important to realize that this restricted, this exceedingly reduced behavior-configuration now mediating man's behavior entails a correspondingly restricted feeling-reaction."[62] Burrow relied on the work of the biologist George Coghill for the description of the interorganic relationship of conditioned symbolic affect and total reaction pattern. Coghill's work on the neurological development of the salamander *Amblystoma* led him to understand reflexes as a behavior pattern consisting of two parts, an overt or excitory reaction of a particular component coupled with a covert or inhibitory reaction of the remaining components.[63] The local reflex is possible because the overall behavior pattern has sensitized a set of organs to respond. In the salamander this mechanism is simple—certain postures of the organism allow the limbs to respond reflexively to stimuli.[64] This dual behavior pattern presents no difficulty for the organism unless the reflex is in some way separated or isolated from the total integrative pattern. Such a condition constitutes, for Coghill, a pathological disturbance. He wrote:

> Normal behavior requires that the total pattern maintain sovereignty over all partial patterns; but through decadence of the organ of the total pattern, or hypertrophy of mechanisms of partial patterns, that sovereignty may give way to the dominance of parts that are normally its subjects, and, as a result of this, behavior may cease to serve the individual as a whole appropriately; that is to say, it may cease to be normal.[65]

Coghill went on to suggest that there is an inherent antagonism between the mechanisms of the total pattern and the mechanisms of the partial patterns and that this kind of antagonism "may constitute the organic basis of psychic conflicts."

For example, Kurt Goldstein's patients behaved abnormally because of damage of the "organ of the total pattern" or central nervous system. This damage allowed many of their reflexes to become isolated. Goldstein observed the following alterations in their partial reactions: (1)"The reactions to stimuli in an isolated part are *abnormally strong;*" (2) "The reactions are of abnormal duration"; (3) "The reactions are bound to the stimulus in an abnormal way. We call this phenomenon . . . forced responsiveness to stimuli"; (4) "A further change of the form of reaction . . . is the appearance of abnormal rigidity on the one hand and alternating reactions to a single stimulus on the other"; (5) "The detachment of part of the organism from the rest more or less deprives the activities of that part of content. . . . Actions in isolation are simpler or . . . more 'primitive.' " Such "isolation phenomena" are possible occurrences, Goldstein says, under conditions of stimulation of abnormal strength or abnormal duration as well as in situations of organic damage.[67]

The characteristics of the partial behavior reactions of Goldstein's patients seem to be analogous to the behavior reactions in terms of the social image that Burrow describes. Since we are not dealing with brain-damaged individuals, but with apparently normal men and women, the resulting neurotic behavior patterns must be due to abnormal conditions of stimulation. What is damaging about these conditions? According to Burrow, man's use and development of complex symbolization creates a special set of conditions.

In each human organism, internal conflict between the local or partitive reactions to affective symbols and the integrative response to the environment is present because "the symbolic zone of responses has encroached . . . upon the zone of the organism's reaction as a whole."[68] That is, "the neuromuscular modifications which attend the ideas the patient has in his head—in his socio-symbolic system—are incompatible with the neuromuscular modifications which motivate his organism as a whole."[69] In short, "man . . . who first enlisted the symbol in his service, has now become the conscript of the symbol."[70] Man's social behavior is not then primarily motivated by the internal biological needs of the human organism. Such behavior can be irrelevant or even destructive in terms of life. Obviously, biological needs do not cease, nor does awareness of them. But Burrow maintains that such awareness is no longer directly or proprioceptively available. Rather it is projected onto an image of internal awareness or onto an outer appearance of awareness.[71] We treat or understand our own sensations as responses to symbolic stimuli and give them symbolic expression in the form of words like "happiness," "sadness," "anger," "love." The result is a systemic misunderstanding of ourselves and the world. "Dealing cognitively (objectively) with our affects and affectively (subjectively) with our cognitions, we fail to envisage what is actually before us."[72]

The social image is not then just a "diplomatic code" camouflaging the conflict of each advantageously motivated substantive "I" with all others. Its vacillating configurations of reactions are an expression of the internal conflicts and tension found in each human being. As Burrow expressed it:

> The social image is that purely psychological factor in man's interideational or sociosymbolic exchange which results when a primary total sensation attempts to push through the restricted, partitive path of the symbol or image and becomes impacted and artificially converted into the distorted composite of an image affect.[73]

The coordination of social interaction on the basis of the social image is thus a fruitless task. That is, the formulation of a set of superior values, rules, and concepts accompanied by an appropriate set of political institutions cannot solve the problem of the social neurosis. For it is not our symbolic formulations which need to be reformed so much as our lives, our work, and our experience. Our symbolic expressions are improved only to the extent that our symbol usage is subordinated to the needs of human life.[74] In short, health or socially adequate conduct can be determined only on biological grounds. Burrow declared, "It is only when we have established in social man a principle of behavior that is universal and constant that we may determine those reactions which deviate from this universal principle."[75]

Symbolization and Conditioned Reflex

The substitution of affective symbols for the total integrative responses of the organism is illustrated throughout Burrow's works by two examples. One example we have considered is the insistence on the part of parents and teachers that children alter their behavior according to the "rightness" or "wrongness" arbitrarily attributed to acts, whether for personal convenience or allegiance to social prescription. Another example is that of the experimentally conditioned animal. In the case of Pavlov's classical experiments with dogs, a certain sign such as a bell or a light is presented just before food is given the animal. After some occurrences of this sequence the dog will begin to respond to the sign *as if* it were the food or in some way stood for the food.[76] Such a sign is responded to by salivation, for example. Burrow remarks that, by means of the techniques of conditioning demonstrated by Pavlov, a dog could be made to salivate to a spoken word as well as to various graphic symbols. Pavlov's conditioned reflexes are, according to Burrow, "an example of an organism's response to the symbol or index in its elementary cortical form."[77] Although the conditioned responses of Pavlov's dogs parallel or are analogous to the human response to the symbols of language, the former is extremely elementary in comparison to the latter, especially as we envisage a social situation of conditioned responses.

In order to get a sense of an overall pattern of conditioning, Burrow suggests the following thought experiment. In this experiment we imagine that, instead of conditioning dogs to respond to metronomes or whistles, we condition them to the cries or gestures of other dogs. For example, we condition one set of dogs to howl when they see another dog scratch. Another set we condition to leap when they hear a howl, another to bark when they see a dog leap, another to scratch when they hear a dog bark, and so on. In the absence of the experimenter an accidental stimulus like, say, a flea would set off a chain of conditioned responses that theoretically could go on for the life of the animals.

Such a situation models the social condition Burrow is trying to describe. First the conditioned responses of each dog to the stimuli of the others is unrelated to ordinary perceptions. That is, the conditioned reflex emitted in the form of a howl is unrelated biologically to the dog's perception of a friendly animal scratching. Burrow comments that "we have introduced among the dogs a system of interactions which is biologically new and represents a group or inter-individual reflex."[78] These new responses are, in his words, "extraorganic." "A restricted, partial or symbolic lamina of contact and communication, having become established as an organic variation among the dogs, now allows the animals to react to one another upon a wholly new segmental plane."[79] Before the experiment the dogs related to each other according to total response patterns—smelling, looking, licking, and all the subtle means of interaction according to posture, expression, and the like. After the experiment their responses are partial and confined to the organs involved in the conditioned reflex. Of course, the total pattern is still there, but its behavioral expressions are stilted or distorted in their primarily symbolic forms.

Burrow's imaginary experiment in "social conditioning" gives us a grasp of the way he sees the social neurosis. Note that in observing the interactions of our imaginary dog society we would find patterns that seem to indicate rationality or conscious purpose from time to time. This was Walter's experience when observing his machine society. His automatons possessed reflexes triggered by environmental stimuli as well as a light emitted by each machine. In turn, these reflexes were controlled by negative feedback loops. Walter writes that the simple design of his machine society "again illustrates an important general principle in the study of animal behavior—that any psychological or ecological situation in which such a reflexive mechanism exists may result in behavior that will seem, at least, to suggest self-consciousness or social consciousness."

It may well be, however, that our concepts of self-consciousness and social consciousness are based on the reflexive mechanisms that constitute only a part of the human repertoire of responses. Thus many of the correlations of behavior patterns with various environmental and social phenomena may not be simply spurious but rather may refer to only one dimension of the human activity involved. The patterns that emerge from such studies may, in fact, be predictive over limited periods of time, but they are doomed to fail inexplicably at any moment. For, if Burrow's description is correct, the symbolic or partial responses of the organism are unstable or vacillating over time (as Thucydides and Machiavelli among others stress) and they never completely supplant the total integrative pattern of responses. Thus, though symbolic behavior may be destructive because of its isolation from biological verification, human organisms still will struggle to survive on the biological level.[81] The resulting pattern of vacillating reflexes and shrewd realism, fanatic idealism and biological sabotage, abstract rationalism and concrete pragmatism makes it difficult to describe human behavior in any definitive way. It is all too easy to stress parts of the pattern as the correct form of behavior or to take such parts for the whole by interpreting other responses as disguised forms.

Social behavior, viewed in this way, is not so different from what social investigators have described over the centuries.[82] But it is now perhaps easier to understand why Burrow judges these descriptions to be exercises in symptomatology. If we understand that we too share these same symptoms, then it is also easier to comprehend why our own descriptions of symptoms will be biased, partial, and distorted in advantageous ways. The self-inclusive perspective that Burrow says we must attain in order to get beyond the symptoms to the disease means initially that our primary investigations must not be simply verbal or symbolic but must involve direct perception of our physiological reactions as well as those of others in a laboratory situation. Or, to put it another way, while statistical techniques may prove to be useful in some phases of social investigation, to limit our studies from their beginning to events (verbal or nonverbal) that such techniques can handle is to remain at the symptomatic level. Our resulting indices may then tell us something about the course of social disease and disintegration but nothing about its cure or prevention.

Consensual Observation

But how is it possible to be human, let alone be a social investigator, without utilizing symbols?[83] Has not Burrow described pathogenic situations from which it is not possible for the human race to escape? According to Burrow, it is impossible for human beings to escape their present derangement of symbol usage by symbolic means.[84] What is required is the use, development, and improvement of our nonsymbolic perception and behavior. Burrow puts it this way:

> Man has taken his intellect to the university for centuries, but never his feeling. There have been no courses for the education of feeling, for instruction and training in the emotions. This education of the intellect to the exclusion of the mood of man inevitably entails a distortion of both.[85]

By learning something directly about our emotions we gain a means to reconstruct our symbol use. For Burrow stresses again and again that it is not the use of symbols itself that causes the social neurosis.[86] Symbol use in the form of language is acknowledged to be a great labor-saving device as well as the basis for developing "a definitive scientific criterion of observation." That is, man's part function of symbol use is basic to man's complex social structures as well as to the project of science itself. By means of symbolic expression, Burrow believed, human beings come to understand that they share sense impressions of the external world. But the symbolic means of consensual observation of external events and objects is completely unsuited to observing and designating the internal physiological events of the individual organism. The attempt to treat organic reactions symbolically or, as Burrow expresses it, the displacement of the physiological reality of feeling and thinking by an external cypher, symbol, or code, represents to him a fundamental mistake or *faux pas* in the development of the species. The result is, for him, "an inadvertent but nevertheless unwarranted overemphasis on both the word and the head that produces the word."[87] The *faux pas* consists of an "error of perception," that is, of perceiving internal states as if they were external categories.[88] By means of this mistake the human condition becomes "semiopathic," that is, one in which feelings are expressed not in direct organic responses but symbolically.[89] It would seem, however, to take something more than a simple mistake or an inadvertence to incapacitate a species.

Symbols and Intermodal Association

Why does symbol use lead to distortions of perception? Significantly, human language differs from other primate communication systems by reason of its ability to refer to environmental objects and states. Although gibbons, chimpanzees, macaques, and other simians have repertoires of "calls," such vocalizations refer to the state of the animal's organism and, by such means, only indirectly to environmental conditions. Thus, a monkey's cry communicates fear, anger, hunger, and joy, but not danger, food, and sunsets. An anthropologist, Jane Lancaster, has made an interesting comparison of primate communication systems. She notes that "nonhuman primates can send complex messages about their motivational states but they communicate almost nothing about the state of their environments."[90]

This ability to form intermodal associations between vocal sounds and printed words, or vocal sounds and pictures, or sounds and events, or sounds and environmental objects, to name only a few possible combinations, is easily accomplished by *homo sapiens* because of special structural features of the human brain, according to Lancaster.[91] The significance of these features is that humans can "name" or associate two sensory images directly and easily, nearly independently of visceral responses or the limbic system.[92] Thus such associations are arbitrary and somewhat independent of the biological needs of the organisms. However, Lancaster maintains that all learning involves visceral responses to some extent:

> All learning, i.e., the formation of association chains, whether in a monkey or in a man eventually is related to the limbic system. The distinction being made here is between a monkey which can form a nonlimbic-limbic association and man who can form a stable nonlimbic-nonlimbic-limbic associative chain. Neither a man nor a monkey can learn or function effectively without ultimately relating his sensory experiences to the limbic system.[93]

Lawrence S. Kubie makes a similar point when he asserts that "every symbol must have roots simultaneously in the internal perceptual experiences of the body and in the external perceptual experiences of the outer world."[94] Kubie likens symbolic units to hammocks hanging "between two poles, one internal or bodily ('the I') and one external ('the non-I'); so that whenever we consciously think and speak of the outer world, we are wittingly or unwittingly thinking and speaking of the innerworld."[95]

In all this we see the possibilities for the development of complex communication systems and scientific knowledge of the environment created by the human capacity for symbol use as well as possibilities for delusions. For while people are learning to use arbitrary symbol units to stand for events or objects in the environment, it is possible for those units to become associated also with visceral states. The resulting symbolic expression may therefore possess both a "meaning" in the sense of an environmental referent and an "affect" or associated feeling or mood. Such an affect may be disclosed in dreams or more seriously in neurotic obsessions or psychosis when the external pole of the symbol is disregarded. Also the external referent may come to be perceived in a distorted manner consistent with an entirely accidental affect. This "tendency to add to the symbol a quality or attribute not inherent in it," as Burrow expressed it, represents an "inescapable pitfall in man's mental outlook."[96]

Symbol Capacity and Derangement

Burrow's way of relating man's symbolic capacity to the deranged tendencies of the species leads to difficulties. The connection between symbol use and delusions can seem analogous to the connection between the capacity to walk upright and the likelihood of sometimes falling on your face. In a sense, upright posture does make it possible, if not likely, that human beings will fall and hurt themselves. But it does not clarify the conditions under which falling is likely, nor does stressing the connection help us avoid serious falls. By pointing out this causal connection between walking and falling we inadvertently suggest that the safest course is the humanly impossible or incapacitating course of refusing to walk. Analogously, Burrow's reiterated emphasis on the connection of symbol uses with pathological states seems to imply that a refusal to use symbols would result in health.

Burrow denies this conclusion time and again, but his formulation does suggest it and such a conclusion can keep us from investigating those social and political situations and conditions that promote a disturbance in the relationship of the symbolic process to the organic reponses of the human being. Such disturbances do seem to be uniquely human or at least rare in the case of other animals, just as falling is more often a problem for the human animal than for four-legged species. But this observation is not instrumental to either the analysis or the treatment of such disturbances. Here is a frontier disclosed by Burrow's work—we need to find out what contexts promote conflict between symbolic and organic responses, and we need to know how and why such conflict comes about. Here we must push on and attempt to discover under what conditions disturbances in symbol use are likely to take place. We have noted that Burrow again and again asserted that thinking or symbol use is a biological process to be evaluated on the basis of its productivity. However, he also argues that the symbolic system or part-brain of the human organism operates independently of biological needs and satisfactions. The two statements are reconcilable.[97] For example, Craik argues that it is the biological independence of man's reasoning, or symbolic process which makes it so productive as a means to survival. By modeling the world symbolically we can estimate the probable outcome of our actions and thereby choose appropriately. Our choices must still be tested in practice. But by using symbols we have reduced to a reasonable level the number of choices to be thus tested. Craik uses the example of bridge building. By calculating the stresses of various bridge designs we can arrive at a design appropriate to our resources and our needs without having to go through the expensive process of building a series of bridges until the best design is discovered.[98]

The biological independence of linguistic symbols—their arbitrariness seen in the fact that the word "salt" is not salty nor the word "fish" fishy—is intrinsic to their productive function.[99] But this independence is not the "isolation phenomena" described by Goldstein, nor does it represent a domination of a local reflex over the total integrative pattern that Coghill finds to be the source of pathological disturbance.[100] The conditions which Goldstein and Coghill describe occur when the symbolizing process becomes cut off from the biological needs of the organism. While some authors, like Leslie A. White and Von Bertalanffy, treat this condition as normal, it seems clear that Burrow does not wish to do this. Here he suggests that human beings have committed a *faux pas* in attempting to deal with the problems of life on a symbolic level.

Conditioning and Conflict

Burrow saw a parallel between human neurosis and the pathological states that occurred during Pavlov's conditioning experiments with dogs. Pavlov found that "a confusion, a conflict, an overlapping between two discrete conditioning stimuli may cause in animals obvious symptoms of behavior disorder."[100] Pavlov described experiments in discrimination that resulted in neurosis. For example, a dog was conditioned to respond to a luminous circle, that is, a projection of the circle was followed by feeding. After the reflex had become established, the dog was trained to differentiate between the circle and an ellipse. As the shape of the ellipse was altered to approach that of a perfect circle, the dog had greater and greater difficulty making the differentiation. When an ellipse with a ratio of semiaxes 9 : 8 was reached, the differentiation not only failed to improve but began to deteriorate and finally ceased. At this stage pathological disturbances in the dog became obvious.[101]

As we have seen, two processes are involved in acquiring a conditioned reflex—an excitory process in the local area of response and an inhibitory process in the total integrative pattern of the organism. Pavlov theorized that in the case of the neurotic dog "the clashing of excitation with inhibition led to a profound disturbance of the usual balance between these two processes, and led in a greater or less degree and for a longer or shorter time to pathological disturbances of the nervous system."[103] The experimenter found two conditions that produced such pathological disturbances in his dogs: an unusually acute clashing of the excitory and inhibitory processes and the influence of an extraordinary or extremely strong stimulus.[104] We would find the first case when a human being is forced to drastically change a habitual pattern of behavior. The second case might be found when a shocking, unexpected, or threatening event occurred.

While Burrow read and cited Pavlov's examples of experimentally induced neurosis, and while he also relied heavily on the neurophysiological work of Coghill and Goldstein, he consistently underestimated the environmental or situational factors involved in the pathological disturbances those authors described. Instead of seeing in Pavlov's example a case in which situational factors (the manipulations of the animal experimenter) cause a neurotic disturbance as Pavlov diagnosed it, Burrow saw it only as a metaphor. That is, Burrow argued that in man "there has come to be a too close approximation not of two discrete conditioned responses, but of two *systems* of responses, namely the extrinsic, partitive or logical system and the instrinsic, total or primarily integrated system; the one conditioned, the other unconditioned."[105]

Burrow noted that brain areas involved in the symbolic processes were connected or neurologically entangled with older, subcortical parts of the brain. This observation is anatomically correct. He concludes that a "phyletic anomaly" has occured, consisting of a convergence or overlapping of the partitive system of responses with the total or integrated system of responses. This seems to me a misinterpretation, since the physiological conditions that Pavlov, Coghill, Goldstein, and Burrow himself describe are situations of conflict, not of confusion or overlapping. The latter occurs, as Burrow points out, when the system of partitive responses becomes dominant. But Burrow is entranced by the idea of a genetic mistake and slips again and again into a position which implies that the partitive, symbolic system of the human organism is deficient, or as he puts it, is "projective." Thus he writes: "The behavior that arises out of man's motivation to wishfulness and fantasy is the expression genetically of a newly acquired projective mechanism."[106]

Burrow's insistence on a genetic factor underlying the social neurosis is a consequence of his distaste for political and social reform movements with their moralism, as well as of his insight that the establishment of biological criteria and direct laboratory observation of physiological reactions were necessary steps to the development of the social sciences. Burrow's emphasis on the primacy of human biology, his insistence that "we are dealing with neuromuscular phenomena and . . . they are decisive in determining the behavior of man as a species," in sum his throughgoing materialism, is an understandable and even useful corrective to the idealistic, speculative, and moralistic approach of most social investigators.[107] For him, it was most important that men and women learn the means (or social techniques, as he sometimes call them) to evaluate and understand both the social and physical environment in terms of their own biological requirements. Thus Burrow's work was oriented in its early stages toward "the establishment of objectively valid principles of evaluation in the sphere of human behavior," which for him depended on learning to discriminate internal physiological patterns. This orientation led him to the laboratory or group method of social investigation.

Modes of Attention

As we have seen, the first product was the demonstration of a generally "unrecognized confederacy of self-protection and resistance throughout the social system."[108] Initially, Burrow and his associates wanted to free themselves from autistic image dependence or to disassociate affects of goodness and badness from specific symbols and images in order to evaluate behavior patterns from a biological perspective. They wanted to move from statements like "I don't like John (*or* communism *or* baseball)" to inclusive statements like "my autistic 'I'-persona (or individualistic image of myself) is threatened by John's behavior," or "our mutual autistic self-images have agreed to confirm the autocracy of each on the basis of a diplomatic agreement to collectively despise communism." Ordinarily such statements are difficult to make or to understand. For example. Burrow comments that such statements imply that there are two terms not in agreement ("I" and "John," "We" and "communism," for examples) "but that it is impossible to say that one of them should be invariably held accountable and that the other should invariably hold it accountable."[109] These inclusive statements run counter to the implications of ordinary expressions of subjective autocracy and make them appear ridiculous.

But the mere recognition of the ridiculous nature of our autocratic judgments can result in the negative relativism or nihilism expressed in the theater and literature of the absurd. Men and women can be understood as venal fools while the "I"-persona of the critic remains impregnable in its skepticism. Burrow and his associates were searching for something more than the debunking of autocratic judgment and the cataloguing of the foibles of the species. They wished to find the basis of a healthy species and, more, they sought to learn how to investigate that basis. They sought, in short, a method of "species seeing" or consensual observation.

In order to establish a method of consensual observation, Burrow had to achieve a perspective other than the socially common one of autocratic individualism. Given pervasive autism, any attempt at consensus was likely to lead to the compounding of bias rather than to an elimination of personal aberrations.[110] There is no better example of this likelihood than situations which develop from time to time in the social sciences. In these cases attempts to develop objective methods and a scientific consensus lead to the establishment of academies or orthodoxies that punish or threaten deviant views. Such academies or orthodoxies are then unmasked as ideologically motivated, particularly as they attempt to utilize institutional and governmental support as a means of defending their consensus. One generation's "objective" revolt becomes the next generation's model of nonobjective, personally biased research. Recognizing this difficulty, Burrow distinguished between the consensus of the social image and a consensus based on shared sense impressions or a "phyletic principle of observation." The first consensus is typical of governments; the latter consensus is typical of the laboratory.

We find many instances of consensual observation in scientific communities, in hunting and gathering tribes, and in work teams. Consensus of the type Burrow endorses seems possible when there is a high premium on the accuracy of environmental description and the appropriateness of human response. The problem, as Burrow sees it, is not with the notion of consensus itself, but whether the basis of such a consensus is observation or fantasy—experimentation or wish fulfillment. We err when, having experienced the arbitrary nature of the consensual social image and observed the manipulative techniques that maintain it, we assume that a consensus is always arbitrary and manipulated. On biological expectation, an accurate if changing consensus should be available to a species with a common anatomical structure and a capacity for communication. The problem is one of establishing the necessary social conditions for such a consensus. Burrow has identified the nature and the damaging features of the consensual social image. This leaves us with a formidable task.

The "biological group principle" that Burrow sought access to was posited by him on the basis of his early researches into the primary identification of child and mother; on the work of biologists like Coghill, Goldstein, and Von Bertalanffy, which insisted on a holistic or organismic approach to the understanding of protoplasm; on the ideas of researchers in group animal behavior like W. C. Allee and Peter Kropotkin, which stressed instinctual cooperation; and on the recognition of the fundamental biological similarity of human organisms to one another with respect to patterns of neural, muscular, vascular, and visceral interconnections.[111] Burrow took the following position, as summarized by William Galt:

> Contrary to our beliefs, our fancies and our cherished supposi-
> tions, the individual does not constitute the unit of social motiva-
> tion and behavior. He no more represents the unit of social
> behavior than the discrete reflex represents the unit of physio-
> logical behavior. The social group, the race or species, is the
> fundamental unit. The behavior of the individual can only be
> sane and effective when it is in alignment with this principle.[112]

Burrow's approach is different from that of other social investigators who employ the organic metaphor in that it is based on a more sophisticated knowledge of biology and is employed as an investigatory principle rather than as a standard of institutional design. Burrow approached society not in order to redesign it to be more organic, nor to discover superficial analogies between social and biological patterns, but to seek and find the "organic substrate" of behavior underlying the mechanical and competitive norms insisted upon by bureaucratic institutions. His perspective is the opposite of the prevailing one which views the intense and extensive cooperation of, say, hunting and gathering tribes or scientific communities as the result of the mechanical process of socialization. Such a view suggests that if human beings were the malleable creatures we often assume them to be there would be no or little occurrence of internal conflicts. Such conflicts have long been noted as ubiquitous by social investigators and have been accounted for by assuming men to be inherently asocial or defective in terms of their social needs. Burrow's perspective helps us to understand that the occurrence of such conflicts is not necessarily evidence for such an asocial nature; rather asocial and antisocial behavior can be viewed as the result of these conflicts. Burrow's position is that

> the stress of civilization has unconsciously stimulated us as a
> people to the represssion or elimination of an instinct that is
> inalienable to the organism of man as race, as is the instinct of
> sex inalienable to his organism as an individual.[113]

Therefore,

> the disorders represented by the psychoses and neuroses are due
> to the represssion of this instinct of man's tribal life as well as to
> the repression of the individual's sex instinct. Hence the logical
> recourse is a societal analysis that will permit the envisagement
> of our social complexes in a manner comparable to the analysis
> that now permits the envisagement of complexes as they occur in
> the individual.[114]

Burrow's view not only has psychological, physiological, and anthropological support, but its Copernican reversal of perspective also avoids the nagging contradictory assertions and paradoxes of classical Western political thought.

Cotention

The altered perspective sought in Burrow's laboratory was found to be accessible through a nonconceptual reorientation. Burrow called this new perspective or "mode of attention" by the name "cotention." He was now able to distinguish between two fundamentally different types of attention on the basis of his research. Understanding attention as a "process that primarily relates the organism to the outer world," Burrow argued that besides the simpler mode of attention to be found in all animals (relating "the whole organism physiologically to the whole environment"), men were capable of other modes.[115] Through group experimentation he could distinguish between a basic and older form of attention and a more specialized but deranged form of attention distorted by affect or self-advantage. This second mode of attention Burrow labeled "ditention" to emphasize its divisive affect on social interaction.

In cotention, the human organism responds by means of its sensory organs to the features of the object; in ditention, the organism is responding primarily to its self-image and the possibilities of utilizing the object for the secret gains of neurosis maintenance. For example, in cotention I would respond to an object, say a tree, in terms of my biological needs (for shelter, fuel, food, stimulation, relaxation, among others) as they relate to features of the tree (its size, its shape, its type, and like qualities). In ditention, I would respond to the tree in terms of what it might mean to my image of self. Trees might be important to my belief that I am a historically displaced frontiersman, to my image as a defender of the environment against the ravages of industrial capitalism, or to my intellectual conceit, in which case I must know the name, history, and some obscure facts about the unique features of the tree. Trees might have no or little relation to my self-image, in which case having seen one I would have seen them all. If this way of relating to trees seems at all far fetched, note the example of Bismarck, who required even visiting dignitaries to remove their hats while in German forests.[116]

Burrow's distinction between cotention and ditention is clear and decisive. But perhaps the dichotomy is too simple. Burrow's writings cite examples of at least three types of attention—cotention, ditention, and a third mode of symbolic attention. This third mode of attention is, of course, a unique aspect of man's evolution. It is, as Burrow notes, the attention basic to a scientific outlook.[117] This third mode, however, is often treated in Burrow's writings as if it were identical with ditention. Burrow is not consistent in this inconsistency. He suggests in one place that a harmonious integration of the two modes of attention (symbolic attention and cotention) would bring man "into a relationship with the objects of the outer environment which [would] give to them apperceptive significance of scientific organization and meaning."[118]

Are Symbols Pathogenic?

If we take the formulations of Coghill and Pavlov as the model with which Burrow is working, then it is clear that symbolic attention itself cannot be exclusively pathogenic. For in their researches the two found that the source of disturbance was either a conflict between, or a separation of, two neurological and tensional processes. Such a conflict or isolation phenomenon occurs when an exclusively symbolic approach is attempted by the organism. For, as Burrow points out, cotention is essential to survival. That is, the attempt to maintain an exclusively symbolic or partitive mode is doomed to fail since so much of the organism's orientation to the environment is unavailable to the specialized organs of that mode. Our posture, respiration, temperature maintenance, surveillance, and the like, go on "automatically" while we are thinking symbolically. Indeed the technical details of these processes of physical maintenance and orientation are probably too complex to be handled symbolically even on a mathematical level.[119] For example, a man who has learned to drive a car is said to have established habits and reflexes that no longer require thought or direction. His mind is supposedly free from such routine matters and can attend to the higher complexities of daydreams, plans, and verbal articulations. Our way of talking about this division reveals to what extent we accept symbolic attention as a "superior" process, discounting or "making unconscious" the processes of cotention. The reflexes of car driving are integrated with or imbedded in cotention, while in the ditentive mode the verbal and eidetic reflexes of "thinking" are isolated and divorced from cotention.

Take my present situation. My body is continuously attentive to and interacting with the environment. Not only do I remain upright on a chair in the face of gravity, but I also sort out and file information on variations in temperature, lighting, physiological needs, and a complex array of patterned sounds, shapes, and smells, while my fingers translate my thought into the English-language symbols of a written page. To try to describe verbally even a minute of this activity would require not only literary skills greater than those of James Joyce, but also volumes larger than an encyclopedia. And yet, if anyone asks me what I am doing, I answer simply, "writing a book." But what a world of actions and objects lies behind that verbal representation—indeed, what an adventure! All this represents, in Burrow's terms, "a crafts-man's response to his tools," one of the examples that he offers of naturally occurring cotention. Yet my tools are symbols and words. I cannot exercise my craft without them. Presumably the symbolic pro-cesses of my organism are operating (or, at least, sometimes operate) in the context of an integrative pattern rather than attempting to domi-nate it.[120]

Employing the inclusive method that Burrow insists on requires me to note how defensive I am at this point. Obviously if symbols are themselves pathogenic then I am a promoter of disease. This accusa-tion makes me a less than fair critic. My "I"-persona as a writer and a symbol maker is in conflict with Burrow's theory. Therefore I or Bur-row must be wrong. It cannot be I, of course. But it cannot be Burrow either. Thus I react to my own defensiveness by defending Burrow at every turn, jealously guarding his statements against misinterpreta-tions, surely, but also against falsification and improved articulation. Again I finally react to this "true believer" mood by becoming hyper-critical. I think I understand why Burrow's reception by intellectuals in general and social scientists in particular has been so disappointing. He seems to threaten us with extinction, although he is only challenging us to do better work.

While Burrow's techniques were important and useful to his re-search and should be helpful in further research, I do not see them as an isolated solution to the problems of the species. A recent experi-ment showed that those trained in Zen Buddhism can attain a physio-logical state which appears identical with cotention by following Bur-row's instructions.[121] Similar results probably could be obtained by using subjects trained in Yoga or in any number of spiritual and mystical disciplines. Yet these techniques of meditation have not done much to improve the life of the species but instead have served as compensations and psychological crutches. Burrow's techniques, in themselves, could become misused as a means to keep us going in the midst of the species-wide madness that he so devastatingly described. His techniques promise to be more useful as tools of investigation, that is, as means to help social investigators avoid their own autocratic biases and defensive postures.

Burrow does not give a complete nor an adequate account of the etiology of the physiological conflict he describes. Reflexes do not dominate integrative patterns except under extraordinary conditions. Further, any extended domination of reflexes or of symbolic processes would seem to mean the end of the species involved. The job remains to examine and explore the detailed connections between social structures, their resulting roles, communication patterns, and norms, and the pathogenic domination of symbolic affect. It has always troubled me that Burrow's work has had so little impact on improving the condition of the species. Indeed, this failure suggests that his approach may have been flawed. But another, and, I think more productive evaluation, is to understand that Burrow was a pioneer in a vast and complex undertaking. He offers no solace, only a profound and even frightening challenge.

Differentiating Modes of Attention

Burrow was successful in establishing that the two modes of attention he demarcated were physiologically distinct. From 1937 on, he and his associates worked to establish instrumental indexes differentiating cotention and ditention. Specifically, they established the following:

> In cotention, the breathing is slower and deeper, the eyes steadier, and there is a marked change in brainwave pattern in the parietal or motor area. This change consists in a reduction in the amplitude of the alpha waves and in the percentage time of the alpha rhythm. Control experiments indicated that these changes are specific to cotention and that they occur automatically as an integral part of the cotentive response.[122]

As I understand these findings, it becomes clear that what Burrow called ditention was not simply the organism using symbols to relate to the environment, but the organism attempting to use symbols exclusively. Perhaps ditention is primarily a defensive mode of attention.[123] The symbolic processes usurp direction of the organism's responses in order to preserve it under certain conditions of threat. In my opinion, this assumption is the best way to make sense out of Burrow's findings. It is important that Burrow has shown that such a usurpation involves a distortion of the human biological processes tantamount to functional damage. The behavior patterns of individuals whose primary mode of relationship to the environment is ditention are thus analogous to those of Pavlov's neurotic dogs. Burrow is, therefore, correct in maintaining that no symbolic adjustment can relieve the basic physiological conflict, but he leaves to us the task of describing and explaining those features of the social situation that promote such conflict.

Burrow takes account of the environmental context of cotention when he writes:

> Cotention originated as a group process and is, therefore, essentially a social as well as an individual phenomenon. This is

of interest in connection with our observation that the individual is assisted in recovering his organism's cotentive pattern to the degree in which he himself finds himself one of a group whose purpose is, in general, hospitable to this altered mode of adaptation.[124]

Syz offers that "while Burrow emphasized socio-individual totality and the emergence of conflict within man in the course of his evolution, he also placed great stress on noxious social conditioning."[125] This stress is not so apparent to me and seems to be limited to the citing of biased parental standards of good and bad and general notices of the arbitrary nature of social images.

Burrow's laboratory method did reveal something of the contextual nature of cotention, but he did not fully explore the conditions of ditention. Clues to the understanding of these conditions are found throughout Burrow's writings—most importantly the idea that the represssion of social instincts is basic to the generation of human neurosis. This suggests that institutions which thwart, disguise, or discourage the development of social skills in communicating and working with others will be conducive to disease. While the examination and description of the morphology and behavior of a species is necessary for establishing standards of health and normality, it also reveals information about that species' environment. If distortions of structure or functional damage are consistently found, then we may infer an environment that is in some degree pathogenic. To conclude, as Burrow does, that we are dealing instead with an evolutionary mischance seems unnecessary and unwarranted. We need to see the social environment of mankind in a new way that emphasizes the relational processes between it and the species. Not merely any new way will do, especially not the mere substitution of new images that can only perpetuate our confusion about the context of our lives. Finding such a new way is a most difficult task, but a task that has been made recognizable and even possible, thanks to the outstanding efforts of Trigant Burrow.

The Shift to Basic Causation

Burrow's efforts "to shift the whole problem of human conduct from the field of individual psychology to that of the more basic behavioral causations that affect both the individual and the community as a whole" provide us with the outlines of a new framework for the investigation of social ignorance.[126] Significantly this framework is not only a new conceptual structure but is also an open perspective demanding critical practice in the form of unfettered empirical experimentation. That is, it recognizes that the continuous symbolic recoding required for the successful adaptation and survival of the species is not an end in itself, not even a determining or directing activity of human life.

Burrow recognized and analyzed the widespread phenomenon of "semiomorphism"[127]—that inverted and erroneous investment of the symbol with substance and causation which has haunted Western political thought and contained it within Platonic limits. His demystifying assertion that "the symbol is nothing more than a sign-board and as such it is merely the hand-maid of the organism as a whole" is a slogan of liberation for intellectuals.[128] For if symbols are but our tools, then we want appropriate ones that can be used productively—not perfect symbols, nor certain symbols, but relevant, precise, reliable, and novel symbols that help us to expand the range of responses available to the race. The symbol producer need not stand apart and above the social world as a founder of institutions or a reformer of men. Nor need he slavishly serve those who rule or the dialectic of history. Like those anonymous geniuses of neolithic pottery production, he must learn to serve his fellow beings with the social sensitivity, the creativity, and the attention to detail of the skilled artisan. For those ancient potters did not mold human life, but did expand its possibilities, enhance its enjoyments, and enrich its experience.[129]

This new and open perspective requires the redefinition of the role of the social investigator from that of the philosopher king or revolutionary hero to that of the social biologist. Based on Burrow's work, the investigatory framework of the social biologist has the following characteristics:

1. Investigatory results are judged on the basis of their "productivity" or contribution to the quality of life.

2. Schemas of investigation are inclusive, embodying the responses and situation of the investigator and denying to him any fixed and absolutist sanctuary (or, all indicative statements are accompanied by stated or implied accounts of the limiting context).

3. The unit of analysis is the social aggregate, not the individual human organism.

4. Human criteria of health and normality are based on morphological rather than statistical standards.

5. Symbolic expressions are considered improved only to the extent that they demonstrably contribute to expanding the range of human action.

6. Laboratory methods employing techniques of direct consensual observation are used.

The social-biologist perspective also entails the following cautionary statements:

1. Symbolic expressions cannot of themselves effectively improve or expand the possibilities of human behavior.

2. Denial and/or suppression of the social instincts of human beings is a basic source of pathological behavior.

3. Unfalsifiable injunctions, whether in the form of commands or value statements, are arbitrary and require structures of domination to be accepted.

4. The process of socialization, as we now understand it, generates arbitrary valuations, personal autism, and social conflict.

5. The isolation of given reflexes through overtraining, overfrustration, or overemphasis creates internal and biological conflicts in the human organism.

6. Symbols are not suited for use in observing and designating internal physiological tensions.

7. The use of symbols alone to determine the behavior of human beings is pathogenic.

The social biologist sees from an industrial, rather than an administrative, context. Burrow tried to express this deceptively simple idea throughout his writings. He understood his stated goal—of finding and applying a technique that would enable men to be more skillful in understanding their own physiological tension and relate them to the objects and processes of the environment—as both social and industrial. Burrow wrote:

> We need more and more to bring home to us that the meaning of attention is adaptation, that it means man's relation to the objects about him and the employment of these objects in the service of those needs which contribute to his maintenance and survival as an individual and as a race. Thus adaptation or attention is essentially industrial. *It is the industry of the organism as a whole in its application to the environment as a whole.*[130]

The industrial context from which Burrow sees is not a context of masterful destruction but rather is one that encompasses both the race and the environment in a process of development ensuring the integrity of both. It was Burrow's belief that such "industrialization" would mean the eventual end of image dependence and of the hierarchical structures of reward and control that dependence entails. Or, as he expressed it in terms of the stultifying socialization processes of education:

> When schools will have become the productive plants of natural childish industry, there will not any longer be the absurd invention by the schools of ulterior rewards such as now supply the artificial stimulus necessary to lend vitality to their essential dullness.[131]

Conclusion

It may be fruitful to view the problems of social knowledge and ignorance through a medical focus such as that which Burrow pioneered. But there are some dangers. Deeming the race sick may have much the same consequences as deeming it inherently deficient unless we understand that we, the social investigators and critics, share the common disease. Also, the modern medical perspective includes an implicit utopianism which suggests that scientific investigation and informed medical practice will eventually eliminate disease. Dubos cautions that "science provides methods of control for the problems inherited from past generations, but it cannot prepare solutions for the specific problems of tomorrow because it does not know what these problems will be." He argues that each civilization "creates its own diseases" and that techniques developed to aid one generation may not help another. Dubos concludes:

> What may be worth asking is whether medical science can help the individual and society to develop a greater ability to meet successfully the unpredictable problems of tomorrow. This is an ill-defined task for which there is hardly any background of knowledge.[132]

The same question must be put to the investigations of society and politics.

The medical perspective also emphasizes the physiological aspects of problems. While these aspects are often neglected by social investigators and are important to understand, as I believe Burrow has demonstrated, emphasizing them may imply that the "cure" for a physiological conflict must be physiological. This implication is an unfortunate product of the mind-body dualism that runs through our language and our medicine. It is so insistent that in most discussions of social biology the emphasis falls on the biological and the social gets neglected. From the social Darwinist of the nineteenth century until the territorialist of our own times such an approach has often been a reactionary justification of whatever political and social institutions exist. If hierarchies are harmful to human adaptation, it matters not that ants, bees, buffalo, and other creatures are organized socially in hierarchies. The deeper and more radical element in the sociobiological perspective lies in describing the links or relations between social structures and their biological consequences. This view requires that the social and the biological spheres be understood as complementary frames of analysis that are not reducible. What is biological or physiological about any human organization consists of its living members. What is social or political consists of the structures and norms of organization.

What is important about Burrow's insight is the notion that our knowledge of the world is dependent upon its social, not its metaphysical or individual, grounding. That is, we see and know no better than our institutional arrangements of cooperation and coordination allow us to. Thus, if the ground of our knowledge is social—not individual and not methodological—then epistemology is a political and sociological study rather than merely a psychological and philosophical one. Such a study requires that the relations between institutional patterns and patterns of social knowledge must be established empirically, of course. Whether such relations are causal or only limiting remains to be seen. If hierarchical organizations limit or restrict certain types of learning and knowing, as I believe they do, they must be altered to provide for wider ranges of human growth. If hierarchies promote some kinds of knowing, then they are to be retained or to be available when that kind of knowledge is required. The age-old justification of hierarchy—that we cannot stop to take a vote at times of immediate emergency but must rely on the direction of those who know or at least have a plan—is not entirely facetious. But justifying in the emergency does not mean that hierarchies can be justified in exploratory, placid, or even continuously turbulent situations.

Frederick Thayer is right in maintaining that alienation ultimately is caused by hierarchy.[133] But it is likely that the immediate causes of alienation are the exaggerated claims to efficiency, reason, and piety made and enforced by hierarchies. Whether hierarchical organizations can function without such claims is questionable. But we can see that nonhierarchical structures also will promote alienation to the extent that they make supernatural or ideological claims to certainty. Testing in use is the only justificatory procedure for human organizations, and even such testing does not permit the prohibition of further experimentation. In sum, the critical question for contemporary social investigators is, as Meehan states:

> What are the characteristics of a social structure and an individual that is able to learn from experience and improve its performance, and how can these characteristics be taught?[134]

Burrow understood the same question as one of establishing a standard of species health. His work gives us evidence that we can create or hypothesize such a standard in a manner that is empirical in the Hippocratic tradition. But this is possible only so long as the investigation of human and social health is understood as a collective and cooperative enterprise in which the assumptions and standards of evidence of the investigators are open to continuous criticism. No matter how difficult this task may be, it offers an escape from the fruitless confines of the hierarchical myth of the framework: (1) there must be assumptions in order to know, (2) yet assumptions are always contaminated by subjectivity, and therefore (3) knowledge, especially social knowledge is impossible, so that (4) efficacious social ignorance in the form of noble lies enforced by hierarchical institutions is the very best we can do. If social investigators can learn to discriminate between the autistic use of smbols to defend or dominate and the cooperative use of symbols to know by means of a laboratory approach, then the prospects for the species are great indeed.

8　The Contexts of Social Ignorance

Patient: This treatment is unpleasant. Here I must talk about things that I do not want to see.
Stekel: People get sick from "not wanting to see." . . . Whoever wants to get well must see everything openly and consciously.

—Wilhelm Stekel

To summarize the argument at this point: (1) what purports to be Western social knowledge concerning human nature and the consequent hierarchical structure of social order is unfalsifiable myth; (2) the social ignorance found to pervade human institutions cannot be accounted for within the traditions of the sociology of knowledge and socialization theories without the result of making social knowledge impossible; (3) patterns of cognitive deprivation which are often cited as the cause of social ignorance are instead the results of the severe role restriction and impoverished organizational structures of hierarchical institutions; (4) social knowledge requires imaginative theorizing grounded in the concrete experience of human work; (5) the necessity for theory in the creation of knowledge does not justify dogmatism or cognitive hegemony in any form; (6) social ignorance and the belief that this ignorance can be overcome through the adoption and propagation of proper symbols and values are both symptoms of a sick species; (7) the human susceptibility to symbolic distortion must be investigated and understood in order to establish criteria for the design of political and social institutions that are favorable to human growth, autonomy, and maturity.

In this chapter I will take up that seventh and last point. The question I will try to answer is: Within what general type of organizational contexts is the domination of the symbolic processes over the total responses of human beings promoted? The approach employed is adapted from the perspective of communication theory as outlined in general by Jurgen Ruesch and as developed in particular as a way of understanding human pathology by R.D. Laing and Gregory Bateson. Ruesch argues that what we perceive as psychopathology is a disturbance of communicative behavior resulting from faulty procedures and networks of communication.[1] He posits that humans have an innate need for communication and that interference with or disturbances of this need are always frustrating and frequently incapacitating.[2]

The phenomenon of social ignorance within the perspective of communication theory is therefore evidence of institutional inadequacies. This view is based on the assumption, as Ruesch expresses it, that "information controls behavior and . . . by studying information and its exchange one can obtain a better understanding of human behavior."[3] If the prediction and control of human behavior require the manipulation of information, and if information manipulation necessarily results in a basic conflict between symbolic processes and physiological responses as Burrow indicates, then organizational contexts designed to control human behavior promote social ignorance at best and pervasive pathology at worst. Thus the increasing attempts to design and apply a technology of social control are self-defeating. The greater the attempts to control human behavior, the greater the resistance and the pathology. Thus the quest for the simplistic order of hierarchy promotes chaos instead. As Ruesch remarks: "We are moving in a direction which is so often depicted by the cartoonist of *Homo sapiens* as a species with a frail body and oversized head, the personification of schizophrenia."[4]

Laing's approach to psychopathology is to understand human neurosis and psychosis as behavioral critiques of, and as challenges to, defective structures of communication and symbol use. Neurotic and psychotic disturbances are seen by Laing not as diseases to be treated by hospitalization but as adaptations that are the beginning point for the critical reform of damaging social contexts. Bateson has attempted to develop a means for talking about the interaction of social contexts with communication disturbances that avoids problems of reification and determinism. In particular he and his associates have described the results of human interactions of a type called "double bind" that can result in learned incapacities to process symbolic messages in the extreme as well as less drastic stupidities.

Double binds may result whenever we have a hierarchical institution that requires an elite to direct and control the behavior of a membership. For real control would result in an automatism that demands omniscient direction. What we get is a semblance of control and an illusion of administrative competence that result from the issuance of self-negating or paradoxical injunctions. Since these injunctions are self-negating they cannot result in faulty action. For no matter what action is taken, if successful it follows from the injunction and if unsuccessful it does not follow. Therefore the hierarch is always right. The subordinate is either obedient or always wrong. And everyone is deceived.

The Heroic Perspective

The traditional investigator tries to separate himself from the social context that he wants to study, even though such a separation is impossible and leads him to deny his own experience and knowledge. This separate or polarized perspective is heroic. It assumes an isolated knower who performs for an audience, serving them through entertainment, astonishment, and exhortation. The heroic investigator further separates himself from the experimental situation by becoming methodologically self-conscious, watching his every move or statement for signs of bias, passion, or the corruption of direct experience. This heroic role and the metaphysical assumptions on which it is based lead to the dividing of society, as Marx put it, "into two parts, one of which is superior to society."[5] Heroic epistemology—in which evil, error, and ignorance haunt every attempt at knowing—results in an administrative view of social processes that prescribes class distinctions and hierarchical forms for human organizations.

Trigant Burrow saw such attempted separation as basic to the structure of insanity in the individual and society. He argued, "It is precisely this division of the individual into actor and onlooker, and its extension within the social mind to which we owe the birth of the hero."[6] And he added, "This is the division that is insanity. This is the division that is the hero. As there can be no hero without an audience, there can be no insanity without an audience."[7] Such division is typical of that most frightening mental state of the modern world, schizophrenia.[8] For Burrow, the individual manifestations of schizophrenic division in the individual social investigator are only exaggerated symptoms of a general social situation. That is, a polarized social situation is conducive to or even requires a "compulsive form of compensatory *mental* polarization."[9]

But to charge that the perspective of social investigator is heroic is not simply an indictment. The investigator, whether a theorist retiring to his study or an empiricist retreating to his computer is an attractive figure who evokes our admiration and sympathy. Of course, some of this response is due to self-dramatization and some to the Western heritage of hero worship. But the hero performs a vital task. As the paradigm of the social investigator, Socrates offers us a model of the hero at work trying to awaken his fellow citizens from their ignorance only to be martyred for his efforts. The story makes it plain that martyrdom was chosen and that death to Socrates was a welcome end to a task that meant a painful existence.

Looking at this exemplary life, it is hard to see how a decent man, a serious man, a dedicated man, could have gone about the investigation and improvement of his society in any other way. But that way failed for Socrates and has continued to fail for lesser men and women who have taken up the quest for social knowledge in some capacity. If we are to adopt another model of social investigation, we cannot do so by simply rejecting the old. The slogan "No more heroes" is a heroic attempt in itself. The heroic perspective must be understood in terms of its relationship to the pathogenic social situation it at once atempts to cure and to defend. For the paradox that we must avoid is the effort to sustain and strengthen those very conditions of social ignorance that have goaded us to heroic activity. This is the paradox which means that there could be no Plato in the Republic, no Machiavelli in the Princedom, no Hobbes in the Commonwealth, no Marx after the Revolution, no scientists in the preplanned Future. The rules of ignorance prescribed by each of these thinkers for the social contexts they advocated would make it impossible for them to carry out their investigations. Each in his way precludes the possiblility of social criticism for which each is rightfully remembered. It is this paradox that makes the heroic investigator's role schizophrenic. For schizophrenia is a state of living paradox. In this final chapter we will look at some recent attempts to understand this state which will help us to further illuminate the structural details of the social context in which ignorance is both a means of survival and a dangerous and potentially fatal restriction of adaption.

Schizophrenia

While the occurrence of schizophrenic adaptations in individuals has reached reportedly epidemic proportions, the nature of schizophrenia itself, whether disease or orientation, is hotly disputed.[10] It is a frightening phenomenon to witness either in oneself or in others. The typical characteristics (in clinical language) include depersonalization, derealization, autism, nihilistic delusions, delusions of persecution, feelings of omnipotence, end-of-the-world fantasies, auditory hallucinations, impoverished affects, and numerous other manifestations.[11] Indeed, the list of schizophrenic symptoms reads like a cultural inventory of post industrial society. These characterstics are difficult enough to deal with, but combined with them in many cases is an acuity of social and psychological insight that may be expressed in important artistic or critical form. Further, persons diagnosed as schizophrenic seem to have many common physical symptoms and thus present a challenge to assumptions of mind-body dualism. The language of those labeled schizophrenic is rich in metaphor, expressive, and yet almost incomprehensible.[12] These individuals seem to get extremely important things said, but in a form called schizophrenic "salad," which must be laboriously deciphered. The behavior patterns of clinical cases, whether the acute fears of the paranoid, the zombielike obedience and rage of the hebephrenic, or the living death of the catatonic, seem to be devastating parodies of normal patterns of accommodation. The suffering entailed is enormous and quite excruciating to observe, particularly since so few of us understand how to respond in a helpful way. It is little wonder that the "schizophrenic" evokes fear and hostility. He seems to be a living witness to the pain of seeing clearly what is going on in the social world. His insights and his delusions, his compelling honesty and elaborate deceptions, his insistent demands and absolute withdrawals, all seem to be a testimony to the survival value of social ignorance. The truth, it would seem, cannot make us free, but only mad.

The question of the etiology of schizophrenia is a political one. If this is understood, then much of the heated and often sterile controversy in the literature can be better understood.[13] On the one hand, there are those who argue that schizophrenia is determined genetically or exclusively physiologically. They cite evidence that there are hereditary patterns of schizophrenia occurrence and that persons diagnosed as schizophrenic apparently have distinctive characteristics of body chemistry. But their evidence can be interpreted in many ways and hardly closes the question. That it does close the question for many is due, I think, to the ability of this interpretation to ignore what those diagnosed as schizophrenic are saying about human conditions.[14] That is, if social insight results in madness, then we are lost. However, if the madness is caused like any other disease, then we can ignore the need for insight (in effect saying that basically there is nothing wrong with present institutional arrangements to those who are healthy and normal) or we can deny any connection between social insight and self-punishment and derangement.

Those who attend to what schizophrenics say and do are entranced by the insights they find and attribute their suffering to the perceptual restrictions of society and the defensive rage that violation of those rules entail. In this view schizophrenics are heroes living out within themselves the disturbances of society. They may be understood as dramatic protesters against the split perceptions required to live a normal life within the institutional structures of modern hierarchies.[15] Or they may be seen as R. D. Laing views them, as people attempting to "get well" under pathogenic conditions. He argues that 'if we look at the extraordinary behavior of the psychotic from his point of view, much of it will become understandable.'[16] Specifically, Laing's clinical investigations of schizophrenics and their families has led him to conclude

> that *without exception* the experience and behavior that gets labeled schizophrenic is *a special strategy that a person invents in order to live in an unliveable situation.* In his life situation the person has come to feel he is in an untenable position. He cannot make a move, or make no move, without being beset by contradictory and paradoxical pressures and demands, pushes and pulls, both internally from himself, and externally from those around him. He is, as it were, in a position of checkmate.[17]

Laing's position on schizophrenia is more complex than the statements of both his critics and his disciples would lead us to suppose.[18] He is not simply prescribing madness as a means of handling impossible social situations, nor is he arguing that certain social situations "cause" schizophrenia. Rather, his position is that the concept of a disease called schizophrenia is a hypothesis or an assumption or a theory, but it is by no means a fact.[19] It is not a fact; that is, schizophrenia is not a clearly recognizable disease caused by something, because the present evidence does not support this conclusion.

For example, Laing and Esterson note that (1) there are no objective clinical criteria for diagnosis; (2) there is no discovered consistency in the prepsychotic personality; (3) there is a wide variety of expert views as to whether schizophrenia is a disease or cluster of diseases or whether an identifiable organic pathology can be found; (4) there are no generally proven forms of successful treatment; (5) schizophrenia observes no genetically clear law, although it runs in families.[20] The question for these authors is: "Are the experience and behavior that psychiatrists take as symptoms and signs of schizophrenia more socially intelligible than has come to be supposed?"[21] Their answer is that the behavior labeled schizophrenic, when investigated in the family context, is coherent and understandable. In the investigation of over two hundred families of schizophrenics, the authors found the statements and actions of patients which seem socially senseless when viewed without reference to the family situation make sense when that context is investigated and taken into account.[22]

Laing's findings suggest a change in framework is required for analyzing and treating those whose behavior is culturally and biologically so defective as to dangerously limit interaction with the social and physical environment. This altered framework recognizes that psychiatry is a political matter and that labelling persons as defective or mad is for the most part an admission of social ignorance. It turns our attention to an investigation of the institutional context of behavior and implies that human action and thought are the result of attempts to cope with the problems of such contexts. This recognition and redirection do not mean that the context causes anything in a Newtonian sense, but that we cannot assume *a priori* that all organizational structures are livable to all human beings or that they are a fit environment for human life. Further, we cannot diagnose a minority of disturbed individuals as "diseased" in a given context simply because they are a minority. Their "disease" is likely to be part of a collective disturbance with respect to which their isolation and treatment is an important ritual.

Cybernetic Explanation

Such a framework as a system of explanation has been labeled "cybernetic" by Bateson. Its distinguishing feature is that it is concerned with restraints or why certain events or behaviors or thoughts do not occur in a given context and not with attempting to account for what does occur. Explanation from this viewpoint is negative. Bateson explains:

> From the cybernetic point of view, a word in a sentence, or a letter within the work, or the anatomy of some part within an organism, or the role of a species in an ecosystem, or the behavior of a member within a family—these are all to be (negatively) explained by an analysis of restraints.[23]

He holds that the negative forms of these explanations are analogous to the form of logical proof by *reductio ad absurdum*.

It is possible that much defective behavior (defective in terms of the individual's survival at a level that does not restrict the range of future responses) is actually an acting out in thought and behavior of just such a *reductio*. By means of self-damaging activities, the individual "proves" that the institutional context is unlivable or defective. This "tendency to verify the unpleasant by seeking repeated experience of it," as Bateson describes it,[24] results because it is impossible to act out—at the level of primary processes like dreams or kinesic interactions—a proposition which contains its own negation.[25] "Playing" at combat is a way of saying at this level that "I will not hurt you." However, acting out the existential statement "I cannot live under these circumstances" may proceed to suicide. To mention "hurt" on the primary level is to hurt. To mention "live" is to live. "Not hurt" is thus acted out in the form of minor or playful hurting. "Not living" is acted out in the form of minor or playful forms of life, that is, by superficial play acting marked by the stereotyping and repetitiveness of neurotic behavior patterns.

But one can mention "not living" also by acting out death, that is, by actually dying or killing oneself. The heroic social investigator enacts just such a *reductio*. His life and work prove that the social system is defective. Such lived proofs of the defective nature of certain institutional contexts have paradoxical implications for survivors. They convey both the message that the context is defective and that recognition of such defects will lead to self-destruction. In short, the lived *reductio ad absurdum* in the form labeled "schizophrenia" both indicts and helps reinforce the context of which it is a part. This summation does not imply, however, that recognition of contextual defects is harmful to the individual or that context maintenance requires human sacrifice. The implication is clearly that the articulation of contextual restraints is a prerequisite for dealing with their damaging effects. It is here that we need to construct new verbal tools in order to establish that damaging contexts exist and to investigate their features on a level that does not require self-sacrifice and the resulting collective guilt. Here, then, is the germ of the task of the social scientist.

The Lanugage of Frameworks

How do we go about the construction of a vocabulary with which to investigate the contexts of human action and interaction without falling into the age-old problem of reification? Language about the "social system" or "institutions" or "environments" or "structures" causing such and such to happen resembles the language of schizophrenia. We look with suspicion on those who talk darkly about "system," "capitalism," or "structures" suppressing people, limiting actions, restricting perceptions, and doing comparable ill deeds. Likewise, we are suspicious of the holistic social engineer, whether dedicated revolutionary or high-salaried city planner, who designs total systems that promise the dramatic rehabilitation of the species. We can begin by noting that while context refers to an overall pattern of relations, this pattern does not contain every feature of the situation.

Popper distinguishes between two meanings of "whole" in social-science literature:

> It is used to denote (a) the totality of all the properties or aspects of a thing, and especially of all the relations holding between its constituent parts, and (b) certain special properties or aspects of the thing in question, namely those which make it appear an organized structure rather than a "mere heap."[26]

Wholes in sense (a) are not the proper subject of investigation, according to Popper, because they can neither be described (since description is necessarily selective) nor acted upon (since action is likewise selective). Wholes in sense (b), however, have been and can be studied scientifically and, presumably, can be acted upon since they represent selected aspects of the situation. We can describe and analyze holistic or systemic aspects of things such as the symmetry or assymmetry of their structure, their boundaries, the informational capacities of their communications networks, or the patterns of energic exchange. Thus, if we understand that "context" refers to certain special properties or aspects of a social situation which restrain occurrences and not an unreachable totality, we can proceed to investigate and describe social contexts in ways that can be falsified. Also, we can begin to experiment with various contexts to learn more about their nature and, it is hoped, improve their design.

Bateson reached his idea of context from an earlier concern with "psychological frames," and their function in human communication processes.[27] He discovered that communication always takes place on at least two levels—that of the message itself and that of other messages that delineate the frame within which the first message is to be interpreted. His original example was that of animal play, wherein a bite that occurs within the frame of "this is play" is reacted to quite differently from a bite in another frame. In order for satisfactory interaction to be achieved, at least two levels of abstraction—the communication and the metacommunication—must be present. Bateson explains frame and the related notion of context by means of two sorts of analogy—the picture frame and mathematical set theory. For example, Bateson describes the following functions and uses of psychological frames:

1. Psychological frames are exclusive. They exclude certain messages and meaningful actions by including only certain messages and actions.

2. Psychological frames are inclusive. As a picture frame includes certain features by excluding the background, so psychological frames call attention to certain messages and actions by inhibiting others. The message of the psychological frame, like that of the picture frame, is "Attend to what is within and do not attend to what is outside."

3. Psychological frames function as premises. Just as the picture frames tell us to use a different pespective for judging and responding to signs within its boundaries, so the psychological frame tells us to apply appropriate premises within its boundaries. Or, in set-theory terms, the enclosed messages are defined as members of the class because of their shared premises or mutual relevance.

4. A psychological frame is metacommunicative. It gives instructions about how to understand messages within its boundaries.

5. Conversely, every metacommunicative statement is or defines a psychological frame.

6. The psychological frame functions to delimit a logical type, that is,

it bounds a ground against which figures may be perceived. This function is necessary if Russellian paradoxes are to be avoided. In other words, those messages that are excluded from the frame must be of the same level of abstraction. If the frame is the "class of matchboxes," then the "class of matchboxes" must be understood not to be a member either of the class of matchboxes or the class of nonmatchboxes. No class can be a member of itself.[28]

The Concept of Social Context

Following this list of functions, we might use context to denote the psychosocial frame of a situation. This frame/context would include the more general rules governing the rules of communication and action. Such general rules function as boundaries excluding classes of messages and behavior as inappropriate, or nonsensical, or possibly inhuman. General rules function both as premises and as boundaries that delimit a logical type. Most importantly, the context or set of implicit and explicit general rules delineating a system of rule-governed interactions cannot be acted upon without communicating and interacting at another level of abstraction if paradox is to be avoided. The paradoxical nature of the heroic perspective in social investigation is due in part to the failure to distinguish the levels of abstraction in theoretical discourse.

For example, if the general rules of the context are treated merely as specific rules, then we assume that they are either rules within the context and are therefore relevant, or that they are rules outside of the context and are not relevant. If they are taken as rules within the context, then they should be subject to change and modification. But general rules cannot be changed in the same way that specific rules can. Attempting to change a general rule as if it were a specific rule involves messages of this sort: "This is a rule: don't obey rules."[29] That is, not only are existing rules ignored (and in a sense, therefore, violated) but their very rationale as rules is also undermined in such a way that rules themselves seem implausible.

Likewise, if the general rules are taken as rules of the noncontext, then knowledge of them or attempts to modify them are irrelevant to the context. Discussion of them takes the form: "In a not-here (perhaps nowhere), there is a rule such-and-such." These "utopian" rules are strangely familiar and seem to illuminate in some way the meaning of actions and messages within the context. If we do not move self-consciously in our discourse to another level of abstraction in dealing with the description and analysis of contexts, we end up with the paradoxes of pure anarchism or the ethereal profundities of utopianism. Conversely, both kinds of analysis—the anarchistic and utopian—in the history of Western political thought can be understood as making statements about social contexts. The results of this confusion of levels of abstraction are (1) the judgment that discussions of context are nonsensical or meaningless and should therefore be abrogated or (2) the judgment that discussions of context are to be accorded a special status removed from practical demands of relevance, reliability, and falsifiability. That is, if we do not recognize the need for the movement to another level of abstraction to discuss contexts, we end either by forbidding such discussions or by designating them "pure thought" and isolating them from the needs and actions of human beings. We get silence or metaphysics.

Another kind of problem arises if we commit what Bateson calls the "heuristic error" when discussing contexts. Bateson notes that our conventional way of talking leads us to say that such and such an action or message occurred "in" a particular context. This language construction implies that the context determines the occurrence. This implication leads to the kind of paradoxes found in Marxian theory, for example. That is, if (a) human action (including communicative actions like formulating, transmitting, and receiving symbolic messages) is determined by the social context, and (b) that social context interdicts responses required for survival, then the social context must be altered. But such alterations are either impossible because they are not determined by a context or else they are automatic in being determined by the changing context. Changing the context requires the assumption of another context that does not exist and is therefore a utopian venture of a highly romantic and volunteeristic kind. If we wish to avoid such questionable behavior, we are forced to bear the tides of history in a detached manner in the faith that contexts which hinder the survival of the human species eventually alter themselves.[30] This latter position requires an idealistic position like Hegel's, which presupposes an evolutionary development of social contexts that results in the attainment of human freedom. Marx, of course, was not able to adopt either romanticism or idealism nor to avoid making paradoxical statements about the changing of social contexts. His use of the "dialectical method" and much of the Hegelian vocabulary is an attempt to create a higher level of abstraction to discuss what might be called the transformation and development of social contexts. Marx was acutely aware of the problems involved. Notice his critique of idealistic determinism:

> *History* does *nothing;* it "does *not* fight battles." It is *men,* real, living men, who do all this, who possess things and fight battles. It is not "history" which uses men as a means of achieving—as if it were an individual person—*its* own ends. History is *nothing* but the activity of men in pursuit of their ends.[31]

Contexts do not cause, nor do they determine. As Bateson writes:
> It is important to see the particular utterance or action as *part* of the ecological subsystem called context and not as the product or effect of what remains of the context after the piece which we want to explain has been cut out from it.[32]

The heuristic error results from aping the explanatory vocabularies of physicist and chemist, Bateson maintains. He argues that the Newtonian framework of analysis excludes consideration of contextual levels. Either the notion of context is denied or it is assumed that there is only one Euclidian context for all events. When we employ the cybernetic mode of explanation or communication framework of analysis, statements of context must accompany all statements of description.

Still a third kind of difficulty develops if we mistake the stability of certain contexts and/or the difficulty with which they are altered for a necessary rigidity. For example, Bateson argues that any organism that must alter its context is faced with a pathogenic situation. Neuroses and psychoses occur in organisms when, after learning a set of appropriate responses to a given context, the context is altered in such a way as to require novel responses. This is the way Bateson interprets Pavlov's "experimental neuroses," described in Chapter 7.[33]

Levels of Learning

Bateson's argument is based upon a theory of learning levels. When we talk about animals learning we often fail to discriminate what are at least three and possibly four different levels or types of learning. *Zero learning* is characterized by specificity of response. When the organism is presented with a given stimulus it responds with a specific response time and again, whether or not the response is correct or incorrect. Such learning is a simple reception of information resulting in minimal changes in the organism. Some examples of zero learning would be, according to Bateson, habituation, stereotyped response, and in animal-learning experiments the stage at which the animal gives nearly 100 percent correct responses to a stimulus.[34] *Learning I* is characterized by a change in a previous response. That is, a change in zero learning from one response to another, or a change in the choice of response out of a given repertoire, is Learning I. A stimulus X elicits a response Y, which results in, say, pain, discomfort, or, perhaps, nonreward. Therefore, the response is altered to Z, which is nonpunishing or, perhaps, rewarding. Classical conditioning is an example of Learning I. Learning in contexts of instrumental rewards and punishments is another, as are rote learning, the extinction, disruption, or inhibition of completed learning, and the process of habituation or changes in habituation. Thus, "Learning I is a change in specificity of response by correction of errors of choice within a set of alternatives."[35]

Learning II is characterized by a change in a previous set of responses. That is, Learning II represents a change in the process of Learning I. The organism has learned a set of responses or alternatives and further learned to choose appropriately from this set as a means of correcting errors. Learning II then occurs when the organism learns a new set of responses. An example of this learning would occur if Pavlov's discriminating dogs, when faced with the impossibility of discrimination, would resort to guessing and gambling—a new set of responses different in kind. According to Bateson, Learning II occurs when the animal has been put in the wrong according to its view of the context. Learning II also occurs in the form of "learning to learn."

Bateson notes four experimental examples of Learning II. (1) In his experiments with human rote learning, Hull recorded not only the familiar curves of Learning I, but also a second set of curves which, Bateson argues, record the "learning of rote learning." For the subjects of these experiments there was an improvement in rote learning ability with each successive session, though the content differed. This ability leveled off at a level unique to each subject.[36] (2) There is the "set learning" recorded by Harlow and previously discussed in Chapter 5. That is, when presented with a series of problems to be solved of the same general type, monkeys learned to solve each new problem faster than the last one, as the logical structure or set of the problems was learned.[37] (3) Bateson also cites recent experimentation in "reversal learning" as an example of Learning II. (4) The final example is Pavlov's discrimination experiments, which produced experimental neurosis.

Bateson argues that what we call "character" in human beings, transactional patterns in human relationships, and the "transference" in psychotherapy, all refer to cases of Learning II. Character refers to the limited set of responses available to an individual described by adjectives like dependent, fatalistic, resourceful. Transactional patterns refer to more complex sets of interpersonal responses between two or more people, which we describe as domination, friendship, mentorship, rivalry, and the like. "Transference" refers to the set of responses to parental behavior learned in childhood.[38] In each of these cases we observe that the person or persons involved have developed a set of behaviors which in turn governs their interpretation or the way they perceive the meanings of certain events, stimuli, and actions of significant others. Bateson cites these cases of Learning II in order to argue that (a) Learning II is self-validating and therefore (b) nearly impossible and always dangerous to undertake. That is, if after having learned a set of responses in infancy the individual is forced to learn a new set, then pathological reactions are likely. According to Bateson, Learning II is a way of *punctuating events*. And "*a way of punctuating* is not true or false. There is nothing contained in the propositions of this learning that can be tested against reality. It is like a picture seen in an inkblot; it has neither correctness nor incorrectness. It is only a *way* of seeing the inkblot."[39] Thus Bateson sees Learning II as "a necessary preparation for the behavioral disturbance."[40] The individual having learned a set of responses and accompanying interpretations of a context, any novel occurrences, anomalies, or other changes in the context will result in what he has called a "double bind." Bateson's argument seems to vindicate socialization theory, to bolster Kuhn's defense of dogmatisms in science, and to prescribe as necessary the polarized perspective of the social investigator.

The demand to abandon the elements of Learning II for a new set of elements creates what Bateson has called a "transcontextual" genus of syndromes.[41] Such syndromes generated by so-called double-bind situations may result in *Learning III*. Bateson offers the following examples of Learning III: learning more readily to form sets of responses which we have called Learning II; learning to change the habits of Learning II; learning that one is a creature capable of Learning II; learning to limit or direct Learning II; learning to avoid the loopholes for preventing Learning III; and finally learning the contexts of Learning II.[42] The author notes that the list proposes a paradox. Learning about Learning II may lead "either to an increase in Learning II or to a limitation and perhaps a reduction of that phenomenon."[43] But he adds, "Certainly it must lead to a greater flexibility in the premises acquired by the process of Learning II—a freedom from their bondage."

The persistence of the behavior patterns of Learning II cited by Bateson mean to him that Learning III is most often avoided or escaped. Persistence in Learning II is the loophole by which Learning III is avoided. Bateson argues that organisms frequently encounter environments in which the reinforcement of essential behavior is infrequent—pigs searching for truffles, a man looking for the keys to his car, a robin seeking worms, a gambler feeding a slot machine. In such cases Learning II simplifies the universe: The subject learns a set of habits and "punctuates" events in a certain way; the required behavior is thereby maintained. But if this simplification is the case, then Learning III is dysfunctional, for it would mean weakening or eliminating these necessary behavior patterns of Learning II. We come to a familiar point in these arguments as we once again learn that ignorance pays and that knowledge is damaging.

The researches of Bateson and his associates indicate, however, that requirements of Learning III (that is, making a change in the sets of alternatives from which the choice of a particular response is to be made) are pathogenic only in certain contexts. There are instances in which persistence of Learning II precludes Learning III, but despite some of Bateson's generalizations about such persistence they seem to be of a narrow and particular kind. For example, let us return again to Pavlov's dogs, who learned to discriminate between circles and ellipses (Learning I). In Bateson's opinion, the dog first learned the experimental context labeled "this is an experiment in discrimination of stimuli" (Learning II). This learning is the necessary preparation for the experimental neurosis that resulted from the alteration of that context.

This is a weak argument paralleling Burrow's contention that man's symbolic ability was a necessary preparation for neurotic conflicts. Why not breathing, eating, procreation, or any number of other prerequisites of animal life that could be taken as necessary preparations for some disease? It is not Learning II which prepares the way to paradox, but rather the drastic and unilateral alteration of the context. Other researchers on double-bind situations interpret the Pavlovian experiments with a different emphasis.[44] They point out that the experimenter first imposed on the animal the necessity of correct discrimination; that is, correct answers meant food, incorrect answers meant no food, and there was no way for the animal to escape. Then the experimenter made it impossible for a correct discrimination to be made. Thus the dogs were faced with a paradoxical injunction—make a correct discrimination without perceptual cues. It is this injunction and the dogs' inability to avoid it that creates the situation of a double bind.

The traditional Western myths of social knowledge have a structure analogous to Bateson's description of double-bind situations. The characteristics of these situations are important clues to understanding the relations between social structures and social ignorance. To anticipate, communication pathologies develop when human beings must live with the paradoxical injunctions of medicinal lies. Such lies require that human beings understand the social context well enough to be good citizens and workers and that they misunderstand it well enough to prevent criticism or threat of conscious alteration. From Plato to the Founding Fathers of the United States, reformers have understood that institutions are human designs at the same time they have publicly argued for their sacred and timeless qualities.

The Double Bind

A double bind occurs under the following circumstances.[45] First there must be a two-person (or more) relationship which to its members is sufficiently intense or vital (that is, important) to make the correct discrimination of message types salient. Second, an individual in the relationship is faced with two orders of messages, one of which denies or negates the other. Third, the victim can neither leave the field nor comment upon the paradoxical nature of the messages.[46] It is important to note that a double bind is possible only if there are two levels of messages present—a message and metamessage indicating what type of message it is. If the metamessage indicates, for example, that the message is false and the message itself is an injunction such as "come here," then it is impossible to respond without distorting perceptions of the situation. If the subject obeys the injunction, then he must disregard the metacommunication. If he attends to the metacommunication, then he must disregard the injunction. The subject cannot be right, no matter what he does, and he cannot do anything unless he denies part of his perception of the situation.

Conversely, the double-binder cannot be wrong: No matter what the victim does, if that action turns out badly, for example, the double-binder is not responsible and, in fact, can claim that the action was done against his orders. Because of the internal negation of the double-binder's comunication, he has succeeded in saying nothing for which he can be held responsible and yet has made it imperative for the victim to act. The double-binder's statements and injunctions are unfalsifiable and he appears to be infallible. And while these messages are not, of course, empirical or in any way guides to action and thought in the world, they do succeed in maintaining a given social context by interdicting all learning except zero learning and Learning I. The double bind is thus related to social ignorance, social myth, and the paradoxes of social investigtion.

Some of the possible reactions of repeated double-bind situations are the shifting of concern away from the situation to a search for "missing" clues or information, literal compliance with all injunctions, and some form of avoidance such as withdrawal or hyperactivity.[47] These "normal" reactions are lesser versions of the psychotic reactions of paranoia, hebephrenia, and catatonia typical of those labeled "schizophrenics." What these reactions indicate is the loss on the part of the double-bind victim of the feedback necessary for correcting and creating appropriate behavior. As Bateson and his colleagues noted:

> These three alternatives are not the only ones. The point is that he cannot choose the one alternative which would help him to discover what people mean; he cannot, without considerable help, discuss the messages of others. Without being able to do that, the human being is like any self-correcting system which has lost its governor; it spirals into never-ending, but always systematic, distortions.[48]

This lack of self-correction is in some ways deliberate, not in the sense that some member of the context wishes to deny to others the ability to discover meaning, but in the sense that someone wishes to preserve and defend the context at all costs.

Weakland points out that not only is the double-bind message self-contradictory; responding to it is made difficult by reason of the concealment, denial, and inhibition inherent in it or added to it. The paradox is concealed because the contradicting messages are on different communication levels or of different logical types. Because of this basic concealment, mention of the paradox can be denied overtly by further messages or covertly by accusing the victim of confusion or misunderstanding by means of messages about the importance and wisdom of the double-binder. Finally, any investigation or discussion of the situation may be inhibited by prohibition or by systemically ignoring the complexities and difficulties of communication and treating them, in Weakland's words, "as though they were out of the question."[49] Bateson summarizes the communication restrictions involved in a family double-bind situation:

> By preventing the child from talking about the situation, the mother forbids him using the metacommunicative level—the level we use to correct our perceptions of communicative behavior. The ability to communicate about communication, to comment upon the meaningful actions of oneself and others, is essential for successful social intercourse.[50]

It is the prohibitions—against altering the context, leaving the context, or discussing or commenting on the paradoxes encountered—that create the situation of the double bind. Behind every double bind is the commandment "Thou shalt love and worship the structure and norms of the context." And this commandment—expressed in myriad forms of concealment, deception, and censorship—is the pathogenic factor in these situations. Bateson does not discriminate between (a) situations of ordinary falsification, when a set of responses is found wanting and a new set devised, and (b) situations of the double bind, when a set of responses is found inadequate but either an alternative is not available, or the means—communication, search, experimentation—for the creation of an alternative set is prohibited by elements (members and rules) of the context. Thus Bateson, like Laing, confuses the pathological responses of schizophrenia with creativity. By characterizing the double-bind situation according to the contradiction involved, Bateson and his colleagues have failed to designate rigorously the criteria for a double-bind situation; this omission in turn has greatly hampered attempts to test their hypothesis experimentally.[51]

Overcompetence and Paradox

An alternative is to see that any context which involves rules against altering the context produces paradoxes. That is, rules about contexts in general are transcontextual and cannot be maintained as rules of a given context without paradoxical injunctions. If, then, the context is not altered when new conditions are required, this rigidity will promote double-bind situations and the resulting patterns of social ignorance. For example, when the social investigator bids fellow citizens to attend to his criticisms of the context while insisting that any criticisms they might offer are either reactionary or promote the dissolution of social order, he presents a paradoxical injunction that requires others not to see or to understand what he means. We can attend to only part of the paradox at a time and must therefore distort the teachings. This distortion can lead to centuries of exegesis, but not to social knowledge.

As Bateson notes, double-bind situations are asymmetrical. In a schizophrenic family, for example,

> the identified patient sacrifices himself to maintain the sacred illusion that what the parent says makes sense. To be close to that parent, he must sacrifice his right to indicate that he sees any metacommunicative incongruencies, even when his perception of these incongruencies is correct. There is, therefore, a curious disparity in the distribution of awareness of what is happening. The patient may know but must not tell, and thereby enables the parent to not know what he or she is doing. The patient is an accomplice in the parent's unconscious hypocrisy. The result may be very great unhappiness and very gross, but always systematic, distortions of communication.[52]

This suggests that institutionalized ignorance in the form of hierarchical social roles, which like these parents include as part of their designation assertions of superior knowledge or skill, promotes double-bind situations whenever incumbents of such roles are not competent. That is, schizophrenogenic families are often characterized by overcompetent and/or undercompetent parents. Both types of parents project an image of their abilities which are not realistic or subject to verification. The overcompetent parent apparently can do everything well and has no difficulties with the role. The undercompetent parent can do nothing well and retreats from the role or enacts only its supportive and effacing operations. In the case of the overcompetent parent, the image of omniscience and omnipotence is maintained by means of the double bind. Such parents are, like all humans, at least partial failures at the demanding role of parent, but rather than face or admit these failures they deny them as if their recognition would evoke a catastrophic situation. Unable to fulfill the demands of the role and further incapacitated by the anxiety caused by that failure, the parent uses the child's responses to enact a ritual of adequate performance. The parent is always right, as all good parents are, while the child is always wrong, as, I suppose, children are supposed to be.

The overcompetent heroic role of the social investigator—separate, exclusive, and polarized—is promoted to the extent that the knowledge necessary to guide social development is absent. Like a parent faced with a task he cannot perform, the social investigator is tempted to enact a ritual of omniscience at the expense of distorting his own vision and drastically restricting the perceptions and communications of fellow citizens. By asserting a general, contextless knowledge of social order he reduces himself to being a mythmaker, paradox spinner, play actor—but never a knower, a builder, a scientist. The investigator's failure to distinguish levels of abstraction is part of this role. In this quest for unshakeable certainty in a world of dissolution, he finds instead a kind of ignorance that cannot be falsified. Likewise, in his quest for knowledge of how to order human life, he finds instead a way to victimize it and further ways to blame the victims for the resulting social entropy.

The Schizophrenogenic Family

The clinical data from the investigation of the structure and process of schizophrenogenic families provide many suggestive and potentially important hypotheses about the formal characteristics of contexts of social ignorance. For example, such families are remarkably stable, according to Bateson, and this stability is purchased at the price of a continuous degradation and denial of each member. The maneuvers involved are at once self-protective and self-denying. Further, the organization is both dynamic and stable. The double-binding parent is constantly shifting the communication context, for it is by this means that identifiable failure is avoided.

Examples from the communications of schizophrenogenic parents illustrated this shifting well. They systematically interpret the messages falsely by denying that they are the type of message that the child thought was being communicated and they systematically contradict their own messages with identifying messages of denial.[53] The ground or context of communication is constantly moving in such families, while the role structure is rigid and unchanging. The incumbent of the parental role maintains the ideal attributes of the role—wisdom, love, direction, protection, and the like—by being flexible in the extreme in designating the context. By this means again we see how the parent may be always correct and the child (as well as others who enter significantly into the interaction) always in the wrong.

This flexibility makes possible "an endless taking of the other person's message and replying to it as if it were either a statement of weakness on the part of the speaker [a patient's mother] or an attack on her which should be turned into a weakness on the part of the speaker; and so on."[54] These clinical descriptions indicate a human organization that is systematically ignorant and permanently structured, possessed of an elaborate and eternally correct account of the world and possessed at the same time of dynamism. The schizophrenogenic family may be a closed system, but its features are much more complex, flexible, and adaptive than our standard conceptualizations of hierarchical institutions of domination. As Bateson sums it up:

> The schizophrenic family is an organization with great ongoing stability whose dynamics and inner workings are such that each member is continually undergoing the experience of negation of self.[55]

Laing points out that what is shared in such a family is the concerted resistance to discovering what is going on.[56] This concert requires what he calls a "family image," which parallels in structure the "social image" of Burrow. There is a set of conditioned symbols to which each family member gives allegiance for the private advantage of selectively refusing to learn from experience. To illustrate: We learn to share images of fantasy and escape by means of such innocent-appearing devices as Santa Claus conventions. Indeed, this systematic deception, practiced on nearly every child, is a kind of paradigm of social lying. The child is told a fantasy about an elf that flies through the sky and delivers presents on Christmas eve. The fantasy itself is pleasant enough, like other tales of childhood. Adults, however, act as if the story were true (1) by asserting its validity through repetition of the story, discussion of details of the story, and the presentation of evidence, and (2) by a series of auxiliary operations which are realistic, such as helping the child write letters to Santa, taking the child to see imitations of Santa, cleaning out the chimney, leaving snacks, hiding presents until Christmas, and the like. The child encounters much evidence that Santa Claus is "not real." There are too many "Santas" for one thing, and their makeup does not bear a close inspection. For the child to argue against the reality of the fantasy is punishing. It makes adults angry, it excludes him from participation in many of the preparations and rituals of Christmas, it makes playmates anxious and hostile, and, finally, it robs the child of belief in a supposedly more pleasant world of magic, love, and generosity. What Santa Claus conventions teach children is how to deny their critical and empirical capabilities in order to share in a collective lie. The experience of this lesson in deception in American society makes plausible our belief that knowledge is dangerous, if not destructive. While all the deceptions concerning Santa Claus conventions are only "pretend" and the results probably are not serious, the example illustrates how a growing child can learn self-deception.

The parents in a schizophrenogenic family are a far cry from the standard pictures of paternal and maternal tyrants found in fairy tales and Freudian case histories. They are flexible, rather than rigid, although Bateson feels that "they are rigidly committed to their patterns of inconsistency."[57] This is to be expected, of course, for what is purchased by their inconsistency is the infallible enactment of their roles. A parent who is never wrong is a parent whose authority is nearly unlimited and nearly impossible to challenge.

The family in postindustrial society is particularly prone to distortion because of the greater emotional demands made on it at the same time that its functions have been drastically reduced and its material resources increased. As sociologists have pointed out, the family is no longer an important economic, educational, or administrative unit. However, as social relationships become fewer, more perfunctory, and more temporary, the family becomes the one place where the individual can form lasting and committed relationships.[58] Bennis and Slater argue that the typical American family is basically democratic, nonauthoritarian and antibureaucratic.[59] But much of their descriptions and that of other authors, like Sennett, present the picture of an institution of intense deception. The middle-class family in the United States is a kind of permanent Christmas in which consumption, fairy tales, and stereotyped responses of happiness and sentimentality substitute for producing, learning, and loving. The combination of surplus resources, reduced productive functions, and intense manipulation of perceptions is becoming typical of advanced bureaucratic structures. The postindustrial family gives us a picture of the institutions of the future as Bennis and Slater maintain, but that picture is not one of democratic participation, rather one of mutual deception and increased pathological disturbances.

Symbolic Distortion as Adaptation

How is it possible to live in such pathogenic contexts? One way of doing it is by means of the various stratagems of not seeing, labeled "schizophrenic." These stratagems are possible because of man's ability to adapt to the environment by means of his symbolic processes. The essence of schizophrenia is the distortion of these symbolic processes. In particular, Bateson maintains the schizophrenic is unable to discriminate modes of communications.

> (a) He has difficulty in assigning the correct communicational mode to the messages he receives from other persons. (b) He has difficulty in assigning the correct communicational mode to those messages which he himself utters or emits nonverbally. (c)

He has difficulty in assigning the correct communicational mode
to his own thoughts, sensations, and percepts.[60]
This inability to discriminate enables the schizophrenic to avoid the
paradoxes of the double bind and to eschew any responsibility for the
metacommunicative aspect of his messages.[61] Bateson notes that the
schizophrenic may flood the environment with messages that are
difficult to type, may withdraw and send no overt messages, or may
constantly employ unlabeled metaphors.[62] The results, whether schizophrenic salad or silence, effectively protect the individual from paradoxes produced by the communication of contradictory messages of
different logical types. In this sense, the schizophrenic response is a
learned defense mechanism differing from other perceptual and symbolic distortions employed to deal with double-bind situations only in
its conspicuousness and in its particular way of blocking feedback.

Schizophrenia results not from the utilization of symbolic processes
but from their distortion. It seems clear that the individual learns to
substitute symbolic processes for organic responses, rather than that
there is any natural propensity for such a substitution. While it is true
that other animals cannot become schizophrenic because of their rudimentary symbolic processes, the phenomenon of schizophrenia does
not represent a species weakness. As learned responses, schizophrenic
stratagems result not only from parental attempts to substitute moralistic symbolic standards for biological standards, but also from consistent
parental inconsistencies that invalidate all standards except the parent's
infallible judgment. This is important to understand because the pattern of authoritarian behavior—flexible infallibility—is becoming more
likely to be encountered in the contemporary family and organization.
It is a particularly dangerous pattern because it is seldom recognized as
authoritarian at all.

People who frequently confront this pattern—namely students and
middle-class married women—often understand their situation as that
of too much freedom. Either the difficulties of the situation are understood as personal failures, or the situation is redefined in demonologi-
cal terms to conform to the authoritarian patterns of the past. Thus, at
a time when American male virility and assertiveness are probably at an
all-time low, the Women's Liberation Movement has launched a full-
scale attack on patriarchy. While all hierarchical social organizations
promote double-binding behavior because they involve roles of ascrip-
tive ability, such behavior is probably most prevalent in times of dissolution when institutional failures are acute. The consequence is an increase in schizophrenic reactions. The prevalence of such reactions
makes prescriptions of social ignorance plausible, because the schizophrenic seems to be seeing too well, to be ignoring rules of behavior,

and to be acting in frivolous and childlike ways. The recurring portrait of a remarkable parental figure—whether philosopher-king, conquering prince, representative sovereign, wise legislator, revolutionary leader, or scientific expert—to be found in Western political thought seems a response to this situation. Also in the same category are the various descriptions and discussions of sovereignty, power, authority, decision making, administrative science, ruling elites, and the like.

Other Responses to the Double Bind

Researchers on double-bind situations emphasize that "the double-bind does not *cause* schizophrenia."[63] I take them to mean that those symbolic responses of extreme disturbance are not necessarily typical of double-bind situations. Individuals may defend themselves in such situations by less extreme defense mechanisms which result in only partial or selective distortion and withdrawal. Bateson argues that hereditary characteristics play some part in the strategy developed by the individual. He notes that "to get confused about the logical types, one presumably has to be intelligent enough to know that there is something wrong and not so intelligent as to be able to see what it is that is wrong.[64] Elsewhere he maintains that schizophrenia-susceptible individuals must be "habit-prone" or overly committed to patterns of learned behavior. Others maintain that vulnerability to paradox requires both logical ability and a high degree of trust.[65] All this implies that nonlogical thinking, cynicism, fickleness, and stupidity are less drastic defenses against the double bind. Hence the impression of clinical observers that if their patients were only less intelligent or less perceptive they might escape psychosis. While all of these forms of resistance and malingering are indeed defenses against psychosis, it is not clear that intelligence, insight, and commitment produce psychosis, as Bateson seems to imply. In other words, it is false that Learning II or learning certain sets of responses sets the stage for double-bind situations and schizophrenic responses. Rather it is the inability to learn how to learn or to form learning sets that is promoted by contexts in which double-bind situations are frequent. In turn, such limitations of the human learning capacity set the stage for schizophrenic reactions.

Critique of Bateson's Theory of Learning

Bateson misunderstands the characteristics of Learning II, or rather describes a phenomenon I will call "ersatz learning," and erroneously considers it the same type of learning as that described by Harlow, Tolman, and others. He maintains that the persistence of Learning II is necessary to survival and cites exploratory behavior as an example of behavior patterns that persist in spite of failure. But he has refuted his own example. He notes that the object of exploratory behavior is to get information about the environment. Thus, finding punishing objects does not discourage further exploration.[66] The same is also true of search behavior and gambling, or at least it may be true, and since it is a more economical explanation of such behavior it should be investigated.[67]

In short, many repeating behavior patterns having to do with the generation of information and the skill development of organisms, like exploration and risk-taking, are intrinsically rewarding.[68] Such behavior is not rigid and frozen, although there is a superficial resemblance between the regular and disciplined patterns of exploration and production and the mechanical repetition of neurotic responses. To put it another way: the rules or response set of a given context may be a product of learning environmental features and adaptive responses; they may be imposed in order to prevent such learning; or they may be so fluid and inconsistent as to make learning impossible on any level except that of zero learning or invariant reactions to specific stimuli. The important thing is to be able to discriminate between these situations.

Falsification is the end result of any learning other than zero learning. Put another way, falsification is possible only if a response or set of responses has been learned and applied with success. On a theoretical level we know that any such set will sooner or later fail since it cannot exhaust the logical possibilities of the physical environment, and the operations it entails change the environment in unforeseeable ways. In contrast to other species of the animal world, human beings have shown the highest capacity to modify their response sets. Particularly, if we look at the technological development of man we find historical periods of extensive and rapid change of such sets. There seems to be nothing inherent in the physiological and psychological capacities of the species to make Learning III any more problematic than Learning I. I suggest that falsifying situations are pathogenic only when either no set of responses has been learned and articulated or when a set of ersatz responses has been learned. Ersatz learning would consist of adopting a symbolic response (verbal, iconic, or ritualistic) that could accompany any event or action. A set of such responses constitutes an ideology—a collection of unfalsifiable statements, gestures, and rituals. Ersatz learning is authoritarian in structure. It is the learning of a "social image," that is, the linking of conditioned affective responses to events and behaviors in the world.

Bateson's confusion leads him to see Learning II as an unfalsifiable way of punctuating events. Ersatz learning is just that. For example, recall Maier's experiments with rats in contexts in which Learning I was not possible. In this experiment it was impossible for the animals to make the connection between a sign and food reward, and further it was made impossible for the animals not to choose between two signs because (1) the correct sign was assigned randomly for each trial and (2) air-blasts or electric shocks forced the rats to jump at one of the two symbols. Under these conditions of high frustration each rat adopted some invariant reaction such as jumping always at circles or jumping always to the left. According to Maier, habits become abnormally fixated in such contexts of frustration.[69] This is zero learning, or an invariant reaction to a stimulus without the possibility of feedback.[70] It occurs in contexts in which environmental cues are insufficient to develop consistently rewarding responses (Learning I) or sets of rewarding responses (Learning II). Such a context is exactly like staring at an ink blot. You can see it or "punctuate" it any way you want because there are not enough perceptual cues to indicate its being any one thing.

A context promoting social ignorance is one of overprotection and flexible infallibility. Its effect on the human being was summed up by a patient interviewed by Laing and Esterson:

> I was never allowed to do anything for myself so I never learned to do things. The world doesn't seem quite real. If you don't do things then things are never quite real.[71]

Or, to recall Tolman's findings about the conditions producing narrow cognitive maps, if the environment is disguised or lied about, if learning takes place under conditions of extreme motivation, or if learning exercises are over-repeated, the learning animal's cognitive map will tend to be narrow, abstract, and rigid, making further learning difficult if not impossible.[72] It is the lack of Learning II that results in the persistence of contexts, not any inherent rigidity in the contexts of human interactions, as Bateson supposes. Thus, Learning III poses no paradoxes and does not result in faulty Learning II. At least, this is the case if we do not mistake the defensive flexibility of the new bureaucratic administrator to be Learning III.

Protean Man

The new "protean man" celebrated as an authoritative facilitator rather than a dominator is similar to the schizophrenogenic parent. Playful, tolerant of ambiguity, various, uncommitted, and irresponsible, this combination of intellectual and administrator maintains the role of positional authority by means of flexibility.[73] His world may seem to be a transcontextual one but actually it is noncontextual. Upon close inspection his claims to authority are formal and without content.[74]

Slater writes of the new "temporary" man—"He must be acutely sensitive and responsive to group norms while recognizing the essential arbitrariness, particularity, and limited relevance of all moral imperatives.[75] This sentence reveals much of the confusion involved in the conceiving of a new level of consciousness concerned with the "context of contexts." For there is an important difference between arbitrary and nonarbitrary norms and between the imperatives of adaptation and survival and imperatives of morality. To understand that Learning II always leads to falsification does not mean that such learning is arbitrary, nor that its validity in specific situations is simply imposed by the will of men. Slater's description is indicative of the curious combination of conformity and fickleness that results from such a false view.

Bateson speaks of the "freedom from the bondage of habit" that for him represents Learning III.[76] He admits that to attempt such "learning" is dangerous. The results may be (a) psychosis, (b) "a collapsing of much that was learned at Level II, revealing a simplicity in which hunger leads directly to eating, and the identified self is no longer in charge of organizing the behavior," or (c) "the resolution of contraries [revealing] a world in which personal identity merges into all the processes of relationship in some vast ecology or aesthetics of cosmic interaction."[77] He comments that those "creative" people who attain this last conception of the universe "are perhaps saved from being swept away on oceanic feeling by their ability to focus in on the minutiae of life."[78]

All this is revealing of the difficulties of discourse about the context of contexts. It seems evident that Learning II is a requisite of Learning III and cannot be bypassed. Much of what is described as Learning III represents attempts to learn in the absence of concrete experience or rather in a situation in which the richness of haptic experience is restricted. The examples offered by these authors of a new, flexible, and adaptable man appear to me to be portraits of the victims of several generations of intense propaganda activities.[79] Those labeled schizophrenic try to escape a world in which experience is reduced to mechanical habit without sense, or habit accompanied by symbolic affirmations of goodness, loyalty, dutifulness, and the like. Such a context is desemanticized, and offers no possibility of developing a stable, broad, and thick cognitive map that could be articulated as a schema of investigation and directed learning. Without such sets of cognitive postulates, we are incapable of becoming creatures who learn from our experience. The schizophrenic tries to develop such a map by ignoring the continuously shifting ground that promotes double binds and tries to defend it by preventing the testing of its contents.

Schizophrenia is an extreme derangement of the theoretical capacities of human beings—an attempt to build up symbolic models and pictures of the world out of the verbalization of egocentric needs and losses.

As Theodore Lidz writes:

> All egocentrism has the common characteristic of reliance upon the "omnipotence of thought"—an unconscious belief in the efficacy of thought. The schizophrenic again can give precedence to wish over reality; believe that the word is equivalent to the object, the signifier to the signified; to think that thoughts can injure; that he is central to all events.[80]

The resulting visions of schizophrenia are delusions, not patterns to guide action in the world. Their genesis is probably related to the hallucinations experimentally produced through sensory deprivation.[81] Tactile and practical deprivation or lack of opportunities for efficacious action promote the belief in the effectiveness of symbolic solutions. Or, to put it differently, these visions are attempts to create and to substitute a symbolic existence for the detailed and contingent complexity of human existence. To the extent that it proceeds in this heroic attempt to substitute thought for life, political theory shares the structure of a psychosis.

The Double Bind and Hierarchy

The double-bind hypothesis developed by Bateson and his associates promises to be a useful conceptual tool for the understanding and analysis of social ignorance as well as to suggest a more useful way of conceiving the role of the social investigator. Weakland notes:

> Certainly the great institutions of business, government, and religion can hardly be completely free of these problems, involving inconsistent messages and their concealment, the denial of personal behavior and responsibility and the assertion of unity and benevolence that have been causing such difficulty with the family and mental hospital systems.[82]

He is probably too modest in this statement. As Crozier noted, the major means of action of hierarchical organizations "can only be the manipulation of information, or at least the strict regulation of access to information."[83] Or, as M. F. Hall put it, "It is the information-structuring clique in an organization which is the one in which decisional (as opposed to merely formal) power resides."[84] The detailed mechanics of how information is manipulated, restricted, and structured by the asymmetrical and simplistic communication networks typical of hierarchies is too extensive and complex to be discussed here and I expect to devote a second volume in this project to it.

What is important to note is that the hierarchical form of organization represents an attempt to predict and control human behavior by utilizing techniques of information management having to do with the restricting and channeling of human symbolic processes. Such restricting and channeling necessarily involves double binds since it requires men and women to respond to symbolic criteria of judgment rather than biological criteria. Further, hierarchical organizations produce a schism and conflict between those with information and ability and those with access to the communications network and the authorization to make decisions. Crozier writes: "Those who have the necessary information do not have the power to decide and those who have the power to decide cannot get the necessary information."[85] This contradiction creates more double-bind situations, since the gap between the official symbolic expression of what is to be done (the rules) and the actual requirements of the task (the work operations) tends to increase over time. Thus, if the worker follows the rules, he ruins the job, but if he does the job, he must disobey the rules.

The control of human behavior is impossible in the strict sense. Organizations based on the belief that such control is possible can sustain their authority structures only by means of overt or covert techniques of damaging human organisms enough to cripple their learning and perceptual capacities.[86] These techniques range from the terror of concentration camps to the interlocking double binds of the modern bureaucracy. Those men and women who attempt to control the behavior of others end by hating the human species for its recalcitrance and apathy and by hating themselves for their own weakness. Attempts at behavior control create pathogenic contexts that drastically cripple the cooperative, learning, and productive capacities of mankind.[87] So long as the results of this crippling—in the form of restricted output, excess resource consumptions, and high rates of human debilitation—can be tolerated because of continuous expansion of economic and industrial activities, the availability of environmental reserves, and population growth, the delusion of behavior control can be maintained as a social goal. But if any or all of these parameters become restricted (as indeed they all must in time), then the control of human behavior must be assigned to the dust-bin of lost causes and hopeless dreams. Social ignorance is a luxury purchased at the price of cannibalizing other nations, the environment, and the wellsprings of human life itself.

The Task of the Social Sciences

The prediction of the effects of social contexts on human capacities for adaptation and the control of such contexts seems to be a worthy goal for human social effort. It is a goal toward which the social sciences can make a great contribution. It involves, however, complex problems, difficult work, and risky enterprises. For example, Bateson and his associates have noted that a double-bind situation does not result in the victim's restriction of perceptions if the paradoxical nature of the communications involved can be discussed. That is, if it is possible to point out the discrepancy between the explicit message and the implicit message designating the type of message, by means of a further commentary, then the paradox can be dissolved. This, of course, is what I have attempted to do in this book—to write a commentary on the discrepancy between the explicit messages of social investigators criticizing institutions and the implicit message of their exclusive autocratic stance that such criticism is destructive.

Double binds can be exploded, so to speak, by discussing the levels of communication and the contradictions involved. The human use of symbols makes possible the occurrence of double-bind situations because, as Bateson and Burrow point out, human linguistic and symbolic capacities are additions to the ordinary kinesic and paralanguage capacities of other species.[88] We are always communicating on at least two levels. Doing so makes possible the attempt to control human behavior through control of linguistic communication. For were we one-dimensional verbal animals we might be controllable, that is, unable to recode or learn to learn, and the failure and limits of such control would be immediately evident as those in "control" watched their automatons wreak havoc by exact and minute compliance with the letter of each verbal instruction.[89] But as complex communicating animals, we are susceptible to the double bind. The result is the appearance of control and the actuality of disturbed human responses. These appearances can be kept up only through concealment, disguise, and denial. Thus there are three prerequisites of systemic double-binds: (1) both linguistic and kinesic communication capacities; (2) the felt need to control the behavior of others; and (3) prohibitions against discourse concerning the levels of communication.

We cannot do anything about the human species' communication capabilities without drastic changes amounting to genocide. We have perhaps spent too much energy moralizing about those who feel the need to control others. It seems to be a natural enough reaction to those moments when we are ignorant, clumsy, and impatient as well as when extraordinary demands are made upon us. Controlling behavior is a short-cut substitute for knowledge, ability, and responsiveness.[90] If it were more clearly understood as this, it might be less tempting. But as long as we exaggerate its possibilities for evil and good and attack those who attempt it with various *post hoc* moralisms based mostly on our own biases and private advantage, the short-cut will remain to tempt the best and worst of us. However, we can do something about the institutional concealment and prohibitions against discourse about communication levels.

We can begin by noting that certain and unfalsifiable social and political propositions are reflections of the pragmatic unfalsifiability of the dominator's injunctions. To the extent that social scientists perpetrate such certainties they are accomplices in the promotion of social ignorance. Remaining silent about these dogmas, even as we retreat to safer ground to be meticulously scientific, is to further obscurantism. Bateson notes that an erroneous epistemology results in a proliferation of verbalisms or an extremely narrow focus if consistency is attempted.[91] The social disciplines show just these characteristics—theoretical profundity and meticulously irrelevant investigation. Despite our obsession with epistemology, the problems of social investigation are due to empirical ignorance, not methodological ineptitude—to poor information, not bad logic. The problems of creating social knowledge are more political than philosophical. For the social sciences to live up to their name, they must face these political problems. Rather than deny or avoid the relevance of social knowledge for developing a higher quality of life, we should cultivate such relevance.

In 1942 Bateson wrote:

> The conflict is now a life-or-death struggle over the role which the social sciences shall play in the ordering of human relationships. It is hardly an exaggeration to say that this war [World War II] is ideologically about just this—the role of the social sciences. Are we to reserve the techniques and the right to manipulate people as the privilege of a few planning, goal-oriented, and power-hungry individuals to whom the instrumentality of science makes a natural appeal? Now that we have the techniques, are we, in cold blood, going to treat people as things?[92]

World War II did not answer his question; it only kept it open. Bateson's attempt to answer the question negatively and avoid treating people as things was derived from Margaret Mead. She argued that "when we apply the social sciences we look for 'direction' and 'value' in our very acts, rather than orient ourselves to some blue-printed goal."[93] In short, our goals are to be made corrigible in terms of the immediate outcomes of our acts. Thus if we find we must murder or maim to reach our goal, then that is good reason to reject the goal. Or more likely, if we find that the unintended results of our acts contradict our goal to lower immediately the quality of life, then we must more carefully and rigorously redefine the details of that goal. This answer to the question is more promising especially if we note that Bateson's optimistic views about the efficacy of social techniques were grossly exaggerated and consider that, when we develop social science and do not just apply it, we should look for direction or value in our means or methods. That is, manipulative heroic methods of theory and research result in perpetuating the myths of social control and of the inevitability of hierarchy. They do not, however, produce knowledge that is a basis for the improvement of human life or institutions. They do not produce science. The social investigators who study the social and political world from an exclusive autocratic viewpoint produce mystification, whatever their motives and however brilliant their insights.

The task of the social scientist does not involve standing apart from or transcending the social context that he studies. The goal is not to prove our intellectual or moral superiority to the context. Such heroism is not at all the point. Our methodological (rather spiritual) exercises go far beyond utility to become expressions of *hubris*—whether the content of these exercises is mathematics and logic or history and philosophy. The objectivity of the absolute spectator is based upon a discounting of our feelings, needs, and information. Another kind of objectivity is required, based upon our immersion in, observations of, and participation with the human and structural elements of the context. This objectivity is evidenced by our ability to contribute to solving social problems.[94] Such ability involves not the creation and imposition of wholesale palliatives, but the systematic trial and correction of proposed solutions. It involves being able to learn how to learn and teach others to learn how to learn.[95] It requires that we learn what it is we hope to teach—how to live productive, healthy lives.

The task is not to speculate about ideal worlds with which to measure the deficiencies of the present or to provide goals for our efforts. The task is rather to speculate about this world, as it is or as it might be. If our hypotheses seem to be outrageous, as Robert Lynd once recommended, let them be about the world in which we live and let them be based on the felt terrors and joys of our lives so that by means of them we may learn something that we can use to improve, here and now, the quality of life. We must understand that empiricism and opportunism are quite different things. To be empirical does not mean merely to describe the formal structure of a given social order and to develop an ideology for it. What contexts are here are one issue; the contexts that might be are another. And knowledge, particularly scientific knowledge, entails the ability to create, or change to, the kind of political and social context required by human needs.

Putting the same thought another way, we note that physicists have not just observed the world, they have probed it; it was the surprising results of their experiments which prodded them to develop the more useful theories which ran counter to commonsense dogma and myth. Successful social investigation would lead to the discovery of new and unexpected social and political phenomena. Since a given political context would not recognize such phenomena, their discovery would demand changes in the procedures and structures of politics. Such changes are likely to be viewed as radical and threatening if the institutions of the context are hierarchical in structure. They will be resisted. Resistance may be only sluggishness, or it may comprise outright attempts to silence and suppress social scientists. The way to escape this danger is obvious: avoid successful, relevant, and novel theories.

A more productive strategy of social investigation is Kurt Lewin's "action research."[96] The basic assumption of this approach is that, in order to understand a social or organizational process or structure, changes in it must be initiated so that the resulting effects can be observed. Initially a desirable goal is posited for the context to be studied. Then the goal is evaluated in the light of the means available to reach it. This requires an initial fact finding or reconnoitering to establish a representation of the organizational situation. Sanford argues that such fact finding should always begin with the lowest levels of the organization in order to precipitate latent resistance.[97] Organizational resistance to research, or more simply to demystification, must be interpreted by the researchers to lay the basis for the education of personnel. Sanford writes:

> Resistance is an expression of the organization's underlying dynamics. To understand it, is to understand some of the organization's basic processes, and to interpret it, or even to wait it out while remaining on the scene, is to become an important factor in the determination of the organizational processes.[98]

Social investigators must be willing to take up the therapeutic task of making explicit the expectations and assumptions implicit in the structure and proceedings of the social context.

After the first round of establishing a goal for change, fact finding, and resistance interpretation, a modified goal or plan for improvement is created and the attempt is made to achieve it. The results of this attempt are then observed and a new plan and new means proposed. Further, investigators teach members of the organization to undertake their own planning, research, and execution. Sanford maintains that research "which is not educational in process as well as in the use of its final results, is inadequately based in theory . . . probably trivial, and dubious in respect to ethics."[99] The three areas of activity in action research are, according to Lewin, action, research, and training. Thus, the approach emphasizes reform, the development of scientific knowledge, and the improvement of social techniques. Indeed, it may be that the only way to develop scientific knowledge of the social and political world is through such consciously directed attempts at reform.[100] The results of successful action research would be measured in terms of change in performance from the original situation to the planned goal, plus the ability of the organization's members to develop procedures for continued planning, research, and action. The social investigator would be part of the process of organizational change and development but would not be an autocratic director of the process.

A good theory aims ultimately at changing the world, but it is not a blueprint of change. A novel theory changes the political world by revealing new possibilities, which is another way of saying that a novel political theory redefines the limits of political practice. While traditional political theorists have attempted to do just this and are therefore to be emulated, they have erred by focusing on the limits rather than the content of practice. That is, the task of the theorist is to develop and discover new practices that can better serve the needs of the species but not to limit practice in some new way. The theorist has only a different job, not a superior one. Consider Meehan's question: "What are the characteristics of a social structure, and an individual, that is able to learn from experience and improve its performance, and how can those characteristics be taught, created and encouraged?"[101] To answer it requires that we confront and combat the concealment necessary to the success of communication disturbances such as the double bind and the perpetuation of the myth of social control.[102] The answer also requires that we look at all aspects of social life, not just the activities of elites or the data gathered conveniently by government agencies or the information easily utilized by our particular computing skills. It also requires that, in Laing's terms, we become aware of the overt and covert rules against seeing or talking about the rules and constraints of the political context and do not mistake them for epistemological contraints. Panegyrics to freedom are always ideological and irrelevant; free men and women never need to be told of their good fortune. Denunciations of domination are equally ideological and irrelevant; repressed men and women do not need to be told of their repression.

To say we do not understand or that we are ignorant of the contemporary political situation is to say that we are not individually or collectively responding to it in a life-enhancing way. To put it another way, our current patterns of adaptation are biologically disastrous. Such patterns are typical of species in the processes of decimation or extinction. Rather than learning, in the sense of discovering, new ways of remaking our social and physical environment, we are pathologically and defensively learning not to feel, not to see, and not to touch. We are discovering naught but ways to rearrange, to dampen, and to destroy the physiological reactions and responses of our bodies. To continue this behavior under the banner of reason over passion is suicide.

The essence of science is to discard conceptual schemes that do not work as guides to successful survival and to continuously propose and try new schemes that might work better than those in vogue. Proposing is only part of the effort. Trying out is another. Much of what I have written has not been tested in ways promoting confidence. Nor is it formulated in ways that are easy to test. That is not the issue here. I want to persuade you that this approach is worth the arduous task of deriving testable hypotheses and testing them. And that it is worth the even more difficult task of deriving workable political strategies and tactics and putting them into practice. Without this kind of treatment, any conceptual structure becomes a mummified corpus and at best an entertaining subject for dissection.

Men and women can act collectively only on those issues on which they can communicate effectively. Collective activities involve everything from laboratory experiments to massive social changes. A political theory is a vocabulary or code by means of which certain interpersonal phenomena can be acted on, or about, in a collective or public manner. A specific code or vocabulary does not determine what a community will experience, but it does make some forms of experience more difficult to understand or explain. Basil Bernstein writes:

> Language represents the world of the possible. On the one hand, it contains a finite set of options and the rules of their regulation at the structural level and a set of options at the level of vocabulary. Language then represents the totality of options and the attendant rules for doing things with words. It symbolizes what can be done.[103]

What is new about a political theory is the additional set of social options it proposes in the forms of names and descriptions of human experience. These options may be only new reasons for being loyal to old institutions, or they may involve new communal actions and social forms. A superior political theory will increase the options available to a community, thereby leading to an increase in the range of adaptive responses available both to its members and also to the larger collectivity.

I have tried to clean up, relate, and sometimes create verbal concepts and categories that will enable us to discuss and act on the problems of social ignorance and social knowledge in a public and political way. It is well known that men and women hate domination and hierarchical social structures based on domination. What I hope to do in this and subsequent volumes is to initiate discussions and research about why they do, while avoiding the dogmatic moralisms of the past. With such a discussion must go the nurturing of nondominant relationships to ourselves, our fellow humans, and our environment. We must humbly ask some very bold questions and learn to be more attentive to what goes on in our immediate vicinity.

Notes

Introduction

1. Sigmund Freud, *The Future of an Illusion*, p. 8.
2. Montague Ullman, "Societal Factors in Dreaming," *Contemporary Psycho-analysis*, Vol. 9, No. 3, May 1973, p. 291.

Chapter 1

1. I am indebted to Ronald Sampson for the basic form of the psychological argument. See his *The Psychology of Power*, pp. 9–11. Sampson concludes: "The acceptance of the idea that the struggle for inequality is endemic and ineradicable in human nature involves us either in a logical contradiction or a metaphysical nightmare."

2. The need for hypocrisy is most clearly stated by Machiavelli: "For how we live is so far removed from how we ought to live, that he who abandons what is done for what ought to be done, will rather learn to bring about his own ruin than his preservation. A man who wishes to make a profession out of goodness in everything must necessarily come to grief among so many who are not good. Therefore, it is necessary for a prince, who wishes to maintain himself, *to learn how not to be good*, and to use this knowledge and not to use it, according to the necessity of the case." (Niccoló Machiavelli, *The Prince and The Discourses*, p. 56; my emphasis)

3. "The decline of the old elite appears as an increased humanitarian and altruistic sentiment; the rise of the new elite appears as the vindication of the humble and weak against the powerful and strong." (Vilfredo Pareto, *The Rise and Fall of Elites*, p. 41) See also Gaetano Mosca, *The Ruling Class*, p. 118.

4. For sheer force Hobbes's description is remarkable: "Whatsoever therefore is consequent to a time of Warre, where every man is Enemy to every man; the same is consequent to the time, wherein men live without other security, than what their own strength, and their own invention shall furnish them withall. In such condition, there is no place for Industry; because the fruit thereof is uncertain: and consequently no Culture of the Earth; no Navigation, nor use of the commodities that may be imported by Sea; no commodious Building; no instruments of moving, and removing such things as require much force; no Knowledge of the face of the Earth; no account of Time; no Arts; no Letters; no Society; and which is worst of all continual feare, and danger of violent death; and the life of man, solitary, poore, nasty, brutish, and short." (Thomas Hobbes, *Leviathan*, p. 96) For a more modern formulation try, "Instead of fostering freedom, the absence of a social code creates a thralldom of fear and anxiety that becomes insupportable. One cannot turn every choice into an endless philosophical appraisal without verging on madness; and even if one could, one can regress only so far in definition and analysis without coming to a dead stop against unanalyzable, indoctrinated preferences." (Robert Dahl and Charles Lindblom, *Politics, Economics, and Welfare* p. 67)

5. The relationship between natural equality and social hierarchy is most dramati-

cally expressed by the paradox that opens Rousseau's *Social Contract.* "Man is born free; and everywhere he is in chains. One thinks himself the master of others, and still remains a greater slave than they. How did this change come about? I do not know. What can make it legitimate? That question I think I can answer."

6. See George D. Beam, *Usual Politics*, esp. pp. 3–73.

7. An example of a sociological expression of this premise runs, "The human organism lacks the necessary biological means to provide stability for human conduct. Human existence, if it were thrown back on its organismic resources by themselves, would be existence in some sort of chaos. Such chaos is, however, empirically unavailable, even though one may theoretically conceive of it." (Peter L. Berger and Thomas Luchman, *The Social Construction of Reality*, pp. 51–52) Notice that while the threat of chaos is considered real and requires a "social order" as a defense, it is also admitted to be "empirically unavailable" as, I suppose, are unicorns.

8. An amusing and poetic description of the terrors of chaos comes from a supposedly hard-headed cybernetician: "Chaos would permit transitions from any state to any other state, mountains transforming themselves into flying pink elephants, pink elephants turning into yellow goo, etc. Not only are organisms impossible in this world, for by definition, there is no law that holds the organism together, but also this world is indescribable, for description requires names, and names refer to the 'invariabilia'—the constraints in the environment." (Heinz Von Foerster, "From Stimulus to Symbol: The Economy of Biological Computation," in Walter Buckley, ed., *Modern Systems Research for the Behavioral Scientist*, p. 172)

9. Stafford Beer has labeled the metaphysical argument for hierarchy the "mythology of order." "The basic myth . . . is made up of four propositions: that the raw state of nature is chaotic; that order is something introduced into chaos and imposed therein as a monolithic structure to be weathered by random noise; that within this structure a second-order chaos lies invisible; and that once the energy necessary to maintain this order ceases to be available all reverts to chaos once again." ("A Mythology of Systems," p. 2)

10. This viewpoint was best articulated by Saint Augustine and echoed by other Christian writers. While from a Christian standpoint the state is a crime, nevertheless, Augustine advised Christians to submit to it as an alternative to social chaos. "What are kingdoms but great robberies: for what are robberies themselves, but little kingdoms? The band itself is made up of men; it is ruled by the authority of a prince, it is knit together by the pact of the confederacy; the booty is divided by the law agreed on. If, by the admittance of abandoned men, this evil increases to such a degree that it holds places, fixes abodes, takes possessions of cities and subdues peoples, it assumes the more plainly the name of a kingdom, because the reality is now manifestly conferred on it, not by the removal of covetousness, but by the addition of impunity." (Henry Paolucci, *The Political Writings of St. Augustine*, p. 29)

11. "In all societies—from societies that are very meagerly developed and have barely attained the dawnings of civilization, down to the most advanced and powerful societies—two classes of people appear—a class that rules and a class that is ruled. The first class, always the less numerous, performs all political functions, monopolizes power, and enjoys the advantages that power brings, whereas the second, the more numerous class, is directed and controlled by the first, in a manner that is now more or less legal, now more or less arbitrary and violent, and supplies the first, in appearance, at least, with material means of subsistence and with the instrumentalities that are essential to the vitality of the political organism." (Gaetano Mosca, *The Ruling Class*, p. 50)

12. "The near universality of hierarchy in the composition of complex systems suggests that there is something fundamental in the structural principle that goes beyond the

peculiarities of human organization." (Herbert A. Simon, *The Shape of Automation for Men and Management*, p.99) See also Ludwig Von Bertalanffy, *Problems of Life*, p.37, and Koestler, *The Ghost in the Machine*, p. 62.

13. "Every explanation must be testable in principle: *some* body of evidence, some set of outcomes, must in principle be sufficient to demonstrate the inadequacy (not the adequacy) of the explanation. Any structure that excludes nothing, that can fit every situation, that cannot be challenged by any body of evidence, is worthless. And when everything that can be done to evaluate an explanation has been done uncertainty will remain. No experiment is conclusive, no test is final, no sequence of actions can establish an explanation for all times or kill it once and for all. As knowledge expands, new reasons for accepting or rejecting an explanation may at any time appear and they must be honored." (Eugene Meehan, *The Foundations of Political Analysis: Empirical and Normative*, p. 70)

14. One author begins with this dictum: "All known societies have classified their members into categories above or below one another on some scale of superiority and inferiority." He then cites a source that describes societies in which "there is an absence of slavery, nobility, and other major rank or wealth distinctions," and adds, "However, it is not permissible to conclude that rank differences are completely absent in these societies. Such analysis would fail to support a theory of primordial equality in human relationships." Kaare Svalastoga, *Social Differentiation*, pp. 2, 3) Evidently any skimpy data are a basis for concluding hierarchy is present. Notice that the author is such a superior scientist that he is certain of the outcome of the investigation he prescribes.

15. Svalastoga, pp. 39–40.

16. "Wherever we find orderly, stable systems in Nature, we find that they are hierarchically structured, for the simple reason that without such structuring of complex systems into sub-assemblies, there could be no order and stability—except the order of a dead universe filled with a uniformly distributed gas. And even so, each discrete gas molecule would be a microscopic hierarchy. If this sounds by now like a tautology, all the better." (Arthur Koestler, *The Ghost in the Machine*, p. 62)

17. See Robert A. Dahl, "The Concept of Power," *Behavioral Science*, Vol. 2, July 1957, pp. 201–215. Also James G. March, "The Power of Power" in David Easton, ed., *Varieties of Political Theory*) for a discussion of the limited utility of the concept of power in creating predictive models of social choice. March concludes (p. 70) that "power is a disappointing concept."

18. P. K. Feyerabend, *Knowledge without Foundations*, pp. 19–20. See also Malinowski, who defines myth as "a story which is told in order to establish a belief, to serve as a precedent in ceremony or ritual, or to rank as a pattern of moral or religious conduct. Mythology, therefore, or the sacred tradition of a society, is a body of narratives woven into their culture, dictating their beliefs, defining their ritual, acting as the chart of their social order and the pattern of their moral behavior." He also remarks that "myth must be studied in its social, ritual, and ethical effects rather than as an imaginative and pseudo-scientific tale. (*Sex, Culture, and Myth*, pp. 249, 246) A colleague, Peter Wissel, points out that it would be less polemical to call the arguments "tautologies," rather than myths, because the latter term has loaded connotations. He is right about the loaded connotations, but I retain the label "myth" advisedly because I am talking about a structure of explanation such as Malinowski describes and not a consciously constructed tautological system like mathematics.

19. *Knowledge without Foundations*, p. 40.

20. *Knowledge without Foundations*, p. 59. "Certainty possessed by a theory is entirely man made. It is due to the way in which the parts of a theory have been related to each other and to the meanings given to these parts. . . . What we must realize here is that

the claim that a myth offers absolute truth is indeed correct. Of course, a myth will usually be much more complex than the simple theory we have just described. It will contain many elements but these elements will again be related to each other in such a manner that the result is the preservation, and even confirmation, of the myth under all possible circumstances."

21. Quoted by Durkheim. See Emile Durkheim, *Montesquieu and Rousseau: Forerunners of Sociology,* p. 15.

22. Jacques Ellul, *The Political Illusion,* p. 57.

23. *Political Economy in the Modern State,* p. 130.

24. John G. Gunnell, *Philosophy, Science, and Political Inquiry.*

25. "Explanation, Reduction, and Empiricism," in Herbert Feigl and Grover Maxwell, eds., *Scientific Explanation, Space, and Time,* pp. 69–70. The dogmatism of contemporary social science, typified by the myths of hierarchy that pervade the literature, has found its justification in the ambiguous writings of Thomas Kuhn, who sometimes implies that mythological structures in the form of paradigms are the necessary prerequisite of scientific investigations. See his *The Structure of Scientific Revolutions.*

26. *Knowledge without Foundations,* p. 52.

27. P. K. Feyerabend, "Linguistic Arguments and Scientific Method," *Telos,* Vol. 2, No. 1 (Spring 1969), pp. 57–58.

28. "Linguistic Arguments," p. 54.

29. Weber does not, however, see this relationship as an obstacle to science. He states, "There is no absolutely 'objective' scientific analysis of culture—or put more narrowly but certainly not essentially differently for our purposes—of 'social phenomena' independent of special and 'one-sided' viewpoints according to which—expressly or tacitly, consciously or unconsciously—they are selected, analyzed, and organized for expository purposes." He later adds, "The points of departure of the cultural sciences remain changeable throughout the limitless future as long as a Chinese ossification of intellectual life does not render mankind incapable of setting new questions to the eternally inexhaustible flow of life." (*The Methodology of the Social Sciences,* pp. 72, 84)

30. Hobbes describes this aspect of modern scientific methodology in a characteristically pithy way: "When we calculate the magnitude and motions of heaven or earth, we do not ascend into heaven that we may divide it into parts, or measure the motions thereof, but we do it sitting still in our closet or in the dark." (Quoted by Richard Peters in his introduction to *Body, Man, and Citizen,* p. 3)

31. *The Rules of the Sociological Method,* pp. xxxvii–xxxviii.

32. For example, of forty-four major articles published in the *American Political Science Review* in 1971, I found only three that involved the gathering of new data by observation, experimentation, or face-to-face interviews. There were thirteen articles dealing with survey research data of some kind. At least two of these dealt with old surveys and two with professional public-opinion polls. None was apparently new. Even if we count these nine, less than 25 percent of the articles published dealt with new data generated by the researchers themselves. From this I concluded that most political scientists get their information from books, government reports, computer printouts, public polls, voting tabulations, census data, official archives, and the like. This practice represents an empiricism of an extraordinarily narrow and special sort.

33. *Knowledge without Foundations,* pp. 50–51.

34. Marshall McLuhan, *The Gutenberg Galaxy,* p. 76.

35. B. F. Skinner, "Freedom and the Control of Men," *The American Scholar,* Vol. 25, Winter 1955–1956, p. 56.

36. V. Gordon Childe, *Society and Knowledge,* p. 105.

Chapter 2

1. Bronislaw Malinowski, *The Sexual Life of Savages*, p. 188. See Chapter VII, "Procreation and Pregnancy in Native Belief and Custom."

2. *The Sexual Life of Savages*, p. 202.

3. *The Sexual Life of Savages*, p. 191.

4. *The Sexual Life of Savages*, p. 192.

5. "We discover then, in the Trobriander language, a sentence composed of essentially disparate and unrelated words. We find that, in his speech, the Trobriander rarely compares, does not express causality or the telic relationship, feels no conventional urge to go beyond the fact into its implications or relationships." (Dorothy D. Lee, "A Primitive System of Values," *Philosophy of Science*, Vol. 7, No. 3, 1940, p. 365)

6. Lee, p. 358.

7. Lee, pp. 359, 360.

8. Lee, p. 367. Lee concludes her article this way: "We find in Trobriand ethics, applied in activity, the logical concepts which are implicit in the Trobriand language. We find that causes and consequences play no part in evaluation. We find that an act or an object is an end, and a reason, unto itself; and that the standard of its evaluation lies within it. We find the telic motivation of no social value, but that supreme value lies in the act which is utterly futile and disparate, enclosing within itself its own beginning and its own end." (p. 378)

9. Gregory Bateson, "Social Planning and the Concept of Deutero-Learning," in *Steps to an Ecology of Mind*, p. 173.

10. *Class Structure in the Social Consciousness*, p. 38.

11. *The Politics of the Family and Other Essays*, p. 113.

12. *The Politics of the Family*, p. 116.

13. Jean-Paul Sartre, *Being and Nothingness*, p. 49.

14. The distinction is Wilhelm Stekel's, who developed it to criticize the Freudian notion of the unconscious: "One might think that it made no difference to therapy whether we called these repressed ideas paraconscious or unconscious. But we recognize that it is far more difficult to cure an unwillingness-to-see than an inability-to-see. We do not fight against mysterious unconscious ideas. We tell the patient, 'you know, but you do not want to know,' " *Compulsion and Doubt*, p. 256)

15. "Totalitarian education must be based in principle upon trying to condition a fault in the conditioning mechanism of the brain, and a fault in this, it was found, is the one physiological activity that cannot be conditioned. You may learn nothing, and get away with it; but you cannot in sanity learn not to learn. The mechanism breaks down, sooner or later, when these natural functions are tampered with; the mind is flattened into a shallow mold; anything can mean anything and untruth be truth." (*The Living Brain*, pp. 265–266)

16. "When the philosopher again descends into the cave, he dare not tell the cave dwellers of his discovery or he will be destroyed and will destroy social order, which rests on illusion. The residents of the cave will not believe him anyway. If he were to tell the residents of the cave what the shadows were they could no longer play the important role they had been playing—the truth would be disruptive to it." (George J. Graham, "Empirical Theory and Classical Evaluation: The Fact-Value Bridge," *The Helderberg Review*, Vol. 2, No. 1, Fall 1972, p. 22)

17. Jean-Paul Sartre, *Search for a Method*, p. 52

18. W. T. Jones, *A History of Western Philosophy*, p. 599.

19. Francis Bacon, "The Great Instauration," in H. G. Dick, ed., *Selected Writings of Francis Bacon*, pp. 435, 437, and 450.

20. Bacon in Dick, ed., p. 437. See Jones' summary in *A History of Western Philosophy:*

"We do not require 'works' for salvation. Knowledge comes to us from outside; the 'Truth' which is supposed to be waiting all the while for faith to work in us, will write its own fair hand upon our intellects as soon as they are made ready to receive it." Rossi summarizes Bacon's position this way: "The only means of enlightening and persuading mankind—since demonstration is impossible without a norm for discussion—is an appeal to the regions of the mind as yet uncontaminated and open to the truth, neither dimmed by prejudice nor burdened with the weight of ancient knowledge. If we discard the baubles of erudition for the bare simplicity of innocence our minds will be prepared to receive the truth." (Paolo Rossi, *Francis Bacon: From Magic to Science*, p. 48)

21. Bacon, "The Great Instauration," p. 423 in Dick, ed., for both quotations.

22. Bacon's description of the way in which theories founded on "plausible fiction" do not suffice for the progress of knowledge and the way that accepted theories are manipulated so as to seem unfalsifiable seem quite contemporary. For example: "It cannot be that axioms established by argumentation should avail for the discovery of new works; since the subtlety of nature is greater many times over than the subtlety of argument. But axioms duly and orderly formed from particulars easily discover the way to new particulars, and thus render sciences active. The axioms now in use, having been suggested by a scanty and manipular experience and a few particulars of most general occurrence, are made for the most part just large enough to fit and take these in; and therefore it is no wonder if they do not lead to new particulars. And if some opposite instance, not observed or not known before, chance to come in the way, the axiom is rescued and preserved by some frivolous distinction; whereas the truer course would be to correct the axiom itself." (*Novum Organum*, in Dick, ed., p. 466)

23. Bacon chastised the Platonic bias against empirical investigation in this way: "He thought also, there was found in the mind of man an affection naturally bred, and fortified and furthered by discourse and doctrine, which did pervert the true proceedings towards active and operative knowledge. This was a false estimation, that it should be as a diminution to the mind of man to be much conversant in experiences and particulars subject to sense and bound in matter, and which are laborious to search, ignoble to meditate, harsh to deliver, illiberal to practice, infinite as is supposed in number, and no ways accommodated to the glory of arts. This opinion or state of mind received much credit from the school of Plato." p. 402)

24. René Dubos, *Reason Awake, Novum Organum*, in Dick, ed., p. 25.

25. Karl Marx, "Contribution to the Critique of Hegel's Philosophy of Right," in T. B. Bottomore, ed., *Karl Marx: Early Writings*, p. 43. Marx might have picked up the notion of an inverted world from Saint-Simon, who wrote: "These suppositions show that society is a world which is upside down ... in every sphere men of greater ability are subject to the control of men who are incapable. From the point of view of morality, the most immoral men have the responsibility of leading the citizens toward virtue; from the point of view of distributive justice, the most guilty men are appointed to punish minor delinquents." (Henri de Saint-Simon, *Social Organization, the Science of Man and Other Writings*, pp. 74–75) However, Feuerbach is the more obvious source. Feuerbach called religion "the dream of the human mind," and noted, "But even in dreams we do not find ourselves in emptiness or in heaven, but on earth, in the realm of reality; we only see real things in the entrancing splendour of imagination and caprice, instead of in the simple daylight of reality and necessity." He also proposed that the way to combat the delusions of religion was to invert them. "We need only ... invert the religious relations—regard that as an end which religion supposes to be a means—exalt that into the primary which in religion is subordinate, the accessory, the condition,—at once we have destroyed the illusion, and the unclouded light of truth streams in upon us." (Ludwig Feuerbach, *The Essence of Christianity*, pp. xxxiv and 274–275)

26. "If the gentlemen who write and speak, some five millennia of them, have not been creating outright lies, but have been inverting reality, then we do not find ourselves confronting ignorance—which could be corrected through the relatively effortless expedient of a properly handled education, but rather peculiarities and defections in understanding that may evolve to an exquisite complexity. The case may well be that civilization's roll call of intellects, one and all, each in his own way, and without necessarily lying, have been twisting knowledge through a plane of strangeness, creating a warpage of the perceptual field, a shimmering aura through which one steps to discover oneself mucked up in little absurdities—such as one glove (just one) being on inside out, or that we have mismatched stockings (though we are certain they were mated when we left home in the morning), or that we are wearing someone else's hat—and it fits. This indeed is a matter of greater enormity than mere ignorance or even of lies invented outright for the well-being of the reader or listener." (Burt Alpert, *Inversions*, p. 51)

27. Marx, "Economic and Philosophical Manuscripts," in Bottomore, ed., *Early Writings*, p. 313.

28. Marx, "Contribution to the Critique of Hegel's Philosophy of Right," in Bottomore, ed., *Early Writings*, p. 43.

29. Marx, "Letter to Arnold Ruge, September 1843," in L. D. Easton and Kurt Guddat, eds., *Writings of the Young Marx on Philosophy and Society*, pp. 212–213.

30. "The criticism which deals with this subject-matter is criticism in a hand-to-hand fight; and in such a fight it is of no interest to know whether the adversary is of the same rank, is noble or *interesting*—all that matters is to strike him. It is a question of denying the Germans an instant of illusion or resignation. The burden must be made still more irksome by awakening a consciousness of it, and shame must be made more shameful still by rendering it public . . . these petrified social relations must be made to dance by singing their own melody to them. The nation must be taught to be *terrified* of itself, in order to give it courage." (Marx, "Contribution to the Critique of Hegel's Philosophy of Right," in Bottomore, ed., *Early Writings*, p. 47)

31. Marx, "Letter to Ruge," in Easton and Guddat, eds.

32. Marx, "Contribution to the Critique of Hegel's Philosophy of Right," in Bottomore, ed., *Early Writings*, pp. 43, 44. The quotations that follow are from p. 44.

33. Marx, "Contribution," in Bottomore, ed., *Early Writings*, p. 52. The quotations that follow are from pp. 52 and 53.

34. "The *alien* being to whom labour and the product of labour belong, to whose service labour is devoted, and to whose enjoyment the product of labour goes, can only be *man* himself. If the product of labour does not belong to the worker, but confirms him as an alien power, this can only be because it belongs to *a man other than the worker*. If his activity is a torment to him it must be a source of *enjoyment* and pleasure to another. Not the gods, nor nature, but only man himself can be this alien power over man." (Marx, "Economic and Philosophical Manuscripts of 1844," in Bottomore, ed., *Early Writings*, p. 130)

35. Marx, "Contribution to the Critique of Hegel's Philosophy of Right," in Bottomore, ed., *Early Writings*, p. 59.

36. Karl Popper defines historicism as "an approach to the social sciences which assumes that historical prediction is their principal aim, and which assumes that this aim is attainable by discovering the 'rhythms' of the 'patterns,' the 'laws' or the 'trends' that underlie the evolution of history." (*The Poverty of Historicism*, p. 3)

37. In Bottomore, ed., *Karl Marx, Selected Writings*, p. 78.

38. Robert Tucker comments: "[To Marx, socialism] meant a religion of revolution, with universal human self-change as the goal." (*Philosophy and Myth in Karl Marx*, p. 202)

39. In Bottomore, ed., *Karl Marx, Selected Writings*, p. 67.

40. "Theses on Feuerbach," in Bottomore, ed., *Selected Writings*, p. 69.

41. Marx, "Economic and Philosophical Manuscripts," in Bottomore, ed., *Early Writings*, p. 164.

42. Karl Mannheim, *Ideology and Utopia*, p. 6.

43. *Ideology and Utopia*, p. 265.

44. Hans Speier, "Karl Mannheim's Ideology and Utopia," in his *Social Order and the Risks of War*, p. 199.

45. Mannheim, *Ideology and Utopia*, p. 297.

46. *Ideology and Utopia*, p. 298.

47. There are difficulties with this argument, as Gustav Bergmann points out, for it is not clear that we are not dealing solely with representations. Bergman argues: "If I show you a snap shot of a person you do not happen to know, it is hardly fair to ask whether you think it is a good likeness. The question remains unfair, no matter how many portraits of this person I show you—snap shots, water colors, oil paintings, or even a montage (composite of synthesis) of all of them. As it is meant, the argument is therefore without force. A subjectivist cannot in this manner define progress and, in particular, approximation toward an objective truth whose very existence he in principle denies. But one may insist on this and yet think that as sociological *aperçu* about the way certain groups function Mannheim's theory of the free intelligentsia is, perhaps, a brilliant insight." (*The Metaphysics of Logical Positivism*, p. 310)

48. *Ideology*, p. 272.

49. *Ideology*, p. 154.

50. Mannheim, *Ideology*, p. 161.

51. *Ideology*, p. 163. Mannheim's position is different from Weber's, however. Speier comments: "[Mannheim] turned Weber upside down. While in Weber's methodology the valuations are subjective and the validity of knowledge objective, Mannheim arrives at a historical-social relativism concerning the validity of knowledge—which he calls 'rationalism'—and confers a sort of objectivity upon the forces which are assumed to determine valuations. He focuses his attention of the origin of valuations and attempts to discover it in the historical process." ("Karl Mannheim's Ideology and Utopia," p. 192)

52. *Ideology and Utopia*, p. 264.

53. Frank E. Hartung, "Problems of the Sociology of Knowledge," *Philosophy of Science*, Vol. 19 (1949), p. 30.

54. "Problems," p. 30.

55. Hans Speier, "The Social Determination of Ideas," *Social Research*, May 1938, p. 186.

56. "The Social Determination," p. 191.

57. "The Social Determination," p. 197.

58. Speier, "Karl Mannheim's Ideology and Utopia," p. 196.

59. "Karl Mannheim's Ideology and Utopia," p. 195.

60. Arthur Child, "The Theoretical Possibility of the Sociology of Knowledge," *Ethics*, July 1941, pp. 392–418.

61. Frank E. Hartung, "Problems," p. 26. See also Jaques J. Maquet, *The Sociology of Knowledge: Its Structure and Its Relation to the Philosophy of Knowledge*, p. 23.

62. Arthur Child, "The Existential Determination of Thought," *Ethics*, January 1942, p. 185.

63. Arthur Child, "The Problem of Imputation in the Sociology of Knowledge," *Ethics*, January 1941, p. 202.

64. "The Problem of Imputation," p. 217.

65. "The Problem of Imputation," p. 218. See Georg Lukács, *History and Class-Consciousness*.

Chapter 3

1. "In order to know that the philosopher's stone did not really exist, it was indispensable that every substance accessible . . . should be observed and examined . . . .But it is precisely in this that we perceive the almost miraculous influence of the idea. The strength of opinion could not be broken till science had reached a certain state of development." (J. Von Liebig, *Familiar Letters on Chemistry;* quoted in John Read, *Prelude to Chemistry: An Outline of Alchemy*, p. 119)

2. John A. Clausen, "A Historical and Comparative View of Socialization Theory and Research," in Clausen, ed., *Socialization and Society*, pp. 20–72.

3. Edward Alsworth Ross, *Social Control: A Survey of the Foundations of Order*, p. 432. Ross acknowledged that the contrast between community and society was analogous to that of Ferdinand Tönnies (published in 1887) but was worked out before he became acquainted with the latter.

4. Ross, p. 13.

5. Ross, p. 61.

6. "In the taming of men there must be provided coil after coil to entangle the unruly one. Man-quellers must use snares as well as leading strings, will-o'-the-wisps as well as lanterns. The Truth by all means if it will promote obedience, but in any case obedience. Hence coupled with the social endeavor to clarify the individual's judgment on certain points, we detect an unmistakable effort to confuse, befuddle, and mislead it on the other points. Taking a leaf from the policy of nature, society learns the trick of deception." Ross, p. 305)

7. Ross, p. 441; the next quotation is from the same page.

8. G.M.A. Grube, *Plato's Republic*, p. 52.

9. Grube, p. 59.

10. Grube, pp. 82–83. Nietzsche calls the theoretical views we are analyzing here Socratic or Alexandrian and expresses their paradox this way: "Alexandrian culture, to be able to exist permanently, requires a slave class, but, with its optimistic view of life, it denies the necessity of such a class, and consequently, when the effect of its beautifully seductive and tranquilizing utterances about the 'dignity of man' and the 'dignity of labor' is over, it gradually drifts towards a dreadful destruction." ("The Birth of Tragedy," in *The Philosophy of Nietzsche*, pp. 1047–1048)

11. Grube, p. 89.

12. "The closer a society is to us and the more that is known about it, the easier it becomes to dispute interpretations of it. One wonders what would happen to the various characterizations of psychologically remote societies if the natives, as well as the investigator's own colleagues who happen to have some knowledge of the society, were able to answer back." (Alfred R. Lindesmith and Anselm L. Strauss, "A Critique of Culture-Personality Writings" *American Sociological Journal*, Vol. 15, No. 5, October 1950, p. 592.

13. A researcher studying children's political socialization in Australia, who carefully interviewed his subjects, remarks: "I was impressed with the development that could be seen from one age to another in their reasoning and arguments about politics, and with the attractively casual way they treated the 'social influences' that were supposed to be molding their outlooks. Try to mold soup."

14. Colin Turnbull, "The Lesson of the Pygmies," *Scientific American*. Vol. 208, No. 1, January 1963).

15. "The Lesson of the Pygmies." For a fuller account of the BamButi see Turnbull's *The Forest People*.

16. Lawrence Kohlberg, "Development of Moral Character and Moral Ideology," in Martin L. Hoffman and Lois W. Hoffman, eds., *Review of Child Development Research*, p. 426.

17. Lawrence Kohlberg, "Stage and Sequence: The Cognitive-Developmental Approach to Socialization," in David A. Goslin, ed., *Handbook of Socialization Theory and Research,* p. 361.

18. Fred Greenstein, "Political Socialization," in D. E. Sills, ed., *International Encyclopedia of the Social Sciences,* 1968, p. 552.

19. Here is a sample of definitions of socialization which illustrate the use of these various names: (a) "Socialization [is] the processes by which individuals selectively acquire the skills, knowledge, attitudes, values, and motives current in the groups of which they are or will become members." William Sewell, "Some Recent Developments in Socialization Theory and Research," *Annals of the American Academy of Political and Social Sciences,* Vol. 349, September 1963, p. 163. (b) "Socialization refers to the process by which individuals with certain behavioral potentialities acquire the values, beliefs, and behavioral patterns of a specific society, culture, or social group." Richard E. Dawson, "Political Socialization," *Political Science Annual,* 1966, ed. James Robinson, p. 5. (c) "We may define socialization as the process by which someone learns the ways of a given society or social group so that he can function within it. Socialization includes both the learning and internalization of appropriate patterns, values and feelings." Frederich Elkin, *The Child and Society,* p. 4. (d) Socialization is "the process by which an individual, born with behavior potentialities of an enormously wide range, is led to develop actual behavior confined within the narrower range of what is customary for him according to the standards of the group." Irvin L. Child, "Socialization," in Gardner Lindzey, ed., *Handbook of Social Psychology,* pp. 655–692. (e) "In its broadest conception, socialization refers to the sum total of past experiences an individual has had which, in turn, may be expected to play some role in shaping his future social behavior." Alex Inkeles, "Social Structure and Socialization" in David E. Goslin, ed., *Handbook of Socialization Research,* p. 615. (f) Socialization is "the attempt to ensure continuity of a social system through time." Vern L. Bengston, "On the Socialization of Values," p. 3.

Socialization has also been defined as the acquisition of culture and as the means by which culture is transmitted from one generation to another. See John W. Whitney, "Socialization IV: Adult Socialization," D. E. Sills, ed., *International Encyclopedia of the Social Sciences,* 1968).

20. David E. Goslin, "Introduction," in Goslin, ed., *Handbook of Socialization Research,* p. 2.

21. Two political scientists characterize work in political socialization as "a body of research which provides a description of *what* people have learned up to a certain point in time rather than an explanation of how they learned their political preferences." Thomas J. Cook and Frank P. Scioli, Jr., "A Critique of the Learning Concept in Political Socialization Research."

22. Alex Inkeles, "Social Structure and Socialization," in Goslin, ed., *Handbook,* p. 617.

23. For example, take the following quotes from Grube's translation of Plato's *Republic* as illustrations of one way of expressing these assumptions. Note that Plato's propositions or expressions are different from my formulations and those of other theorists. I am proposing that such differences can be subsumed under my general categories. *Primacy principle:* "You know that the beginning of any process is most important especially for anything young and tender. For it is at that time that it takes shape, and any mould one may want can be impressed upon it" (p. 7). *Consensus principle:* "Moderation spreads throughout the whole among the weakest and the strongest and those in between, be it in regard to knowledge or, if you wish, in physical strength or in numbers or in wealth or in anything else and makes them sing the same tune" (p. 97). *Passivity principle:* "Dyers who want to dye wool purple, first of all pick out the natural white and then prepare this in a

number of ways so that it will absorb the color as well as possible . . . we are doing something similar when we were selecting our soldiers . . . What we were in fact contriving was that in obeying us they should absorb the laws" (pp. 94–95). *Structuring principle:* "Education then is the knowledge of how the soul can most easily and most effectively be turned around" (p. 171).

24. Freud, *The Future of an Illusion,* p. 9.

25. *The Future of an Illusion,* p. 8.

26. Freud, *Civilization and Its Discontents,* p. 90. Freud's pessimism is expressed also in the following passage: "It is just as impossible to do without government of the masses by a minority as it is to dispense with coercion in the work of civilization, for the masses are lazy and unintelligent, they have no love for instinctual renunciation, they are not to be convinced of its inevitability by argument, and the individuals support each other in giving full play to their unruliness. It is only by the influence of individuals who can set an example, whom the masses recognize as their leaders, that they can be induced to submit to the labours and renunciations on which the existence of culture depends." (*Civilization and Its Discontents,* pp. 6–7)

27. Daniel Miller, "Psychoanalytic Theory of Development: A Re-Evaluation," in Goslin, ed., *Handbook of Socialization,* p. 484. "So close is the neonate's initial world to a *tabula rasa* that he does not know the difference between real events and imagined ones."

28. As Hobbes writes: "Because the constitution of a man's Body, is in continual mutation; it is impossible that all the same things should always cause in him the same Appetites, and Aversions: much less can all men consent, in the Desire of almost any one and the same Object." (*Leviathan,* p. 40) Locke is more sanguine and sees the problem as that of the failure to accurately calculate the pleasure and pains lying in the distant future. See John Locke, "The Art of Medicine," quoted in W. T. Jones, *A History of Western Philosophy,* pp. 737–738. Compare Locke and Hobbes with the psychoanalytic formulation: "The world is perceived according to the instincts as a possible source of satisfaction or as a possible threat: instinctual wishes and fears falsify reality, a more objective perception presupposes a certain psychological distance of the perceiving ego from the data of perception, a judgment about the sources of the experienced sensations and, more than that, a correct judgment, an ability for differential learning, whereas the primitive experiences are felt as still undifferentiated wholes which make their appearance repeatedly. The pleasure principle, that is, the need for immediate discharge, is incompatible with correct judgment, which is based on consideration and postponement of the reaction. The time and energy saved by the postponement are used in the function of judgment." (Otto Fenichel, *The Psychoanalytic Theory of Neurosis,* p. 39)

29. *The Psychoanalytic Theory of Neurosis,* p. 40.

30. *The Psychoanalytic Theory of Neurosis,* p. 102; the two following quotations are from the same page.

31. These suggestions are: "Whenever possible, unnecessary warnings about instinctual drives should be avoided. It can be stated: 1) it is good to avoid letting children witness sexual scenes between grownups; 2) it is good to reduce seductions by grownups or older children as much as possible; 3) it is good to avoid direct castration threats; 4) it is good to train children to cleanliness in the right way, not too early, not too late, not too strictly, not too emotionally; 5) it is good to prepare children ahead of time for extraordinary impending events like the birth of siblings, operations, and so on; 6) it is better to understand the child's needs than to use rigid disciplinary patterns." (*The Psychoanalytic Theory of Neurosis,* p. 584)

32. *The Psychoanalytic Theory of Neurosis,* p. 488.

33. "The character of man is socially determined. The environment enforces specific frustrations, blocks certain modes of reaction to these frustrations, and facilitates others;

it suggests certain ways of dealing with the conflicts between instinctual demands and fears of further frustrations; it even creates desires by setting up and forming specific ideals. Different societies, stressing different values and applying different educational measures, create different anomolies." *The Psychoanalytic Theory of Neurosis*, p. 464)

34. Lasswell's reasoning goes this way: " . . . it may be said that society depends upon a certain amount of pathology, in the sense that society does not encourage the free criticism of social life, but establishes taboos upon reflective thinking about its own pre-suppositions. If the individual is ·pathological to the extent that he is unable to contemplate any fact with equanimity, and [unable] to elaborate impulses through the process of thought, it is obvious that society does much to nurture disease." (*Psychopathology and Politics*, p. 193)

35. *Civilization and Its Discontents*, p. 7.

36. *The Interpretation of Dreams*, in *The Standard Edition of the Complete Psychological Works of Sigmund Freud*, Vol. 5, p. 57.

37. *Moses and Monotheism*, p. 161.

38. *Introductory Lectures on Psycho-Analysis*, in *The Standard Edition*, Vol. 16, p. 356.

39. "The psychoanalyses of individuals have taught us that their earliest impressions, received at a time when they were hardly able to talk, manifest themselves later in an obsessive fashion, although those impressions themselves are not consciously remembered." (Freud, *Moses and Monotheism*, p. 167)

40. Paul Roazen comments: "One of the misleading appeals of personality theory for the liberal mind is the illusory notion that the psyche is the only source of limitation and failure, and that potentially the outside world can be made tractable if only one's inner self were under control." (Paul Roazen, *Freud: Political and Social Thought*, p. 30. Freud assures us, " . . . the genesis of the neurosis always goes back to very early impressions in childhood." (*Moses and Monotheism*, p. 91)

41. *Civilization and Its Discontents*, pp. 10–11.

42. Freud, *The History of the Psychoanalytic Movement*, p. 51. The next quotation is from p. 52.

43. Harold Orlansky, "Infant Care and Personality," *Psychological Bulletin*, Vol. 46, No. 1 (January 1949), p. 2.

44. "Any moment of behavior is neurotic if the processes that set it in motion predetermine its automatic repetition, and this irrespective of the situation or the social or personal values or consequences of the act." (Lawrence S. Kubie, *Neurotic Distortion of the Creative Process*, p. 21)

45. Eleanor R. Maccoby, "The Development of Moral Values and Behavior in Childhood," in Clausen, ed., *Socialization and Society*, p. 232.

46. In Clausen, ed., p. 264.

47. "It is an . . . American misinterpretation to view psychoanalytic theory as directly relevant to an understanding of individual differences in personality traits. In part, it is a theory of development and maturation. In part, it is a theory of psychopathology. It has never claimed, however, to be a theory designed to predict adult individual differences or traits from specific childhood experiences—a task Freud claimed was impossible." (Lawrence Kohlberg, "Stage and Sequence: The Cognitive-Developmental Approach to Socialization," in David E. Goslin, ed., *Handbook of Socialization*, p. 367)

48. Robert Waelder, *Basic Theory of Psychoanalysis*, pp. 53–54. Roazen calls attention to the passage.

49. "Basic responses of personality are conditioned by early experiences. Clearly, then, the early experiences of each individual will be paramount in shaping his social development, according to this [the psychoanalytic] theory." (Roger Burton, "Socialization: Psychological Aspects," in D. E. Sills, ed., *International Encyclopedia of the Social Sciences*, p. 535)

50. Ross, *Social Control,* p. 163.

51. "A standard, general hypothesis in this connection is that the earlier the person adopts a given set of political orientations, the less likely it is that these orientations will be eroded later in life." (Jack Dennis, "Major Problems of Political Socialization Research," *Midwest Journal of Political Science,* Vol. 12, February 1968, p. 99) David Marsh identifies the principle as an unquestioned assumption "not based on sound quantitative evidence." ("Political Socialization: The Implicit Assumptions Questioned," *British Journal of Political Science,* Vol. 1, October 1971, p. 457)

52. "Socialization: Psychological Aspects" in D. E. Sills, ed., *International Encyclopedia of the Social Sciences,* p. 540.

53. Orlansky, "Infant Care and Personality," p. 18. For a more detailed discussion, see the section of this chapter on culture-personality studies.

54. "There are cultures where 'no attention is paid to the filth which accumulates and . . . the babies are caked with dirt,' where the infant's head or feet are deformed, or where its nose, ears, or mouth are subject to piercing and its body to scarification or other painful mutilation. Until contrary evidence is forthcoming, there is no reason to believe that infants reared in a 'foetusphobic' manner are any more neurotic or insecure or differ in any significant aspect of personality from the 'foetusphile' infants because of any single type of treatment to which they are subjected." ("Infant Care and Personality," p. 14) Few middle-class Americans would agree with this statement.

55. "Infant Care and Personality," p. 30. See M. Sherman and I. Sherman, *The Process of Human Behavior,* pp. 122–123, 142.

56. "Infant Care and Personality," p. 25.

57. "Infant Care and Personality," p. 34. See J. McV. Hunt, "The Effects of Infant-feeding Frustration upon Adult Hoarding in the Albino Rat," *Journal of Abnormal and Social Psychology,* Vol. 36, 1941, pp. 338–360.

58. "There are certain conditions that prevent the formation of dispositions as stable as those to be formed later (during the first year of life). There is, for example, a low degree of retentivity for conscious experiences. . . . Then, too, though the infant learns rapidly, he also forgets rapidly. . . . The propensity for an all-or-none type of emotional activity prevents his learning discriminative effective response or the development of a hierarchy of likes and dislikes. His capacity for conceptualization is slight. There are then plenty of reasons why personality should be less stable, less predictable, and less consistent in the early months of life than at any other time." (Gordon Allport, *Personality*)

59. "Infant Care and Personality," p. 38.

60. "Infant Care and Personality," pp. 37–38.

61. William H. Sewell, "Infant Training and the Personality of the Child," *American Journal of Sociology,* Vol. 58, 1952, pp. 150–159. See also John R. Thurston and Paul H. Mussen, "Infant Feeding Gratification and Adult Personality," *Journal of Personality,* Vol. 19, June 1951, pp. 449–458. The authors found no relation between infant feeding gratification and adult personality.

62. "On the basis of the results of this study, the general null hypothesis that the personality adjustments and traits of children who have undergone varying training experiences do not differ significantly cannot be rejected. Of the 460 chi square tests, only 18 were significant at or beyond the 5 percent level. Of these, 11 were in the expected direction and 7 were in the opposite direction from that expected on the basis of psychoanalytic writings. Such practices as breast feeding, gradual weaning, demand schedule, and easy and late induction to bowel and bladder training, which have been so much emphasized in the psychoanalytic literature, were almost barren in terms of relation to personality adjustment as measured in this study. Actually these 6 factors produced only 11 significant chi squares out of a possible total of 276. Of these, 9 are in the

direction which would be predicted on the basis of psychoanalytic writings and 2 are in the opposite direction." ("Infant Training and the Personality of the Child," p. 158)

63. Kohlberg, "Stage and Sequence: The Cognitive-Developmental Approach to Socialization," p. 361.

64. "Stage and Sequence: The Cognitive Developmental Approach to Socialization," p. 367.

65. Donald Searing, Joel J. Swartz, and Alden E. Lind, "The Structuring Principle: Political Socialization and Belief Systems," *American Political Science Review*, Vol. 67, No. 2, June 1973, p. 426.

66. Michael P. Riccards, "The Socialization of Civic Virtue," in Philip Abbot and Michael P. Riccards, eds., *Reflections in American Political Thought*, p. 217.

67. "Having uplifted the expectations of people, it must either make the sacrifices necessary to satisfy them or be willing to face the consequences of public disillusionment. America is learning all too well that while the socialization of civic virtue is an easy process to instill, it can be a frightening yardstick by which to be measured once school is out and events are in the saddle." (Riccards, "The Socialization of Civic Virtue," p. 222)

68. The difficulty of confronting the theory of socialization with the findings of socialization research in such a way to assess the validity of that theory is illustrated in the following passages: "It would appear to be amply demonstrated that differences in moral behavior and values among children of the same age are associated with differences in the socialization practices of their parents," writes Eleanor Maccoby in reviewing much of the same literature as Kohlberg in "Stage and Sequence." She adds, "Even more telling are the findings of the experimental studies, in which it has been possible to have experimenters reproduce at least some aspects of parental behavior and obtain changes in children's behavior which parallel some of the findings of correlational studies." But notice that the experimental studies demonstrate that the supposed behavior patterns and values inculcated by parents can be easily changed by experimenters. This finding would mean that parental effects are not primary since the child's encounter with other agents can change behavior. But the very experimenters who demonstrate this persist, according to Maccoby, in insisting that "the parents are the central figures in early socialization, and this makes them central for the whole of moral development, for in social-learning theory, early learned behavior tends to persist." To further complicate Maccoby's presentation, she reports that the relation of parental socialization practices to specific aspects of moral development is supported, if at all, by inconsistent findings. See Eleanor R. Maccoby, "The Development of Moral Values and Behavior in Childhood," pp. 251, 242, 248.

69. David Marsh, "Political Socialization," p. 458.

70. See D. Butler and D. Stokes, *Political Change in Britain*, and R. J. Benewick, et al., "The Floating Voter and the Liberal View of Representation," *Political Studies*, Vol. 17, 1969, pp. 177–195.

71. Joan Aldous and Reuben Hill, "Social Cohesion, Lineage Type, and Intergenerational Transmission," *Social Forces*, Vol. 43, 1965, pp. 471–482.

72. Vern Bengston, "On the Socialization of Values," pp. 22, 24.

73. Bengston, p. 32.

74. A. J. Reiss, "Social Organization and Socialization: Variations on a Theme about Generations," Working Paper #1, Center for Research on Social Organization, University of Michigan, Ann Arbor, 1965.

75. R. W. Connell, "Political Socialization in the American Family: The Evidence Re-examined," *Public Opinion Quarterly*, Vol. 36, 1972, pp. 323–333.

76. M. Kent Jennings, *The Student-Parent Socialization Study.*

77. If I seem to overstate the principle and its implication, take a look at this recent

formulation: "In blunt and in brief: for Freud the self is an accumulation of encounters between instinct and society, and from the first encounter on the libido has been bent by power like a hairpin. The world which the ego feels it must accommodate desire to is composed of lies and illusion laid down like law. Society itself is a structured set of individuals who have been socially deformed." (William Gass, "The Battered, Triumphant Sage," *The New York Review of Books*, May 15, 1975, p. 12)

78. Thomas A. Harris, *I'm OK—You're OK*, p. 30.

79. McCulloch continues: "His body could not eat enough to energize its mere retention even if we suppose a single molecule of structuring protein would serve as a trace. Actually the mean half-life of a trace in human memory, and of a molecule of protein is only half a day. Some few percent of engrams do survive, presumably because we recreate the traces in our heads, but that is all fate leaves us of our youth. Where written words remain to check our senile recollections they often prove us wrong. We rewrite history, inventing the past so it conforms to present needs. We forget, as our machines forget, because entropic processes incessantly corrupt retention and transmission of all records and signals." (W. S. McCulloch, *Embodiments of Mind*, p. 292)

80. George A. Talland, *Disorders of Memory and Learning*, p. 60.

81. Wilder Penfield, "Memory Mechanisms," *AMA Archives of Neurology and Psychiatry*, Vol. 67 (1952), pp. 178–198.

82. Wilder Penfield and Lamar Roberts, *Speech and Brain Mechanisms*, p. 45. Penfield reports, "Some patients call an experiential response a dream. Others state that it is a 'flashback' from their own life history. All agree that it is more vivid than anything they could recall voluntarily." (p. 51)

83. Penfield and Roberts, p. 48

84. "Though our memory may store some form of record of trivial past events that we would not have thought worth retaining, there is no evidence of anything approaching photographic detail in the quality of such storage. And it is quite an extrapolation from the double handful of observations of the eliciting by cortical stimulation of detailed records of unimportant events to the conclusion that all events are recorded in the memory. It seems more likely that there may have been associated at the time with each of these seemingly trivial events some element that caused them to be remembered, while other events that today would seem as important were not recorded." (Dean E. Wooldridge, *The Machinery of the Brain*, p. 190)

85. Maitland Baldwin, "Electrical Stimulation of the Mesial Temporal Region" in Estelle R. Ramey and Desmond S. O'Doherty, eds., *Electrical Studies on the Unanesthetized Brain*, pp. 159–176.

86. Wooldridge, p. 190.

87. John Von Neumann, *The Computer and The Brain*, p. 62. A "bit" is a term coined by Claude Shannon as a unit for measuring information capacity. It is defined as the number of successive yes-no choices required to determine a specific signal out of a given repertoire. For example, if we ask "How much information is in the statement, 'this is Friday,' " we can calculate the answer in bits if we know the number of answers that are possible in a given context. If we have awakened from a coma and ask what day it is, there are seven possible answers and the statement "This is Friday" contains $\log_2 7$ bits or 2.81 bits of information. See Elwyn Edwards, *Information Transmission*, pp. 28–39.

88. *The Machinery of the Brain*, p. 189.

89. J. Z. Young, *A Model of the Brain*, p. 66.

90. Claude E. Shannon and Warren Weaver, *The Mathematical Theory of Communication*.

91. Ernest G. Schactel, "On Memory and Childhood Amnesia" in Patrick Mullahy, ed., *A Study of Interpersonal Relations*, p. 8.

92. "Memory, in other words, is even more governed by the conventional patterns than perception and experience are. One might say that, while all human experiences, perception, and thought are eminently social—that is, determined by the socially prevailing ways of experiencing, perceiving, and thinking, memory is even more socialized, to an even higher degree dependent on the commonly accepted categories of what and how one remembers." (Schactel, p. 16)

93. Robert Waelder, *Basic Theory of Psychoanalysis*, p. 51.

94. Classics of the genre would include Ruth Benedict, *Patterns of Culture;* Margaret Mead, "National Character" in A. L. Kroeber, ed., *Anthropology Today;* Cora DuBois, *The People of Alor;* Erik Erikson, "Childhood and Tradition in Two American Indian Tribes: With Some Reflections on the Contemporary American Scene," in Clyde Kluckhohn and H. A. Murray, *Personality in Nature, Society and Culture;* Eric Fromm, *Escape from Freedom;* Geoffrey Gorer, *Japanese Character Structure and Propaganda;* Abram Kardiner, *The Individual and His Society;* Clyde Kluckhohn, "Culture and Behavior" in Gardner Lindzey, ed., *Handbook of Social Psychology*, Vol. 2; Weston La Barre, "Some Observations on Character Structure in the Orient," *Psychiatry*, Vol. 8, 1945, pp. 319–342; Ralph Linton, *The Cultural Background of Personality;* Geza Roheim, *The Origin and Function of Culture.*

95. "Cultural relativity demands that every item of cultural behavior be seen as relative to the culture of which it is a part, and in that systematic setting every item has positive or negative meaning and value." (Margaret Mead, "The Comparative Study of Culture and the Purposive Cultivation of Democratic Values" in *Science, Philosophy and Religion: Second Symposium,* p. 58)

96. Mead, "The Comparative Study," p. 58.

97. "To say that culture 'teaches' puts the matter too mildly. Actually culture invades and infests the mind as an obsession. If it does not, culture will not 'work'; only an obsession has the power to withstand the impact of critical differences; to fly in the face of contradiction; to engulf the mind so that it will see the world only as the culture decrees that it shall be seen; to compel a person to be absurd." (Jules Henry, *Culture against Man*) "Man's need for security in an uncertain world leads to the systematization of ideas that run counter to experience. The acceptance of untestable axioms needed to provide emotional security often directs perception and understanding. Such axioms form belief systems when shared and culturally acceptable and delusional systems when idiosyncratic." (Theodore Lidz and Stephen Fleck, "Schizophrenia, Human Integration, and the Role of the Family," in Don D. Jackson, ed., *The Etiology of Schizophrenia*, p. 329)

98. Erik Erikson, "Childhood and Tradition in Two American Indian Tribes," p. 180.

99. Anthony F. C. Wallace, *Culture and Personality*, p. 24.

100. "Each system in its own way tends to make similar people out of all its members, but each in a specific way also permits exemptions and deductions from the demands with which it thus taxes the individuality of the individual ego. It stands to reason that these exemptions are less logical and much less obvious, even to the people themselves, than are the official rules." (Erik Erikson, *Childhood and Society*, p. 185) This formulation is typically maddening when one tries to sort out exactly what is being asserted; indeed, it stands to reason that no conceivable evidence could make it false.

101. Lindesmith and Strauss conclude their critique of culture—personality writings: "Available evidence offered by the writers in support of their conclusions is inadequate and does not justify their conclusions. Positive generalizations made in this area are generally based on unwarranted confidence in rather loose unscientific methods or interpreting data, and upon a relatively uncritical acceptance of a particular conceptual scheme." (Alfred R. Lindesmith and Anselm L. Strauss, "A Critique of Culture-Personality Writings," p. 599)

102. See Clyde Kluckhohn, "Covert Culture and Administrative Problems," *American Anthropologist,* Vol. 45, 1947. Kluckhohn credits the concept of covert culture to Ralph Linton and defines it as "that sector of the culture of which the members of the society are unaware or minimally aware." That definition seems to imply social ignorance, which presents no problems, but Kluckhohn argues further that the covert culture consists of unstated principles or premises of which members must be aware even though they do not verbalize them. I do not know what an unverbalized principle might look like.

103. Lindesmith and Strauss, "A Critique of Culture-Personality Writings," pp. 596–599.

104. Kardiner writes: "The family is where the social emotions are cultivated. Once these are formed, there is no need for admonitions and threats to keep them in operation; if they are malformed, exhortations and threats will certainly have no effect in bringing them into existence. This is another place where our moralists have gone awry. One cannot preach morality at people. It has to be built into them. Preaching and exhortation do not reach the sources of human motivation. They can only reinforce morality, they cannot create it. Morality is built by constant interaction with parents in early life." (*Sex and Morality,* p. 253) Thus moral discourse is an impossibility and to contribute to the improvement of civic values requires the massaging of infant bodies.

105. "If the microscopic view is adopted, then research is not necessary to demonstrate that covariation between personality and culture is exact (given constant 'genetic factors'); this is regarded as true by definition. The problem becomes essentially one of child development." (Wallace, *Culture and Personality,* p. 85) Orlansky complains that "the same childhood experience is arbitrarily read as having one significance for personality formation in one society and the opposite significance in another" ("Infant Care and Personality," p. 287)

106. "The basic personality type for any society is that personality configuration which is shared by the bulk of the society's members as a result of the early experiences which they have in common. It does not correspond to the total personality of the individual but rather to the projective systems or, in different phraseology, the value-attitude systems which are basic to the individual's personality configuration. Thus the same basic personality type may be reflected in many different forms of behavior and may enter into many different total personality configurations." (Ralph Linton in Abram Kardiner and Associates, *The Psychological Frontiers of Society,* pp. vii–viii)

107. *The Psychological Frontiers of Society,* p. 29. See pp. 28–29 for a full description of the process by which individual's attitudes are a product of his care in infancy.

108. "Man in his personality make-up is the product of the adaptive maneuvers he is obliged to institute in order to function in his environment. Adaptive patterns are *not* inherited; each individual creates them anew according to needs, within the framework of culturally determined possibilites." (Abram Kardiner and Lionel Ovesey, *The Mark of Oppression,* p. xvi)

109. See Abram Kardiner, *The Individual and His Society,* and Kardiner, *Sex and Morality.* Wallace uses the material of Cora DuBois as an example of the confusions and difficulties of the basic personality approach. (*Culture and Personality,* p. 86) See Cora A. DuBois, *The People of Alor.*

110. Walter Goldschmidt, "Ethics and the Structure of Society: An Ethnological Contribution to the Sociology of Knowledge," *American Anthropologist,* Vol. 53, 1951, pp. 506–524.

111. Erik Erikson, *Childhood and Society,* p. 178.

112. Erikson writes: "The collective or official character structure of the Yurok shows many of the traits which Freud and Abraham found to be of typical significance in patients with 'anal fixations,' namely compulsiveness, suspiciousness, retentiveness, etc. It

would be hard, however, to find in Yurok childhood an emphasis on feces or on the anal zone that would fulfill the criteria of a collective 'anal fixation.' Yurok attitude toward body content and property is alimentary and rather concerns the total inside of the body with its network of channels and orifices and its mixture of incorporated objects, excreta, and secretions." ("Childhood and Tradition in Two American Indian Tribes," p. 194) See also Erikson, "Observations of the Yurok: Childhood and World Image," *University of California Publications in American Archaeology and Ethnology,* Vol. 35, No. 10. It is difficult to tell if the above passage is a recognition of the defeat of the theory of anal fixation or something of an intellectual epicycle which simultaneously admits failure and reinterprets the data to salvage the theory. Evidently the Yurok suffer from "alimentary fixations" which are identical in terms of personality to "anal fixations" but are generated by other means than toilet training.

113. Daniel Miller, "Psychoanalytic Theory of Development," p. 495.

114. See: A. Bernstein, "Some Relations between Techniques of Feeding and Training during Infancy and Certain Behavior in Childhood," *Genetic Psychology Monographs,* Vol. 55, 1975, pp. 141–172. E. E. Hetherington and Y. Brackbill, "Etiology and Covariation of Obstinacy, Orderliness, and Parsimony in Young Children," *Child Development,* Vol. 34, 1963, pp. 919–943.

115. "A person can hardly hoard money, e.g. or be compulsively punctual if there is no money to hoard and no clocks by which to measure punctuality and need it be added that money and clocks serve rational purposes and that their development can be explained historically without reference to the infant libido?" (Orlansky, "Infant Care," p. 20)

116. Goldschmidt, "Ethics and the Structure of Society," p. 522. Barrows Dunham makes the point bluntly: "Careers within one's own society are easier if one believes what the society says it believes and those same careers may end abruptly if one ceases to hold those same beliefs." (*Heroes and Heretics,* p. vii.)

117. See Christopher Jencks, et al., *Inequality,* p. 8.

118. "Prior to politics, beneath it, enveloping it, restricting it, conditioning it, is the underlying consensus on policy that usually exists in the society among a predominant proportion of the politically active. Without such a consensus no democratic system would long survive the endless irritations and frustrations of elections and party competition." (Robert A. Dahl, *A Preface to Democratic Theory,* p. 132) Notice that Dahl's statement is restricted to what Mosca would call the "political class" and thus cannot be falsified by citing examples of social conflict and deviance. The modern view is that there must be a consensus but that it need not involve all nor even a majority of citizens so long as the most active (read: most powerful) are in basic agreement.

119. Anthony F. C. Wallace, "The Psychic Unity of Human Groups," in B. Kaplan, ed., *Studying Personality Cross-Culturally,* p. 158.

120. Note that much which passes for social science is not only based on assuming the consensus principle, but also attempts to single out those goals, those beliefs, and that public terminology that are considered essential for stability. It further attempts to convince leaders and other intellectuals of the crucial nature of these beliefs and terms and to persuade the public to support the consensus that is deemed necessary. Bernard Crick comments, "Political science as a discipline first arose in the United States to fulfill the practical task of maintaining a belief in the unity of American sentiments." (*The American Science of Politics*) Unless the job of political scientists in the United States is redefined they will continue to have a vested interest in assuming the consensus principle and protecting it from criticism.

121. "It is . . . impossible to demonstrate empirically that any social system is operated by individuals all driven by the same motives; indeed, the data of personality-and-culture

studies, as well as clinical observation, show conclusively that a sharing of motives is not necessary to a sharing of institutions." (Wallace, *Culture and Personality*, p. 29) See also Ralf Dahrendorf, "Out of Utopia: Toward a Reorientation of Sociological Analysis," *American Journal of Sociology*, Vol. 64, September 1958, p. 120: "That societies are held together by some kind of value consensus seems to be either a definition of societies or a statement clearly contradicted by empirical evidence—unless one is concerned not so much with real societies and their problems as with social systems in which anything might be true, including the integration of all socially held values into a religious doctrine. I have yet to see a problem for the explanation of which the assumption of a unified value system is necessary, or a testable prediction that follows from this assumption."

122. "The attitudes of voters in selected Midwestern and Southern communities offer no support for the hypothesis that democracy requires a large measure of consensus among the carriers of the creed, that is, those most consistently in accord with democratic principles. As expected, general consensus was found on the idea of democracy itself and on the broad principles of majority rule and minority rights, but it disappeared when these principles were put in a more specific form. Indeed, the voters in both communities were closer to complete discord than to complete consensus; they did not reach consensus on any of the ten specific statements incorporating the principles of majority rule and minority rights; and majorities expressed the "undemocratic" attitude on about half of the statements." (James W. Prothro and Charles M. Grigg, "Fundamental Principles of Democracy: Bases of Agreement and Disagreement," *Journal of Politics*, May 1960, p. 294)

123. Wallace, *Culture and Personality*, pp. 37–38. Wallace adds, "But the advocate of togetherness may argue, whether or not it is necessary that *all* members of society share *all* cognitive maps, they must share at least *one*. Such an argument, however, is not convincing. No criteria known to the writer would specify what one map is functionally necessary that all members of a given society should share. Recourse cannot be had to the empirical argument that all members of all societies are *known* to share at least one map, for the data to support such an argument do not exist. And merely demonstrating that some defined group of human individuals, or even all the members of some one society, share a particular map, is irrelevant to the discussion. (Such a society would have to be a peculiarly simple and at the same time clairvoyant one, anyway.) Two or more parties may indeed share a common cognitive map, but such a circumstance is, in a sense, wasteful, since at least two, and therefore all, of these maps must be larger than the minimally necessary ones. And only when each actor is cognizant of the other's 'motive' (consummatory act), can the actors' cognitive maps be identical and still contribute to system maintenance."

124. Wallace, "The Psychic Unity," p. 146.

125. "The concepts of identity and equivalence . . . are formal logical concepts. They may be applied to predicates which are the descriptive elements of propositions (for instance, in the proposition, 'The table is round,' 'is round' is the predicate). Two symbols, 'p' and 'q', are said to stand for identical predicates only if the predicates are one and the same. The two symbols 'p' and 'q' are said to stand for strictly equivalent predicates if, whenever p is true, q is true also, and whenever q is true, p is true. Evidently identity implies equivalence; but equivalence does not imply identity." (Wallace, "The Psychic Unity," pp. 158–159)

126. "The Psychic Unity," p. 151.

127. "The Psychic Unity," p. 151.

128. Wallace, *Culture and Personality*, pp. 39–40. Wallace gives as one example of cognitive diversity, the difference between the conceptual framework of the administrator as opposed to those of subordinates. I maintain that such vertical differentiation is

not complimentary but conflictual, since both maps are necessarily partial and restricted. The administrative map is overly abstract and devoid of detail, the subordinate map is overly concrete and lacking in relational predicates. The result is mutual deception, as Marx once noted, not coordination.

129. "The Psychic Unity," p. 41

130. Carl J. Friedrich, *The New Belief in the Common Man,* p. 156.

131. "Where there is no universe of discourse, where the image possessed by the organism is purely private and cannot be communicated to anyone else, we say the person is mad." (Kenneth Boulding, *The Image,* p. 15) Notice that all cognitions are at least partially private and that the struggle is to communicate them to others; Boulding implies that this represents a struggle for sanity rather than the human effort to articulate. The cliché that genius and madness are nearly the same thing clearly stems from the same view.

132. Wallace, "The Psychic Unity," p. 135.

133. "This assumption that primitive peoples think according to radically different rules of logic, and that these 'primitive' logical calculi are needful to account for such irrational beliefs about process in the natural world as mana and taboo, magic, witchcraft, and so forth, is an old one. It has been unfortunately coupled with a psychiatric theory that the psychotic regresses not merely in the direction of his own infancy but in the direction of the infancy of the species, and that—to complete the circle—thought processes of psychotics in modern mental hospitals can be studied as a means of understanding primitive thought. There is, however, no real evidence that any primitive people characteristically and conventionally employs what Western logicians would define as a logical fallacy. And to suppose that the primitive is *unable* to think rationally, for instance, would lead to the expectation that the primitive hunter would perform the following feat of cerebration, with suicidal consequences:

> A rabbit has four legs.
> That animal has four legs.
> Therefore that animal is a rabbit.

"This fallacious piece of reasoning follows the so-called law of von Domarus (subjects are identical if they have a common predicate). Such reasoning has been attributed to primitives and schizophrenics alike, and, had it been in fact widely applied during the Paleolithic period, it would long ago have been the death of our ancestors. . . . The theories of natural process implicit in beliefs about taboo, magic, and witchcraft are not illogical; they are simply wrong." (Wallace, "Culture and Cognition," *Science,* Vol. 135, No. 3501, February 2, 1962, p. 5)

134. Wallace, "The Psychic Unity," p. 136. In particular, Wallace is criticizing the theories of Domarus and Arieti, but his critique could also be applied to the theories of Plato, Hobbes, Pareto, Freud, and many others who deduce a fundamental irrationality in human reasoning from the evidence of defective social actions. All such theories lead to plans for reforming human nature—meaning to restrict cognitive structures to some presumed pattern of "truth" or "rationality." See Silvano Arieti, *Interpretation of Schizophrenia,* and E. Von Domarus, "The Specific Laws of Logic in Schizophrenia," in J. S. Kasanin, ed., *Language in Thought and Schizophrenia.*

135. Wallace, *Culture and Personality,* p. 27.

136. "From the organization-of-diversity standpoint . . . culture change is not necessarily traumatic; indeed it is to be regarded as the natural conditions of man. If we regard most 'living' cultures as heterogenious and in constant, relatively rapid change (rapid change, incidentally, does not necessarily imply either change in material artifacts

or rapid cumulative evolution), we note first that heterogeneity and change by definition no longer imply psychological and cultural disorganization. The causes of such disorganization must be sought elsewhere than in heterogeneity and change per se." (*Culture and Personality,* pp. 118–119)

137. "The psychological reality of an individual is the world as he perceives and knows it, in his own terms; it is his world of meanings. A 'psychologically real' description of a culture thus is a description which approximately reproduces in an observer the world of meanings of the native users of that culture. 'Structural reality,' on the other hand, is a world of meanings, as applied to a given society or individual, which is real to the ethnographer, but it is not *necessarily* the world which constitutes the mazeway of any other individual or individuals. This difference is well illustrated in the difference which sometimes obtains between descriptions of a given society by social anthropologists who are interested in predictive models of relations among groups and in related economic and demographic processes, and by ethnographers who are interested in describing the world as the individual sees it." (Anthony F. C. Wallace and John Atkins, "The Meaning of Kinship Terms," *American Anthropologist,* Vol. 62, February 1960, pp. 75–76)

138. "Social-structural reality can be achieved; psychological reality can only be approximated. But such approximations are sorely needed. The problem of extending the psychological reality of ethnographic description is not just a 'culture-and-personality' problem, it is a general anthropological issue with implications for anyone concerned with the relationship between culture and cognitive processes. Indeed, it is a general issue for the behavioral sciences, because structurally real descriptions do not predict certain phenomena so well as psychologically real descriptions." (Wallace and Atkins, p. 79)

139. Wallace, "The Psychic Unity," p. 137.

140. "The Psychic Unity," p. 146.

141. "Man's nervous system does not merely enable him to acquire culture, it positively demands that he do so if it is going to function at all. Rather than culture acting only to supplement, develop, and extend organically based capacities genetically prior to it, it would seem to be an ingredient to those capacities A cultureless human being would probably turn out to be not an intrinsically talented though unfulfilled ape, but a wholly mindless and consequently unworkable monstrosity. Like the cabbage it so much resembles, the *Homo sapiens* brain, having arisen with the framework of human culture, would not be viable outside of it." (Clifford Geertz, "The transition to Humanity," in Sol Tax, ed., *Horizons of Anthropology,* p. 44)

142. Geertz, p. 141.

143. Geertz, p. 141. I prefer Tolman's notation of "cognitive map" (which is introduced in the next chapter to Wallace's because "mazeway" is both ugly and too reminiscent of the rat laboratory). The two terms seem to be equivalent if not identical. "*Mazeway* is to the individual what *culture* is to the group. Just as every group's history is unique, so every human individual's course of experience is unique. Every human brain contains, at a given point of time, as a product of this experience, a unique mental image of a complex system of objects, dynamically interrelated, which includes the body in which the brain is housed, various other surrounding things, and sometimes even the brain itself. This complex mental image is the mazeway. Its content consists of an extremely large number of assemblages, or cognitive residues of perception. It is used, by its holder, as a true and more or less complete representation of the operating characteristics of a 'real' world." (Wallace, *Culture and Personality,* p. 16)

144. "Social coordination is entirely feasible, given the common possession of a cultural nature, without uniformity of motive or interest. This is, in fact, precisely the achievement of the cultural mode of organization. Such an assumption lies at the root of such notions as the ideas of justice, of law, of convention, and of a minimally necessary

behavioral conformity without sacrifice of individuality, which have been associated with the concept of 'freedom' in sophisticated civilizations. Without such an assumption, indeed, motivational diversity is merely hidden under mutual illusions of motivational identity (and mutual suspicions of 'disloyalty'), by the ritualization of all expression, by the frustration of the drive for maximal meaning and organization of experience, and by the blocking of the evolution of human personalities and cultures. Neither order nor complexity can be immolated on the other's altar without violating the laws of cultural nature." (*Culture and Personality*, p. 158)

145. Carl J. Friedrich, *The New Belief in the Common Man*, p. 181. Friedrich argues: "Almost all mankind is united in condemning dishonesty and murder. The legal codes of people after people will show provisions against these types of anti-social behavior. But just because they are so universally agreed upon as undesirable, they do not represent any issue with which constitutional democracy, as contrasted with authoritarian forms of government, is likely to be specifically concerned. Such simple issues do not provide a problem." (*The New Belief*, p. 172)

146. Edward M. Bruner, "The Psychological Approach in Anthropology," in Sol Tax, ed., *Horizons of Anthropology*, p. 73.

147. A typical example of such reasoning runs: "If all the aggressive, sexual, and acquisitive needs of an individual were immediately and completely gratified, then that individual would never become fully human. We develop ego strength, self-awareness, and a sense of reality as a consequence of external controls and inhibitions. Some degree of frustration is necessary for survival and maturity." (Bruner, "The Psychological Approach," p. 74) The implication is that the rape and sexual exploitation of women, the systematic plundering of human creativity, and the periodically manipulated genocide of the modern world makes us "fully human."

148. *The New Belief in the Common Man*, p. 173.

149. *An Essay Concerning Human Understanding*, p. 100.

150. *An Essay Concerning Human Understanding*, pp. 68, 93.

151. The work of Clark Hull also is relevant here. I have not treated his theories of behavior because of space and time limitations.

152. B. F. Skinner, "Freedom and the Control of Men," *American Scholar*, Vol. 25, Winter 1955–1956, p. 53.

153. B. F. Skinner, *About Behaviorism*.

154. There is a difficulty for Skinner regarding the passivity principle because his own experimental findings stress that the behavior of an animal can only be shaped or molded but not, technically speaking, caused. The original activities of the experimental animal are "emitted" or occur without action on the part of the experimenter. For an interpretation of this difficulty which argues the idea that organisms can and do initiate action is contained within the Skinnerian system, see Finley Carpenter, *The Skinner Primer*, p. 49. Carpenter writes, "Operant behavior . . . is that which is roughly but not technically equivalent to voluntary behavior." (p. 19)

155. See Richard Sennett's review of *Beyond Freedom and Dignity*, *The New York Times Book Review*, October 24, 1971. "Skinner . . . has weakened behaviorism by bending it to an inappropriate goal. Hoping to revive the morality of a less complicated age by invoking the certainties of an antiquated science, he appears to understand so little, indeed to care so little, about society itself that the reader comes totally to distrust him." (p. 18)

156. For a further description and pictures of the basic equipment, see Part II of Skinner's *Cumulative Record*, 3d ed., pp. 69–171.

157. B. F. Skinner, " 'Superstition' in the Pigeon," *Journal of Experimental Psychology*, Vol. 38, April 1948, pp. 168–172. Reprinted in *Cumulative Record*.

158. " 'Superstition' in the Pigeon," p. 171.

159. See B. F. Skinner, "Pigeons in a Pelican," *American Psychologist,* Vol. 15, January 1960, pp. 28–37. In this retrospective article about an abortive World War II contract, Skinner affirms his belief in an approach to the study of psychology which admirably combines "wide-ranging speculation about human affairs, supported by studies of compensating rigor."

160. See Finley Carpenter, *The Skinner Primer,* pp. 32–34, for a simplified glossary of Skinnerian terms. For exact definitions, however, see Skinner's own experimental reports as found in *Cumulative Record,* for example.

161. Noam Chomsky, "The Case Against B. F. Skinner," *New York Review of Books,* Vol. 17, No. 11, December 30, 1971, p. 20.

162. B. F. Skinner, "The Technology of Teaching," *Proceedings of the Royal Society,* B, Vol. 162, 1965, p. 429.

163. "The Case Against B. F. Skinner," p. 22.

164. "The Case Against B. F. Skinner," p. 23.

165. Ludwig Von Bertalanffy, *Robots, Men and Minds,* p. 8.

166. For an excellent critique of Skinner see David J. Bell, *Power, Influence, and Authority,* Appendix B. See also Arthur Koestler, *The Ghost in the Machine,* Chapter I.

167. B. F. Skiner, "Behaviorism at Fifty," *Science,* Vol. 140, No. 3570, May 31, 1963, p. 956.

168. B. F. Skinner, *Verbal Behavior,* p. 253.

169. Noam Chomsky, "Review of Verbal Behavior," *Language,* Vol. 35, January–March 1959, p. 32.

170. *Beyond Freedom and Dignity,* p. 213.

171. John Read, *Prelude to Chemistry,* p. 2.

172. Eleanor R. Maccoby, "The Development of Moral Values and Behavior in Childhood," p. 240.

173. Albert Bandura, "Social-Learning Theory of Identificatory Processes," in David A. Goslin, ed., *Handbook of Socialization Theory and Research,* p. 213.

174. Maccoby, "The Development of Moral Values," p. 241.

175. Kohlberg, "Stage and Sequence: The Cognitive-Developmental Approach to Socialization," p. 363. On the preceding page, Kohlberg elaborates: "With regard to reward, no relations have been found between amount of reward and moral variables in twenty different studies of moral socialization. With regard to physical punishment and *high* moral resistance to temptation: Two studies find *no* correlation between physical punishment and resistance to temptation. Two studies find *high* punishment correlated *with* high delinquency, i.e. *low* resistance to temptation. Three studies find *high* punishment correlated with *low* projective guilt (low morality). Three studies find *no* correlation between punishment and guilt. One is tempted to interpret these findings as representing a pattern of correlations randomly distributed around a base of zero."

176. Bandura, "Social-Learning Theory," p. 216.

177. Lawrence Kohlberg, "Development of Moral Character and Moral Ideology," pp. 412, 388.

178. Justin Aronfreed, "The Concept of Internalization," in D. Goslin, ed., *Handbook of Socialization Theory and Research,* p. 305.

179. Kohlberg, "Development of Moral Character," p. 389.

180. Kohlberg, "Stage and Sequence: The Cognitive-Developmental Approach," p. 365.

181. H. Hartshorne and M. A. May, *Studies in the Nature of Character.*

182. Bandura, "Social-Learning Theory," p. 214.

183. Aronfreed writes: "The more remarkable consequence of socialization is that it gives the child's acquired behavioral dispositions a stability that shows an increasing

independence of external control." ("The Concept of Internalization," p. 263) Remarkable hardly seems the word—perhaps miraculous.

184. Bandura, "Social-Learning Theory." p. 214–215.

185. K. Lazowick, "On the Nature of Identification," *Journal of Abnormal and Social Psychology*, Vol. 51, 1955, pp. 175–183.

186. Bandura, "Social-Learning Theory," p. 215.

187. Bandura, "Social-Learning Theory," p. 216.

188. Bandura comments, "It may seem paradoxical, but under conditions of high diversity of modeling patterns much innovation of social behavior can occur entirely through identification." ("Social-Learning Theory," p. 252)

189. Bandura, "Social-Learning Theory," p. 233.

190. "The conduct may be reinforced by the person's empathic or vicarious response to observable external cues which indicate its immediate effect on others (for example, cues which indicate pleasure or relief of stress)." (Aronfreed, "The Concept of Internalization," p. 269)

191. Vera T. Kanareff and J. T. Lanzetta, "Effects of Task Definition and Probability of Reinforcement upon the Acquisition and Extinction of Imitative Responses," *Journal of Experimental Psychology*, 1960, pp. 430–438.

192. D. M. Baer and J. A. Sherman, "Reinforcement Control of Generalized Imitation in Young Children, *Journal of Experimental Child Psychology*, Vol. 1, 1964, pp. 37–49.

193. Bandura, "Social-Learning Theory," p. 234.

194. "Social-Learning Theory," p. 247.

195. "When a child is exposed to a variety of models, he may select one or more of them as the principal sources of social behavior, but he rarely reproduces all elements of a single model's repertoire or confines his imitation to that person." ("Social-Learning Theory," p. 251)

196. "Social-Learning Theory," pp. 250–251.

197. Maccoby, "The Development of Moral Values," p. 243.

198. Aronfreed, "The Concept of Internalization," p. 263. "[The child's] behavior gradually comes to be governed, to a very considerable extent, by internal monitors. These internal monitors appear to carry many of the functions of internal controls which were originally required to establish behavior."

199. "The Concept of Internalization," pp. 204, 305.

200. Bandura, "Social-Learning Theory," p. 225.

201."Various external stimulus events, including the occurrence of punishment itself, may acquire potential reinforcement value through their association with the reduction of anticipatory anxiety." (Aronfreed, "The Concept of Internalization," p. 289) If you can believe that, you can believe anything.

202. David Marsh, "Political Socialization: The Implicit Assumptions Questioned," *British Journal of Political Science*, October 1971, p. 455.

203. Donald D. Searing, Joel H. Swartz, and Alden E. Lind, "The Structuring Principle: Political Socialization and Belief Systems," *American Political Science Review*, Vol. 67, No. 2, June 1973, pp. 415–416. A typical expression of the primacy principle is: "In many areas of inquiry we may nevertheless hold to the theory [sic] that what is learnt early in life tends to be retained and to shape later attitudes and behavior." (David Easton and Jack Dennis, *Children and the Political System: Origins of Political Legitimacy*, p. 9)

204. Searing et al., p. 416.

205. Searing et al., p. 421.

206. David Marsh, "Political Socialization," p. 464.

207. Richard G. Niemi, "Political Socialization," in Jeane Knutson, ed., *Handbook of Political Psychology*. Researchers have failed to find any spillover.

208. "Now a major finding in socialization research is that benevolent images (affect and trust) of institutions and political leaders are learned by very young children; by contrast political cynicism is known to be learned later during adolescence or young adulthood. Thus for adults we would expect trust in government to be more important than political cynicism in the sense that it should be more strongly related to . . . issue beliefs. This is not borne out by the data, which show substantial differences between the two types of items." (Searing et al., "The Structuring Principle," p. 426)

209. Richard E. Dawson and Kenneth Prewitt, *Political Socialization*, pp. 213–214.

210. Fred Greenstein, "A Note on the Ambiguity of 'Political Socialization': Definitions, Criticism, and Strategies of Inquiry," *Journal of Politics*, November 1970, p. 973.

211. Dawson and Prewitt, *Political Socialization*, p. 215.

212. David B. Truman gives expression to this cynicism in this manner: "To promote a favorable attitude toward individualism would be education in the United States but propaganda in the Soviet Union. To train people in the principles of aerodynamics would be education in both places." (*The Government Process*, p. 223)

213. Greenstein lists four current definitions of political socialization among researchers: (1) "The study of children's political orientations or more simply: 'the study of pre-adult orientations to the adult political process.' " (2) "The study of the acquisition of prevailing norms . . . the focus is on the acquisition of norm-consistent behavior." (3) "The study of any political learning whatsoever, whether of conformity or deviance, and at any stage in the life cycle." (4) "The actual observation of socialization processes in any of the above senses, taking into account both the socialized and the agents of socialization." ("A Note on the Ambiguity," pp. 971–972)

214. "Socialization is an economical tool of government. To the degree that government relies upon the habitual responses of citizens, the necessity of environmental constraints is lessened." (Greenstein, "Political Socialization," in D. E. Sills, ed., *International Encyclopedia of the Social Sciences*, p. 551)

215. Dawson and Prewitt, *Political Socialization*, p. 221.

216. Jack Dennis, "Major Problems of Political Socialization Research," *Midwest Journal of Political Science*, Vol. 12, February 1968, p. 89. The next quotation is from the same page.

217. David Easton, *A Framework for Political Analysis*, pp. 124–125.

218. Dennis, "Major Problems," p. 90.

219. Dennis, "Major Problems," p. 91: "The assumption that every system engages in some program of political socialization needs to be tested; and it needs examination within the context of alternative means for building—or perhaps undermining—the support of the system's membership."

220. In modern political thought Mosca's articulations are usually the most succinct. He measured the failure of liberal democratic theory in terms of its inability to stem the growth of socialism. Thus he manages to connect up the ideas of science, manipulation, antisocialism, realism, and mass irrationalism. He wrote: "In the world in which we are living, socialism will be arrested only if a realistic political science succeeds in demolishing the metaphysical and optimistic methods that prevail at present in social studies—in other words, only if discovery and demonstration of the great constant laws that manifest themselves in all human societies succeed in making visible to the eye the impossibility of realizing the democratic ideal. . . . A whole metaphysical system must be met with a whole scientific system." (*The Ruling Class*, p. 327)

221. James Steintrager, "Political Socialization and Political Theory," *Social Research*, Vol. 35, 1968, p. 129.

222. Hobbes, *Leviathan*, p. 260.

223. "Neither classical nor contemporary scholarship has produced a generally agreed upon framework for analysing political socialization, much less a codified body of knowledge." (Greenstein, "Political Socialization" in D. E. Sills, ed., *International Encyclopedia of the Social Sciences*, p. 552)

224. Marsh, "Political Socialization," p. 460. Marsh notes: "The assumption that political attitudes learnt early are the most important is not based on sound quantitative evidence." (p. 457)

225. "An orientation's importance in adult behavior must be demonstrated before we can be sure that its childhood genesis is of interest to political science." (Searing et al., "The Structuring Principle," p. 431)

226. "The Structuring Principle," p. 425. The following quotation is from the same place.

227. For example, Madison's statement in Federalist 10 that "the most common and durable source of factions, has been the various and unequal distributions of property." A modern version is Beard's statement: "The sentiments and views which arise from the possession of different degrees and kinds of property form the stuff of so-called 'political psychology.' " (Charles A. Beard, *The Economic Basis of Politics*, 3d ed., p. 17)

228. "We sum up the political type in terms of the development of motives as follows: Private Motives — Displaced on Public Objects — Rationalized in Terms of Public Interest." (Harold Lasswell, *Power and Personality*, p. 38)

229. Searing et al., "The Structuring Principle," p. 427. Also: "The effects of personality on political behavior may often be marginal rather than central, circuitous rather than direct." (Greenstein, "Political Socialization," p. 553) Note that such effects may not be present at all. Kohlberg concludes, "The study of socialization in terms of personality formation under the assumption of trait stability is unjustified." "Stage and Sequence: The Cognitive-Developmental Approach," pp. 369–370)

230. For examples from the heyday of this hypothesis see: T. W. Adorno, et al., *The Authoritarian Personality;* Bruno Bettelheim and Morris Janowitz, *Dynamics of Prejudice and Ethics;* Robert Lindner, *Must You Conform?;* Erich Fromm, *Escape From Freedom.*

231. "The Structuring Principle," pp. 428, 430.

232. Philip Converse, "The Nature of Belief Systems," in David E. Apter, ed., *Ideology and Discontent*, p. 239.

233. "Political Socialization," p. 459.

234. R. T. Lapiere, "Attitudes Versus Actions," *Social Forces,* 1934, pp. 230–237. See also M. F. Defleur and R. F. Westie, "Verbal Attitudes and Overt Acts: An Experiment on the Saliency of Attitudes," *American Sociological Review*, Vol. 23, 1958, pp. 667–673; and S. M. Corey, "Professed Attitudes and Actual Behavior," *Journal of Educational Psychology*, Vol. 28, 1937, pp. 271–280. Kohlberg notes that "conformity to a moral rule has not been found to bear much relationship to the strength of stated belief in that rule." ("Development of Moral Character and Moral Ideology," p. 388)

235. A. Wicker, "Attitudes Versus Actions: The Relationship of Verbal and Overt Behavioral Responses to Attitude Objects," *Journal of Social Issues*, Vol. 25, 1969, p. 69.

236. Marsh, "Political Socialization," p. 456.

237. This is a schematic summary of the following works: David Easton and Jack Dennis, *Children in the Political System;* Fred Greenstein, *Children and Politics;* R. Hess and J. Torney, *The Development of Political Attitudes in Children.*

238. R. Hess and J. Torney, *The Development of Political Attitudes in Children*, Chapter 7.

239. D. Jaros, H. Hirsch, and F. Fleron, Jr., "The Malevolent Leader: Political Socialization in an American Subculture," *American Political Science Review*, Vol. 62, 1968, pp. 564–575; and S. Liebschutz and R. Niemi, "Political Socialization among Black Children:

The Development of Attitudes and the Impact of Curriculum and Teachers" (Paper presented at the meeting of the American Political Science Association, Washington, D.C. September 1972)

240. Richard Niemi, "Political Socialization."

241. R. Hess and J. Torney, *The Development of Political Attitudes in Children,* p. 101. See also Edgar Litt, "Civil Education, Community Norms, and Political Indoctrination," *American Sociological Review,* Vol. 28, February 1963, pp. 69–75; Franklin Patterson et al., *High Schools for a Free Society;* H. H. Remmers, *Anti-Democratic Attitudes in American Schools;* Marvin Schick and A. Somit "The Failure to Teach Political Activity," *American Behavioral Scientist,* Vol. 6, January 1963; A. Somit, et al., "The Effect of Introductory Political Science Courses on Student Attitudes Toward Personal Political Participation," *American Political Science Review,* Vol. 52, December 1958, pp. 1129–1132.

242. See D. Sears, "Review of Hess and Torney, 'The Development of Political Attitudes in Children' ", *Harvard Educational Review,* Vol. 38, 1968, pp. 571–578; and R. Niemi, "Review of Hess and Torney, 'The Development of Political Attitudes in Children,' " *Contemporary Psychology,* Vol. 14, 1969, pp. 497–498.

243. K. Prewitt and J. Okello-Oculi, "Political Socialization and Political Education in the New Nations," R. Sigel, ed., *Learning about Politics.*

244. Dawson and Prewitt, *Political Socialization,* pp. 198–199.

245. Richard Niemi, "Political Socialization."

246. Herbert H. Hyman, *Political Socialization,* p. 11.

247. Steintrager, "Political Socialization," p. 123.

248. See for example Lucian W. Pye, *Politics, Personality and Nation Building.*

249. After plowing through the writings of the alchemists, Read commented: "Undoubtedly there is a vein of reason running through the mountainous accumulation of literature which deals with transmutation and the Philosopher's Stone: but the vein is usually so deeply embedded as to be undiscernable without the aid of a divining rod." (J. Read, *Prelude to Chemistry,* p. 121) In this discussion I have tried to provide such a divining rod for those who might wish to plow through the mountainous accumulation of literature on socialization. Or better still, I hope I have shown something of the meagerness of the vein of reason to be found there.

250. Anthony Burgess, *The Clockwork Testament or Enderby's End,* p. 101. For a fuller treatment of Burgess's critique of behavior modification see his more sensational *A Clockwork Orange.*

251. Jean Piaget, *The Moral Development of the Child.* The book was first published in 1932. For the most succinct statement of Kohlberg's contribution, see his "Stage and Sequence: The Cognitive-Developmental Approach to Socialization" in Goslin, ed., pp. 347–481.

252. Kohlberg, "Stage and Sequence," p. 352 and on p. 415: "Developmental theories assume a primary motivation for competence and self-actualization which is organized through an ego or self whose structure is social or shared."

253. Eleanor Maccoby, "The Development of Moral Values," p. 265.

254. "Logic is the morality of thought just as morality is the logic of action." J. Piaget, *The Moral Judgment of the Child,* p. 398.

255. Kohlberg, "Stage and Sequence," pp. 348–349.

256. "Stage and Sequence," p. 352. Kohlberg lists the following characteristics of cognitive stages: "(1)Stages imply . . . qualitative differences in children's modes of thinking or of solving the same problem and different ages. (2) These different modes . . . form an invariant sequence. . . . While cultural factors may speed up, slow down, or stop development, they do not change its sequence. (3) Each of these . . . sequential modes of thought forms a 'structural whole.' A given stage-response . . . represents an underlying

thought-organization . . . which determines responses to tasks which are not manifestly similar . . . (4) Cognitive stages are hierarchical integrations. Stages form an order of increasingly differentiated and integrated structures to fulfill a common function." (pp. 352–353) These characteristics are after Piaget, "The General Problems of the Psycho-biological Development of the Child," in J. M. Tanner and Barbel Inhelder, eds., *Discussions on Child Development: Proceedings of the World Health Organization Study Group on the Psychobiological Development of the Child*. Vol. 4.

257. Kohlberg, "Stage and Sequence," p. 405.

258. Piaget, *The Moral Judgment*, p. 402.

259. Kohlberg, "Development of Moral Character and Moral Ideology," p. 387.

260. Kohlberg, "Stage and Sequences," p. 397.

261. Piaget, *The Moral Judgment*, p. 402.

262. "While peer-group participation appears to be stimulating of moral development, its influence is better conceptualized in terms of providing general role-taking opportunities rather than as having very specific and unique forms of influence." (Kohlberg, "Stage and Sequence," p. 401)

263. "Stage and Sequence," p. 373. See J. H. Anderson, "The Prediction of Adjustment Over Time," in Ira Iscoe and Harold W. Stevenson, eds., *Personality Development in Children*.

264. Kohlberg, "Stage and Sequence," p. 374.

265. J. Piaget, *The Psychology of Intelligence*.

266. J. Piaget, *The Moral Judgment*, pp. 92–93.

267. *The Moral Judgment*, pp. 36–37.

268. *The Moral Judgment*, p. 284.

269. *The Moral Judgment*, pp. 46–47.

270. *The Moral Judgment*, pp. 284–285.

271. *The Moral Judgment*, p. 298.

272. *The Moral Judgment*, p. 302. For example, 82 percent of the six-year-old girls and 50 percent of the six-year-old boys said that hitting back was naughty while no 12-year-old boy or girl agreed with them. Some 78 percent of 12-year old girls said that one should hit back less, while only 12 percent of the boys agreed. No six-year-old reported that one should hit back more or less.

273. Kohlberg, "Stage and Sequence," p. 353.

274. Kohlberg, "Stage and Sequence," pp. 172–173.

275. For summaries and details of the findings see Lawrence Kohlberg, *Stages in the Development of Moral Thought and Action*.

276. Kohlberg, "Stage and Sequence," p. 385.

277. "Stage and Sequence," p. 286. See also J. Rest, E. Turiel, and L. Kohlberg, "Relations Between Levels of Moral Judgment and Preference and Comprehension of the Moral Judgment of Others," *Journal of Personality*, 1969.

278. "Stage and Sequence," p. 387.

279. "Stage and Sequence," pp. 388–389.

280. "Stage and Sequence," pp. 388–389. See also Kohlberg, *Stages in the Development of Moral Thought and Action*.

281. E. Maccoby, "The Development of Moral Values," pp. 236–237. Maccoby notes that social-learning theorists can claim that the progression shown in Kohlberg's studies "stems from systematic changes in the nature of socialization techniques employed with children of different ages." (p. 253) That claim can, of course, be made; but it is more indicative of the unfalsifiable nature of social-learning theories and their *ad hoc* flexibility than any ambiguity in Kohlberg's findings.

282. An example of the use of Kohlberg's theory as a successful predictor of behav-

ior where other explanations fail badly is Robert E. O'Connor, "Political Activism and Moral Reasoning: Political and Apolitical Students in Great Britain and France," *British Journal of Political Science,* Vol. 4, December 1974, pp. 53–78. O'Connor concluded: "Kohlberg's moral reasoning variable was the single best predictor of activism from among the fifty not explicitly political variables employed in the study."

283. Kohlberg, "Stage and Sequence," p. 383.

284. Kohlberg, "Cognitive Stages and Preschool Education," *Human Development,* Vol. 9, 1966, p. 6.

285. "Cognitive Stages," pp. 7–11.

286. "Cognitive Stages," p. 13.

287. "The Atayal's learning of the adult dream ideology did not appear to be a smooth and painless superimposition of social content on an underlying cognitive structure. Rather it appeared to engender complication and conflict in the adolescents' cognitive responses. Atayal children acquired the conservation of mass of a ball of clay at the usual age (7–8). Nevertheless, at age 11–15, the age of dream 'regression,' they partially 'lost' conservation. The loss did not seem to be a genuine regression, but an uncertainty about trusting their own judgment, i.e., there was an increase in 'don't know' responses. Apparently, adolescent confrontation with adult magical beliefs led them to be uncertain of their naturally developing physical beliefs, even when the latter were not in direct conflict with adult ideology." (Kohlberg, "Stage and Sequence," pp. 360–361)

288. J. Langer, "Disequilibrium as a Source of Cognitive Development" (Paper presented to the Society for Research on Child Development. New York, March 21, 1967).

289. Hannah Arendt, *Eichmann in Jerusalem.*

290. Jacques Ellul, *Propaganda.* "Propaganda strips the individual, robs him of part of himself, and makes him live an alien and artificial life." (p. 169)

291. J. Piaget, *The Moral Judgment of the Child,* p. 403. "Parent and child, as Piaget sees it, can never free themselves from the relationship of 'unilateral respect' that is established in early childhood, a circumstance which makes it impossible for the parent to be the socialization agent who will teach the child a mature morality based on mutual respect and cooperation." (Maccoby, "The Development of Moral Values," p. 234)

292. Kohlberg, "Stage and Sequence," p. 414.

293. "Stage and Sequence," p. 416. "In order to *play* a social role in the family, school, or society, the child must implicitly *take* the role of others towards himself and toward others in the group. Moral role-taking involves an emotional empathetic or sympathetic component, but it also involves a cognitive capacity to define situations in terms of rights and duties, in terms of reciprocity and the perspectives of other selves." (Kohlberg, "Development of Moral Character and Moral Ideology," p. 395)

294. Kohlberg, "Development of Moral Character," p. 425.

295. "In all nations studied, there are social-class differences in the direction of earlier intentionality for the middle class. These are not class differences in values, but class differences in the cognitive and social stimulation of development." (Kohlberg, "Stage and Sequence," p. 375) Maccoby summarizes Kohlberg's viewpoint: "Certain positions in society provide greater stimulation for role-taking and hence more rapid development. Greater peer-group participation does this, he believes, as does membership in a higher social class." ("The Development of Moral Values," p. 238)

296. Kohlberg, "Development of Moral Character," p. 399.

297. George C. Homans, *Social Behavior: Elementary Forms,* p. 311.

298. "[The Administrator] creates, as it were, a spurious environment of his own—an environment, if he is a dominant type, of yes men who reflect the executive's own wishes rather than the realities of the world around him; what he thinks are windows are in fact mirrors." (Kenneth Boulding, *The Organizational Revolution,* p. 70)

299. See Peter Nokes, "Feedback as an Explanatory Device in the Study of Certain Interpersonal and Institutional Processes," *Human Relations*, Vol. 14, 1961, pp. 381–387.

300. Orville G. Brim, "Family Structure and Sex Role Learning by Children: A Further Analysis of Helen Koch's Data," *Sociometry*, Vol. 21, 1958, pp. 1–6. Brim tested the hypothesis that because of differences in control of rewards and punishments and in ability to discriminate between self and other roles, the effects of role taking would be more pronounced for those in inferior statuses. He found support, namely that younger girls with older brothers and younger boys with older sisters showed more traits associated with opposite sex roles.

301. See Kant's argument that attempting to guide actions on the basis of the promotion of human happiness leads to unacceptable uncertainty; whereas duty supplies instant certainty about what is to be done. Immanuel Kant, *On the Old Saw: That It May Be Right in Theory but It Won't Work in Practice*.

302. Barbel Inhelder, "Some Aspects of Piaget's Genetic Approach to Cognition," in W. Kessen and C. Kuhlman, eds., *Thought in the Young Child*, Vol. 2, Serial No. 83, 1962, p. 20

303. "The very methods of intelligent inquiry have been excluded from prosperous contact with whole segments of human experience, those of human decision, excluded not because of demonstrated failure but because of institutional blocks. Behind those blocks flourish now what have always flourished there—despair and absolutism." (George Gieger, "Values and Social Science," *Journal of Social Issues*, Vol. 6, No. 4, 1950, p. 16)

304. Karl Popper, *The Open Society and Its Enemies*, Vol. 1, p. 61.

305. *The Open Society and Its Enemies*, p. 65.

306. Eugene Meehan, *The Foundations of Political Analysis: Empirical and Normative*, p. 19.

307. Karl Popper, *The Logic of Scientific Discovery*, p. 47. See also Chapter 2.

308. George S. Klein, "Cognitive Control and Motivation," in Gardner Lindzey, ed., *Assessment of Human Motives*, p. 89.

309. Meeham, *The Foundations*, p. 23.

310. Klein, "Cognitive Control and Motivation," p. 91.

311. Kohlberg, "Stage and Sequence," p. 416.

Chapter 4

1. Sampson, *The Psychology of Power*, p. 63.

2. Kurt Goldstein, *Human Nature in the Light of Psychopathology*, pp. 94–106.

3. Goldstein, pp. 107–108. D. O. Hebb cites a similar example of a patient suffering from tuberculosis of the bone. ("The American Revolution," in Robert J. C. Harper et al., eds., *The Cognitive Process*, p. 10)

4. Goldstein, p. 107.

5. W. R. Bion has clinically investigated this process of denying and suppressing development in group settings. However, his analysis is based on Freudian premises of fundamental human irrationality and laziness. Bion argues that human beings hate the process of development, hate to learn from experience, and have little faith in such learning. Despite this approach his descriptions are provocative and informing. The equivalent of Freud's id in Bion's social psychology is called the "basic assumption mentality." He finds that groups relapse into this primitive and emotional state of awareness as a defense against stimuli to development. "If a group wishes to prevent development, the simplest way to do so is to allow itself to be overwhelmed by basic-assumption mentality and thus become approximated to the one kind of mental life in which a capacity for development is not required. The main compensation for such a shift appears to be an increase in a pleasurable feeling of vitality." (*Experiences in Groups*, p. 159)

6. Goldstein, pp. 58–59.

7. Goldstein, p. 53.

8. Goldstein, pp. 59–60.

9. Goldstein, p. 61.

10. Goldstein, p. 61.

11. Goldstein, p. 66.

12. Goldstein, p. 220.

13. Goldstein, p. 118.

14. See Bion, *Experiences in Groups*, pp. 127–128.

15. Pierre Janet, *Les Névroses*, p. 357. Quoted in Elton Mayo, *The Social Problems of an Industrial Civilization*, p. 24.

16. Mayo, *The Social Problems*, p. 21.

17. *The Uses of Disorder: Personal Identity and City Life*, p. 11.

18. Popper, *The Poverty of Historicism*, pp. 90–91.

19. *The Poverty of Historicism*, p. 89.

20. Karl Deutsch, "Discussion," in Grinker, ed., *Toward a Unified Theory of Human Behavior*, p. 293.

21. "Discussion," p. 294.

22. *Form in Civilization*, p. 187. The statement concludes the following passage: "It is very disgusting to 'pure thought,' but the first of propositions is that we live by daily eating. It is horrid to mention anything so vulgar, and such facts, like legs, are usually handsomely draped. That elegant exercise of high intelligences, 'philosophy,' ignores the legs by cutting in on a superior plane: 'I think, therefore I am,' it says, but this noble brainy structure will not march without legs. I eat, therefore I work, and I work, therefore I think, are necessary preliminaries. Now we are ready for a reasonable and not falsely defined life-philosophy—I eat, work, and think, therefore I am."

23. Victor A. Thompson, *Modern Organization*, p. 152.

24. *Modern Organization*, p. 154.

25. *Modern Organization*, p. 156.

26. We also find courage and a fine, if narrow, sensitivity. For example, the writings of the Emperor Marcus Aurelius reveal the problems involved in trying to live as a healthy bureaucrat. He writes, "Be not disgusted, nor discouraged, nor dissatisfied, if thou dost not succeed in doing everything according to right principles, but when thou hast failed, return back again, and be content if the greater part of which thou doest is consistent with man's nature, and love this to which thou returnest; and do not return to philosophy as if she were a master, but act like those who have sore eyes and apply a bit of sponge and egg, or as another applies a plaster, or drenching with water. For thus thou wilt not fail to obey reason, and thou wilt repose in it." (*Meditations*, p. 35) I take the passage to mean that the administrator should not expect that the application of rules and procedures will actually work, but should learn to be satisfied with whatever results do obtain.

27. *Modern Organization*, p. 172; the two quotations that follow are from pp. 176 and 175.

28. Basil Bernstein, "Some Sociological Determinants of Perception," *British Journal of Sociology*, Vol. 9, January 1958, pp. 159–174.

29. Basil Bernstein, "Language and Social Class," *British Journal of Sociology*, Vol. II, September 1960, p. 271. For a complete inventory of the respective characteristics of public and formal languages see B. Bernstein, "A Public Language: Some Sociological Implications of a Linguistic Form," *British Journal of Sociology*, Vol. 10, 1959, pp. 311, 312.

30. Bernstein later makes a distinction between two modes of formal language—one

concerned with the relationship between things and the other concerned with the relationship between people. He suggests that these correspond roughly to scientific and humanistic orientations. See Basil Bernstein, "Elaborated and Restricted Codes: Their Social Origins and Some Consequences," in John J. Gumperz and Dell Hymes, eds., *The Ethnography of Communication*, special edition of the *American Anthropologist*, Vol. 66, No. 6, December 1964, pp. 65, 68.

31. Bernstein, "A Public Language," p. 315. The brief quotations that follow in the paragraph are from pp. 318 and 319.

32. Bernstein, "Elaborated and Restricted Codes," p. 63.

33. "Elaborated and Restricted Codes," p. 62.

34. "A Public Language," p. 323.

35. "Elaborated and Restricted Codes," p. 66.

36. "A Public Language," p. 332–323.

37. "Democratization of the means of education together with the internalizing of the achievement ethic by members of the working-class strata may lead to an individualizing of failure, to a loss of self-respect which, in turn, modifies an individual's attitude both to his group and to the demands made upon him by society." (Bernstein, "Sociological Determinants of Perception," p. 173)

38. Bernstein, "A Public Language, p. 322. The quotations that follow are from the same page.

39. "It was bipedalism which started man on his separate evolutionary career. But tool use was nearly as early. Biological changes in the hand, brain, and face follow the use of tools, and are due to the new selection pressures which tools created. Tools changed the whole pattern of life, bringing in hunting, cooperation, and the necessity of communication and language. Memory, foresight, and originality were favored as never before, and the complex social system made possible by tools could only be realized by domesticated individuals [sic!]. In a very real sense, tools created *Homo sapiens.*" (S. L. Washburn, "Speculations on the Interrelations of the History of Tools and Biological Evolution," *Evolution of Man's Capacity for Culture*, p. 31. in J. N. Spuhler, ed., *The Evolution of Man's Capacity for Culture*, p. 31.

40. "The Man of flesh and blood can maintain physical and mental sanity only to the extent to which he can have direct contact with a certain kind of reality not very different from the conditions under which he evolved." (R. Dubos, *Reason Awake*, p. 73)

41. Edward C. Tolman, *The Behavior of Psychological Man*, p. 51.

42. Tolman, p. 60. The quotation immediately below is from the same page.

43. Gregory Bateson, "Double Bind, 1969" in *Steps to an Ecology of Mind*, p. 227.

44. Philip Solomon et al., eds., *Sensory Deprivation*.

45. *Behavior and Psychological Man*, pp. 244–245.

46. *Behavior and Psychological Man*, p. 258.

47. Slater, *The Pursuit of Loneliness*, p. 15.

48. Wilhelm Reich, *Character-Analysis*, 3d. ed., p. 145.

49. *Character-Analysis*, p. 146.

50. *Character-Analysis*, p. 148.

51. Wilbert E. Moore and Melvin M. Tumin, "Some Social Functions of Ignorance," *American Sociological Review*, Vol. 14, December 1949, p. 795. E. E. Schattschneider's comment is more candid: "There is no escape from the problem of ignorance, because *nobody knows enough to run the government.* Presidents, senators, governors, judges, professors, doctors of philosophy, editors and the like are only a little less ignorant than the rest of us. Even an expert is a person who chooses to be ignorant about many things so that he may know all about one.... The compulsion to know everything is the road to insanity." (*The Semisovereign People*, pp. 136–137)

52. Graham Wallas, *Human Nature in Politics,* pp. 146–147.

53. Warren Weaver, "The Mathematics of Information," in Ernest Nagel and Arnold Tustin, eds., *Automatic Control,* p. 100.

54. W. S. McCulloch, *Embodiments of Mind,* p. 309.

55. "It is not intellectuality that is important; it is sensibility and consciousness—consciousness of the relations of external phenomena and of one's internal relation to them. The time has come for adult man to recognize that information is not learning. It is the mere mechanics of memory. Yet information is the great desideratum. Apparently, the goal is to make of one's mind the largest possible barrel for containing the largest possible number of mental items." (Trigant Burrow, *Science and Man's Behavior,* p. 304)

56. Douglas H. Lawrence and Leon Festinger, *Deterrents and Reinforcement,* p. 156.

57. Leon Festinger, *A Theory of Cognitive Dissonance,* p. 219.

58. *Deterrents and Reinforcement,* p. 170.

59. William J. McGuire, "The Current Status of Cognitive Consistency Theories," in Shel Feldman, ed., *Cognitive Consistency,* pp. 10–11.

60. J. L. Freedman and D. O. Sears, "Selective Exposure," in L. Berkowitz, ed., *Advances in Experimental Social Psychology,* pp. 57–97.

61. Jerome E. Singer, "Motivation for Consistency," in Feldman, ed., *Cognitive Consistency,* p. 63. Singer cites Festinger and Cannon among other investigators who have found inconsistency to be positively motivating.

62. Singer, "Motivation for Consistency," p. 64.

63. "Motivation for Consistency," p. 64.

64. "The Current Status of Cognitive Consistency Theories," p. 37. Among the complexity theorists the author includes D. E. Berlyne, D. W. Fiske, and S. R. Maddi, and H. Fowler. Berlyne argues, for example, that conceptual conflict is most often resolved through the pursuit and acquisition of knowledge. (D. E. Berlyne, *Conflict, Arousal, and Curiosity,* pp. 283–303.

65. Albert Pepitone, "Some Conceptual and Empirical Problems of Consistency Models," in Feldman, ed., *Cognitive Consistency,* p. 261.

66. Jerome Kagan maintains that the activity of fitting events to cognitive maps or expectations is a source of pleasure when the match is close but not perfect. According to his studies of children's assimilation of novelty: "Stimuli that deviate a critical amount from the child's schema for a pattern are capable of eliciting an active process of recognition, and this process behaves as if it were a source of pleasure. Stimuli that are easily assimilable or too difficult to assimilate do not elicit these reactions." ("On the Need for Relativism," in Liam Hudson, ed., *The Ecology of Human Intelligence,* p. 145)

67. D. J. Ben, "Self-Perception: An Alternative Interpretation of Cognitive Dissonance Phenomena," *Psychological Review,* Vol. 74, No. 3, 1967, p. 189.

68. Feyerabend, *Knowledge without Foundation,* p. 56.

69. Herbert Marcuse, *One Dimensional Man,* p. 125.

70. A. T. W. Simeons, *Man's Presumptuous Brain,* p. 283.

Chapter 5

1. Krechevsky [David Krech], " 'Hypothesis' in Rats," *Psychological Review,* Vol. 39, November 1932, p. 532.

2. J. Z. Young, *Doubt and Certainty in Science,* p. 66.

3. *Doubt and Certainty,* p. 62.

4. *Doubt and Certainty,* p. 75.

5. Robert L. Fantz, "The Origin of Form Perception," *Scientific American,* May 1961.

6. Austin H. Riesen, "The Development of Visual Perception in Man and Chimpanzee," *Science,* August 1, 1947, p. 108.

7. W. H. Ittelson and F. P. Kilpatrick, "Experiments in Perception," *Scientific American*, August 1951 (Reprint 405), p. 7.

8. Ittelson and Kilpatrick, p. 5.

9. Ittelson and Kilpatrick, p. 2.

10. Krechevsky, " 'Hypothesis' in Rats," p. 523.

11. " 'Hypothesis' in Rats," p. 523.

12. " 'Hypothesis' in Rats," p. 529.

13. James J. Gibson and Eleanor J. Gibson, "Perceptual Learning: Differentiation or Enrichment?" *Psychological Review*, Vol. 62, January 1955, p. 34.

14. Harry F. Harlow, "The Formation of Learning Sets," *Psychological Review*, Vol. 56, January 1949, p. 51.

15. D. M. McKay, "The Epistemological Problem for Automata," in C. E. Shannon and J. McCarthy, *Automata Studies*, p. 235.

16. McKay, p. 236.

17. McKay, p. 237.

18. McKay, p. 237.

19. McKay, p. 249.

20. McKay, p. 249.

21. McKay, p. 250.

22. Harry F. Harlow, "Mice, Men, and Motives," *Psychological Review*, Vol. 60, January 1933, p. 28.

23. *Patterns of Discovery*, p. 90.

24. "Review of Patterns of Discovery," *Philosophical Review*, Vol. 69, April 1960, p. 247.

25. For an elaborate example of this position see Joseph H. Woodger, "The Technique of Theory Contruction," in Otto Neurath and C. Morris, eds., *Foundations of the Unity of Science*, Vol. 2, pp. 449–453.

26. "If the Social Scientist Is to Be More Than a Mere Technician," *Journal of Social Issues*, Vol. 24, No. 1, 1968.

27. Hanson, *Patterns of Discovery*, p. 19.

28. *Society and Knowledge*, pp. 38–39.

29. "When children make drawings they tend to show only parts that they can name. In learning a language, therefore, a person not only gains the advantages of communication with his fellows, he also sharpens his own observation. This is a truism that follows from the fact that through the use of words men are able to use the observations of others. What it amounts to is that by the use of words we learn to see the connexions between things that are not obviously related to each other." (J. Z. Young, *Doubt and Certainty in Science*, p. 91)

30. G. C. Homans, *The Human Group*, p. 5.

31. Eugene Meehan, *Value Judgment and Social Science*, p. 6.

32. *Conjectures and Refutatuions*, p. 229.

33. Meehan, *The Foundations of Political Analysis*, p. 206.

34. Popper, *Conjectures and Refutations*, p. 222.

35. Jurgen Ruesch and Gregory Bateson, *Communication: The Social Matrix of Psychiatry*, p. 26.

36. V. Gordon Childe, *Society and Knowledge*, p. 75.

37. "Our ideal reconstruction or theory is certainly not a complete copy or reproduction, and indeed for three reasons cannot aspire to be such. In the first place, the function of knowledge is ultimately practical—to provide rules for action. For that a full and complete reflection of the external world would be useless; and an abstract chart would be more convenient. (2) . . . since a time series is an essential component of the full

pattern. At no moment is the pattern complete. (3) . . . not only is the object of knowledge, the pattern of the external world, itself incomplete, but also in so far as it has been completed, it is so rich and complicated that twenty-two million generations of men just have not had time fully to discover it—or should we say, to extricate it from the minute incoherent fragments, in which it is presented to private experience." (Childe, *Society and Knowledge,* pp. 60, 65, 66)

38. "Experimental sciences justify themselves by orderly control of events, i.e., by introducing order into otherwise chaotic processes. In doing this they may be said to predict, but their predictions are confined, with rare exceptions, to the four walls of the laboratory (Latin) or workshop (Anglo-Saxon) from which they come to and to which they refer. Prediction outside laboratories and workshops is more precarious though not impossible." (A. D. Ritchie, *Studies in the History and Methods of the Sciences,* p. 155)

39. K. J. W. Craik conceives of prediction as successful symbolic modeling. He writes: "One of the most fundamental properties of thought is its power of predicting events. This gives it immense adaptive and constructive significance as noted by Dewey and other pragmatists. It enables us, for instance, to design bridges with a sufficient factor of safety instead of building them haphazard and waiting to see whether they collapse, and to predict consequences of recondite physical or chemical processes whose value may often be more theoretical than practical. In all these cases the process of thought, reduced to its simplest terms, is as follows: a man observes some external event or process and arrives at some conclusion or prediction expressed in words or numbers that 'mean' or refer to or describe some external event or process which come to pass if the man's reasoning was correct." (*The Nature of Explanation,* p. 50)

40. *Patterns of Discovery,* p. 20.

41. There is, however, a basic rule which does not guarantee knowledge but must be part of our procedure if we are to learn at all. Craik states it succinctly: "If we honestly admit our failure and do not have recourse to dogma and belief we may sooner or later hit upon a more promising method of approach." (*The Nature of Explanation,* pp. 93–94)

42. For an example of the richness and complexity of the former, see Daniel Paul Schreber, *Memoires of My Nervous Illness.* Schreber's work has been analyzed by Freud and Canetti. See Sigmund Freud, *Three Case Histories,* pp. 103–183, and Elias Canetti, *Crowds and Power* pp. 434–462.

43. "As the situation now stands, science and its pursuits have become a kind of mental illness, marked by an obsessive-compulsive set of symptoms. (Robert Lindner, *Prescription for Rebellion* p. 35) Unfortunately some scientists (Einstein, for example) describe the scientific enterprise as an escape from, or domination of, the physical world—the same projection as that of the compulsive-neurotic. See Wilhelm Stekel, *Compulsion and Doubt,* pp. 325–326: "Compulsion might be defined as the triumph of a degenerate idea over physical matter." Craik analyzes the situation more carefully, pointing out that only when scientists pontificate and seek to defend their theories against all criticism do their actions and arguments resemble pathological symptoms. According to Craik's view, hysterical conduct "seems to consist in adapting oneself by excluding all parts of the environment to which one's powers and attitudes are inadequate; a form of adaptation is thus achieved by narrowing and distorting the environment until one's conduct appears adequate to it, rather than by altering one's conduct and enlarging one's knowledge till one can cope with the larger, real environment. Dissociation and schizophrenia and repression are further mechanisms for attaining this state of splendid isolation and pseudo-adjustment and excluding difficulties and awkward suspicions. . . . Hence arise the hysterical symptoms in preservation of these 'truths'—the emphasis on their sanctity and immunity from criticism or argument; the refusal to admit their analogy with other human phenomena such as pre-scientific opinion on scientific problems, when this has

proven to be wrong; the strengthening of belief by formula, repetition, ritual and pseudo-scientific systems. The result, as seen by an unsympathetic observer, is a series of repetitive actions and justifications for them, closely analogous to the exaggerated and neurotic conduct of a man who washes his hands a hundred times a day, or hesitates a hundred times before crossing the road, or requires to have his self-confidence reassured every moment of the day by fresh praise and new successes." (Craik, *The Nature of Explanation,* p. 90)

44. Herbert Feigl, "Philosophical Embarrassments of Psychology," *American Psychologist,* Vol. 14, March 1959, p. 126.

45. N. R. Hanson, *Patterns of Discovery,* p. 70.

46. *Patterns of Discovery,* p. 71.

47. *Patterns of Discovery,* p. 86.

48. In Justus Buchler, ed., *Philosophical Writings of Peirce,* pp. 150–157.

49. Peirce, in Buchler, ed., p. 54. Peirce adds: "What is a likely hypothesis? It is one which falls in with our preconceived ideas. But these may be wrong. Their errors are just what the scientific man is out gunning for more particularly."

50. Peirce, in Buchler, ed., p. 156.

51. Benjamin Farrington, *Greek Science,* p. 18. He concludes: "There is no such thing as science *in vacuo.* There is only the science of a particular society at a particular time and place. The history of science can only be understood as a function of the total life of society." (p. 19)

52. Reflect on the reciprocal use of social mystifications as documented in Turnbull's *The Forest People.*

53. See Muzafer Sherif, "If the Social Scientist Is to Be More Than a Mere Technician."

54. Thomas Kuhn, *The Copernican Revolution.*

55. Farrington, *Greek Science,* p. 70.

56. John Chadwick and W. N. Mann, trans,. *The Medical Works of Hippocrates,* p. 12. The brief quotation a few lines up is from the same page.

57. Farrington, *Greek Science,* pp. 75–76. Elsewhere, Farrington offers some examples of plausible fictions founded on mechanical analogies and appled to physiology which the school of Hippocrates was combating: "Empedocles . . . had explained the vertebrate character of the spinal column in man by the contorted position of the foetus in the womb. The back-bone had snapped under the strain! Similarly he explained the cavity of the stomach by the pressure of water trapped in the embryo, and the piercing of the nostrils as the result of a violent outrush of air. Such explanations, which might have had relevance to accidents in the workshop of a potter or glassblower, were the dazzling speculations of fifth-century biology." (*Science in Antiquity,* p. 95–96) The example of Empedocles indicates that model borrowing, while seemingly less arbitrary than speculation, can have equally misleading results. The point of the Hippocratic position is to attend carefully to the matter at hand and the practical processes developed to deal with it.

58. Farrington, *Greek Science,* p. 70.

59. Chadwick and Mann, *The Medical Works of Hippocrates,* p. 21.

60. See Larry D. Spence and Francis M. Sim, "The Use and Abuse of Metaphors in Social Science" (mimeographed, presented at the annual meeting of the Pennsylvania Sociological Society, November 2, 1974, Philadelphia).

61. The example is from Deutsch, *The Nerves of Government,* p. 250.

62. An example of a current text on "theory construction" is Jerald Hage, *Techniques and Problems of Theory Construction.*

63. Cited in Sheldon Wolin, *Politics and Vision,* p. 246.

64. "Social scientists are tempted to regard institutions as beyond man's rational

powers of control. So regarding them gives the social scientist a solid subject matter, impervious to human wish, even as the physicist has. Thus, his claims acquire more credibility, his recommendations nore legitimacy; and he himself acquires respectability." (Victor A. Thompson, *Modern Organization*, p. 194)

65. Young, *Doubt and Certainty in Science*, p. 158.

66. "We ought now to be able to see that theory and practice must not be divorced, if only from experience of the errors that come from divorcing them and specially from misapplied analogies from misunderstood mathematics and physics." (A. D. Ritchie, *Studies in the History and Methods*, p. 178)

67. P. K. Feyerabend, "Science Without Experience," *Journal of Philosophy*, Vol. 66, No. 22, November 20, 1969. He concludes: "In the struggle for better knowledge theory and observation enter on an equal footing" (p. 794)

68. N. R. Hanson, "The Logic of Discovery," *Journal of Philosophy*, Vol. 55, No. 25, December 4, 1958, p. 1008.

69. In T. B. Bottomore, ed., *Karl Marx: Selected Writings*, p. 69.

70. "It is difficult to see how . . . a country can . . . survive . . . under the continual necessity of so controlling education that the people may not become aware of the meaninglessness of the whole elaborate superstructure. It consists of a problem of probable superhuman difficulty to promote enough intelligence to enable the country to maintain its position in the race of material progress, without leaving open the possibility that intelligence may sometime begin asking questions about the foundations of its own society." (P. W. Bridgman, *The Intelligent Individual and Society*, p. 136)

71. Gunnar Myrdal, *Objectivity in Social Research*, p. 129.

72. "If we place ourselves under the obligation to spell out, in as definite terms as possible, a set of instrumental value premises—however they have been reached and whichever they may be—and if we allow them to determine our approach, the definitions of our concepts, and the formulation of our theories, this represents an advance towards the goals of honesty, clarity, and effectiveness in research. These are steps in the direction of 'objectivity' in the only sense [in which] this concept can be understood." (Myrdal, *Objectivity in Social Research*, p. 72)

Chapter 6

1. *The Methodology of the Social Sciences*, p. 7.

2. C. Judson Herrick, *The Evolution of Human Nature*, p. 314.

3. J. Z. Young claims that the brain operates in ways that will return it to regular rhythmic patterns of neuro-excitation after any disturbance. (*Doubt and Certainty in Science*, p. 69) Stekel, in contrast, writes that "doubt is the characteristic symptom of compulsion neurosis" and that "perhaps . . . doubt is only a particular form of anxiety." He concludes: "Perhaps all philosophies were created by men suffering from compulsive neurosis. At the beginning of every new belief there is the doubt in the validity of the old one. Moreover, all compulsive neurotics are given to brooding. Generally, this brooding does not produce any results. But in some cases, the personal conflict can be sublimated and turned into a general problem." (*Compulsion and Doubt*, pp. 91, 377)

4. *Compulsion and Doubt*, p. 600.

5. *Compulsion and Doubt*, pp. 92, 90.

6. Sheldon Wolin, "Paradigms and Politics," in Preston King and B. C. Parekh, eds., *Politics and Experience*, p. 148.

7. Kurt Goldstein, *Human Nature in the Light of Psychopathology*, pp. 114–115.

8. Sheldon S. Wolin, *Politics and Vision*, p. 8.

9. Goldstein, *Human Nature in the Light of Psychopathology*, p. 104.

10. See Karl Deutsch, *The Nerves of Government*. Deutsch writes: "Internal rearrange-

ments that are still relevant to goal-seeking in the outside world we may call 'learning.' Internal arrangements that reduce the net's goal-seeking effectiveness belong to the pathology of learning." (p. 92) And "By pathological learning in the case of an individual or an organization we may understand a learning process, and a corresponding change in inner structure, that will reduce rather than increase the future learning capacity of the person or organization." (p. 248)

11. From a letter to Antoine Gauthier in 1841. Quoted in J. Hampden Jackson, *Marx, Proudhon, and European Socialism,* pp. 27–28.

12. Wolin, *Politics and Vision,* p. 8. Some might argue that prophets of progress (like Turgot, Condorcet, or Comte), entrepeneurs, utopian planners, and advertising executives, as well as revolutionary leaders like Trotsky and Mao Tse-tung, have advocated something like permanent revolution. A discussion of this would require a detailed examination and critique of these positions much too lengthy to include here. To clarify the argument it should be understood that to advocate change, novelty, or social astonishments is to misunderstand the issues involved in permanent revolution—development and successful adaptation.

13. The relative nature of order is well expressed in Goldstein's discussion: "It is impossible to characterize a distribution of objects once and for all as either orderly or disorderly. Total disorder would be a completely haphazard distribution, as far as such an arrangement is possible. Further, what may appear to one person as order may be disorder for another, depending on the attitude of each and the capacity of each to change his attitude. The adequate distribution of certain objects may be one thing for the contemplative individual and quite another for a person whose approach is behavioral. A person with a behavioral approach would find a distribution orderly which enabled him to use the objects easily and as quickly as possible in the situation in which he was acting. Furthermore, the distribution might vary greatly with different tasks. A distribution which is adequate for a simple action may be inadequate for a complex one and may even hinder the person who has to use the same objects in different combinations and in different situations. The distribution of the objects on the desk of a very busy man may seem disorderly if you have no insight into the purposes for which they are to be used. When you have this insight, you see that it may be the best order it is possible to find in the situation. It is not uncommon for housewives or maids to feel an irresistible desire to put such objects in 'good order' to the dismay of the man to whom the desk belongs." (Goldstein, *Human Nature,* pp. 102–103)

14. See Leon Brillouin, *Scientific Uncertainty and Information,* pp. 5–11.

15. *The Political Illusion,* p. 209.

16. "On the Evolution of Social Stratification and the State," in S. Diamond, ed., *Culture in History,* p. 715.

17. See Peter Worsley, *The Trumpet Shall Sound.*

18. Kuhn, *The Structure of Scientific Revolutions,* 2d ed., "Postscript 1969," p. 208.

19. See Wolin, "Paradigms and Politics," p. 149.

20. Thomas S. Kuhn, "The Function of Dogma in Scientific Research," in A. C. Crombie, ed., *Scientific Change,* p. 387.

21. Thomas S. Kuhn, *The Structure of Scientific Revolutions,* p. 100.

22. As Weber put it, "A chaos of 'existential judgments' about countless individual events would be the only result of a serious attempt to 'analyze reality' without presuppositions." *The Methodology of the Social Sciences,* p. 78)

23. "A physical theory is not an explanation. It is a system of mathematical propositions, deduced from a small number of principles, which aim to represent as simply, as completely, and as exactly as possible a set of experimental laws." (Pierre Duhem, *The Aim and Structure of Physical Theory,* p. 19)

24. Duhem, p. 23.

25. "Without adequate conceptual schemes, scientific research is either blind *or fruit-less.* ... Indeed, the history of science, and especially of modern science because of its rapid rate of progress, could be written in terms of the successively greater development of conceptual schemes and the correspondingly greater reduction in the degree of empiricism in science." (Bernard Barber, *Science and the Social Order,* pp. 37–38)

26. P. K. Feyerabend, "Consolations for the Specialists," in Lakatos and Musgrave, eds., *Criticism and the Growth of Knowledge.*

27. Stephen Toulmin, "Discussion," in Crombie, ed., *Scientific Change,* p. 387.

28. Thomas S. Kuhn "Logic of Discovery or Psychology of Research," in Lakatos and Musgrave, eds., *Criticism and the Growth of Knowledge,* p. 21.

29. Kuhn, "Logic of Discovery," pp. 6–7.

30. Kuhn, "Reflections on My Critics," in Lakatos and Musgrave, eds., *Criticism and the Growth of Knowledge,* p. 245. The comment is in answer to Feyerabend's charge that "more than one social scientist has pointed out to me that now at last he had learned how to turn his field into a 'science'—by which of course he meant that he had learned how to *improve* it. The recipe according to these people is to restrict criticism, to reduce the number of comprehensive theories to one, and to create a normal science that has this one theory as its paradigm. Students must be prevented from speculating along different lines and the more restless colleagues must be made to conform and 'to do serious work.' Is this what Kuhn wants to achieve?" (Feyerabend, "Consolations for the Specialist," in Lakatos and Musgrave, eds., *Criticism and the Growth of Knowledge,* p. 98) In his "Postscript 1969" to the second edition of *The Structure of Scientific Revolutions,* Kuhn makes a milder demurrer by stating (p. 179) that "what changes with the transition to maturity is not the presence of a paradigm but rather its nature."

31. "The Function of Dogma," p. 368.

32. A. Rupert Hall, "Commentary," in Crombie, ed., *Scientific Change,* p. 372.

33. Hall, "Commentary," p. 372.

34. P. K. Feyerabend, "Problems of Empiricism," in Robert G. Colodny, ed., *Beyond the Edge of Certainty,* p. 148.

35. "Observation and experience can and must drastically restrict the range of admissible scientific belief, else there would be no science. But they cannot alone determine a particular body of such belief. An apparently arbitrary element, compounded of personal and historical accident, is always a formative ingredient of the beliefs espoused by a given scientific community at a given time." (Kuhn, *The Structure of Scientific Revolutions,* p. 4)

36. Kuhn, "The Function of Dogma," p. 363.

37. "The Function of Dogma," p. 364.

38. *The Structure of Scientific Revolutions,* p. 5.

39. *The Structure of Scientific Revolutions,* p. 24.

40. John W. N. Watkins, "Against 'Normal Science,' " in Lakatos and Musgrave, eds., *Criticism and the Growth of Knowledge* p. 26.

41. This is the way many social scientists read Kuhn. See three recent presidential addresses of the American Political Science Association—David Truman, "Disillusion and Regeneration: The Quest for a Discipline," *American Political Science Review,* December 1965, pp. 865–873; Gabriel Almond, "Political Theory and Political Science," *APSR,* December 1966, pp. 869–879; David Easton, "The New Revolution in Political Science," *APSR,* December 1969, pp. 1051–1061. Kuhn's thesis is interpreted in each case in an oversimplified manner to mean that a "research consensus" is a sign of scientific maturity. A more sophisticated discussion of Kuhn is to be found in the exchange over Eugene F. Miller's "Positivism, Historicism, and Political Inquiry" in *APSR,* September 1972, pp.

796–873. See especially Martin Landau, "Comment: On Objectivity" pp. 846–856 in the same issue. Landau writes: "Kuhn's scenario has overwhelmed political science. Its appeal has been so immediate, so powerful, so universally compelling that it seems as if a massive conversion experience has taken place. In the face of the discord and upheaval that characterize the discipline today, all sides of the 'science' controversy derive sustenance and solace from the Book of Kuhn. It is not stretching the metaphor to suggest that it has appeared as a 'godsend.' " See also the discussion of Kuhn in Landau, *Political Theory and Political Science: Studies in the Methodology of Political Inquiry.*

42. Margaret Masterman, "The Nature of a Paradigm," in Lakatos and Musgrave, eds., *Criticism and the Growth of Knowledge,* p. 61. A description of the twenty-one uses follows on pp. 61–65.

43. Kuhn, "The Function of Dogma," p. 358. The quoted expressions that immediately follow are from the same page.

44. "The Function of Dogma," pp. 392–393.

45. "The Nature of a Paradigm," pp. 66–67. Masterman comments: "Kuhn, alone among philosophers of science, puts himself in a position to dispel the worry which so besets the working scientists confronted for the first time with professional philosophy-of-science, 'How can I be using a theory which isn't there.' "

46. Kuhn, *The Structure of Scientific Revolutions,* 2d ed., p. 176.

47. *The Structure of Scientific Revolutions,* pp. 182–191.

48. *The Structure of Scientific Revolutions,* p. 192.

49. *Communication and Social Order,* p. 37.

50. Anthony F. C. Wallace and John Atkins, "The Meaning of Kinship Terms," *American Anthropologist,* Vol. 62, February 1960, pp. 75–76.

51. Kuhn, *The Structure of Scientific Revolutions,* p. 182.

52. " 'The Myth of the Framework' is, in our time, the central bulwark of irrationalism. My counterthesis is that it simply exaggerates a difficulty into an impossibility. The difficulty of discussion between people brought up in different frameworks is to be admitted. But nothing is more fruitful than such a discussion; than the culture clash which has stimulated some of the greatest intellectual revolutions." (Karl Popper, "Normal Science and Its Dangers." (Lakatos and Musgrave, eds., *Criticism and the Growth of Knowledge,* pp. 56–57)

53. Kuhn continues: "To these shared examples should, however, be added at least some of the technical problem-solutions found in the periodical literature that scientists encounter during their post-educational research careers and also show them by example how their job is to be done." *The Structure of Scientific Revolutions,* p. 187)

54. Kuhn, "The Function of Dogma," p. 351.

55. "The Function of Dogma," p. 351. Others do not agree that this is a proper sort of education for future scientists. B. Glass wrote in reply to Kuhn: "I can at least speak for my fellow biologists of this generation in America. I have found complete unanimity among them in the belief that science must be taught—I do not say *has* been taught —as a variety of methods of investigation and inquiry rather than as a body of authoritative facts and principles. They also agree emphatically that students must be taught that scientific laws and principles are approximations derived from the data of experience and that they remain forever subject to alteration and correction or replacement in the light of new evidence. I am appalled to think that, if Mr. Kuhn is right, we should go back to teaching paradigms and dogmas, not as merely temporary expedients to aid us more clearly to visualize the nature of our scientific problems but rather as part of the regular, approved method of scientific advance." (Bentley Glass, "Discussion," in A. C. Crombie, ed., *Scientific Change,* p. 382) Kuhn replied that he was not to be taken as an apologist for current modes of teaching science in America and this system of education

was a parody. He adds, "But I do insist that it is a parody, i.e., that it is not irrelevant. The fact that it has arisen in the sciences and not in the humanities or social sciences can tell us something about the nature of science." (Kuhn, in Crombie, ed., p. 391) The reply is typical of how Kuhn handles difficulties. He does not seem capable of conceiving that he might be describing American science or twentieth-century science but always Science. Of course the humanities and social sciences have been taught dogmatically using exemplary models, as in the Hellenistic world, and the result was stagnation—many decades of diligent cataloging, listing, and copying.

56. Kuhn, "Logic or Psychology?" in Lakatos and Musgrave, eds., *Criticism and the Growth of Knowledge*, p. 21.

57. Kuhn, *The Structure of Scientific Revolutions*, p. 24. Alfred North Whitehead described the process as "cooking the facts for the sake of exemplifying the law." (*Adventures of Ideas*, p. 94)

58. Kuhn, "The Function of Dogma," p. 364.

59. Kuhn, *The Structure of Scientific Revolutions*, p. 79.

60. *The Structure of Scientific Revolutions*, p. 79.

61. *The Structure of Scientific Revolutions*, p. 77.

62. "Because of the necessarily long delays, because of the amplitude of the scope it must attain, and because of the resistance it must overcome, change in bureaucratic organizations is a deeply felt crisis. The essential rhythm prevalent in such organizations is, therefore, an alternation of long periods of stability with very short periods of crisis and change. . . . Crisis is a distinctive and necessary element of the bureaucratic system. It provides the only means of making the necessary adjustments, and it therefore plays a role in enabling the organization to develop and, indirectly, for centralization and impersonality to grow." (Michel Crozier, *The Bureaucratic Phenomenon*, p. 196)

63. T. C. Schneirla and Gerard Piel, "The Army Ant," *Scientific American*, June 1948 (W. H. Freeman & Company reprint no. 413. p. 4). Schneirla has published *Army Ants: A Study of Social Organization* (San Francisco: W. H. Freeman & Company, 1971) for those interested in a more detailed account.

64. "The Army Ant," reprint, p. 4.

65. "The Army Ant," reprint, p. 7.

66. "The Army Ant," reprint, p. 8.

67. John Von Neumann, "Probabilistic Logics and the Synthesis of Reliable Organisms from Unreliable Components," in Shannon and McCarthy, eds., *Automata Studies*.

68. "In networks which allow feedback . . . when a pulse from an organ gets back to the same organ at some later time, there is danger of strong statistical correlation. Moreover, without randomness, situations may arise where errors tend to be amplified instead of cancelled out. E.g., it is possible that the machine remembers its mistakes, so to speak, and thereafter perpetuates them." ("Probabilistic Logics," p. 88)

69. Jules Henry, "Homeostasis in a Special Life Situation," in Grinker, ed., *Toward a Unified Theory of Human Behavior*, p. 226.

70. "Homeostasis," p. 272.

71. Schneirla and Piel, "The Army Ant," reprint, p. 8.

72. Kuhn writes that the analogy between the evolution of organisms and the evolution of scientific ideas by means of natural selection is particularly appropriate. But he does not consider the difficulties. The theory of natural selection is unfalsifiable, for one thing, and it is impossible to know whether one's species, organization, or ideas are being naturally selected or rejected until it is too late to matter. That is, the analogy is only a way of rationalizing the practices of the *status quo*, but does not and cannot be used to evaluate the present or future appropriateness of an adaptation.

73. Kuhn, *The Structure of Scientific Revolutions*, p. 111.

74. *The Structure of Scientific Revolutions,* p. 122.

75. *The Structure of Scientific Revolutions,* p. 140.

76. "Kuhn sees the scientific community on the analogy of a religious community and sees science as the scientists' religion. If that is so, one can perhaps see why he elevates Normal Science above Extraordinary Science; for Extraordinary Science corresponds, on the religious side, to a period of crisis and schism, confusion and despair, to a spiritual catastrophe." (John W. N. Watkins, "Against 'Normal Science,'" in Lakatos and Musgrave, eds., *Criticism and the Growth of Knowledge,* p. 33)

77. *The Structure of Scientific Revolutions,* p. 150.

78. One critic has disputed Kuhn's notion that succeeding paradigms are not related in some developmental manner. "Complete novelty is most unlikely because scientists are human beings looking at nature through the thought-forms of their culture and environment. Occasionally, through his own particular background, a scientist may contribute a perspective from outside the 'normal' culture to bear on a problem, but generally all that is contributed is a new analogy, a viewpoint taken from some non-scientific activity or from another field of science," comments O. T. Benfey. He goes on to note that in 1858, two scientists, Kekule and Couper, independently described the structural relations of the atoms in organic compounds and that Kekule said his solution came out of his earlier architectural training while Couper said that he employed a linguistic approach based on his training in linguistics and philosophy prior to his study of chemistry. (Otto Theodor Benfey, "An Approach to the Conceptual Analysis of Scientific Crises," in L. von Bertalanffy and A. Rappaport, eds., *General Systems,* Vol. 9. p. 57)

79. Herman Broch, *The Sleep Walkers,* p. 446. See especially the discontinuous essay titled "Disintegration of Values." Kenneth Boulding puts it, "Science might almost be defined as the process of substituting unimportant questions which can be answered for important questions which cannot." (*The Image,* p. 164)

80. Broch, p. 636. "No system of values can exist without an irreducible residue of the irrational which preserves the rational itself from a literally suicidal autonomy." (p. 626)

81. Broch, p. 526.

82. George Gieger, "Values and Social Science," *Journal of Social Issues,* Vol. 6, No. 4, 1950. pp. 12–13.

83. Gieger, p. 11.

84. P. K. Feyerabend, "On the Improvement of the Sciences and the Arts and the Possible Identity of the Two," Cohen and Wartofsky, eds., *Boston Studies in the Philosophy of Science,* Vol. 3, pp. 387–415.

85. "On the Improvement," p. 396.

86. Kuhn, "Logic of Discovery," in Lakatos and Musgrave, eds., *Criticism and the Growth of Knowledge,* p. 19.

87. Kuhn, *The Copernican Revolution,* pp. 75–76.

88. *The Copernican Revolution,* p. 95.

89. *The Copernican Revolution,* p. 95.

90. *The Copernican Revolution,* p. 132. Kuhn takes this all back, apparently, three years later. In *The Structure of Scientific Revolutions* he writes, "By the early sixteenth century an increasing number of Europe's best astronomers were recognizing that the astronomical paradigm was failing in application to its traditional problems." (p. 69) Perhaps Kuhn can reconcile these statements but I cannot.

91. *The Copernican Revolution,* p. 124.

92. Stephen Toulmin, "Conceptual Revolutions in Science," in Cohen and Wartofsky, eds., *Boston Studies in the Philosophy of Science,* Vol. III, p. 341.

93. *The Structure of Scientific Revolutions,* p. 64.

94. *The Structure of Scientific Revolutions.* p. 64.

95. J. S. Bruner and Leo Postman, "On the Perception of Incongruity: A Paradigm," *Journal of Personality.* Vol. 18, 1949, pp. 206–223.

96. Bruner and Postman. pp. 213–215.

97. Bruner and Postman, p. 207.

98. Bruner and Postman, p. 208.

99. Leo Postman and J. S. Bruner, "Perception under Stress," *Psychological Review,* Vol. 55, No. 6, November 1948, pp. 314–323.

100. N. R. F. Maier, Nathan Glaser, and James B. Klee, "Studies of Abnormal Behavior in the Rat III. The Development of Behavior Fixations through Frustration," *Journal of Experimental Psychology,* Vol. 26, June 1940, pp. 521–546.

101. An early statement of this finding is L. G. Humphreys, 'The Effect of Random Alternation of Reinforcement on the Acquisition and Extinction of Conditioned Eyelid Reactions," *Journal of Experimental Psychology,* Vol. 25, 1939, pp. 141–158.

102. Maier et al., p. 539

103. Maier et al., p. 541

104. Maier et al., p. 538.

105. Karl Popper, *Conjectures and Refutations,* p. 346.

106. Toulmin, "Conceptual Revolutions," p. 339.

107. *The Structure of Scientific Revolutions,* p. 175.

108. Masterman, "The Nature of a Paradigm," in Lakatos and Musgrave, eds., *Criticism and the Growth of Knowledge,* p. 78.

109. From the *Metaphysics,* quoted in Farrington, *Greek Science,* p. 168.

110. Kuhn, "Logic of Discovery or Psychology of Research," in Lakatos and Musgrave, eds., *Criticism and the Growth of Knowledge,* p. 16.

111. Farrington, *Greek Science,* p. 41.

112. René Dubos, *Pasteur and Modern Science.*

113. René Dubos, *Reason Awake: Science for Man,* pp. 142–143.

114. *Reason Awake,* p. 77. "Many aspects of sixteenth-century life in Europe had been revolutionized by the practical inventions and advances in knowledge that occurred during the Renaissance, long before experimental science began to influence technology or act as an effective social force. Invention and new knowledge, in fact, had caused social upheavals long before the Renaissance." (p. 76) Also see Lynn Whyte, Jr., *Medieval Technology and Social Change.*

115. Bottomore, ed., *Karl Marx: Early Writings,* pp. 163–164.

116. Bottomore, ed., *Karl Marx: Early Writings,* p. 43.

117. *Greek Science,* p. 141.

118. Kuhn, "Logic of Discovery or Psychology of Research," in Lakatos and Musgrave, eds., *Criticism and the Growth of Knowledge.* Kuhn's argument here is important and more explicit than most. Basically it says that theory articulation means that falsification of the theory becomes likely.

119. Judith Merkle, *Command and Control: The Social Implication of Nuclear Defense.* p. 5.

120. *Command and Control,* p. 5.

121. Kuhn, "Reflections of My Critics," in Lakatos and Musgrave, eds., *Criticism and the Growth of Knowledge,* p. 249.

122. Childe, *Society and Knowledge,* p. 124.

123. "Experience of *touch* in the traditional wide meaning of the term includes the whole exploratory process of handling or dealing with things, as well as being passively pushed or touched. This is pre-eminently the sensory field in which we confirm or corroborate. It is therefore the realm of causal, substantial, mechanical relations . . . I

suggest 'haptic' experience as a convenient compendious term, emphasizing active grasping and including all processes needed for bodily movement and posture." (A. D. Ritchie, *Studies in the History and Methods of Sciences*, p. 209)

124. N. R. F. Maier, "Reasoning in Humans. III. The Mechanisms of Equivalent Stimuli and of Reasoning," *Journal of Experimental Psychology*, Vol. 35, 1945, p. 358.

125. "Reasoning," p. 357.

126. Karl Duncker, "On Problem Solving," H. G. Birch and H. S. Rabinowitz, "The Negative Effect of Previous Experience on Productive Thinking," and P. Saugstad and K. Raaheim, "Problem Solving, Past Experience, and Availability of Functions," in P. C. Wason and P. N. Johnson-Laird, eds., *Thinking and Reasoning*.

127. Saugstad and Raaheim, "Problem Solving," pp. 56–57.

128. Duncker, "On Problem Solving," p. 34.

129. "On Problem Solving," p. 37.

130. The question of whether Kuhn's theory adequately accounts for the historical developemnt of scientific knowledge, for actual scientific practice, or whether it is even logically tenable, has been addressed by several authors. By all accounts familiar to me, his theory fails badly in these regards. For example, see: Dudley Shapere, "Meaning and Scientific Change" in R. Colodny, ed., *Mind and Cosmos;* Carl R. Kordig, *The Justification of Scientific Change;* as well as the articles by L. Pierce Williams, John W. N. Watkins, and Stephen E. Toulmin in the Lakatos and Musgrave volume, *Criticism and the Growth of Knowledge.* Feyerabend's and Popper's criticisms have been cited throughout the chapter.

131. "Consolation for the Specialist," in Lakatos and Musgrave, eds., *Criticism and the Growth of Knowledge.*

132. A contemporary description of the institutional context of scientific research is pertinent. "Where do scientists work? There are 29 per cent in educational institutions; 45 per cent in industry, business, or are self-employed; 18 per cent in government organizations; and 8 per cent are classified as 'nonprofit' or other types. . . . My main point is that the scientist today is typically an 'organization man,' and that most scientists are not working in the institutional setting which has been traditionally identified as the citadel of pure research, namely the academic instititien.

"Consequently when we speak today of the 'scientific ethos' we must take account of the specific organizational setting in which it operates. It is simply not realistic to expect the chemist who works for Dupont or the physicist who works at IBM to have the same motivations as a Lavoisier or a Newton." (Walter Hirsch in the *Bulletin of the Atomic Scientists*, Vol. 21, 1965. Quoted by Michael Reagan, "Basic and Applied Research: A Meaningful Distinction?" *Science*, Vol. 155, No. 3768, 1967, p. 1385)

133. Trigant Burrow, *Science and Man's Behavior*, p. 144.

Chapter 7

1. As we have noted, this inherent deficiency is sometimes discussed in terms of man's "natural goodness"—a goodness which is always easily corrupted and hence of little use. That is, the deficiency can be expressed as either sin or gullibility; in either case the defective characteristics of observed behavior—laziness, irrationality, are the same. Labeling human beings as either evil geniuses or good fools does not seem to be a distinction worth making.

2. Alvin Gouldner, *Patterns of Industrial Bureaucracy*, p. 245.

3. Trigant Burrow, "Altering Frames of Reference in the Sphere of Human Behavior," *Journal of Social Philosophy*, Vol. 2, pp. 118–141.

4. "Altering Frames," pp. 119–120.

5. Burrow, "Our Mass Neurosis," *The Psychological Bulletin*, Vol. 23, 1926, pp. 305–

306. See also "A Relative Concept of Consciousness," *Psycho-Analytic Review*, Vol. 12, No. 1, 1925, pp. 1–15.

6. "Our Mass Neurosis," p. 311.

7. Biographical material is from Hans Syz, "A Summary Note on the Work of Trigant Burrow" (*International Journal of Social Psychiatry*, Vol. 7, No. 4, 1961, pp. 283–291) and William E. Galt, ed., *A Search for Man's Sanity: The Selected Letters of Trigant Burrow*.

8. H. Syz, "Reflections on Group- or Phylo-Analysis," supplement to *Acta Psychotherapeutica et Psychosomatica*, Vol. 2, 1963, p. 38.

9. Burrow, *Preconscious Foundations of Human Experience*, p. 3. Note: this is a posthumous volume consisting of early articles collected and edited by William Galt.

10. Burrow, *Science and Man's Behavior*, p. 182.

11. Burrow, *Preconscious Foundations*, pp. 40–41.

12. Burrow, *The Social Basis of Consciousness*, p. 13.

13. Burrow, "Our Social Evasion," *Medical Journal and Record*, Vol. 123, 1926, p. 795.

14. Burrow, "The Laboratory Method in Psychoanalysis, Its Inception and Development," *American Journal of Psychiatry*, Vol. 5, No. 3, January 1926, pp. 349–350.

15. Burrow, *The Biology of Human Conflict*, p. 148.

16. "Everybody who has to do with human behavior is irresistibly prone to correct it rather than observe it." (*The Biology of Human Conflict*, p. 197)

17. Burrow, "The Autonomy of the 'I' from the Standpoint of Group Analysis," *Psyche*, Vol. 8, No. 31, 1928, p. 45. Freud wrote: "We have long observed that every neurosis has the result, and therefore probably the purpose, of forcing the patient out of real life, of alienating him from actuality. . . . The neurotic turns away from reality because he finds it unbearable—either the whole or parts of it." (Freud, "Formulations Regarding the Two Principles in Mental Functioning," in Philip Rieff, ed., *The Collected Papers of Sigmund Freud: General Psychological Theory*, p. 21)

18. Freud, "The Loss of Reality in Neurosis and Psychosis," in Philip Rieff, ed., *General Psychological Theory*, p. 214.

19. "The Loss of Reality," p. 203.

20. Burrow, *The Social Basis of Consciousness*, p. 246.

21. Burrow, *The Biology of Human Conflict*, p. 46.

22. Burrow, *The Social Basis of Consciousness*, p. 54. Laing makes a similar indictment in *The Politics of the Family*, pp. 9–10.

23. *The Social Basis of Consciousness*, p. 54.

24. *A Search for Man's Sanity*, p. 50.

25. *The Structure of Insanity*, pp. 38–39.

26. *The Structure of Insanity*, p. 181.

27. Hans Syz, "Problems of Perspective against the Background of Trigant Burrow's Group-Analytic Researches," *International Journal of Group Psycho-Therapy*, Vol. 2, No. 2, April 1961, p. 151.

28. Syz, "Reflections," p. 63.

29. *Preconscious Foundations of Human Experience*, p. 35. Note the full implication of this, which Burrow was careful to spell out. "The very criterion which by universal agreement constitutes the test of an individual's sanity, namely, his capacity to discriminate between right and wrong, constitutes in fact the precise index of his imbalance or insanity." (*The Biology of Human Conflict*, p. 379)

30. Burrow suggested in a letter to H. L. Mencken that the relation of his ideas to those of Hobbes was analogous to the relationship of Darwin's theory of evolution to the book of Genesis. (*A Search for Sanity*, pp. 276–277)

31. Burrow, "Social Images versus Reality," *Journal of Abnormal and Social Psychology*, Vol. 19, 1924, p. 230.

32. "Social Images," p. 231.

33. "Social Images," p. 231.

34. "Social Images," p. 231.

35. My favorite description of such conceptual structures or social images is Nietzsche's account of truth: "What therefore is truth? A mobile army of metaphors, metonymies, anthropomorphisms: in short, a sum of human relations which become poetically and rhetorically intensified, metamorphosed, adorned, and after long usage seem to a nation fixed, canonic, and binding; truths are illusions of which one has forgotten that they *are* illusions; worn-out metaphors which have become powerless to affect the senses; coins which have their obverse effaced and now are no longer of account as coins but merely as metal." (Friedrich Nietzsche, *Early Greek Philosophy*, p. 180) See also the following accounts: Jacques Ellul, *The Political Illusion*, pp. 116–171; Kenneth E. Boulding, *The Image*, pp. 47–48; Eric A. Havelock, *Preface to Plato*, pp. 41–42; Harold Innis, *The Bias of Communication*, p. 132; Abram Kardiner and Associates, *The Psychological Frontiers of Society*, pp. 1–2, 37; Elton Mayo, *The Human Problems of an Industrial Civilization*, p. 151; C. Wright Mills, *Power, Politics, and People*, p. 405; Robert Presthus, *The Organizational Society*, p. 94; Jurgen Ruesch and Gregory Bateson, *Communication*, pp. 41–42; Alfred North Whitehead, *Adventures of Ideas*, pp. 19–20; Raymond Williams, *The Long Revolution*, p. 18; J. Z. Young, *Doubt and Certainty in Science*, p. 153; and R. D. Laing, *The Politics of the Family*, p. 9.

36. "Social Images vs. Reality," p. 235.

37. Mills writes, "No man stands alone directly confronting a world of solid fact. No such world is available, The closest men come to it is when they are infants or when they become insane: then, in a terrifying scene of meaningless events and senseless confusion, they are often seized with the panic of near-total insecurity." (*Power, Politics, and People*, p. 405). Jacques Ellul is an exception; he writes: "Because we live in a universe of images, affecting the masses can be reduced to manipulating symbols. If we lived in a microcosm of direct experience, such symbol manipulation would have little effect on us." (*The Political Illusion*, p. 116)

38. *The Biology of Human Conflict*, p. 28.

39. *The Biology of Human Conflict*, pp. 268–269.

40. *The Biology of Human Conflict*, p. 111.

41. *The Biology of Human Conflict*, p. 112.

42. *Science and Man's Behavior*, pp. 212–213.

43. *Science and Man's Behavior*, p. 223. J. Z. Young notes that any system of language involves acts of communication which presuppose "agents, persons, egos," and the like. "But our way of speaking has magnified these egos to such an extent as to obscure the reason for which we originally postulated them, namely to speak about their communication. We learn very early in life to talk like this about ourselves, so that it becomes the obvious thing to do. It may seem absurd to doubt the primacy of oneself. . . . But biology has shown us to what an extraordinary extent our ways of observing and speaking are not our own, but, like our whole organization, are inherited and learned. We are in fact already coming to speak of ourselves in quite a different way—not as one thing but as a great variety of them." (Young, *Doubt and Certainty in Science*, p. 154)

44. "By the term 'I'-persona, . . . I mean the artificial system of prefabricated affects and prejudices that underlies man's present level of 'normal' feeling and thinking and that leads to interferences that are lacking in biological warrant. I mean the social conditioning that has placed a premium upon man's subjective emotions at the expense of his objective relationships." (*Science and Man's Behavior*, p. 291)

45. *The Social Basis of Consciousness,* p. 31.

46. Syz, "Problems of Perspective," p. 152.

47. *The Biology of Human Conflict,* p. 92.

48. "Either component of the individual's criterion necessarily contains the other. Whoever tends to feel his own importance entertains an equal conviction of his own insignificance. A criterion of goodness necessarily entails an alternative of badness." (Burrow, "Our Mass Neurosis," pp. 308–309)

49. Burrow, "Physiological Behavior-Reactions in the Individual and the Community: A Study in Phyloanalysis," *Psyche,* Vol. 2, No. 42, 1930, p. 79.

50. See the article "Schizophrenia and Perception: A Critique of the Liberal Theory of Externality," by James Glass, *Inquiry,* Vol. 15, 1972, pp. 114–115, for a discussion of Hobbes's theory of common names as the basis of political order and perceptual objectivity. Glass notes that although such a system allows a sense of security about the public acts of the sovereign, it creates a situation of extreme anxiety concerning the intentions of other citizens. He writes, "While politically the public rules could not be mistaken, the contingencies, and hidden motives, the 'secret thoughts' of the existential realm, the space of interpersonal being, posed a whole set of different problems."

51. "The Autonomy of the 'I' from the Standpoint of Group Analysis," *Psyche,* Vol. 8. No. 31, 1928, p. 39.

52. "The Autonomy," p. 42.

53. "The Autonomy," p. 43.

54. "Whatever the postulate, belief or argument, there lurks beneath it, in the mind of each of us, the unconscious determination to preserve intact the secret illusion of his own separateness." (Burrow, *The Social Basis of Consciousness,* p. 134)

55. "The Autonomy," p. 47.

56. "A Relative Concept of Consciousness," p. 3.

57. "Our Mass Neurosis," p. 306.

58. "Our Mass Neurosis," p. 307.

59. Burrow, "Physiological Behavior Reactions," p. 78.

60. *Science and Man's Behavior,* p. 136.

61. Burrow, "Physiological Behavior-Reactions," p. 69.

62. *Science and Man's Behavior,* p. 439.

63. "There is no direct evidence for the hypothesis that behavior in so far as the form of the pattern is concerned, is simply a combination or co-ordination of reflexes. On the contrary, there is conclusive evidence of a dominant organic unity from the beginning. The evidence appears not only in the manner in which behavior develops, but particularly in the manner in which the nervous system puts the principle into effect, for . . . the nervous system concerns itself first with the maintenance of the integrity of the individual, and only later makes provision for local reflexes." (George E. Coghill, *Anatomy and the Problem of Behavior,* p. 89) See also C. Judson Herrick, *The Evolution of Human Nature,* p. 254.

64. Coghill, *Anatomy,* p. 21.

65. Coghill, "The Biological Basis of Conflict in Behavior," *Psychoanalytic Review,* Vol. 20, No. 1, January 1933, p. 4. See Burrow, "Bio-Physical Factors in Relation to Functional Imbalances," *Human Biology,* Vol. 10, 1938, pp. 93–105.

66. Kurt Goldstein, *Human Nature in the Light of Psychopathology,* pp. 16–18.

67. Goldstein, *Human Nature,* p. 18.

68. Burrow, *The Biology of Human Conflict,* p. 394.

69. *The Biology of Human Conflict,* p. 133.

70. *The Biology of Human Conflict,* p. 182. Burrow also summarizes the result this way: "The Sign controls the organism; the semaphore runs the train!" (p. 184)

71. Burrow, *The Structure of Insanity,* p. 40.

72. Burrow, *The Social Basis of Consciousness,* p. 121. A body of experimental literature indicates that there is divergence between emotional states and physiological states.
That is, we do not know what we feel except as we learn, from what Skinner calls the
"verbal community," how to label them. See Stanley Schachter and Jerome Singer, "Cognitive, Social, and Physiological Determinants of Emotional States," *Psychological Review.*
Vol. 69, No. 5, September 1962, p. 398. They conclude from their experiments that
"given a state of physiological arousal for which an individual has no immediate explanation, he will label this state and describe his feelings in terms of the cognitions available to
him. To the extent that cognitive factors are potent determiners of emotional states, it
should be anticipated that precisely the same physiological arousal could be labeled 'joy'
or 'fury' or 'jealousy' or any of a great diversity of emotional labels depending on the
cognitive aspects of the situation."

73. *The Biology of Human Conflict,* p. 123.

74. Burrow writes: "No formulation of life can function as life. It is only life itself in
its organic confluence that may abrogate the separateness that is the essence of resistance.
Whether in the societal or in the individual sphere, whether in the sphere we call functional (physiological) the question of health or disease hangs solely upon the issue as to
whether the element—cell or system—functions integrally or separatively, congruently or
resistantly." (*The Social Basis,* p. 155)

75. Burrow, "The Social Neurosis: A Study in 'Clinical Anthropology,'" *Philosophy of
Science,* Vol. 16, 1949, p. 33. In the same paper the author expresses essentially the same
idea this way: "In the sphere of human behavior, a method of inquiry that does not
possess value for everyone is not a scientific method." (p. 39.)

76. The most general and useful definition of a symbol I find to be that of Wheelwright. He writes: "A symbol . . . is a relatively stable and repeatable element of perceptual experience, standing for some larger meaning or set of meanings which cannot be
given, or not fully give, in perceptual experience itself." Thus a symbol can be anything
from a signal like a bell, through an elaborate representation like a picture, to abstractions like words. See Philip Wheelwright, *Metaphor and Reality,* p. 92.

77. Burrow, "Altering Frames of Reference," p. 124.

78. "Altering Frames of Reference," p. 125.

79. "Altering Frames of Reference," p. 125. Burrow notes that his imaginary experiment could not be carried out because of the extreme costs in terms of time and equipment required, but adds that "at least in theory the procedure cited is not at all to be
excluded physiologically." A situation such as he describes has been simulated by simple
reflexive machines constructed by W. Grey Walter. His ingenious mechanism, *M. specula-
trix,* responds to and also emits light signals. When several of these devices are placed
together the effect is that of a society of machines. Walter comments: "In a sense, then, a
population of machines forms a sort of community, with a special code of behavior.
When an external stimulus is applied to all members of such a community, they will of
course see it independently and the community will break up; then, the more individuals
there are, the smaller the chance of any one achieving its goal, for each individual finds
in the others converging obstacles." (Walter, *The Living Brain,* p. 129. See Chapter 5 of
the work for a full description.)

80. *The Living Brain,* p. 180.

81. "By and large (although with exceptions) biologically disadvantageous behavior
will be quickly eliminated by selection. In contrast, symbolic behavior is not only creative
in its roots . . . it also far transcends biological advantage. . . . The biological and adaptive
value of just the highest symbolic and cultural activities is questionable; and in suicide,
war, etc., biological values are sacrificed to symbolic ones. This is the biological back-

ground of the antithesis of 'nature' and 'culture.'" (Von Bertalanffy, *Robots, Men and Minds*, p. 27) Also: "Symbols may come to be manipulated without much regard to what they represent biologically; when this happens with the symbols which constitute language, one has metaphysics; when it happens with economic symbols, one has high-finance. Either may have significant biological consequences." (Charles F. Hockett, "Biophysics, Linguistics, and the Unity of Science," *American Scientist*, Vol. 36, 1948, p. 568) See also Leslie A. White, *The Science of Culture*, Chapter 2. White stresses the "extrasomatic" nature of symbols, arguing that "the meaning of a symbol can be grasped only by nonsensory, symbolic means." (p. 26) Noam Chomsky comments on linguistic symbols, "The normal use of language is not only innovative and potentially infinite in scope, but also free from the control of detectable stimuli, either external or internal. It is because of this freedom from stimulus control that language can serve as an instrument of thought and self-expression, as it does not only for the exceptionally gifted and talented, but, in fact, for every normal human." (*Linguistic Contributions to the Study of Mind*, pp. 10–11)

82. Pareto seems to have captured the flavor of what Burrow calls the "social neurosis" in his massive but faulty attempt to describe the reflexes involved (residues) and resulting social images (derivations), while also noting the rational aspects of human behavior. See Vilfredo Pareto, *The Mind and Society*.

83. "The anthropological importance of the symbol as a time and labor-saving device need hardly be pointed out. It affords man a shorthand means of communication that is an incalculable asset to the individual and the species." (Burrow, *Science and Man's Behavior*, p. 103) Wheelwright makes the same point. "Now action on the human level is symbolic action. Man is, perhaps uniquely, the symbolizing animal; he not only performs, he also means and intends and seeks to know. Somehow in the long temporal mystery of evolution there emerged the power and disposition to let something—whether a body, an image, a sound, or later a written word—stand as surrogate for something else. Therein man became . . . a linguistic animal." (Wheelwright, *Metaphor and Reality*, p. 19)

84. Throughout his career Burrow's ideas were often linked with those of general semanticists like Korzybski and Hayakawa. But he differed with them fundamentally, as he often pointed out. Basically his position is that "it is not the distorted meaning or symbol that is responsible for the incited affect; it is the incited affect that is responsible for the distorted meaning or symbol." (*Science and Man's Behavior*, p. 277) See also Burrow's letter to Hayakawa dated November 16, 1949, in Galt, ed., *A Search for Man's Sanity*, pp. 587–589.

85. *Preconscious Foundations of Human Experience*, p. 110.

86. "I repeat that the sign, symbol, or word has been and will continue to be a great asset in man's communication with man." (*Preconscious Foundations*, p. 111) And "I must not be understood as derogating in any sense this specialized part equipment of man." (*The Structure of Insanity*, p. 29) Burrow, later in life, wrote, "It may be that my manner of emphasizing the joint origin of language and man's ditentive behavior has been misleading." (Letter in Galt, ed., *A Search for Man's Sanity*, p. 589)

87. Burrow, *Preconscious Foundations of Human Experience*, pp. 111–112.

88. Burrow, *The Biological Basis of Human Conflict*, p. 185.

89. *The Biological Basis of Human Conflict*, p. 191.

90. Jane B. Lancaster, "Primate Communication Systems and the Emergence of Human Language," (Ph. D. dissertation, University of California, Berkeley, n.d.), p. 22.

91. "Primate Communication Systems," p. 41. "Subhuman primates readily form associations between environmental stimuli and sensations closely related to the limbic systems, such as pain, or to a limbic modality, such as an olfactory or gustatory sensation. The majority of classic learning experiments demonstrate this fact when a monkey is

expected to form an association between an arbitrary stimulus such as a light flash or a bell and a limbic stimulus such as food, water, or sex as a reinforcer. What the monkey cannot do is to readily form associations between two nonlimbic stimuli."

92. "Primate Communication Systems," pp. 33–34. "The term 'limbic system' refers to the phylogenetically old parts of the cortex and its related nuclei. . . . The limbic lobe is common to the brains of all mammals. In contrast to phylogenetically new cortex, limbic cortex has strong connections with the hypothalamus and midbrain tegmentum, areas that are important in the integrative mechanisms for activities involved with self-preservation and reproduction. Just as the limbic system is found as a common denominator in the brains of all mammals, so the categories of behavior that it controls are common to all mammals. This group of activities is characterized by their intimate connections with the basic needs of the organism, survival and reproduction. Stimulation of a part of the limbic system usually elicits not only physiological changes, but also emotional sensations that provide the animal with a state of heightened motivation to perform a behavior pattern that is critical in its survival. . . . The limbic system is closely associated with emotion—it makes the animal want to do what it has to do to survive and reproduce." The limbic system appears to be the neurophysiological basis of what Burrow calls the "total integrative pattern" of the human organism.

93. "Primate Communication Systems," p. 75.

94. *Neurotic Distortion of the Creative Process,* p. 85.

95. "Some Implications for Psychoanalysis of Modern Concepts of the Organization of the Brain," *Psychoanalytic Quarterly,* Vol. 22, 1953, p. 42. See also Count's discussion of these issues from which he concludes; "Our problem henceforth is that of a symbolizing brain operation on a primate biogram." (Earle W. Count, "The Biological Basis of Human Sociality," *American Anthropologist,* Vol. 60, 1958, p. 1073)

96. *Science and Man's Behavior,* p. 235.

97. Burrow reconciles these statements somewhat differently. He argues that while we have come to accept the symbolic or partitive mode of human behavior as the biological expression of the species, in fact this mode cannot make organic inroads on the organism's pattern of total reaction. While the symbolic mode can interfere with primary reaction patterns, it cannot substitute for them nor can it eliminate them. "The Law of the Organism," *American Journal of Sociology,* Vol. 42, 1937, p. 819)

98. K. J. W. Craik, *The Nature of Explanation,* pp. 50–51.

99. "In a semantic communicative system the ties between meaningful message-elements and their meanings can be arbitrary or non arbitrary. The word 'salt' is not salty or granular; 'dog' is not 'canine'; 'whale' is a small word for a large object; 'microorganism' is the reverse. A picture on the other hand looks like what it is a picture of. A bee dances faster if the source of the nectar he is reporting is closer. . . . The design-feature of 'arbitrariness' has the disadvantage of being arbitrary, but the great advantage that there is no limit to what can be communicated about." (Charles F. Hockett, "The Origin of Speech," *Scientific American,* September 1960)

100. The fallibility of symbol use is likewise no reason to indict it as a cause of man's delusions. For it is not the making of mistakes which seems to produce pathological reactions, it is the nonrecognition of mistakes. Craik comments: "A particular type of symbolism may always fail in a particular case, as Euclidean geometry apparently fails to represent stellar space; but if all types of symbolism always failed we should be unable to recognize any objects . . . at all." (*The Nature of Explanation,* p. 29)

101. Burrow, *The Biology of Human Conflict,* p. 279.

102. Ivan P. Pavlov, *Conditioned Reflexes,* p. 291.

103. *Conditioned Reflexes,* p. 293.

104. *Conditioned Reflexes,* p. 297.

105. *The Biology of Human Conflict,* p. 208.

106. Burrow,"The Law of the Organism," p. 280.

107. *"The Law of the Organism,"* p. 821.

108. Burrow, *"The Laboratory Method,"* p. 354.

109. Burrow, *"The Autonomy,"* p. 41.

110. Syz, *"Problems of Perspective,"* p. 153.

111. See William Galt, "The Principle of Cooperation in Behavior," *Quarterly Review of Biology,* Vol. 15, December 1940, pp. 401–410.

112. "The Principle of Cooperation," p. 403.

113. Burrow, "An Ethnic Aspect of Consciousness," *Sociological Review* (London) Vol. 19, 1927, p. 71.

114. "An Ethnic Aspect," p. 76.

115. Burrow, *Science and Man's Behavior,* p. 202.

116. See the discussion of crowd symbols in Elias Canetti, *Crowds and Power,* pp. 75–70, 169–183.

117. *Science and Man's Behavior,* pp. 202, 203.

118. *The Structure of Insanity,* p. 75. Also, "Inherently there is no conflict between the total system and the symbolic system of behavior." (*The Biology of Human Conflict,* p. 197)

119. See John Von Neumann, *The Computer and the Brain.*

120. Since first writing this passage I ran across the pioneering work of Ray Birdwhistell in studying kinesics, or the language of body movements and gestures. He notes that by the adoption of a special code and other techniques the recording and analysis time for one second of human interaction had been reduced from 100 hours to one hour. This gives some idea of the complexity of visible human behavior, not to speak of the even more complex internal processes. See Ray L. Birdwhistell, *Kinesics and Context,* p. xii.

121. Kunio Shiomi, "Respiratory and EEG Changes by Cotention of Trigant Burrow," *Psychologia,* 1969, pp. 24–28.

122. Burrow, *Preconscious Foundations of Human Experience,* p. 147. See the following for details: Burrow, "Kymograph Records of Neuromuscular (Respiratory) Patterns in Relation to Behavior, Disorder," *Psychosomatic Medicine,* Vol. 3, No. 2, April 1941, pp. 174–186; Burrow,"Preliminary Report of Electroencephalographic Recordings in Relation to Behavior Modifications," *Journal of Psychology,* Vol. 15, 1943, pp. 109–114; Burrow and Galt, "Electroencephalographic Recordings of Varying Aspects of Attention in Relation to Behavior." *Journal of General Psychology,* Vol. 32, 1945, pp. 269–288. Also see the appendixes to *Science and Man's Behavior.*

123. Burrow recognizes this very often but without drawing the conclusion that the symbols of the neurotic and of the social image are employed to defend and disguise, not communicate.

124. Burrow, "Kymograph Records," p. 183.

125. Syz, "Problems of Perspective," p. 157.

126. Burrow, in Galt, ed., *A Search for Man's Sanity,* p. 277. Letter to to Julian Huxley, January 31, 1934.

127. *A Search for Man's Sanity,* p. 356. Letter to William Galt, December 15, 1937.

128. Burrow, *The Biology of Human Conflict,* p. 255.

129. For an attempt to express the outlook of the artisan, see Michael Ayrton, *The Maze Maker.* Ayrton creates the following testament of Daedalus, the mythical craftsman: "I am not impious nor insensitive to the vision of poets and other sacred persons, but in general they are less observant than they think, suffering as they do from revelation, which blinds them. I accept that poets celebrate important things such as honor and beauty and birth and valor and man's relations with the gods, but when you come down

to it, what they most celebrate are heroes, which is not surprising. Poets have much in common with heroes. They are neither of them aware of the world, of its true appearance nor its real consequence, its structure nor its marvelous imperfection. They are blind to that and because my methods of gaining experience have been observation, deduction and experiment, I have been no worse off and much better instructed than any poets or heroes known to me. In fact, since I am not beset by my own personality I am better off. I prefer cognition to revelation and in my view the valiant act is to live as long and as fully as possible, but then I make things which take time. . . .

"I am involved in matters which I do not wish disturbed nor interrupted by eloquent activities, the facile assumption of power, speculation or immeasurable phenomena, nor any apotheosis. What I make exists." (p. 137)

130. *The Structure of Insanity*, pp. 67–68.

131. *The Social Basis of Consciousness*, p. 93.

132. René Dubos, *The Dreams of Reason*, pp. 85, 71, 86.

133. Frederick C. Thayer, *An End to Hierarchy! An End to Competition!*

134. Eugene Meehan, *The Foundations of Political Analysis*, p. 255.

Chapter 8

1. Jurgen Ruesch, *Therapeutic Communication*.

2. Jurgen Ruesch, *Disturbed Communication*, pp. 113 and 115.

3. *Disturbed Communication*, p. 173.

4. *Disturbed Communication*, p. 131.

5. In Bottomore, ed., *Karl Marx: Selected Writings*, p. 67.

6. Burrow, "The Heroic Role: An Historical Retrospect," *Psyche*, Vol. 6, No. 25, 1926, p. 44.

7. "The Heroic Role," p. 45.

8. "Schizophrenia or the divided mind has become the paradigm of the insanities. . . . Thus in his autocratic image of himself, the schizophrenic stands as Prometheus or Christ ministering between God and man. He occupies toward his environment the same intermediary role as those historic heroes. As the emissary of God or the forces of good, he would, like them, bring salvation unto men, and through his mediation deliver them from evil. But though he is the savior of men they at the same time persecute and deny him." ("The Heroic Role," pp. 45–46)

9. "The Heroic Role," p. 46.

10. A report of a 1967 survey of the National Institute of Mental Health gives the following figures: 1.75 million schizophrenic or potentially schizophrenic persons, 0.5 million schizophrenic persons in hospitals and possibly "60 million Americans are borderline schizophrenics or exhibit other deviant behavior in the schizophrenic category." The reporter of the survey, Dr. David Rosenthal, said the rate of psychoneurosis "is so prevalent in the population that it is almost impossible to estimate." (Associated Press in *The Centre Daily Times*, State College, Pa., April 24, 1972) For a survey of the literature concerning the "causes" of schizophrenia, see Don D. Jackson's collection, *The Etiology of Schizophrenia*.

11. R. D. Laing, *The Divided Self*, p. 178.

12. See J. S. Kasanin, ed., *Language and Thought in Schizophrenia*. Also Langdon Winner, "Language, Comedy and Madness in the Art of Captain Beefheart" (Berkeley, Unpublished, 1970).

13. A thorough review of this literature is not feasible here. For an introduction, see Don D. Jackson's collection *The Etiology of Schizophrenia* and Theodore Lidz, *The Origin and Treatment of Schizophrenic Disorders*.

14. Jackson makes the following comment on the arguments for genetic causes of schizophrenia: "However much the geneticists may ignore the cultural, they have been able by their figures to convince many people to such an extent that they have led to unwarranted genetic counseling and in some cases to sterilization laws. Genetic arguments in general have a way of attaching themselves to the socio-political feelings." (Don D. Jackson, "A Critique of the Literature on the Genetics of Schizophrenia," in Jackson, ed., *The Etiology of Schizophrenia*, p. 81)

Lidz notes that "there probably always is some genetic component to any disorder or human characteristic, even as a predisposition enters into contracting tuberculosis or poliomyelitis . . . but confusing 'familial' with 'genetic' probably impeded the study of these and other illnesses. A genetic etiology means little unless it can suggest a specific means of transmission. . . . I oppose accepting the belief that a specific genetic factor is a prime determinant of schizophrenic disorders until more definitive evidence for it appears primarily because such genetic hypotheses have interfered with the appreciation of how greatly the behavior of one generation influences the next, the central importance of the family to the integrated development of its offspring, and the central moment of language and thought in human integration and adaptation." (Theodore Lidz, *The Origin and Treatment of Schizophrenic Disorders*, p. 12) For a critique of studies purporting to prove a genetic factor causing schizophrenia, see pages 67–68.

15. See James Glass, "Schizophrenia and Perception" "[The schizophrenic's flouting of society], by moving away from even the most rudimentary canons of behavior goes beyond mere rhetoric, or 'dangerous' ideas, or even life-style. He attacks the mores at their roots: the perceptual schema conditioning behavior and action." (p. 135)

16. Laing, *The Divided Self*, p. 161.

17. Laing, *The Politics of Experience*, p. 79.

18. Lidz argues that the therapeutic attitude toward patients labeled schizophrenic by Laing and his followers can lead to a "therapeutic nihilism." "These psychiatrists, themselves caught up in existential despair, convey to their patients as well as to the world at large, that, in this meaningless and corrupt world, no one who is sensitive and aware can remain sane in the usual social sense of being sane. Schizophrenic episodes are deemed to have a beneficial effect. . . . As unhappy as one might be about the state of civilization, it is an error to equate schizophrenic disorders with a deeper sanity." (Lidz, *The Origin and Treatment of Schizophrenic Disorders*, p. 128) Laing frequently lays himself open to the charge of therapeutic nihilism and often seems to imply that the solution to the mystifications of the modern family and by implication modern society is destruction. For example, see D. David Cooper, *The Death of the Family*.

19. R. D. Laing and Aaron Esterson, *Sanity, Madness and the Family*, p. 11.

20. Laing and Esterson, p. 17.

21. Laing and Esterson, p. 12.

22. Laing and Esterson, p. 13.

23. Gregory Bateson, "Cybernetic Explanation," in *Steps to an Ecology of Mind*, p. 400.

24. Bateson, "The Cybernetics of 'Self': A Theory of Alcoholism," in *Steps to an Ecology of Mind*, p. 328.

25. Bateson, "Style, Grace, and Information in Primitive Art," in *Steps to an Ecology of Mind*, pp. 140–141.

26. *The Poverty of Historicism*, p. 76.

27. "A Theory of Play and Fantasy," in *Steps to an Ecology of Mind*, pp. 177–193.

28. My paraphrasing from "A Theory of Play and Fantasy," pp. 187–189.

29. A student's critique of my attempt to state the limits of American politics expresses well the paradoxical impact of the discussion of contextual general rules: "You have presented a theory of institutions which both criticizes their social and political

effects and precludes the reader's conceptualizing any way to deal with these effects without destroying his society."

30. See George V. Plekhanov, *The Role of the Individual*, pp. 60–61.

31. In Bottomore, ed., *Karl Marx: Selected Writings*, p. 63.

32. *Steps to an Ecology of Mind*, p. 338.

33. "The Logical Categories of Learning and Communication," *Steps to an Ecology of Mind*, p. 297.

34. "The Logical Categories," pp. 283–287.

35. "The Logical Categories," p. 293. See also pp. 287–289.

36. "The Logical Categories," pp. 294–295. See C. L. Hull et al., *Mathematico-Deductive Theory of Rote Learning*.

37. Again, see H. Harlow, "The Formation of Learning Sets." Bateson might also cite other examples of Learning II which we have previously discussed, such as the learning of "rules of seeing" noted by Young, Reisen, Ittleson, Kilpatrick, and other investigators, the learning of hypotheses described by Krech, the learning of cognitive maps noted by Tolman, as well as the hypothetical learning of conceptual frameworks by McKay's automaton and the learning of exemplars depicted by Kuhn for the student of physics.

38. "The Logical Categories," pp. 299–300.

39. "The Logical Categories," p. 300.

40. "The Logical Categories," p. 297.

41. "Double-bind theory asserts that there is an experiential component in the determination or etiology of schizophrenic symptoms and related behavioral patterns, such as humor, art, poetry, etc. Notably, the theory does not distinguish between the subspecies. Within its terms there is nothing to determine whether a given individual shall become a clown, a poet, a schizophrenic or some combination of these. We deal not with a single syndrome but with a genus of syndromes, most of which are not conventionally regarded as pathological." ("The Logical Categories," p. 272)

42. "The Logical Categories," pp. 303–304.

43. "The Logical Categories," p. 304.

44. Paul Watzlawick, Janet Beavin, and Don D. Jackson, *Pragmatics of Human Communication*, pp. 216–217.

45. Gregory Bateson, Don D. Jackson, Jay Haley, and John H. Weakland, "Toward a Theory of Schizophrenia," in Bateson, *Steps to an Ecology of Mind*, pp. 201–227. Originally published in *Behavioral Science*, Vol. 1, No. 4, 1956.

46. Bateson et al., "Toward a Theory of Schizophrenia," pp. 206–209. See also John H. Weakland, "The 'Double-Bind' Hypothesis and Three-Party Interaction," in Jackson, ed., *The Etiology of Schizophrenia*, pp. 374–375, 376–378. See also Watzlawick et al., *Pragmatics of Human Communication*, pp. 212–213.

47. Bateson et al., "Toward a Theory of Schizophrenia," pp. 210–211. My paraphrase.

48. "Toward a Theory of Schizophrenia," pp. 211–212.

49. Weakland, "The 'Double-Bind' Hypothesis," pp. 377–378.

50. Bateson et al., "Toward a Theory of Schizophrenia," p. 215.

51. Anthony Schuham, "The Double-Bind Hypothesis a Decade Later," *Psychological Bulletin*, Vol. 68, No. 6, December 1967, pp. 412–413.

52. "The Group Dynamics of Schizophrenia," p. 237.

53. "Epidemiology of a Schizophrenia," p. 199.

54. "Epidemiology of a Schizophrenia," p. 199.

55. "The Group Dynamics of Schizophrenia," p. 243.

56. *The Politics of the Family*, p. 9. "The family as a shared fantasy image is usually a container of some kind *in* which all members of the family feel themselves to be, and *for*

which image all members of the family may feel each should sacrifice themselves. Since this fantasy exists only in so far as it is 'in' everyone who shares 'in' it, anyone who gives it up, shatters the 'family' and everyone else."

57. Bateson, "Minimal Requirements for a Theory of Schizophrenia," p. 263.

58. Warren G. Bennis and Philip Slater, *The Temporary Society*, pp. 88–89.

59. Bennis and Slater, Chapter 2.

60. Bateson et al., "Toward a Theory of Schizophrenia," p. 205.

61. Bateson, "Minimal Requirements," p. 261.

62. "Minimal Requirements," p. 261. See also Bateson et al., "Toward a Theory of Schizophrenia," p. 210.

63. Watzlawick et al., *Pragmatics of Human Communication*, pp. 214–215.

64. Bateson, "Epidemiology of a Schizophrenia," p. 197.

65. Watzlawick et al., *Pragmatics of Human Communication*, pp. 223–224.

66. Bateson, "The Logical Categories of Learning and Communication," p. 282.

67. A song by P. and V. Garvey expresses the rewards of the human experience of search and gambling eloquently. The song is entitled, "Lovin' of the Game." A sample verse runs: "But beside the lookin' for / Oh, the findin's always tame. / There ain't nothin' drives a gambler / Like the lovin' of the game." The lyrics were taken from the record album, "Travlin' Lady," by Rosalie Sorrels (Sire Records, Sl 5902).

68. See the work of Frederick Herzberg, *Work and the Nature of Man*.

69. See N. R. F. Maier, Nathan Glazer, and James B. Klee, "Studies of Abnormal Behavior in the Rat III: The Development of Behavior Fixations through Frustration." Also see N. R. F. Maier, *Frustration*.

70. Karl Deutsch characterizes the form of learning this way: "If you can predict a relatively invariant reaction, you have essentially a built-in bias. The individual with a bias has by-passed his memory, closed the library, and built himself a simple, low order decision point which says, 'If you come to the intersection, go to the left—one way only.' No decision is necessary any more and no memory." ("Autonomy and Boundaries According to Communication Theory," in R. Grinker, ed., *Toward a Unified Theory of Human Behavior*, pp. 280–281)

71. *Sanity, Madness and the Family*, p. 45.

72. See the conclusion of Chapter 4.

73. Robert Jay Lifton developed the notion of "protean man" to describe this phenomenon. He took the name from Proteus of Greek mythology, who was capable of transforming himself into any shape. Lifton comments on the myth, "Proteus was able to change his shape with relative ease from wild boar to lion to dragon to fire to flood. What he found difficult, and would not do unless seized and chained, was to commit himself to a single form, a form most his own, and carry out his function of prophecy." By "protean man" Lifton means an individual who can maintain no clear boundaries. See *Boundaries: Psychological Man in Revolution*, p. 44. See also Bennis and Slater, *The Temporary Society*, Chapter 5, and Henry S. Kariel, *Open Systems: Arenas for Political Action*, for other discussions of this style of leadership and adaptation.

74. See John H. Schaar, "Reflections on Authority," *New American Review*, No. 8, January 1970. Schaar writes, "Events, institutions, and moral epistemological ideas which, taken together, constitute modernity, have virtually driven humanly meaningful authority and leadership from the field, replacing them with bureaucratic coordination and automatic control processes, supplemented when necessary by ideology and phony charisma." (p. 80) Victor A. Thompson analyzes this gutting of authority in organizational terms: "Authority is centralized, but ability is inherently decentralized because it comes from practice rather than from definition. Whereas the boss retains his full rights to make all decisions, he has less and less ability to do so because of the advance of science

and technology. For these reasons the man-boss relationship has become curiously distorted and unstable; formally unilateral boss-to-man, informally unilateral man-to-boss. Each has power in the relationship, but the power of the man does not have the sanction of legitimacy." (*Modern Organization,* p. 47)

75. Bennis and Slater, *The Temporary Society,* p. 87. The discoverer of this new temporary man, Slater points out, is David Riesman, who labeled him "other directed." See the classic David Riesman, Nathan Glazer, and Reuel Denney, *The Lonely Crowd.*

76. "The Logical Categories of Learning and Communication," p. 304.

77. "The Logical Categories," p. 306.

78. "The Logical Categories," p. 306.

79. "Obviously propaganda limits the application of thought. It limits the propagandee's field of thought to the extent that it provides him with ready-made (and moreover, unreal) thoughts and stereotypes. It orients him toward very limited ends and prevents him from using his mind or experimenting on his own. It determines the core from which all his thoughts must derive and draws from the beginning a sort of guideline that permits neither criticism nor imagination." (Jacques Ellul, *Propaganda*)

80. *The Origin and Treatment of Schizophrenic Disorders,* p. 83.

81. See Philip Solomon et al., *Sensory Deprivation.*

82. "The 'Double-Bind' Hypothesis of Schizophrenia," p. 387.

83. Michel Crozier, *The Bureaucratic Phenomenon,* p. 163. See also Lewis Mumford, *The Myth of the Machine.* Mumford correctly identifies bureaucracy as a "communication machine."

84. M. F. Hall, "Communication within Organizations," in Walter A. Hill and Douglas M. Egan, eds., *Readings in Organization Theory,* p. 408.

85. Michel Crozier, *The Bureaucratic Phenomenon,* p. 51. See also Victor A. Thompson, *Modern Organization.*

86. Thompson notes: "Status rank is a function of ignorance." (*Modern Organization,* p. 493) See also Moore and Tumin, "Some Social Functions of Ignorance," p. 789: "Any power structure may depend in part [sic] upon ignorance, not only of its specific activities, but also of its basic intentions."

87. See Larry D. Spence, Robert E. O'Connor et al., *Communication Disturbances and Their Consequences: Information Flow in the Welfare Delivery System of the Pennsylvania Department of Public Welfare.*

88. Bateson, "Redundancy and Coding," *Steps to an Ecology of Mind,* p. 412: "The kinesics of men have become richer and more complex, and paralanguage has blossomed side by side with the evolution of verbal language."

89. Samuel Butler refers to "this miraculous provision of nature, this buffer against collisions, this friction which upsets our calculations but without which existence would be intolerable, this crowning glory of human invention whereby we can be blind and see at one and the same moment." (*Erewhon,* pp. 129–130)

90. H. G. Wells wrote a parable about Jesus Christ in his last years. The temptation and disappointment of attempting a behavior-controlling strategy are keenly expressed; thus: " 'Never have disciples,' said Jesus of Nazareth. 'It was my greatest mistake. I imitated the tradition of having such divisional commanders to marshal the rabble I led to Jerusalem. It has been the common mistake of all world-menders, and I fell into it in my turn as a matter of course. I had no idea what a real revolution had to be; how it had to go on from and to and fro between man and man, each one making his contribution. I was just another young man in a hurry. I thought I would carry the whole load, and I picked my dozen almost haphazard.' " (*Mind at the End of Its Tether and The Happy Turning,* pp. 15-16)

91. Bateson, "The Cybernetics of Self," p. 321.

92. "Social Planning and the Concept of Deutero-Learning," p. 162, in *Steps to an Ecology of Mind.*

93. "The Comparative Study of Religion and the Purposive Cultivation of Democratic Values," Chapter IV in Lyman Bryson and Louis Finkelstein, eds., *Science, Philosophy, and Religion: Second Symposium.* Bateson's essay, quoted above, was a comment on this essay of Mead's.

94. "The brutal truth is that we have very little knowledge indeed of how to get things done, or what to do," writes Eugene Meehan of political scientists. (*The Foundations of Political Analysis,* p. 255)

95. See Robert P. Biller, "Some Implications of Adaptation Capacity for Organizational and Political Development," in Frank Marini, ed., *Toward a New Public Administration: The Minnowbrook Perspective,* p. 115.

96. Kurt Lewin, *Resolving Social Conflicts.* See Chapter 13, "Action Research and Minority Problems."

97. Nevitt Sanford, "Research with Students as Action and Education," *American Psychologist,* Vol. 24, 1969, p. 546.

98. "Social Science and Social Reform," *Journal of Social Issues,* Vol. 21, 1958, p. 67. See also W. L. Yancy, "Intervention as a Strategy of Social Inquiry," *Social Science Quarterly,* Vol. 50, No. 2, December 1969, pp. 582–588.

99. "Research with Students," p. 545.

100. Sanford states his thesis this way: "As social scientists we have values of our own. These derive from the nature of science itself. We cannot separate our quest for knowledge from our desires respecting what ought to be, nor can we make any clear distinction between means and ends. Our research function cannot be separated from our helping or reformist function." ("Social Science and Social Reform," p. 56) See also Sanford, "Whatever Happened to Action Research?" *Journal of Social Issues,* Vol. 26, No. 4, 1970.

103. Basil Bernstein, "Elaborated and Restricted Codes: Their Social Origin and Some Consequences," in John J. Gumperz and Dell Hymes, eds., *The Ethnography of Communication (American Anthropologist,* Vol. 66, No. 6, December 1964), pp. 55–56.

101. Eugene Meehan, *The Foundations of Political Analysis,* p. 255.

102. "The situation is complex, but once one begins to break some of the rules against seeing the rules, one realizes that much of one's difficulty is not due to the intrinsic complexity of the subject but one's inhibitions against seeing what may be obvious, once the inhibition against seeing it is undone. There remain inhibitions against putting into words, such real or imagined insights." (R. D. Laing, *The Politics of the Family,* p. 38)

Bibliography

Adorno, T. W., et al. *The Authoritarian Personality. New York: Harper, 1950.*

Aldous, Joan, and Reuben Hill. "Social Cohesion, Lineage Type, and Intergenerational Transmission." *Social Forces,* Vol. 13, 1965.

Almond, Gabriel. "Political Theory and Political Science." *American Political Science Review,* December 1966.

Allport, Gordon. *Personality.* New York: Holt, 1937.

Alpert, Burt. *Inversions.* San Francisco: Burt Alpert, 1972.

Altmann, Stuart A. *Social Communication among Primates.* Chicago: University of Chicago Press, 1967.

Anderson, J. "The Prediction of Adjustment over Time." In Ira Iscoe and Harold W. Stevenson, eds., *Personality Development in Children.* Austin: University of Texas Press, 1960.

Arendt, Hannah. *Eichmann in Jerusalem.* New York: Viking, 1963.

Arieti, Silvano. *Interpretation of Schizophrenia.* New York: Robert Bruner, 1955.

Aronfreed, Justin. "The Concept of Internalization." In David A. Goslin, ed., *Handbook of Socialization Theory and Research.*

Ashby, W. Ross. *An Introduction to Cybernetics.* New York: Wiley, 1963.

Augustine, St. *See* Paolucci, Henry.

Aurelius, Marcus. *Meditations.* New York: Washington Square Press, 1964.

Ayrton, Michael. *The Maze Maker.* New York: Holt, 1967.

Bachrach, Peter. *The Theory of Democratic Elitism.* Boston: Little, Brown, 1967.

Bacon, Francis. *Selected Writings of Francis Bacon,* ed. Hugh G. Dick. New York: Modern Library, 1955.

Baer, D. M., and J. A. Sherman. "Reinforcement Control of Generalized Imitation in Young Children." *Journal of Experimental Child Psychology,* Vol. 1, 1964.

Baldwin, Maitland. "Electrical Stimulation of the Mesial Temporal Region." In Estelle R. Ramey and Desmond S. O'Doherty, eds., *Electrical Studies on the Unanesthetized Brain.* New York: Harper, 1960.

Bandura, Albert. "Social-Learning Theory in Identificatory Processes." In David A. Goslin, ed., *Handbook of Socialization Theory and Research.*

Barber, Bernard. *Science and the Social Order.* New York: Collier Books. 1962.

Bateson, Gregory. "Comment on M. Mead." In Lyman Bryson and Louis Finkelstein, eds., *Science, Philosophy, and Religion: Second Symposium.* Reprinted in Bateson, *Steps to an Ecology of Mind,* as "Social Planning and the Concept of Deutero-Learning."

———. "Cybernetic Explanation." In *Steps to an Ecology of Mind.*

———. "The Cybernetics of 'Self': A Theory of Alcoholism." In *Steps to an Ecology of Mind.*

———. "Double Bind, 1969." In *Steps to an Ecology of Mind.*

———. "Epidemiology of a Schizophrenia." In *Steps to an Ecology of Mind.*

———. "The Logical Categories of Learning and Communication." In *Steps to an Ecology of Mind.*

———. "Minimal Requirements for a Theory of Schizophrenia." In *Steps to an Ecology of Mind.*

———. "Redundancy and Coding." In *Steps to an Ecology of Mind.*

———. "Social Planning and the Concept of Deutero-Learning." In *Steps to an Ecology of Mind.*

———. *Steps to an Ecology of Mind.* New York: Ballantine Books, 1972. (This is the paperback version, cited in the present book; it differs in pagination and content from the hardback version published also in 1972 by Chandler Publishing Company.)

———. "A Theory of Play and Fantasy." In *Steps to an Ecology of Mind.*

———, Don D. Jackson, Jay Haley, and John H. Weakland. "Toward a Theory of Schizophrenia." In *Steps to an Ecology of Mind;* reprinted from *Behavioral Science,* Vol. 1, No. 4, 1956.

Beam, George D. *Usual Politics.* New York: Holt, 1970.

Beard, Charles A. *The Economic Basis of Politics,* 3d ed. New York: Knopf, 1945.

Beer, Stafford. "A Mythology of Systems." Banquet Address to the First Systems Symposium. The Systems Research Center of Case Institute of Technology, April 26, 27, 1960.

Bell, David J. *Power, Influence and Authority.* New York: Oxford University Press, 1975.

Bell, Richard Q. "A Reinterpretation of the Direction of Effects in Studies and Socialization." *Psychological Review,* Vol. 75, March 1968.

Ben, D. J. "Self-Perception: An Alternative Interpretation of Cognitive Dissonance Phenomena." *Psychological Review,* Vol. 74. No. 3, 1967.

Benedict, Ruth. *Patterns of Culture.* Boston: Houghton Mifflin, 1934.

Benewick, R. J., et al. "The Floating Voter and the Liberal View of Representation." *Political Studies,* Vol. 17, 1969.

Benfey, Otto Theodor. "An Approach to the Conceptual Analysis of Scientific Crises." In Ludwig Von Bertalanffy and A. Rappaport, eds., *General Systems.*

Bengston, Vern L. "On the Socialization of Values: Cohort and Lineage Effects in Inter-Generational Transmission." Paper given at the annual meeting of the American Sociological Association, New York, August 28, 1973.

Bennis, Warren G., and Philip Slater. *The Temporary Society.* New York: Harper, 1968.

Berger, Peter L., and Thomas Luchmann. *The Social Construction of Reality: A Treatise in the Sociology of Knowledge.* New York: Doubleday Anchor, 1967.

Bergmann, Gustav. *The Metaphysics of Logical Positivism.* New York: Longmans, 1954.

Berlyne, D. E. *Conflict, Arousal, and Curiosity.* New York: McGraw-Hill, 1960.

Bernstein, A. "Some Relations between Techniques of Feeding and Training During Infancy and Certain Behavior in Childhood." *Genetic Psychology Monographs,* Vol. 55, 1957.

Bernstein, Basil. "Elaborated and Restricted Codes: Their Social Origins and Some Consequences." In John J. Gumperz and Dell Hymes, eds., *The Ethnography of Communication (American Anthropologist,* Vol. 66, No. 6, December 1964).

———. "Language and Social Class." *British Journal of Sociology,* Vol. 11, September 1960.

———. "A Public Language: Some Sociological Implications of a Linguistic Form." *British Journal of Sociology,* Vol. 10, 1959.

———. "Some Sociological Determinants of Perception." *British Journal of Sociology,* Vol. 9, January 1958, pp.159–174.

Bettelheim, Bruno, and Morris Janowitz. *Dynamics of Prejudice and Ethics.* Springfield, Ill.: Charles C. Thomas, 1955.

Biller, Robert P. "Some Implications of Adaptation Capacity for Organizational and Political Development." In Frank Marini, ed., *Toward a New Public Administration: The Minnowbrook Perspective.* Scranton, Pa.: Chandler Publishing Company, 1971.

Bion, W. R. *Experience in Groups.* New York: Basic Books, 1959.

Birch, H. G., and H. S. Rabinowitz. "The Negative Effects of Previous Experience on Productive Thinking." In P. C. Wason and P. N. Johnson-Laird, eds., *Thinking and Reasoning.*

Birdwhistell, Ray L. *Kinesics and Context.* New York: Ballantine Books, 1972.

Birnbach, Martin. *Neo-Freudian Social Philosophy.* Stanford, Ca.: Stanford University Press, 1961.

Blau, Peter M., and W. Richard Scott. *Formal Organizations.* San Francisco: Chandler Publishing Company, 1962.

Bottomore, T. B., ed. *Karl Marx: Early Writings.* New York: McGraw-Hill, 1963.

———. *Karl Marx: Selected Writings.* New York: McGraw-Hill, 1956.

Boulding, Kenneth E. *The Image: Knowledge in Life and Society.* Ann Arbor: University of Michigan Press, 1961.

———. *The Organizational Revolution.* New York: Harper, 1953.

Bridgman, P. W. *The Intelligent Individual and Society.* New York: Macmillan, 1938.

Brillouin, Leon. *Scientific Uncertainty and Information.* New York: Academic Press, 1964.

Brim, Orville G. "Family Structure and Sex Role Learning by Children: A Further Analysis of Helen Koch's Data." *Sociometry,* Vol. 21, 1958.

Broadbent, D. E. *Perception and Communication.* London: Pergamon, 1958.

Broch, Herman. *The Sleep Walkers.* New York: Grosset, 1964.

Brown, Norman O. *Life Against Death.* New York: Vintage Books, 1959.

Bruner, Edward M. "The Psychological Approach in Anthropology." In Sol Tax, ed., *Horizons of Anthropology.*

Bruner, J. S., and Leo Postman. "On the Perception of Incongruity: A Paradigm." *Journal of Personality,* Vol. 18, 1949.

Bryson, Lyman, ed. *The Communication of Ideas.* New York: Harper, 1948.

Bryson, Lyman, and Louis Finkelstein, eds. *Science, Philosophy, and Religion: Second Symposium.* New York: Harper, 1942.

Buchler, Justus, ed. *Philosophical Writings of Peirce.* New York: Dover, 1955.

Buckley, Walter, ed. *Modern Systems Research for the Behavioral Scientist.* Chicago: Aldine, 1968.

Burgess, Anthony. *The Clockwork Testament or Enderby's End.* New York: Knopf, 1975.

Burrow, Trigant. "Altering Frames of Reference in the Sphere of Human Behavior." *Journal of Social Philosophy,* Vol. 2, 1937.

———. "The Autonomy of the 'I' from the Standpoint of Group Analysis." *Psyche,* Vol. 8, No. 31, 1928.

———. *The Biology of Human Conflict: An Anatomy of Behavior—Individual and Social.* New York: Macmillan, 1937.

———. "Bio-Physical Factors in Relation to Functional Imbalances." *Human Biology,* Vol. 10, 1938.

———. "An Ethnic Aspect of Consciousness." *Sociological Review,* London, Vol. 19, 1937.

———. "The Heroic Role: An Historical Retrospect." *Psyche,* Vol. 6, No. 25, 1926.

———. "Kymograph Records of Neuromuscular (Respiratory) Patterns in Relation to Behavior Disorder." *Psychosomatic Medicine,* Vol. 3, No. 2, April 1941.

———. "The Laboratory Method in PsychoAnalysis, Its Inception and Development." *American Journal of Psychiatry,* Vol. 5, No. 3, January 1926.

———. "The Law of the Organism." *American Journal of Sociology,* Vol. 42, 1937.

———. "Neuropathology and the Internal Environment: A Study of the Neuromuscular Factors in Attention and Their Bearing upon Man's Disorders of Adaptation." *Human Biology,* Vol. 7, 1935.

———. "Our Mass Neurosis." *Psychological Bulletin,* Vol. 23, 1926.

————. "Our Social Evasion." *Medical Journal and Record,* Vol. 123, 1926.

————. "Physiological Behavior-Reactions in the Individual and the Community: A Study in Phylo-analysis." *Psyche,* Vol. 2, No. 2, 1930.

————. *Preconscious Foundations of Human Experience.* New York: Basic Books, 1964.

————. "Preliminary Report of Electroencephalic Recordings in Relation to Behavior Modification." *Journal of Psychology,* Vol. 15, 1943.

————. "A Relative Concept of Consciousness." *Psychoanalytic Review,* Vol. 12, No. 1, 1925.

————. *Science and Man's Behavior: The Contribution of Phylo-biology.* New York: Philosophical Library, 1953.

————. *Selected Letters.* See William E. Galt, ed.

————. *The Social Basis of Consciousness.* New York: Harcourt, 1927.

————. "Social Images versus Reality." *Journal of Abnormal and Social Psychology,* Vol. 19, 1924.

————. "The Social Neurosis: A Study in 'Clinical Anthropology.' " *Philosophy of Science,* Vol. 16, 1949.

————. *The Structure of Insanity.* London: Kegan Paul, 1932.

————, and William E. Galt. "Electroencephalograph Recordings of Varying Aspects of Attention in Relation to Behavior." *Journal of General Psychology,* Vol. 32, 1945.

Burton, Roger. "Socialization: Psychological Aspects," In D. E. Sills, ed., *International Encyclopedia of the Social Sciences.*

Burtt, E. A. *The Metaphysical Foundations of Modern Science,* rev. ed. Garden City, N.Y.: Doubleday Anchor, 1931.

Butler, D., and D. Stokes. *Political Change in Britain.* London: Macmillan, 1969.

Butler, Samuel. *Erewhon.* New York: Modern Library, 1927.

Canetti, Elias. *Crowds and Power.* New York: Viking, 1962.

Cannon, Walter B. *The Wisdom of the Body,* rev. ed. New York: Norton, 1939.

Carpenter, Finley. *The Skinner Primer.* New York: Free Press, 1964.

Cartwright, Dorwin, and Alvin Zander, eds. *Group Dynamics: Research and Theory,* 3d ed. New York: Harper, 1968.

Chadwick, John, and W. N. Mann, trans. *The Medical Works of Hippocrates.* Oxford: Blackwell, 1950.

Child, Arthur. "The Existential Determination of Thought." *Ethics,* January 1942.

————. "The Problem of Imputation in the Sociology of Knowledge." *Ethics,* January 1941.

————. "The Theoretical Possibility of the Sociology of Knowledge." *Ethics,* July 1941.

Child, Irvin L. "Socialization." In Gardner Lindzey, ed., *Handbook of Social Psychology.*

Childe, V. Gordon. *Society and Knowledge.* New York: Harper, 1956.

————. "The Prehistory of Science: Archeological Documents." In Guy Métraux and François Crouzet, eds., *The Evolution of Science.* New York: Mentor, 1963.

Chomsky, Noam. "The Case Against B. F. Skinner." *New York Review of Books,* Vol. 17, No. 11, December 30, 1971.

————. *Linguistic Contributions to the Study of Mind.* Berkeley, Ca.: Academic Publishing, 1967.

————. "Review of Verbal Behavior." *Language,* Vol. 35, January-March 1959.

Clausen, John A., ed. *Socialization and Society.* Boston: Little, Brown, 1968.

Coghill, George E. *Anatomy and the Problem of Behavior.* Cambridge: Cambridge University Press, 1929.

————. "The Biological Basis of Conflict in Behavior." *Psychoanalytic Review,* Vol. 20, No. 1, January 1933.

Cohen, Robert S., and Marx W. Wartofsky, eds. *Boston Studies in the Philosophy of Science,* Vol. 3. Dordrecht and Boston: Reidel, 1967.

Cohn-Bendit, Daniel, and Gabriel Cohn-Bendit. *Obsolete Communism, the Left-Wing Alternative.* New York: McGraw-Hill, 1968.

Connell, R. W. *The Child's Construction of Politics.* Melbourne: Melbourne University Press, 1971.

———. "Political Socialization in the American Family: The Evidence Re-examined." *Public Opinion Quarterly,* Vol. 36, 1972.

Converse, Philip. "The Nature of Belief Systems." In David E. Apter, ed., *Ideology and Discontent.* New York: Free Press, 1964.

Cook, Thomas J., and Frank P. Scioli, Jr. "A Critique of the Learning Concept in Political Socialization Research," Unpublished, 1971.

Cooper, David. *The Death of the Family.* New York: Pantheon, 1971.

Corey, S. M. "Professed Attitudes and Actual Behavior." *Journal of Educational Psychology,* Vol. 28, 1937.

Count, Earl W. "The Biological Basis of Human Sociality." *American Anthropologist,* Vol. 60, 1958.

Craik, K. J. W. *The Nature of Explanation.* London: Cambridge University Press, 1943.

Crick, Bernard. *The American Science of Politics.* Berkeley: University of California Press, 1959.

Crombie, A. C., ed. *Scientific Change.* New York: Basic Books, 1963.

Crozier, Michel. *The Bureaucratic Phenomenon.* Chicago: University of Chicago Press, 1963.

Dahl, Robert A. *A Preface to Democratic Theory.* Chicago: University of Chicago Press, 1963.

———. "The Concept of Power." *Behavioral Science,* Vol. 2, July 1957.

———, and Charles Lindblom. *Politics, Economics, and Welfare.* New York: Harper Torchbooks, 1963.

Dahrendorf, Ralf. "Out of Utopia: Toward a Reorientation of Sociological Analysis." *American Journal of Sociology,* Vol. 64, 1968.

Dawson, Richard E. *"Political Socialization."* In James A. Robinson, ed., *Political Science Annual.* New York: Bobbs-Merrill, 1966.

———, and Kenneth Prewitt. *Political Socialization.* Boston: Little, Brown, 1969.

Defleur, M. F., and R. F. Westie. "Verbal Attitudes and Overt Acts: An Experiment on the Saliency of Attitudes." *American Sociological Review,* Vol. 23, 1958.

Degré, Gérard. "The Sociology of Knowledge and the Problem of Truth." *Journal of the History of Ideas,* January 1941.

Dennis, Jack. "Major Problems of Political Socialization Research." *Midwest Journal of Political Science,* Vol. 12, February 1968.

Deutsch, Karl. "Autonomy and Boundaries According to Communication Theory." In Roy R. Grinker, ed., *Toward a Unified Theory of Human Behavior.*

———. "Discussion," in Roy R. Grinker, ed., *Toward a Unified Theory of Human Behavior.*

———. *The Nerves of Government.* New York: Free Press, 1966.

Dick, Hugh G., ed. *Selected Writings of Francis Bacon.* New York: Modern Library, 1955.

Du Bois, Cora A. *The People of Alor.* Minneapolis: University of Minnesota Press, 1944.

Dubos, René. *The Dreams of Reason.* New York: Columbia University Press, 1961.

———. *Pasteur and Modern Science.* New York: Doubleday Anchor, 1960.

———. *Reason Awake: Science for Man.* New York: Columbia University Press, 1970.

Duhem, Pierre. *The Aim and Structure of Physical Theory.* New York: Atheneum, 1962.

Duncan, Hugh Dalziel. *Communication and Social Order.* New York: Oxford University Press, 1968.

Duncker, Karl. "On Problem Solving." In P. C. Wason and P. N. Johnson-Laird, eds., *Thinking and Reasoning.*

Dunham, Barrows. *Heroes and Heretics.* New York: Knopf, 1964.

Durkheim, Emile. *The Elementary Forms of Religious Life.* New York: Collier Books, 1961.

———. *Montesquieu and Rousseau: Forerunners of Sociology.* Ann Arbor: University of Michigan Press, 1960.

———. *The Rules of Sociological Method.* Glencoe, Ill.: Free Press, 1964.

Easton, David. *A Framework for Political Analysis.* Englewood Cliffs, N.J.: Prentice-Hall, 1965.

———. "The New Revolution in Political Science." *American Political Science Review,* December 1969.

———, ed. *Varieties of Political Theory.* Englewood Cliffs, N.J.: Prentice-Hall, 1967.

———, and Jack Dennis. *Children in the Political System.* New York: McGraw-Hill, 1969.

Easton, L. D., and Kurt Guddat, eds. *Writings of the Young Marx on Philosophy and Society.* Garden City, N.Y.: Doubleday Anchor, 1967.

Edwards, Elwyn. *Information Transmission.* London: Chapman and Hall, 1964.

Elkin, Frederick. *The Child and Society: The Process of Socialization.* New York: Random House, 1960.

Ellul, Jacques. *The Political Illusion.* New York: Knopf, 1967.

———. *Propaganda: The Formation of Men's Attitudes.* New York: Knopf, 1965.

———. "The Technological Order." In C. F. Stover, ed., *The Technological Order.* Detroit: Wayne State University Press, 1963.

Engels, Frederick. *Dialectics of Nature.* Moscow: Foreign Languages Publishing House, 1954.

Erikson, Erik. *Childhood and Society.* New York: Norton, 1963.

———. "Childhood and Tradition in Two American Indian Tribes: With Some Reflections on the Contemporary American Scene." In Clyde Kluckhohn and Henry A. Murray, eds., *Personality in Nature, Society, and Culture.*

———. "Observations on the Yurok: Childhood and World Image." *University of California Publications in American Archaeology and Ethnology,* Vol. 35, No. 10.

Fantz, Robert L. "The Origin of Form Perception." *Scientific American,* May 1961.

Farrington, Benjamin. *Greek Science: Its Meaning for Us.* Baltimore: Penguin, 1963.

———. *Science in Antiquity,* 2d ed. New York: Oxford University Press, 1969.

Feigl, Herbert. "Philosophical Embarrassments of Psychology." *American Psychologist,* Vol. 14, March 1959.

———, and Grover Maxwell, eds. *Scientific Explanation, Space, and Time,* Vol. 3 of *Minnesota Studies in the Philosophy of Science.* Minneapolis: University of Minnesota Press, 1962.

Feldman, Shel, ed. *Cognitive Consistency.* New York: Academic Press, 1966.

Fenichel, Otto. *The Psychoanalytic Theory of Neurosis.* New York: Norton, 1945.

Festinger, Leon. "Informal Social Communication." *Psychological Review,* Vol. 57, 1950.

———. *A Theory of Cognitive Dissonance.* Stanford, Ca.: Stanford University Press, 1957.

———, and Elliott Aronson. "The Arousal and Reduction of Dissonance in Social Contexts." In Dorwin Cartwright and Alvin Zander, eds. *Group Dynamics: Research and Theory.*

———, Henry W. Riecken, Jr., and Stanley Schacter. *When Prophecy Fails.* Minneapolis: University of Minnesota Press, 1965.

———, Stanley Schacter, and Kurt Back. *Social Pressures in Informal Groups.* Stanford, Ca.: Stanford University Press, 1963.

Feuerbach, Ludwig. *The Essence of Christianity.* New York: Harper Torchbooks, 1957.

Feyerabend, P. K. "Consolations for the Specialists." In Imre Lakatos and Alan Musgrave, eds., *Criticism and the Growth of Knowledge.*

———. "Explanation, Reduction, and Criticism." In Herbert Feigl and G. Maxwell, eds., *Scientific Explanation, Space, and Time.*

———. *Knowledge without Foundations.* Oberlin, Ohio: Oberlin Printing Company, 1952.

―――. "Linguistic Arguments and Scientific Method." *Telos*, Vol. 2, No. 1, Spring 1969.

―――. "On the Improvement of the Sciences and the Arts and the Possible Identity of the Two." In Robert S. Cohen and Marx W. Wartofsky, eds., *Boston Studies in the Philosophy of Science*.

―――. "Problems of Empiricism." In Robert G. Colodny, ed., *Beyond the Edge of Certainty*. Englewood Cliffs, N.J.: Prentice-Hall, 1965.

―――. "Review of Patterns of Discovery." *Philosophical Review*, Vol. 69, April 1960.

―――. "Science without Experience." *Journal of Philosophy*, Vol. 66, No. 22, November 20, 1969.

Freedman, J. L., and D. O. Sears. "Selective Exposure." In L. Berkowitz, ed., *Advances in Experimental Social Psychology*. New York: Academic Press, 1965.

Freud, Sigmund. *Civilization and Its Discontents*. New York: Doubleday Anchor, n.d.

―――. *The Collected Papers of Sigmund Freud: General Psychological Theory*. Philip Rieff, ed. New York: Collier Books, 1963.

―――. "Formulations Regarding the Two Principles in Mental Functioning." In Philip Rieff, ed., *The Collected Papers of Sigmund Freud*.

―――. *The Future of an Illusion*. New York: Doubleday Anchor, n.d.

―――. *The History of the Psychoanalytic Movement*. New York: Collier Books, 1963.

―――. "The Loss of Reality in Neurosis and Psychosis." In Philip Rieff, ed., *The Collected Papers of Sigmund Freud*.

―――. *Moses and Monotheism*. New York: Vintage Books, 1939.

―――. *The Standard Edition of the Complete Psychological Works of Sigmund Freud*, ed. James Strachey. London: Hogarth Press, 1953.

―――. *Three Case Histories*. New York: Collier Books, 1963.

―――. "The 'Uncanny.'" In Freud, *Studies in Parapsychology*, ed. Philip Rieff. New York: Collier Books, 1963.

Fried, Morton. "On the Evolution of Social Stratification and the State." In Stanley Diamond, ed., *Culture in History*. New York: Columbia University Press, 1960.

Friedrich, Carl J. *The New Belief in the Common Man*. Boston: Little, Brown, 1942.

Fromm, Eric. *Escape from Freedom*. New York: Farrar, 1941.

Galt, William E. "The Principle of Cooperation in Behavior." *Quarterly Review of Biology*, Vol. 15, December 1940.

―――, ed. *A Search for Man's Sanity: The Selected Letters of Trigant Burrow*. New York: Oxford University Press, 1958.

Gass, William. "The Battered, Triumphant Sage." *New York Review of Books*, May 15, 1975.

Geertz, Clifford. "The Transition to Humanity." In Sol Tax, ed., *Horizons of Anthropology*.

Gerth, Hans, and C. Wright Mills, eds. and trans. *From Max Weber: Essays in Sociology*. New York: Oxford University Press, 1958.

Gibson, James J., and Eleanor J. Gibson. "Perceptual Learning: Differentiation or Enrichment?" *Psychological Review*, Vol. 62, January 1955.

Giedion, Siegfried. *Mechanization Takes Command: A Contribution to Anonymous History*. New York: Oxford University Press, 1948.

Gieger, George. "Values and Social Science." *Journal of Social Issues*, Vol. 6, No. 9, 1950.

Glass, Bentley. "Discussion." In A. C. Crombie, ed., *Scientific Change*.

Glass, James. "Schizophrenia and Perception: A Critique of the Liberal Theory of Externality." *Inquiry*, Vol. 15, 1972.

Goldschmidt, Walter. "Ethics and the Structure of Society: An Ethnological Contribution to the Sociology of Knowledge." *American Anthropologist*, Vol. 53, 1951.

Goldstein, Kurt. *Human Nature in the Light of Psychopathology*. New York: Schocken, 1963.

Gorer, Geoffrey. *Japanese Character Structure and Propaganda.* New Haven: Mimeographed, 1942.

Goslin, David A., ed. *Handbook of Socialization Theory and Research.* Chicago: Rand McNally, 1969.

Gouldner, Alvin. *Patterns of Industrial Bureaucracy.* New York: Free Press, 1954.

Graham, George J. "Empirical Theory and Classical Evaluation: The Fact-Value Bridge." *Helderberg Review,* Vol. 2, No. 1, Fall 1972.

Greenstein, Fred. *Children and Politics.* New Haven: Yale University Press, 1965.

————. "A Note on the Ambiguity of 'Political Socialization': Definitions, Criticism, and Strategies of Inquiry." *Journal of Politics,* Vol. 32, November 1970.

————. "Political Socialization." In D. E. Sills, ed., *Encyclopedia of the Social Sciences.*

Grinker, Roy R., ed. *Toward a Unified Theory of Human Behavior.* New York: Basic Books, 1956.

Grube, G. M. A. *Plato's Republic.* Indianapolis: Hackett, 1974.

Gunnell, John G. *Philosophy, Science, and Political Inquiry.* Morristown, N.J.: General Learning Press, 1975.

Hage, Jerald. *Techniques and Problems of Theory Construction.* New York: Wiley, 1972.

Hall, A. Rupert. "Commentary." In A. C. Crombie, ed., *Scientific Change.*

Hall, M. F. "Communication within Organizations." *Journal of Management Studies,* Vol. 2, No. 1, February 1965.

Hanson, Norwood Russell. "The Logic of Discovery." *Journal of Philosophy,* Vol. 55, No. 25, December 4, 1958.

————. *Patterns of Discovery.* Cambridge: Cambridge University Press, 1958.

Harlow, Harry F. "The Formation of Learning Sets." *Psychological Review,* Vol. 56, January 1949.

————. "Mice, Men, and Motives." *Psychological Review,* Vol. 60, January 1953.

Harris, Thomas A. *I'm OK—You're OK.* New York: Avon, 1973.

Hartshorne, H., and M. A. May. *Studies in the Nature of Character.* 3 vols. New York: Macmillan, 1928–1930.

Hartung, Frank E. "Problems in the Sociology of Knowledge." *Philosophy of Science,* Vol. 19, 1949.

Havelock, Eric A. *Preface to Plato.* Cambridge, Mass.: Harvard University Press, 1963.

Hebb, D. O. "The American Revolution." In Robert J. C. Harper, et al., eds., *The Cognitive Process.* Englewood Cliffs, N.J.: Prentice-Hall, 1964.

Henry, Jules. *Culture Against Man.* New York: Random House, 1963.

————. "Homeostasis in a Special Life Situation." In Roy R. Grinker, ed., *Toward a Unified Theory of Human Behavior.*

Herrick, C. Judson. *The Evolution of Human Nature.* New York: Harper Torchbooks, 1961.

Herzberg, Frederick. *Work and the Nature of Man.* New York: World Publishing Company, 1966.

Hess, R., and J. Torney. *The Development of Political Attitudes in Children.* Chicago: Aldine, 1967.

Hetherington, E. E., and Y. Brackbill. "Etiology and Covariation of Obstinacy, Orderliness, and Parsimony in Young Children." *Child Development,* Vol. 34, 1963.

Hill, Walter A., and Douglas M. Egan, eds. *Readings in Organization Theory.* Boston: Allyn and Bacon, 1966.

Hippocrates. *The Medical Works of Hippocrates,* trans. John Chadwick and W. N. Mann. Oxford: Blackwell, 1950.

Hobbes, Thomas. *Body, Man and Citizen.* New York: Collier Books, 1962.

————. *Leviathan.* Oxford: Oxford University Press, 1962.

Hockett, Charles F. "Biophysics, Linguistics and the Unity of Science." *American Scientist,* Vol. 36, 1948.

———. "The Origin of Speech." *Scientific American,* September 1960.

———, and Robert Ascher. "The Human Revolution." *Current Anthropology,* Vol. 5, No. 3, June 1964.

Homans, George C. *The Human Group.* New York: Harcourt, 1950.

———. *Social Behavior: Elementary Forms.* New York: Harcourt, 1961.

Hull, C. L. *Mathematico-Deductive Theory of Rote Learning.* New Haven: Yale University Institute of Human Relations, 1940.

Humphreys, L. G. "The Effect of Random Alternation of Reinforcement on the Acquisition and Extinction of Conditioned Eyelid Reactions." *Journal of Experimental Psychology,* Vol. 25, 1939.

Hunt, J. McV. "The Effects of Infant-feeding Frustration upon Adult Hoarding in the Albino Rat." *Journal of Abnormal and Social Psychology,* Vol. 36, 1941.

Hyman, Herbert H. *Political Socialization.* New York: Free Press, 1969. (First publication 1959.)

Inhelder, Barbel. "Some Aspects of Piaget's Genetic Approach to Cognition." In W. Kessen and C. Kuhlman, eds., *Thought in the Young Child.* (Monographs of the Society for Research in Child Development, Vol. 2, Serial No. 83, 1962.)

Inkeles, Alex. "Social Structure and Socialization." In David A. Goslin, ed., *Handbook of Socialization Research.*

Innis, Harold A. *The Bias of Communication.* Toronto: University of Toronto Press, 1964.

———. *Political Economy in the Modern State.* Toronto: Ryerson, 1946.

International Encyclopedia of the Social Sciences. D. E. Sills, ed. New York: Macmillan, 1968.

Ittelson, W. H., and F. P. Kilpatrick. "Experiments in Perception." *Scientific American,* August 1951.

Jackson, Don D. "A Critique of the Literature on the Genetics of Schizophrenia." In Jackson, ed., *The Etiology of Schizophrenia.*

Jackson, Don D., ed. *The Etiology of Schizophrenia.* New York: Basic Books, 1960.

Jackson, J. Hampden. *Marx, Proudhon and European Socialism.* New York: Collier Books, 1962.

Janet, Pierre. *Les Névroses.* Paris: Flammarion, 1915. Quoted in Elton Mayo, *The Social Problems of an Industrial Civilization.* Boston: Harvard University Press, 1945.

Jaros, D., H. Hirsch, and F. Fleron, Jr. "The Malevolent Leader: Political Socialization in an American Subculture." *American Political Science Review,* Vol. 62, 1968.

Jencks, Christopher, et al. *Inequality.* New York: Harper, 1972.

Jennings, M. Kent. *The Student-Parent Socialization Study.* Ann Arbor: University of Michigan Inter-University Consortium of Political Research, 1971.

Jones, W. T. *A History of Western Philosophy.* New York: Harcourt, 1952.

Juenger, Friedrich Georg. *The Failure of Technology.* New York: Regnery, 1956.

Kagan, Jerome. "On the Need for Relativism." In Liam Hudson, ed., *The Ecology of Human Understanding.* Baltimore: Penguin Books, 1970.

Kanareff, Vera T., and J. T. Lanzetta. "Effects of Task Definition and Probability of Reinforcement upon the Acquisition of Extinction and Imitative Responses." *Journal of Experimental Psychology,* 1960.

Kant, Immanuel. *On the Old Saw: That It May Be Right in Theory but It Won't Work in Practice.* Philadelphia: University of Pennsylvania Press, 1974.

Kardiner, Abram. *The Individual and His Society.* New York: Columbia University Press, 1939.

———. *Sex and Morality.* New York: Bobbs-Merrill, 1954.

————, and Associates. *The Psychological Frontiers of Society*. New York: Columbia University Press, 1945.

————, and Lionel Ovesey. *The Mark of Oppression*. New York: Norton, 1951.

Kariel, Henry S. *Open Systems: Arenas for Political Action*. Ithaca, Ill.: Peacock, 1969.

Kasanin, J. S., ed. *Language and Thought in Schizophrenia*. Los Angeles: University of California Press, 1954.

Katz, Daniel, and Robert L. Kahn. *The Social Psychology of Organizations*. New York: Wiley, 1966.

Kaufman, Herbert. "Organization Theory and Political Theory." *American Political Science Review*, Vol. 58, No. 1, March 1964.

Kecskemeti, Paul. *Meaning, Communication and Value*. Chicago: University of Chicago Press, 1952.

King, Preston, and B. C. Parekh. *Politics and Experience*. Cambridge: Cambridge University Press, 1968.

Klein, George S. "Cognitive Control and Motivation." In Gardner Lindzey, ed., *Assessment of Human Motives*. New York: Rinehart, 1958.

Kluckhohn, Clyde. "Covert Culture and Administrative Problems." *American Anthropologist*, Vol. 45, 1947.

————. "Culture and Behavior." In Gardner Lindzey, ed., *Handbook of Social Psychology*.

————, and Henry A. Murray, eds. *Personality in Nature, Society and Culture*. New York: Knopf, 1948.

Koestler, Arthur. *The Ghost in the Machine*. New York: Macmillan, 1968.

Kogon, Eugene. *The Theory and Practice of Hell*. New York: Berkley, 1958.

Kohlberg, Lawrence. "Cognitive Stages and Preschool Education." *Human Development*, Vol. 9, 1966.

————. "Development of Moral Character and Moral Ideology." In Martin L. Hoffman and Lois W. Hoffman, eds., *Review of Child Development Research*. New York: Russell Sage Foundation, 1964.

————. "Moral and Religious Education and the Public Schools." In T. Sizer, ed., *Religion and Public Education*. Boston: Houghton Mifflin, 1967.

————. "Stage and Sequence: The Cognitive-Developmental Approach to Socialization." In David A. Goslin, ed., *Handbook of Socialization Theory and Research*.

————. *Stages in the Development of Moral Thought and Action*. New York: Holt, 1969.

Kordig, Carl R. *The Justification of Scientific Change*. Dordrecht: Reidel, 1971.

Krechevsky, I. [David Krech]. "'Hypothesis' in Rats." *Psychological Review*, Vol. 39, November 1932.

Kroeber, A. L., ed. *Anthropology Today*. Chicago: University of Chicago Press, 1953.

Kubie, Lawrence S. *Neurotic Distortion of the Creative Process*. New York: Noonday Press, 1961.

————. "Some Implications for Psychoanalysis of Modern Concepts of the Organization of the Brain." *Psychoanalytic Quarterly*, Vol. 22, 1953.

Kuhn, Thomas S. *The Copernican Revolution*. New York: Vintage Books, 1959.

————. "The Function of Dogma in Scientific Research." In A. C. Crombie, ed., *Scientific Change*.

————. "Logic of Discovery or Psychology of Research." In Imre Lakatos and Alan Musgrave, eds., *Criticism and the Growth of Knowledge*.

————. "Reflections on My Critics." In Imre Lakatos and Alan Musgrave, eds., *Criticism and the Growth of Knowledge*.

————. *The Structure of Scientific Revolution*, 2d ed. Chicago: University of Chicago Press, 1970. (First published 1962.)

La Barre, Weston. "Some Observations on Character Structure in the Orient." *Psychiatry*, Vol. 8, 1945.

Laing, R. D. *The Divided Self.* Baltimore: Penguin Books, 1965.

———. *The Politics of Experience.* New York: Pantheon, 1967.

———. *Politics of the Family and Other Essays.* New York: Vintage Books, 1972.

———, and Aaron Esterson. *Sanity, Madness and the Family.* Baltimore: Penguin Books, 1970.

Lakatos, Imre, and Alan Musgrave, eds. *Criticism and the Growth of Knowledge.* Cambridge: Cambridge University Press, 1970.

Lancaster, Jane B. "Primate Communication Systems and the Emergence of Human Language." Ph. D. Dissertation, University of California, Berkeley, n.d.

Landau, Martin. "Comment: On Objectivity." *American Political Science Review*, September 1972.

———. *Political Theory and Political Science: Studies in the Methodology of Political Inquiry.* New York: Macmillan, 1972.

Langer, J. "Disequilibrium as a Source of Cognitive Development." New York: Society for Research on Child Development, March 21, 1967.

Lapiere, R. T. "Attitudes versus Actions." *Social Forces*, 1934, pp. 230–237.

Lasswell, Harold. "Attention Structure and Social Structure." In Lyman Bryson, ed., *The Communication of Ideas.*

———. *Power and Personality.* New York: Viking, 1948.

———. *Psychopathology and Politics.* Chicago: University of Chicago Press, 1930.

———. "The Structure and Function of Communication in Society." In Lyman Bryson, ed., *The Communication of Ideas.*

Lawrence, Douglas H., and Leon Festinger. *Deterrents and Reinforcement: The Psychology of Insufficient Reward.* Stanford, Ca.: Stanford University Press, 1962.

Lazowick, K. "On the Psychology of Identification." *Journal of Abnormal and Social Psychology*, Vol. 51, 1955.

Lee, Dorothy D. "A Primitive System of Values." *Philosophy of Science*, Vol. 7, No. 3, 1940.

Lethaby, W. R. *Form in Civilization.* London: Oxford University Press, 1957.

Lewin, Kurt. *Resolving Social Conflicts.* New York: Harper, 1948.

Lidz, Theodore. *The Origin and Treatment of Schizophrenic Disorders.* New York: Basic Books, 1973.

———, and Stephen Fleck. "Schizophrenia, Human Integration, and the Role of the Family." In Don D. Jackson, ed., *The Etiology of Schizophrenia.*

Liebschutz, S., and R. Niemi. "Political Socialization among Black Children: The Development of Attitudes and the Impact of Curriculum and Teachers." Paper presented at the meeting of the American Political Science Association, Washington, D.C., September 1972.

Lifton, Robert Jay. *Boundaries: Psychological Man in Revolution.* New York: Vintage Books, 1970.

Lindesmith, Alfred R., and Anselm L. Strauss. "A Critique of Culture-and-Personality Writings." *American Sociological Review*, Vol. 15, No. 5, October 1950.

Lindner, Robert. *Must You Conform?* New York: Grove Press, 1961.

———. *Prescription for Rebellion.* New York: Grove Press, 1952.

Lindzey, Gardner, ed. *Assessment of Human Motives.* New York: Rinehart, 1958.

———, ed. *Handbook of Social Psychology.* Cambridge, Mass.: Addison-Wesley, 1954.

Linton, Ralph. *The Cultural Background of Personality.* NewYork: Appleton-Century, 1945.

Litt, Edgar. "Civil Education, Community Norms, and Political Indoctrination." *American Sociological Review*, Vol. 28, February 1963.

Locke, John. *An Essay Concerning Human Understanding.* Maurice Cranston, ed. New York: Collier Books, 1965.

Lukács, Georg. *History and Class Consciousness.* Cambridge, Mass.: M.I.T. Press, 1971.

Maccoby, Eleanor R. "The Development of Moral Values and Behavior in Childhood." In John A. Clausen, ed., *Socialization and Society.*

McCulloch, Warren S. *Embodiments of Mind.* Cambridge, Mass.: M.I.T. Press, 1970.

McGuire, William J. "The Current Status of Cognitive Consistency Theories." In Shel Feldman, ed., *Cognitive Consistency.*

Machiavelli, Niccoló. *The Prince and The Discourses.* New York: Modern Library, 1950.

McKay, D. M. "The Epistemological Problem for Automata." In C. E. Shannon and J. McCarthy, eds., *Automata Studies.*

McLuhan, Marshall. *The Gutenberg Galaxy.* Toronto: University of Toronto Press, 1962.

Maier, N. R. F. *Frustration.* New York: McGraw-Hill, 1949.

————. "Reasoning in Humans III. The Mechanisms of Equivalent Stimuli and Reasoning." *Journal of Experimental Psychology,* Vol. 35, 1945.

————, Nathan Glaser, and James B. Klee. "Studies of Abnormal Behavior in the Rat III. The Development of Behavior Fixations Through Frustration." *Journal of Experimental Psychology,* Vol. 26, June 1940.

Malinowski, Bronislaw. *Sex, Culture and Myth.* New York: Harcourt, 1962.

————. *The Sexual Life of Savages.* New York: Harcourt, 1929.

Mannheim, Karl. *Essays on the Sociology of Knowledge.* New York: Oxford University Press, 1952.

————. *Ideology and Utopia: An Introduction to the Sociology of Knowledge.* New York: Harcourt, 1955.

Maquet, Jacques J. *The Sociology of Knowledge: Its Structure and Relation to the Philosophy of Knowledge.* Boston: Beacon, 1951.

March, James G. "The Power of Power." In David Easton, ed., *Varieties of Political Theory.* Englewood Cliffs, N.J.: Prentice-Hall, 1967.

————, ed. *Handbook of Organizations.* Chicago: Rand McNally, 1965.

Marcuse, Herbert. *One Dimensional Man.* Boston: Beacon, 1964.

Marsh, David. "Political Socialization: The Implicit Assumptions Questioned." *British Journal of Political Science,* Vol. 1, October 1971.

Marx, Karl. *Capital,* Vol. 1. New York: International Publishers, 1967.

Marx, Karl. *See* Bottomore, T. B., ed.; Easton, L. D., and Kurt Guddat, eds.

Masterman, Margaret. "The Nature of a Paradigm." In Imre Lakatos and Alan Musgrave, eds., *Criticism and the Growth of Knowledge.*

Mayo, Elton. *The Human Problems of an Industrial Civilization.* New York: Viking, 1960.

————. *The Social Problems of an Industrial Civilization.* Boston: Harvard University Press, 1945.

Mead, Margaret. "The Comparative Study of Culture and the Purposive Cultivation of Democratic Values." In Lyman Bryson and Louis Finkelstein, eds., *Science, Philosophy and Religion: Second Symposium.*

————. "National Character." In A. L. Kroeber, ed., *Anthropology Today.*

Meehan, Eugene. *The Foundations of Political Analysis: Empirical and Normative.* Homewood, Ill.: Dorsey Press, 1971.

————. *Value Judgment and Social Science.* Homewood, Ill.: Dorsey Press, 1969.

Merkle, Judith. *Command and Control: The Social Implication of Nuclear Defense.* New York: General Learning Press, 1971.

Merriam, Charles E. *Political Power.* New York: McGraw-Hill, 1934.

Michels, Robert. *Political Parties.* New York: Dover, 1959.

Miller, Daniel. "Psychoanalytic Theory of Development: A Re-evaluation." In David A. Goslin, ed., *Handbook of Socialization Theory and Research.*

Miller, Eugene F. "Positivism, Historicism, and Political Inquiry." *American Political Science Review,* September 1972.

Mills, C. Wright. *Power, Politics, and People.* New York: Ballantine, 1963.

Moore, Wilbert E., and Melvin M. Tumin. "Some Social Functions of Ignorance." *American Sociological Review,* Vol. 14, December 1949.

Mosca, Gaetano. *The Ruling Class.* New York: McGraw-Hill, 1939.

Mullahy, Patrick, ed. *A Study of Interpersonal Relations.* New York: Grove Press, 1957.

Mumford, Lewis. *The Myth of the Machine.* New York: Harcourt, 1966.

Myrdal, Gunnar. *Objectivity in Social Research.* New York: Pantheon, 1969.

Nadel, S. F. "Social Control and Self-Regulation." *Social Forces,* Vol. 31, March 1953.

Niemi, Richard G. "Political Socialization." In Jeane Knutson, ed., *Handbook of Political Psychology.* San Francisco: Jossey-Bass, 1974.

———. "Review of Hess and Torney, 'The Development of Attitudes in Children.' " *Contemporary Psychology,* Vol. 14, 1969.

Nietzsche, Friedrich. "The Birth of Tragedy." In *The Philosophy of Nietzsche.* New York: Random House, 1954.

———. *Early Greek Philosophy.* Oscar Levy, ed. New York: Russell and Russell, 1964.

Nokes, Peter. "Feedback as an Explanatory Device in the Study of Certain Interpersonal and Institutional Processes." *Human Relations,* Vol. 14, 1961.

O'Connor, Robert E. "Political Activism and Moral Reasoning: Political and Apolitical Students in Great Britain and France." *British Journal of Political Science,* Vol. 4, December 1974.

Olson, Mancur. "The Relationship between Economics and the Other Social Sciences." In Seymour M. Lipset, ed., *Politics and the Social Sciences.* New York: Oxford University Press, 1969.

Orlansky, Harold. "Infant Care and Personality." *Psychological Bulletin,* Vol. 46, No. 1, January 1949.

Ossowski, Stanislaw. *Class Structure in the Social Consciousness.* London: Routledge, 1963.

Paolucci, Henry. *The Political Writings of St. Augustine.* Chicago: Regnery, 1962.

Pappenheim, Fritz. *The Alienation of Modern Man.* New York: *Monthly Review Press,* 1959.

Pareto, Vilfredo. *The Mind and Society.* 4 vols. New York: Harcourt, 1935.

———. *The Rise and Fall of Elites.* Totowa, N.J.: Bedminster, 1968.

Parker, Carleton H. *The Casual Laborer and Other Essays.* New York: Harcourt, 1920.

Patterson, Franklin, et al. *High Schools for a Free Society.* New York: Free Press, 1960.

Pavlov, Ivan P. *Conditioned Reflexes.* New York: Dover, 1960.

Peirce, Charles S. *See* Buchler, Justus, ed.

Penfield, Wilder. "Memory Mechanisms." *AMA Archives of Neurology and Psychiatry,* Vol. 67, 1952.

———, and Lamar Roberts. *Speech and Brain Mechanisms.* New York: Atheneum, 1959.

Pepitone, Albert. "Some Conceptual and Empirical Problems of Consistency Models." In Shel Feldman, ed., *Cognitive Consistency.*

Peters, Richard, ed. *Thomas Hobbes: Body, Man, and Citizen.* New York: Collier Books, 1962.

Piaget, Jean. "The General Problems of the Psychological Development of the Child." In J. M. Tanner and Barbel Inhelder, eds., *Discussions on Child Development: Proceedings of the World Health Organization Study Group on the Psychological Development of the Child,* Vol. 4. New York: International Universities Press, 1960.

———. *The Moral Judgment of the Child.* New York: Collier Books, 1962. Originally published by Routledge & Kegan Paul, 1962.

————. *The Psychology of Intelligence.* London: Routledge, 1947.

Pigors, Paul. *Leadership or Domination?* London: Harrap, 1935.

Plato. *Plato's Republic. See* G. M. A. Grube.

Plekhanov, George. *The Role of the Individual in History.* New York: International Publishers, 1940.

Polanyi, Michael. *Science, Faith, and Society.* Chicago: University of Chicago Press, 1964.

Popper, Karl. *Conjectures and Refutations.* London: Routledge, 1963.

————. *The Logic of Scientific Discovery.* New York: Science Editions, 1961.

————. "Normal Science and Its Dangers." In Imre Lakatos and Alan Musgrave, eds., *Criticism and the Growth of Knowledge.*

————. *The Open Society and Its Enemies,* Vol. 1. New York: Harper, 1963.

————. *The Poverty of Historicism.* New York: Harper, 1957.

Postman, Leo, and J. S. Bruner. "Perception under Stress." *Psychological Review,* Vol. 55, No. 6, Nov. 1948.

Presthus, Robert. *The Organizational Society: An Analysis and a Theory.* New York: Knopf, 1962.

Prewitt, K., and J. Okello-Oculi, "Political Specialization and Political Education in New Nations." In R. Sigel, ed., *Learning about Politics.* New York: Random House, 1970.

Prothro, James W., and Charles M. Grigg. "Fundamental Principles of Democracy: Ba˜es of Agreement and Disagreement." *Journal of Politics,* May 1960.

Pye, Lucian W. *Politics, Personality, and Nation Building.* New Haven: Yale University Press, 1962.

Read, John. *Prelude to Chemistry: An Outline of Alchemy.* Cambridge, Mass.: M.I.T. Press, 1966.

Reagan, Michael. "Basic and Applied Research: A Meaningful Distinction?" *Science,* Vol. 155, No. 3768, 1967.

Reich, Wilhelm. *Character-Analysis.* New York: Noonday Press, 1961.

————. *Ether, God and Devil.* Rangeley, Maine: Orgone Institute Press, 1949.

————. *The Murder of Christ.* Rangeley, Maine: Orgone Institute Press, 1953.

Reiss, A. J. "Social Organization and Socialization: Variations on a Theme about Generations." Working Paper No. 1, Center for Research on Social Organization. Ann Arbor, Mich., 1965.

Remmers, H. H. *Anti-Democratic Attitudes in American Schools.* Chicago: Northwestern University Press, 1963.

Rest, J., E. Turiel, and L. Kohlberg. "Relations between Levels of Moral Judgment and Preference and Comprehension of the Moral Judgment of Others." *Journal of Personality.* 1969.

Riccards, Michael P. "The Socialization of Civic Virtue." In Philip Abbott and Michael P. Riccards, eds., *Reflections in American Political Thought: Readings from Past and Present.* New York: Chandler Publishing Company, 1971.

Rieff, Philip., ed. *The Collected Papers of Sigmund Freud: General Psychological Theory.* New York: Collier Books, 1963.

Riesen, Austin H. "The Development of Visual Perception in Man and Chimpanzee." *Science,* August 1, 1947.

Riesman, David, Nathan Glazer, and Reuel Denney. *The Lonely Crowd.* Garden City, N.Y.: Doubleday, 1955.

Ritchie, A. D. *Studies in the History and Methods of the Sciences.* Edinburgh: Edinburgh University Press, 1958.

Roazen, Paul. *Freud: Political and Social Thought.* New York: Knopf, 1968.

Roheim, Geza. *The Origin and Function of Cultures.* New York: Nervous and Mental Disease Publications, 1943.

Rosenthal, David. Article in the *Centre Daily Times,* Associated Press, State College, Pa., April 24, 1972.

Ross, Edward Alsworth. *Social Control: A Survey of the Foundations of Order.* Cleveland: The Press of Case Western Reserve University, 1969. Originally published in 1901 by Macmillan.

Rossi, Paolo. *Francis Bacon: From Magic to Science.* London: Routledge, 1968.

Rousseau, Jean Jacques. *The Social Contract.* New York: Hafner, 1947.

Ruesch, Jurgen. *Disturbed Communication.* New York: Norton, 1957.

———. *Therapeutic Communication.* New York: Norton, 1961.

———, and Gregory Bateson. *Communication: The Social Matrix of Psychiatry.* New York: Norton, 1951.

Saint-Simon, Henri de. *Social Organization, The Science of Man, and Other Writings.* New York: Harper Torchbooks, 1964.

Sampson, Ronald V. *The Psychology of Power.* New York: Pantheon, 1965.

Sanford, Nevitt. "Research with Students as Action and Education." *American Psychologist,* Vol. 24, 1969.

———. "Social Science and Social Reform." *Journal of Social Issues,* Vol. 21, 1958.

———. "Whatever Happened to Action Research?" *Journal of Social Issues,* Vol. 26, No. 4, 1970.

Sartre, Jean-Paul. *Being and Nothingness.* New York: Philosophical Library, 1956.

———. *Search for a Method.* New York: Knopf, 1963.

Saugstad, P., and K. Raaheim. "Problem Solving, Past Experience, and Availability of Functions." In P. C. Wason and P. N. Johnson-Laird, eds., *Thinking and Reasoning.*

Schaar, John H. "Reflections on Authority." *New American Review,* No. 8, January 1970.

Schactel, Ernest G. "On Memory and Childhood Amnesia." In Patrick Mullahy, ed., *A Study of Interpersonal Relations.*

Schachter, Stanley G. and Jerome Singer. "Cognitive, Social, and Physiological Determinants of Emotional States." *Psychological Review,* Vol. 69, No. 5, September 1962.

Schattschneider, E. E. *The Semi-Sovereign People: A Realist's View of Democracy in America.* New York: Holt, 1960.

Schick, Marvin, and A. Somit. "The Failure to Teach Political Activity." *American Behavioral Scientist,* Vol. 6, January 1963.

Schneirla, T. C., and Gerard Piel. "The Army Ant." *Scientific American,* June 1948. Reprint: W. H. Freeman & Company, San Francisco.

Schreber, Daniel Paul. *Memoires of My Nervous Illness.* London: Dawson, 1955.

Schuham, Anthony. "The Double-Bind Hypothesis a Decade Later." *Psychological Bulletin,* Vol. 68, No. 6, December 1967.

Searing, Donald, Joel J. Swartz, and Alden E. Lind. "The Structuring Principle: Political Socialization and Belief Systems." *American Political Science Review,* Vol. 67, No. 2, June 1973.

Sears, D. "Review of Hess and Torney, *The Development of Political Attitudes in Children.*" *Harvard Educational Review,* Vol. 38, 1968.

Sennett, Richard. *Families against the Cities: Middle-Class Homes of Industrial Chicago.* New York: Knopf, 1970.

———. "Review of *Beyond Freedom and Dignity.*" *New York Times Book Review,* October 24, 1971.

———. *The Uses of Disorder: Personal Identity and City Life.* New York: Knopf, 1970.

Sewell, William H. "Infant Training and the Personality of the Child." *American Journal of Sociology,* Vol. 58, 1952.

———. "Some Recent Developments in Socialization Theory and Research." *Annals of the American Academy of Political and Social Sciences,* Vol. 32, 1963.

Shannon, Claude E., and J. McCarthy, eds. *Automata Studies.* Princeton: Princeton University Press, 1956.

Shannon, Claude E., and Warren Weaver. *The Mathematical Theory of Communication.* Urbana: University of Illinois Press, 1949.

Shapere, Dudley. "Meaning and Scientific Change." In R. Colodny, ed., *Mind and Cosmos.* Pittsburgh: University of Pittsburgh Press, 1966.

Sherif, Muzafer. "If the Social Scientist Is to Be More Than a Mere Technician." *Journal of Social Issues,* Vol. 24, No. 1, 1968.

Sherman, M., and I. Sherman. *The Process of Human Behavior.* New York: Norton, 1929.

Shiomi, Kunio. "Respiratory and EEG Changes by Cotention of Trigant Burrow." *Psychologia,* 1969.

Sills, D. E., ed. *International Encyclopedia of the Social Sciences.* New York: Macmillan, 1968.

Simeons, Albert T. *Man's Presumptuous Brain.* New York: Dutton, 1962.

Simon, Herbert A. *The Shape of Automation for Men and Management.* New York: Harper Torchbooks, 1965.

Skinner, B. F. *About Behaviorism.* New York: Knopf, 1971.

——. "Behaviorism at Fifty." *Science,* Vol. 140, No. 3570, May 31, 1963.

——. *Beyond Freedom and Dignity.* New York: Knopf, 1971.

——. *Cumulative Record,* Part II, 3d ed. New York: Appleton-Century, 1972.

——. "Freedom and the Control of Men." *American Scholar,* Vol. 25, Winter 1955–1956.

——. "Pigeons in a Pelican." *American Psychologist,* Vol. 15, January 1960.

——. "Superstition in the Pigeon." *Journal of Experimental Psychology,* Vol. 38, April 1948. Reprinted in Skinner, *Cumulative Record.*

——. "The Technology of Teaching." *Proceedings of the Royal Society,* B, Vol. 162, 1965.

——. *Verbal Behavior.* Appleton-Century-Crofts, 1957.

Slater, Philip. *The Pursuit of Loneliness.* Boston: Beacon, 1970.

Solomon, Philip, et al. *Sensory Deprivation.* Cambridge, Mass.: Harvard University Press, 1961.

Somit, A., et al. "The Effect of Introductory Political Science Courses on Student Attitudes toward Personal Political Participation." *American Political Science Review,* Vol. 52, December 1958.

Speier, Hans. "Karl Mannheim's Ideology and Utopia." In Speier, *Social Order and the Risks of War.* Cambridge, Mass.: M.I.T. Press, 1969. From *The American Journal of Sociology.*

——. "The Social Determination of Ideas." *Social Research,* May 1938.

Spence, Larry D., Robert E. O'Connor, et al. *Communication Disturbances and Their Consequences: Information Flow in the Welfare System of the Pennsylvania Department of Public Welfare.* University Park, Pa.: Center for Human Services Development, Report No. 5, 1974.

Spence, Larry D., and Francis M. Sim. "The Use and Abuse of Metaphors in Social Science." Mimeographed; presented at the annual meeting of the Pennsylvania Sociological Society, Philadelphia, November 2, 1974.

Spuhler, J. N., ed. *The Evolution of Man's Capacity for Culture.* Detroit: Wayne State University Press, 1965.

Stark, Werner. *The Fundamental Forms of Social Thought.* London: Routledge, 1962.

Stavaren, Herbert. "Suggested Specificity of Certain Dynamisms in a Case of Schizophrenia." In Patrick Mullahy, ed., *A Study of Interpersonal Relations.*

Steintrager, James. "Political Socialization and Political Theory." *Social Research,* Vol. 35, 1968.

Stekel, Wilhelm. *Compulsion and Doubt,* trans. Emil Gutheil. New York: Grosset, 1962.

Strachey, James, ed. *See* Sigmund Freud, *The Standard Edition.*

Svalastoga, Kaare. *Social Differentiation.* New York: David McKay, 1965.

Syz, Hans. "Problems of Perspective against the Background of Trigant Burrow's Group-Analysis Researches." *International Journal of Group Psycho-Therapy,* Vol. 2, No. 2, April 1961.

————. "Reflections on Group- or Phylo-Analysis." Supplement to *Acta Psychotherapeutica et Psychosomatica,* Vol. 2, 1963.

————. "A Summary Note on the Work of Trigant Burrow." *International Journal of Social Psychiatry,* Vol. 7, No. 4, 1961.

Szasz, Thomas. *The Manufacture of Madness.* New York: Harper, 1970.

Talland, George A. *Disorders of Memory and Learning.* Baltimore: Penguin Books, 1968.

Tax, Sol, ed. *Horizons of Anthropology.* Chicago: Aldine, 1964.

Thayer, Frederick C. *An End to Hierarchy! An End to Competition!* New York: Franklin Watts, 1973.

Theophrastus. *Metaphysics.* W. D. Ross and F. H. Forbes, trans. Oxford: Clarendon Press, 1929.

Thompson, Charles B., and Alfreda P. Sill. *Our Common Neurosis—Notes on a Group Experi-ment.* New York: Exposition Press, 1952.

Thompson, Victor A. *Modern Organization.* New York: Knopf, 1965.

Thurston, John R., and Paul H. Mussen. "Infant Feeding Gratification and Adult Personality." *Journal of Personality,* Vol. 19, June 1951.

Tocqueville, Alexis de. *Democracy in America.* New York: Vintage Books, 1945.

Tolman, Edward C. *Behavior and Psychological Man.* Berkeley: University of California Press, 1966.

Toulmin, Stephen E. "Conceptual Revolutions in Science." In Robert S. Cohen and Marx W. Wartofsky, eds., *Boston Studies in the Philosophy of Science,* Vol. 3.

————. "Discussion." In A. C. Crombie, ed., *Scientific Change.*

Truman, David. "Disillusion and Regeneration: The Quest for a Discipline." *American Political Science Review,* December 1965.

————. *The Governmental Process.* New York: Knopf, 1960.

Tucker, Robert. *Philosophy and Myth in Karl Marx.* London: Cambridge University Press, 1961.

Turnbull, Colin. *The Forest People.* Simon and Schuster, 1961.

————. "The Lesson of the Pygmies." *Scientific American,* Vol. 208, No. 1, January 1963.

Ullman, Montague. "Societal Factors in Dreaming." *Contemporary Psycho-analysis,* Vol. 9, No. 3, May 1973.

Von Bertalanffy, Ludwig. *Problems of Life.* New York: Harper Torchbooks, 1960.

————. *Robots, Men and Minds.* New York: Braziller, 1967.

————, and A. Rappaport, eds. *General Systems,* Vol. 9. Yearbook of the Society for General Systems Research, Ann Arbor, Mich. (16 volumes, 1956-1971).

Von Domarus, E. "The Specific Laws of Logic in Schizophrenia." In J. S. Kasanin, ed., *Language in Thought and Schizophrenia.*

Von Foerster, Heinz. "From Stimulus to Symbol: The Economy of Biological Computation." In Walter Buckley, ed., *Modern Systems Research for the Behavioral Scientist.*

Von Neumann, John. "Probabilistic Logics and the Synthesis of Reliable Organisms from Unreliable Components." In Claude E. Shannon and J. McCarthy, eds., *Automata Studies.*

————. *The Computer and the Brain.* New Haven: Yale University Press, 1958.

Waelder, Robert. *Basic Theory of Psychoanalysis.* New York: International Universities Press, 1960.

Wallace, Anthony F. C. "Culture and Cognition." *Science,* Vol. 135, No. 3501, February 2, 1962.

———. *Culture and Personality.* New York: Random House, 1963.

———. "The Psychic Unity of Human Groups." In B. Kaplan, ed., *Studying Personality Cross-Culturally.* Evanston, Ill.: Row, Peterson, 1961.

———, and John Atkins. "The Meaning of Kinship Terms." *American Anthropologist,* Vol. 62, February 1960.

Wallas, Graham. *Human Nature in Politics.* Lincoln: University of Nebraska Press, 1962.

Walter, W. Grey. *The Living Brain.* New York: Norton, 1963.

Washburn, S. L. "Speculations on the Interrelations of the History of Tools and Biological Evolution." In J. N. Spuhler, ed., *The Evolution of Man's Capacity for Culture.*

Wason, P. C., and P. N. Johnson-Laird, eds. *Thinking and Reasoning.* Baltimore: Penguin Books, 1968.

Watkins, John W. N. "Against 'Normal Science.' " In Imre Lakatos and Alan Musgrave, eds., *Criticism and the Growth of Knowledge.*

Watzlawick, Paul, Janet Beavin, and Don D. Jackson. *Pragmatics of Human Communication.* New York: Norton, 1967.

Weakland, John H. "The 'Double-Bind' Hypothesis of Schizophrenia and Three-Party Interaction." In Don D. Jackson, ed., *The Etiology of Schizophrenia.*

Weaver, Warren. "The Mathematics of Information." In Ernest Nagel and Arnold Tustin, eds., *Automatic Control.* New York: Simon and Schuster, 1955.

Weber, Max. *From Max Weber: Essays in Sociology,* trans. and ed. Hans Gerth and C. Wright Mills. New York: Oxford University Press, 1958.

———. *The Methodology of the Social Sciences.* Glencoe, Ill.: Free Press, 1949.

Wells, H. G. *Mind at the End of its Tether and The Happy Turning.* New York: Didier, 1946.

Wheelwright, Philip. *Metaphor and Reality.* Bloomington: Indiana University Press, 1962.

White, Leslie A. *The Science of Culture.* New York: Farrar, Straus, and Cudahy, 1949.

Whitehead, Alfred N. *Adventures of Ideas.* New York, Mentor Books, 1933.

Whitney, John W. "Socialization IV: Adult Socialization." In D. E. Sills, ed., *International Encyclopedia of the Social Sciences.*

Whyte, Lynn, Jr. *Medieval Technology and Social Change.* Oxford: Oxford University Press, 1962.

Wicker, A. "Attitudes versus Actions: The Relationship of Verbal and Overt Behavioral Responses to Attitude Objects." *Journal of Social Issues,* Vol. 25, 1969.

Williams, Raymond. *The Long Revolution.* New York: Harper, 1966.

Wolin, Sheldon. "Paradigms and Politics." In Preston King and B. C. Parekh, *Politics and Experience.*

———. *Politics and Vision.* New York: Little, Brown, 1960.

Woodger, Joseph S. "The Technique of Theory Construction." In Otto Neurath and C. Morris, eds., *Foundations of the Unity of Science,* Vol. 2. Chicago: University of Chicago Press, 1970.

Wooldridge, Dean E. *The Machinery of the Brain.* New York: McGraw-Hill, 1963.

Worsley, Peter. *The Trumpet Shall Sound: A Study of Cargo Cults in Melanesia.* New York: Schocken, 1968.

Yancy, W. L. "Intervention as a Strategy of Social Inquiry." *Social Science Quarterly,* Vol. 50, No. 3, December 1968.

Young, J. Z. *A Model of the Brain.* Oxford: Clarendon Press, 1964.

———. *Doubt and Certainty in Science.* Oxford: Oxford University Press, 1951.

Name Index

Subject Index